Pro JavaScript™ RIA Techniques

Best Practices, Performance, and Presentation

Den Odell

Apress®

Pro JavaScript™ RIA Techniques: Best Practices, Performance, and Presentation

Copyright © 2009 by Den Odell

ISBN-13 (pbk): 978-1-4302-1934-7

ISBN-13 (electronic): 978-1-4302-1935-4

9 8 7 6 5 4 3 2 1

Lead Editors: Clay Andres and Jonathan Hassell
Technical Reviewer: Kunal Mittal
Editorial Board: Clay Andres, Steve Anglin, Mark Beckner, Ewan Buckingham, Tony Campbell, Gary Cornell, Jonathan Gennick, Jonathan Hassell, Michelle Lowman, Matthew Moodie, Duncan Parkes, Jeffrey Pepper, Frank Pohlmann, Ben Renow-Clarke, Dominic Shakeshaft, Matt Wade, Tom Welsh
Project Manager: Sofia Marchant
Copy Editor: Marilyn Smith
Associate Production Director: Kari Brooks-Copony
Production Editor: Laura Esterman
Compositor: Lynn L'Heureux
Proofreader: Martha Whitt
Indexer: Carol Burbo
Artist: April Milne
Cover Designer: Kurt Krames
Manufacturing Director: Tom Debolski

Distributed to the book trade worldwide by Springer-Verlag New York, Inc., 233 Spring Street, 6th Floor, New York, NY 10013. Phone 1-800-SPRINGER, fax 201-348-4505, e-mail orders-ny@springer-sbm.com, or visit http://www.springeronline.com.

For information on translations, please contact Apress directly at 2855 Telegraph Avenue, Suite 600, Berkeley, CA 94705. Phone 510-549-5930, fax 510-549-5939, e-mail info@apress.com, or visit http://www.apress.com.

Apress and friends of ED books may be purchased in bulk for academic, corporate, or promotional use. eBook versions and licenses are also available for most titles. For more information, reference our Special Bulk Sales–eBook Licensing web page at http://www.apress.com/info/bulksales.

The source code for this book is available to readers at http://www.apress.com.

For my family, friends, and loved ones

Contents at a Glance

Contents

PART 2 ■ ■ ■ Performance

CHAPTER 10 Binary Ajax 331

CHAPTER 11 Drawing in the Browser 357

CHAPTER 12 Accessibility in Rich Internet Applications 375

About the Author

DEN ODELL is a multidisciplined web developer with expert JavaScript skills. He is a web standards and accessibility advocate, with a special passion for user interface development.

As a front-end technical architect at the AKQA digital service agency in London, Den built and architected several large-scale web sites and rich Internet applications for a number of clients, including Ferrari, Nike, and Nokia. He now lives in Sweden, where he has been using his technical skills and passion for music to help record labels and artists develop their presence on the Web.

In his spare time, Den runs nightclub events, plays records at clubs across Europe, and has a keen eye for digital photography.

About the Technical Reviewer

KUNAL MITTAL serves as Executive Director of Technology at Sony Pictures Entertainment, where he is responsible for the SOA and Identity Management programs. He provides a centralized engineering service to different lines of business and consults on content management, collaboration, and mobile strategies.

Kunal is an entrepreneur who helps startups define their technology strategy, product road map, and development plans. With strong relationships with several development partners worldwide, he is able to help startups and even large companies build appropriate development partnerships. He generally works in an advisor or a consulting CTO capacity, and serves actively in the project management and technical architect functions.

Kunal has authored and edited several books and articles on J2EE, WebLogic, and SOA. He holds a Master's degree in Software Engineering and is an instrument-rated private pilot.

Acknowledgments

Throughout the course of my career, I have met and worked alongside many incredibly intelligent people who have inspired me to improve my technical skills, and to varying degrees, have had an impact on this book and its material. There are way too many people to name, but I would like to thank you all—you know who you are.

Thanks to Clay Andres for seeing the potential in my book and allowing me to run with it. I'd also like to offer my sincere thanks to Kunal, Sofia, Jon, Marilyn, Laura, and the rest of the team at Apress who worked so diligently and effectively to run a tight ship for delivering such a high-quality product from my source material.

I want to offer massive thanks to Maria for supporting me when I was busy for what must have seemed like endless evenings and weekends as I wrote this book. Thank you for calming my stress, keeping me together, encouraging me to keep on when times were tough, and going above and beyond what anyone could expect. You are an amazing, beautiful, insightful, and intelligent person; I love you, and I can't imagine my life without you.

Thanks most of all to you, my readers, for taking the time to read and study this book. I hope you are able to understand, learn from, and put into practice its contents and build better web applications, and to advance your career as a result.

Introduction

Rich Internet applications (RIAs), or web applications, are those web sites that blur the boundary between the web browser and standard desktop applications. Managing your e-mail through web sites such as Google Gmail, Yahoo! Mail, and Microsoft Windows Live Hotmail is every bit as simple and intuitive as using a desktop e-mail client such as Microsoft Outlook or Apple Mail. Web page refreshes are not expected when performing actions, and if a new message is received by the mail server, we expect to see it appear in our inbox immediately.

Building web sites that behave in this way is seen as a departure from the traditional model on the Web, where performing actions such as a submitting a form or clicking a link to refresh an online forum to see the latest posts were considered the norm. It is this difference that has led some to label these RIAs as Web 2.0, as if an upgrade to the Web were taking place.

In some respects an upgrade has been taking place, but not an upgrade of the Web itself. The improvements are actually in the web browsers we use to browse our favorite sites. Gradually over the past few years, features have been added to each of the major web browsers. Additionally, some attempts at conformance among browser manufacturers have meant that finally, through the power of JavaScript and standardized Document Object Model (DOM) scripting, live page updates are possible using data loaded dynamically from the web server. The Web is no longer a static place.

I have written this book primarily to help you harness the power of JavaScript to add dynamic components to your pages and to create entire RIAs of your own. (I assume you already have some knowledge of HTML, CSS, and JavaScript.) With great power comes great responsibility, however. I put emphasis on ensuring that you understand the importance of creating a responsive user experience that excites, rather than frustrates, your site visitors. I also stress that you have the ability to apply creativity through your design, to make your application look and behave superior to any static web site. You'll see how you can use custom-built user interface components that don't sacrifice usability or accessibility,

By the end of this book, you should have the confidence to build your own web site or RIA, safe in the knowledge that it has been constructed in a robust, reliable, efficient, beautiful, and highly accessible manner.

PART 1

■ ■ ■

Best Practices

In this first part of the book, I will present some tried-and-tested guidelines for building rich Internet applications (RIAs). Applying these guidelines will allow you to build the foundations of a web site structure that's scalable from a single page with a few lines of code up to many thousands of pages and thousands of lines of code. I will show you how to follow best practices in a sensible, pragmatic way that won't make the tasks of application maintenance and bug fixing daunting—during construction or in the future.

Building a Solid Foundation

If you're reading this book, chances are that you have felt the proud sense of achievement that comes with building and releasing a web site. Perhaps you completed the project solo; perhaps you built it as part of a team. Maybe it's a simple site, with just a few pages you're using to establish a presence for yourself on the Internet for an audience of a few of your friends, or maybe it's a cutting-edge rich Internet application (RIA) with social networking features for a potential audience of millions. In any case, congratulations on completing your project! You deserve to feel proud.

Looking back to the start of your project with the knowledge and experience you have garnered, I bet you can think of at least one thing that, if done differently, would have saved you from bashing your head against the wall. If you're just starting out in the web development industry, it might be that you wish you had kept a backup of a previous version of your files, because it cost you precious time trying to recover your changes after an unexpected power outage. Or it might be that you wish you hadn't decided to rely on that third-party software library that seemed like it would be up to the task at the start of the project, but soon proved itself to be a huge waste of time and effort. In the course of my own career, I've been in exactly these situations and come out the other side a little wiser. I've learned from those mistakes and fed that new knowledge back into the next project.

Based on my experiences and what I've learned from others, I've developed an effective, sensible approach to web development. This approach, along with a handful of smart techniques thrown in the mix, should minimize those head-bashing moments and ensure things run more smoothly right from the get-go all the way through to the launch of your next web site or application.

Best Practice Overview

Let's start by considering what is meant by the term *best practice*. If you've been in the development profession for long, you'll have heard this expression being tossed around quite a lot to justify a particular coding technique or approach. It is a bit of a loaded phrase, however, and should be treated with caution. I'll explain why.

Who Put the "Best" in Best Practice?

The landscape of web development is constantly changing. Browsers rise and fall in popularity, feature adoption between them is not always in parallel, and the technologies we use to construct web sites for display in such browsers are still fairly immature, constantly undergoing revisions and updates. In an environment that is in flux, what we might consider to be a best-practice solution to a problem right now could be obsolete in six months' time.

The use of the word *best* implies that a benchmark exists for comparison or that some kind of scientific testing has been adopted to make the distinction. However, very rarely have such tests been undertaken. You should consider carefully any techniques, technologies, and components that have been labeled as *best practice*. Evaluate them for yourself and decide if they meet a set of criteria that benefit you as a developer, the end users of your site, and if relevant, the client for whom you are undertaking the work.

The guidelines, rules, and techniques I set out in this chapter are ones that I have personally tried out and can attest to their suitability for real-world web development. I consider them to be the best we have right now. Of course, some of these could be irrelevant by the time you are reading this book, so my advice to you is to stay up-to-date with changes in the industry. Read magazines, subscribe to blog feeds, chat with other developers, and scour the Web for knowledge. I will maintain a comprehensive list of sources I recommend on my personal web site at `http://www.denodell.com/` to give you a place to start.

By staying abreast of changes to these best practices, you should be able to remain at the forefront of the web development industry, armed with a set of tools and techniques that will help you make your day-to-day work more efficient, constructive, and rewarding.

Finally, don't be afraid to review, rewrite, or refactor the code you write as you build your sites. No one has built a web site from scratch without needing to make code alterations. Don't believe for a second that any code examples you see on the Web, or in this or any other book, were written in a way that worked perfectly the first time. With that said, knowledge and experience make things easier, so practice every chance you get to become the best web developer you can be.

Who Benefits from Best Practices?

The truth is that everyone should be able to benefit from the use of best practices in your code. Take a look at the following lists, and use these criteria to assess any guidelines, techniques, or technologies you come across for their suitability for your site.

Web Developers

Best practice starts at home. A site structure and code that work well for you and your web developer colleagues will make all your lives a lot easier, and reduce the pain that can be caused by poor coding.

- Will my code adhere to World Wide Web Consortium recommendations?
- Will my site be usable if a proprietary technology or plug-in is unavailable?
- Will my code pass testing and validation?

- Is my code easily understood, well structured, and maintainable?

- Can extra pages, sections, and assets be added to the site without significant unnecessary effort?

- Can my code be localized for different languages and world regions without a lot of extra effort?

Search Engines and Other Automated Systems

Believe it or not, a large percentage of site traffic is from automated machines and scripts, such as search engines, screen scrapers, and site analysis tools. Designing for these robots is every bit as important as for any other group of users.

- Will my code appear appropriately in search engine results according to sensible search terms used to find it?

- Can my code be read simply and easily by a machine or script that wishes to read or parse its contents for whatever reason?

End Users

The most important users of your code are your site visitors, so making your code work effectively for them is the number one priority.

- Will my code be usable in and accessible to any web browser or device, regardless of its age, screen size, or input method?

- If my site were read aloud by screen reader software, would the content and its order make sense to the listener?

- Can I be confident my code will not demonstrate erroneous behavior or display error messages when used in a certain way I have not anticipated?

- Can my site be found through search engines or other online tools when using appropriate search terms?

- Can my users access a localized version of my site easily if one is available?

General Best Practices

If you're like most developers, you probably want to spend as much of your time as possible constructing attractive user interface components and great-looking web sites, rather than refactoring your code base because of an unfortunate architectural decision. It's very important to keep your code well maintained. Without sensible structure and readability, it will become harder and harder to maintain your code as time passes. Bear in mind that all the guidelines in this chapter have been put together with a view to making things as easy on you, the developer, as possible.

Define the Project Goals

The following are the two most important things to consider while coding a web page:

- How will end users want to use this?

- How will other developers want to make changes to this?

Bear in mind that the end users may not be human. If you were to check the server request logs for one of your existing sites, you would discover that many of your site visitors are actually search engine spiders, RSS readers, or other online services capable of reading your raw page content and transforming it into something else.

This kind of machine-based access is likely to become more widespread over the coming years, as automatic content syndication, such as RSS feeds, becomes more commonplace. For example, content from the popular knowledge-sharing site Wikipedia (`http://www.wikipedia.org/`) is already being used in other places around the Web, including within Google Maps (`http://maps.google.com/`), where articles are placed according to the geographical position of the content described in each article.

Yahoo! and other search engine companies have been pushing for some time for web developers to incorporate extra context-specific markup within pages, so that they can better understand the content and perhaps present the results in their search engine in a different way. Recipes could be presented with images and ingredients, for example; movie-related results could contain reviews and a list of where the movie is showing near you. The possibilities of connecting your code together with other developers' code online like this are vast. By marking up your content in the correct way, you ensure the whole system fits together in a sensible, coherent, connected way, which helps users get the information they are looking for faster.

As for ensuring other developers (including yourself, if only for your own sanity when you return to a project after a long break) can follow your code, you need to consider what the usual site maintenance tasks might be. These usually fall into the following four categories:

- Making alterations to existing pages

- Adding new pages

- Redesigning or modifying the page layout

- Adding support for end users who need the page in other languages, or in region- or country-specific versions

By thinking about these tasks up-front, you reduce the likelihood of needing to refactor your code or rearrange and split up files, so the job of maintenance is made easier. Welcome back, sanity!

Know the Basic Rules

So how do we go about making sure that we get it right in the first place? The following seven rules of thumb seem to sum it up succinctly:

- Always follow mature, open, and well-supported web standards.

- Be aware of cross-browser differences between HTML, CSS, and JavaScript implementations, and learn how to deal with them.

- Assume HTML support, but allow your site to be usable regardless of whether any other technologies—such as CSS, JavaScript, or any plug-ins—are present in the browser.

- Name your folders and files consistently, and consider grouping files together according to purpose, site structure, and/or language.

- Regularly purge redundant code, files, and folders for a clean and tidy code base.

- Design your code for performance.

- Don't overuse technology for its own sake.

Let's go through each of these basic rules in order.

Follow Mature, Open, and Well-Supported Web Standards

Back in the early 1990s, a very clever man who worked at the technology research organization CERN (European Organization for Nuclear Research, `http://www.cern.ch/`), Tim Berners-Lee, invented what we know today as the World Wide Web. He developed the concepts of home pages, Hypertext Markup Language (HTML), and interconnected hyperlinks that form the foundation of web browsing. He also created the world's first web browser to demonstrate his invention.

The project became quite large and eventually took up many resources at CERN. When the decision was made to redirect funding and talent toward building the recently completed Large Hadron Collider project instead, Tim Berners-Lee made the decision to create a separate organization to manage the continuation of standards development for HTML and its related technologies. This new organization, the World Wide Web Consortium (W3C, `http://www.w3.org/`), was born in October 1994.

Since its inception, the W3C organization has documented more than 110 recommended standards and practices relating to the Web. The three that are most useful to readers of this book are those pertaining to HTML (including XHTML), Cascading Style Sheets (CSS), and Domain Object Model (DOM) scripting with JavaScript (also known as ECMAScript, since the JavaScript name is trademarked by Sun Microsystems).

Two popular browsers emerged in those early days of the Web: Netscape Navigator, released in December 1994, and Microsoft's Internet Explorer (IE), released in August 1995. Both browsers were based on similar underlying source code and rendered web pages in a similar way. Of course, a web page at the time was visibly very different from what we see today, so this wasn't particularly difficult for both to achieve.

Roll on a year to 1996, and things get a little more interesting. Microsoft introduced basic support for a new W3C recommendation, CSS level 1, in IE 3. This recommendation defined a way for web developers to apply font and color formatting; text alignment; and margins, borders, and padding to most page elements. Netscape soon followed suit, and competition began to intensify between the two browser manufacturers. They both were attempting to implement new and upcoming W3C recommendations, often before those recommendations were ready for the mainstream.

Naturally, such a variation in browser support for standards led to confusion for web developers, who often tended to design for an either/or scenario. This resulted in end users facing web sites that displayed the message "This web site works only in Internet Explorer. Please upgrade your browser."

Of course, the W3C recommendations are just that: recommendations for browser manufacturers and developers to follow. As developers, we must consider them only as useful as
their actual implementation in common web browsers. Over time, browsers have certainly
made strides toward convergence on their implementations of these web standards. Unfortunately, older versions of browsers with poorer quality of standards adoption in their rendering
of web pages still exist, and these must be taken into account by web developers.

The principle here is to ensure you are up-to-date on common standards support in
browsers, rather than just on the latest recommendations to emerge from the W3C. If the standard is well supported, you should use it. If not, it is best avoided.

Deal with Cross-Browser Issues

Web browsers are regularly updated, and they quite often feature better support for existing W3C recommendations and some first attempts at implementations of upcoming
recommendations.

Historically, browsers have varied in their implementations of existing recommendations.
This is also true of browser support for the newer recommendations. This means that developers must aim to stay up-to-date with changes made to browser software and be aware of the
features and limitations of different browsers.

Most browser users, on the other hand, tend not to be quite as up-to-date with new
browser releases as developers would wish. Even browsers that are capable of automatically
updating themselves to the latest version often require the user to authorize the upgrade first.
Many users actually find these notifications distracting to what they're trying to achieve in
their web browser then and there, and so they tend to put off the upgrade.

As developers, we must be aware and acknowledge that there are many different web
browsers and versions of web browsers in the world (some 10,000 different versions in total,
and counting). We have no control over which particular piece of software the end user is
using to browse our pages, nor should we.

What we do know from browser statistics sites, such as Net Applications' Market Share
(http://marketshare.hitslink.com/), is that the five main web browsers in the world today are
Microsoft's IE, Mozilla's Firefox, Apple's Safari, Opera Software's Opera, and Google's Chrome.
These five browsers account for around 99% of all access to web pages through the desktop.
However, just relying on testing in these browsers misses out on the burgeoning market in
mobile web browsing, for example, so it is worth staying up-to-date with the latest progress in
the web browser market.

Testing your pages across a multitude of browsers and operating systems allows you to
locate the portions of your code that cause different browsers to interpret it in different ways.
Minimizing these differences is one of the hardest tasks for any web developer and separates
this role from most other software-related professions. This is a task that needs to be attacked
from the get-go of a new project, as leaving it until too late can result in frantic midnight coding sessions and missed deadlines—never fun!

The smartest approach is to build the HTML, CSS, and JavaScript code that form the basic
template or outline of the site before writing any page-specific code. Then test this bare-bones
structure in as wide a range of browsers on as many different operating systems, and with as
varied a range of monitor and window sizes, as possible. Tweak the code to ensure the template displays correctly before adding any page-specific code or content.

A particular source of variation is in the different interpretations of color within browsers. Some support the reading of color profile information from image files; some don't support this. Some apply a gamma correction value; some don't apply this value. Consequently, the same image or color can appear slightly different in various browsers, so it's worth checking that your design doesn't cause color mismatching to occur between objects on your page.

You should build and test individual page components one at a time in as many browsers as possible during development. Again, by bringing most of the testing up-front to coincide with development, you will experience fewer problems later on and have fewer bugs to squish. By the end of a project, developers are often feeling the pressure of last-minute client requests for changes, so minimizing bugs by this stage in the proceedings is a smart idea.

Assume Support for HTML Only

Your HTML markup must be visible and operate functionally in any available browser, device, or user agent without reliance on CSS, JavaScript, or plug-ins. Where CSS, JavaScript, or plug-ins provide additional content, layout, or functionality over and above the HTML, the end users should be able to access the content and a functional equivalent of the behavior in a sensible way, without reliance on these technologies. For example, if you're using a Flash movie to provide an animated navigation menu for your site, you need to ensure the same navigation is available through HTML; otherwise, you are preventing a whole group of users from accessing your site.

Obviously, this has a massive impact on the way you develop your web pages. You will build from the HTML foundations upward, ensuring no functionality gets lost when certain browser features are switched off or are nonexistent. Each "layer" of code should be unobtrusive; that is to say that no CSS style rules or JavaScript code should exist within the HTML markup—each should be in a separate file and stand alone.

In the context of modern web applications, which are often written in such a way so that communication between the browser and the server is handled via JavaScript, this means that those communication points must exist when JavaScript is switched off in the browser. For example, modern JavaScript allows data to be sent to and received from a web server without the need for the page to refresh when sending a form. In this case, you must ensure that the form can be submitted without the need for JavaScript—treat it like an optional extra, rather than a requirement.

You might hear this principle called *progressive enhancement*, referring to the adding or layering of extra functionality on top of the HTML, or *graceful degradation*, referring to the fact that the removal of features from the browser always results in a working web page. It is the central principle of what is termed *accessibility*, which refers to providing access to a web page regardless of browser or device.

This principle is best understood through real-life examples, so let's go through two of them now.

First, suppose that in your web application, you have a button that, when clicked, launches a login modal dialog box within the page, as shown in Figure 1-1. After the user fills in the form and clicks the submit button, JavaScript is used to send the supplied login credentials to the server, and then to perform a refresh of certain page elements, instead of the entire page, based on the user's logged-in status as shown in Figure 1-2.

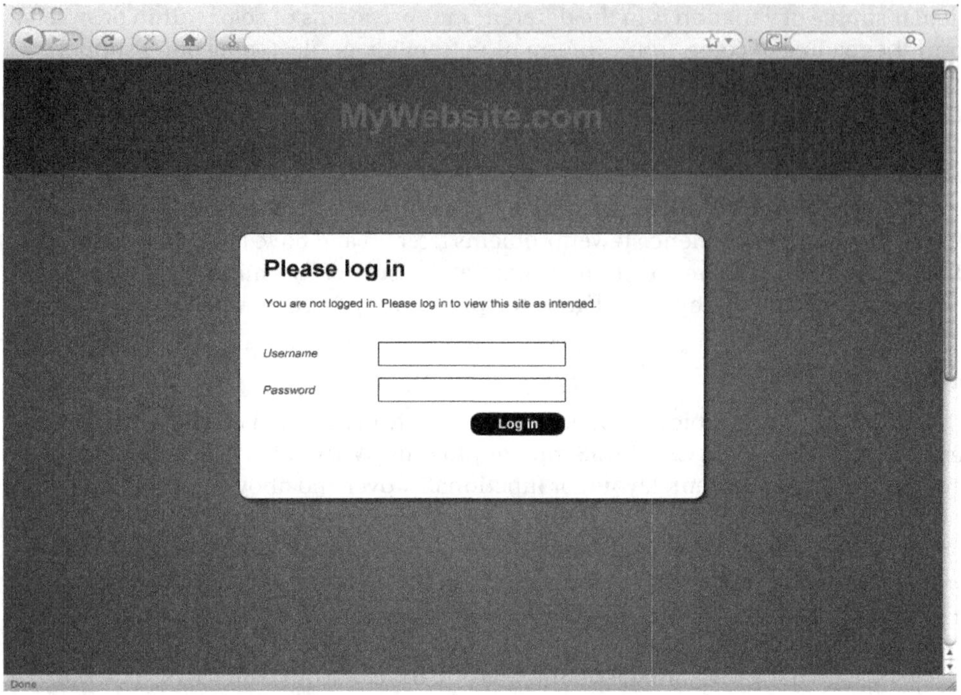

Figure 1-1. *A modal-style login box*

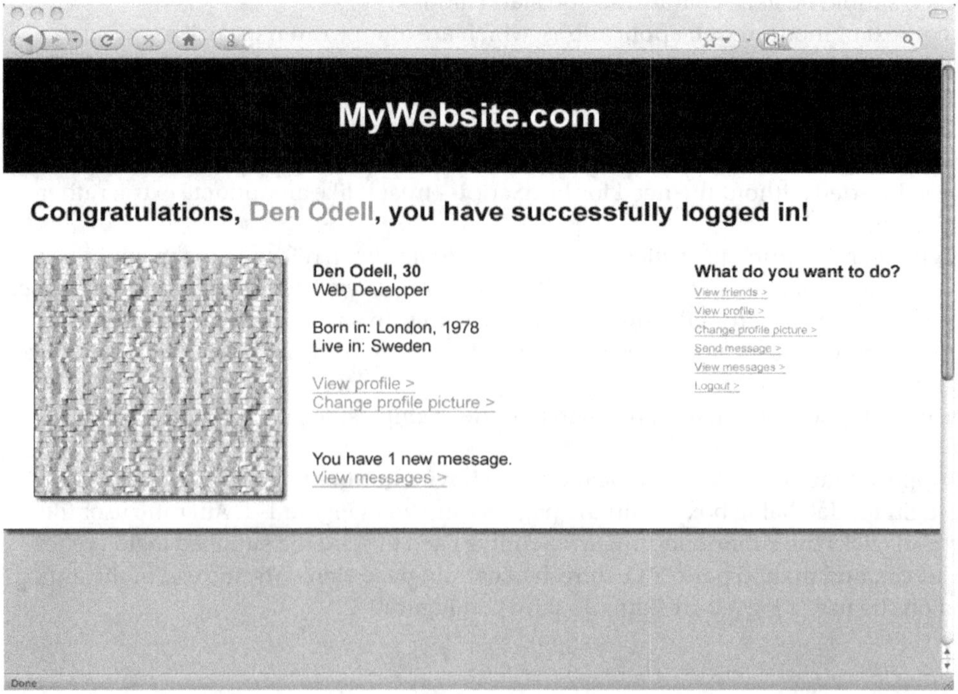

Figure 1-2. *Successful login, loaded without a refresh if JavaScript is enabled*

But what if JavaScript is disabled? You would need to ensure that your HTML code was structured such that the user would be taken to a separate page with the login form. Submitting this form would post the data back to the server, causing a refresh, and the server-side code would decide which page to send according to the user's status—either successfully logged in or not logged in. In this way, both scenarios are made to be functionally equivalent, although their user flow and creative treatment could potentially be different.

As another example, suppose you have a page that contains a form used for collecting payment information for an online booking system. Within this form, depending on the type of credit card selected, you would like certain fields to display only if the user selects a credit card, as shown in Figure 1-3, rather than a debit card, as shown in Figure 1-4. For instance, the Issue Number field is applicable only to debit cards, and perhaps you want to display the Valid from Date fields only for cards from certain suppliers. You probably also want to make it impossible for the user to submit an incorrect date, such as February 30.

As web developers, we use JavaScript to make this happen. JavaScript fires events when the user performs certain actions within the browser, and we are able to assign code to execute when these events are fired. We even have the power to cancel the event, meaning that if the user attempted to submit a form, for example, we could cancel that submission if we decided that form wasn't suitable for submission because it had failed some validation tests.

We use JavaScript to "listen" for changes to the Card Type field. This event gets fired when the user selects a different radio button option. When this event is fired, we can execute a piece of code that, depending on the card type selected, shows or hides the desired fields.

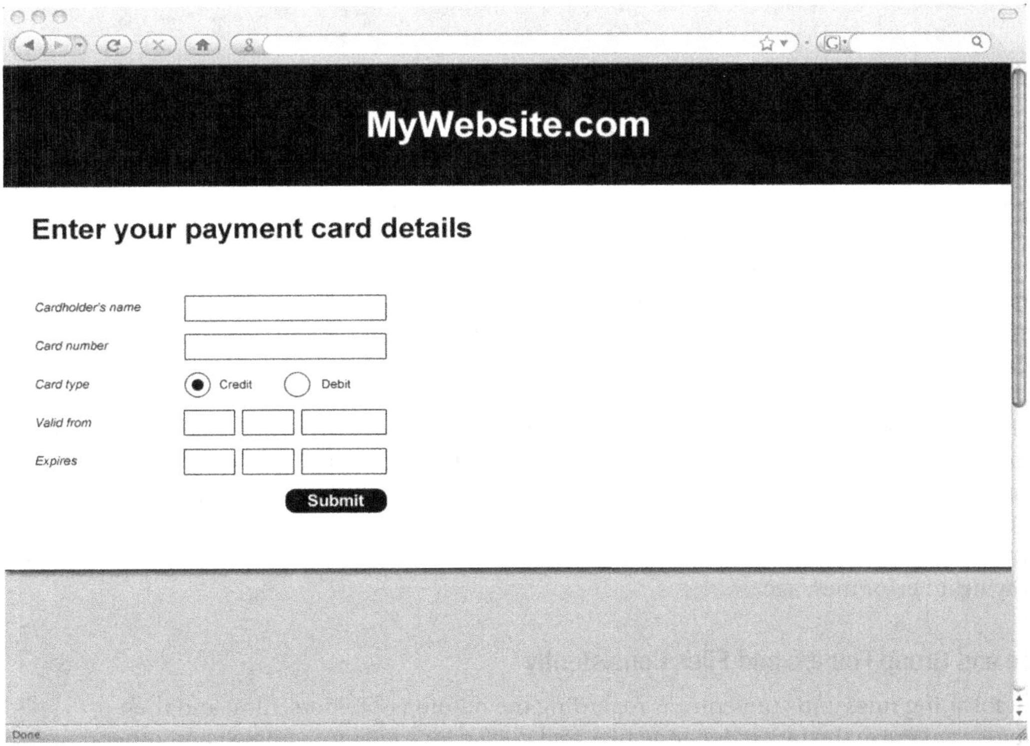

Figure 1-3. *A payment card form showing credit card fields*

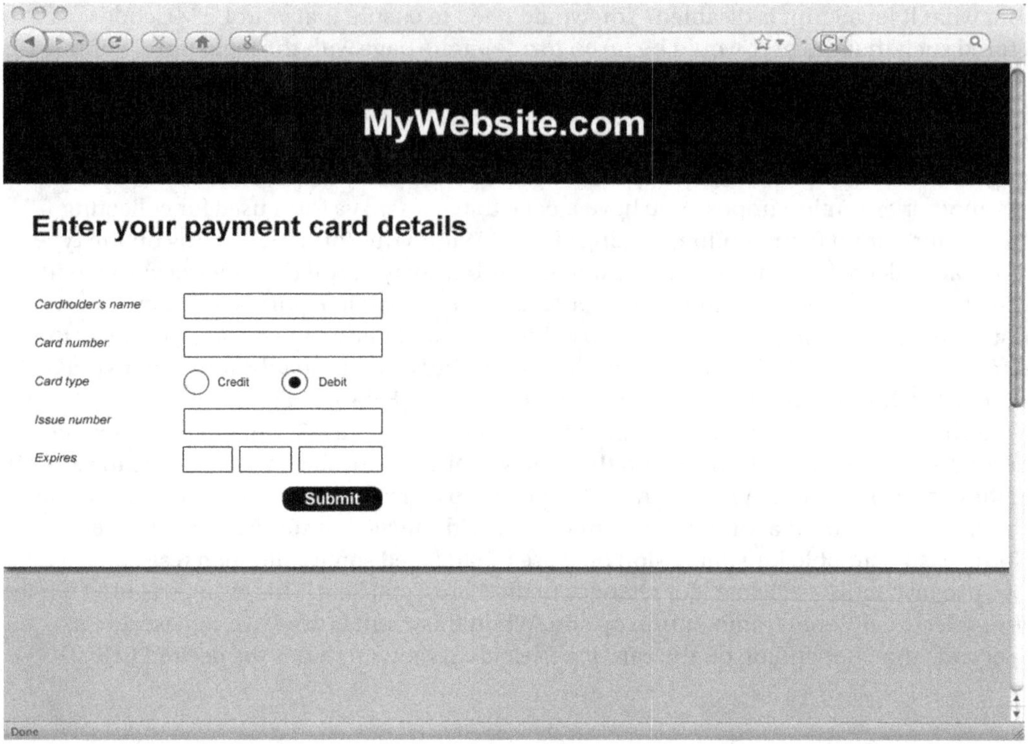

Figure 1-4. *A payment card form showing debit card fields*

We also listen for the submit event of the form to fire and, when it does, we run a small JavaScript routine to check that the date fields contain valid values. We can force the form submission to fail if we decide the values entered are not up to scratch.

Now what happens when someone visits your web page with a browser that doesn't support JavaScript? She selects her card type using the radio button, but nothing changes. In fact, in order to instantiate a change to the appearance of the page, the form must be submitted to the server to allow the server to perform the kind of processing you had been performing using JavaScript.

In terms of usability, you might consider it odd to ask the users to submit the form after they have selected their card type, as the fields are already displayed below. Probably the ideal way to structure your page in this case is to have all of the fields existing in the page's HTML, and simply allow the users to fill in the information they have available on their card. When they finally submit the form, the processing that exists on the server can validate their card data and check whether they have entered a valid date, and if there is an error, reload the page displaying an error message.

Name and Group Folders and Files Consistently

By establishing rules and conventions regarding the naming of folders, files, and their contents, you make the task of locating files and code a lot easier for yourself and other developers. The task of maintenance and future additions is made simpler with a consistent naming convention, ensuring developers always know how to name their assets. See the "Structuring

Your Folders, Files, and Assets" section later in this chapter for some examples of directory structures you might adopt.

Maintain a Tidy Code Base

You should ensure that the files and code associated with a project are the only ones necessary for the web site to do its job—no more and no less. Over time, certain files may be superseded by others, and certain CSS style rules or JavaScript files by others.

I recommend that you purge all redundant files, folders, and code from your code base on a regular basis during development. This reduces the size of the project, which aids comprehension of the code by other developers and ensures the end users of your site are not downloading files that are never used, consuming bandwidth that they could potentially be paying for.

To avoid problems with the accidental deletion of files or the situation where you later require files you've deleted, you should consider using a source code management system. Such a system will keep backups of changes made to project files and ensure you can always revert to a previous version of a particular folder or file—even a deleted one. See the "Storing Your Files: Version Control System" section later in this chapter for more information.

Design Your Code for Performance

Your site visitors, whether they realize it or not, demand a responsive user interface on the Web. If a button is clicked, the users expect some kind of reaction to indicate that their action was recognized and is being acted upon.

HTML, CSS, and JavaScript code run within the browser and are reliant on the power of the end user's machine or device. Your code needs to be lightweight and efficient so it downloads quickly, displays correctly, and reacts promptly. Part 2 of this book focuses on performance and explains how you can make your code lighter, leaner, and faster for the benefit of your end users.

Don't Use Technology for Its Own Sake

Within the wider web development community, you will often hear hype about new technologies that will make your web pages better in some way. Most recently, this hype has focused around the Asynchronous JavaScript and XML (Ajax) technique, which is the practice of communicating with the server using JavaScript within the browser, meaning that page refreshes can be less frequent. This became the favorite technique to be used by web developers on any new project.

The problem is that sites were built so that they worked only with the Ajax technique, and so relied exclusively upon JavaScript. Those users without this capability in their browsers—users with some mobile web browsers, users with restrictions in place in their office environment, users with special browser requirements due to a disability, and external robots such as search engine spiders—could not access the information that would normally have been provided through HTML pages, connected together through hyperlinks and buttons. Conversely, some users with capable browsers were finding that if they remained on certain sites that relied heavily on the Ajax technique, eventually their browser would become slow or unresponsive. Some web developers, keen to jump onboard the new craze, forgot to code in a way that would prevent memory leaks from occurring in the browser.

Build your sites on sound foundations and solid principles, ensuring you test and push new technologies to usable limits before deciding they are a good choice for your project. You'll learn about the Ajax technique in Chapter 2, and how to deal with memory leaks in browsers in Chapter 4.

Markup Best Practice: Semantic HTML

HTML or XHTML forms the basic foundation of every web page. Technically, these are the only web standards that need to be supported by all web browsers and user agents out there in the wild. The term *semantic* in this context refers to applying the correct tags to match the meaning behind the content (according to the dictionary, the word *semantic* literally means *meaning*).

Knowledge of as many of the HTML/XHTML tags and attributes as possible will put you in good stead. Make sure that your content is marked up with exactly the right tag for the content it encompasses: table tags for tabular data, heading tags for section headlines, and so on. The more meaning you are able to give your content, the more capable web browsers, search engine spiders, and other software will be at interpreting your content in the intended way.

It is advisable to include all semantic information in your markup for a page, even if you chose to use CSS style rules to hide some elements visually within the browser. A useful guideline is that you should code your markup according to how it would sound if read aloud. Imagine the tag name were read aloud, followed by the contents of that tag. In fact, this is how most screen reader browsers work, providing audio descriptions of web pages for those with visual impairments.

For example, suppose you've built a web site for movie reviews, and you want to display an image that denotes the movie has scored four out of five possible stars. Now consider how you would want this information to be read aloud—something like, "rated four out of a possible five stars." Say you put this text within the HTML, so that everyone can access it. But you don't want this text to be displayed on the page; you want only the image of four stars to appear. This is where CSS comes into play. You can apply a `class` attribute to the tag surrounding this text, and target this class using CSS to specify that the text be hidden and an image displayed according to a specified size. The style rules for hiding portions of text in a way that works for all browsers, including screen readers, are covered in the "Formatting Best Practice: CSS" section later in this chapter. The HTML for this part of the page might look like this:

```
<div class="rated-four-out-of-five">
    This movie was rated four out of a possible five stars.
</div>
```

Learn the HTML Tags

If you're an experienced web developer who has worked on multiple sites, and you've been marking up your content semantically, you're already familiar with a whole host of tags: `<h1>`, `<h2>`, `<p>`, `<img>`, `<ul>`, and `<li>`, to name a few. However, a number of less common tags are rarely at the forefront of developers' minds. Without some of these tags, you risk marking up your documents in the wrong way, missing an opportunity to add meaning to your content for the benefit of your users, search engines, and others.

The following are a few tags that add important meaning for the browser or end user, but are commonly forgotten:

`<abbr>`: Abbreviation, used for marking up inline text as an abbreviation. In many browsers, hovering the mouse over the text reveals the unabbreviated version.

```
<abbr title="et cetera">etc.</abbr>
```

`<acronym>`: Acronym, used for marking up inline text as an acronym. In many browsers, hovering the mouse over the text reveals the elongated version.

```
<acronym title="World Wide Web">WWW</acronym>
```

`<address>`: Contact information for page. At first glance, you may think this tag should be used to mark up postal addresses listed on the page. However, that is an incorrect usage of the tag. It should be used only to mark up the contact details of the page author. (Of course, a postal address could be part of that information.)

```
<address>
    Author: Den Odell<br />
    <a href="mailto:me@denodell.com">Email the author</a>
</address>
```

`<blockquote>`: Long quotation. An important point to note about block quotes that often gets missed is that the tag may contain only block-level elements. Therefore, the quote itself must, at the very least, be enclosed by a paragraph or other block-level element.

```
<blockquote>
    <p>If music be the food of love, play on,<br />
    Give me excess of it, that surfeiting,<br />
    The appetite may sicken, and so die.</p>
</blockquote>
```

`<ins>` and `<del>`: Inserted and deleted copy. `<del>` is used to show that one piece of content has been deleted. `<ins>` shows that another piece has been inserted into a page. For example, these tags might be used on a blog post where the author has, after publication, returned to the piece and edited it to alter a particular sentence. The tags can be used to show this in a semantic way. Often, content within a `<del>` tag will be rendered in the browser as struck through with a line.

```
There are <del>50</del> <ins>60</ins> million inhabitants of the UK
```

Keep these tags in mind as you code your pages. See if you can spot opportunities to work them into your markup to denote the correct meaning of your content.

Tip Keep a reference list of tags and attributes on hand when developing, and revise that list occasionally. A great online resource for XHTML tags and attributes can be found at `http://www.w3schools.com/tags/`.

Start with a Document Type Definition

You should start every HTML or XHTML page with a Document Type Definition (DTD, or DOCTYPE). This should appear before any other HTML tags in a page. The DTD indicates the HTML standard used for the page content, which is important information for any software parsing the page contents. For example, if the browser knows that the content in the rest of the document is XHTML, it then may assume that each tag is closed, that the casing of tags and attributes is consistent, and that tags are properly nested, as these are the rules that apply to XHTML documents.

The DTD is not a standard tag and does not need to be closed, Here is an example:

```
<!DOCTYPE html PUBLIC "-//W3C//DTD XHTML 1.0 Transitional//EN" ➥
    "http://www.w3.org/TR/xhtml1/DTD/xhtml1-transitional.dtd">
```

This DTD declares the rest of the page contents to be in the XHTML 1.0 Transitional format and tells the content reader which URL it can visit to get the specification to follow.

By omitting the DTD, you run the risk of having the browser itself try to figure out which standard to use, which can result in some odd rendering bugs.

DOCTYPE Switching

One of the huge complaints that arose from earlier releases of Microsoft's IE browser (up to and including version 5.5) was that it would not actually render some styles as the W3C recommendation suggested. More specifically, the *box model*, which determines how the browser should apply CSS width and height dimensions to a block-level element that also has padding, was not in line with the W3C's recommendation, nor with implementations in other browsers.

Microsoft developers faced a predicament with the release of IE 6: they could either adopt the correct implementation and break the rendering of all existing pages designed for previous versions of the browser, or they could leave it as is and force all developers to use different style sheets for IE than for other browsers. Obviously, neither option was desirable. As a solution, they built in both rendering methods and came up with a way of switching between them using the DTD at the start of the document.

By supplying a DTD that omitted the URL portion, the developer forced the browser into *quirks mode*—the original but incorrect way of rendering the box model within IE. By supplying a DTD with the full URL portion, the developer forced the browser into *standards mode*, complying with W3C standards. Thus, the choice was left to developers to pick which rendering method to use for their site.

DTD Selection

As developers, we want to push forward standards adoption across the Web, both in terms of our code and the software used to interpret it. However, we must realize that simply adopting the latest recommendation from the W3C is not always the smartest move. We must take into account the proportion of existing browsers that support that recommendation.

As it stands at the time of printing, the following selection of DTDs have full cross-browser support and are recommended:

- HTML 4.01 Strict
- HTML 4.01 Transitional

- HTML 4.01 Frameset

- XHTML 1.0 Strict

- XHTML 1.0 Transitional

- XHTML 1.0 Frameset

HTML 4.01 is a trimmed-down version of HTML 4 that emphasizes structure over presentation. HTML 4.01 Strict should be used as a default DTD, unless there is an overriding reason to use another version. It renders the document in the strictest, most standards-compliant mode.

HTML 4.01 Transitional includes all elements and attributes of HTML 4.01 Strict, but adds presentational attributes, deprecated elements, and link targets. HTML 4.01 Transitional should be used if integration with legacy code is required.

HTML 4.01 Frameset includes all elements and attributes of HTML 4.01 Transitional but adds support for framesets. You should not use it, except in cases where using framesets is unavoidable.

As discussed shortly, XHTML is essentially HTML in the format of XML. It can be read by XML parsers, and transformed using Extensible Stylesheet Language Transformations (XSLT) to any other text-based form.

DTD Validation

Selecting a DTD to describe your document doesn't mean that the markup you have written adheres to the specification contained within that DTD. To avoid errors, you should run your page through an HTML validator, which will check your page's adherence to the DTD you specified.

One of the best validators is the online tool supplied by the W3C, at `http://validator.w3.org/`. You can run the validation from a public-facing URL by uploading your HTML file or by directly entering your markup into a text field on the site. Clicking the Check button on the W3C validator site runs the validation. Any resulting errors are listed in document source code order.

How Do You Put the X in XHTML?

As XHTML is essentially HTML with XML rules applied, the rules are the same as for XML:

- All tags must be well formed.

- All elements and attribute names should be in either lowercase or uppercase, as XML is case-sensitive. Many find lowercase to be easier to read.

- Values for attributes must be quoted and provided. Even simple numeric values must be quoted. In instances where the attribute serves as a Boolean on-or-off type of value (for example, the `checked` and `disabled` attributes for `<input>` elements), the value should be set to be the same as the attribute name, as in this example:

```
<input checked="checked" type="checkbox" name="item1" id="item1" value="1" />
```

Unlike HTML, XHTML is well formed—every tag that's opened must be closed. This means that it is simpler for a browser to parse XHTML than HTML, and therefore its use is also suited for mobile applications, where processors are slow and memory small. Specifically for mobile usage, there is XHTML Mobile Profile (now known as XHTML Basic), a subset of full XHTML.

In fact, the general transformability and readability of XHTML makes it suitable for other web services and computer programs to access and parse, meaning it is incredibly versatile, and as such, its use is highly recommended. All examples in the rest of this book will favor XHTML over HTML.

Well-Formed Documents

An XHTML document is well formed when all elements have closing tags or are self-closing and all elements are nested properly with respect to others. That is to say that any tag opened must be closed before its parent tag is closed.

Here is an example of the correct nesting of tags:

```
<p>
    Here is a paragraph with <em>emphasized</em> text.
</p>
```

And here is an example that shows incorrect nesting:

```
<p>
    Here is a paragraph with <em>emphasized</p> text.
</em>
```

In XHTML documents, elements with no inner content, such as `<br />` and `<img />`, must be self-closing. A space should be placed between the final character of the tag name and the slash character at the end of the tag. Omitting this space has been known to cause issues with rendering in some older browsers, including Netscape 4.

Element Prohibitions

XHTML does place some restrictions on the nesting of elements. Inline elements cannot be placed directly inside the `<body>` element, for example, and must be wholly nested inside block-level elements. Block-level elements cannot be placed inside inline elements. Certain elements are considered both block and inline, depending on the content within them, such as `<ins>` and `<del>`. It is worth noting which elements these are by looking through your HTML reference guide. Be aware that certain elements cannot contain other elements, such as those listed in Table 1-1.

Table 1-1. *Some Tags with Content Restrictions*

Tag	Restriction
`<a>`	Cannot contain other `<a>` tags
`<pre>`	Cannot contain the `<img>`, `<object>`, `<big>`, `<small>`, `<sub>`, or `<sup>` elements
`<button>`	Cannot contain the `<input>`, `<select>`, `<textarea>`, `<label>`, `<button>`, `<form>`, `<fieldset>`, `<iframe>`, or `<isindex>` elements
`<label>`	Cannot contain other `<label>` elements
`<form>`	Cannot contain other `<form>` elements

Put Best Practice into Practice

So you're sitting in front of your computer ready to code up an HTML page according to best practices. How do you go about doing that?

Remember that your goal is to write code that is consistent and easy to follow for other developers, and results in a web page that is correctly marked up and accessible to end users. Let's go through some guidelines and rules that should help you follow best practices.

Write Code That's Neat and Tidy

Code indentation enhances code readability. By indenting sections of code based on their grouping or degree of nesting, your code will be easier to read and understand. Remember that one of the goals here is for maintainability by other developers. Just as you tidy up your living room in case you have guests, you should keep your code tidy for when you might have visitors.

Tab characters should be used for indentation instead of whitespace. This facilitates maintenance as well as readability, while reducing the overall weight of a page. In your development environment, you can configure tab spacing to map to a certain number of character spaces. Usually two, four, or eight character spaces are sufficient for readability.

Code blocks residing inside other tags should be indented. For every level of nesting, the code should be indented one tab inward. Tags that contain only text content for display, or inline elements, need not have their content indented with respect to their parent. Take a look at the following example, which shows some typical spacing.

```
<div id="container">
    <p>A paragraph of content</p>
    <table>
        <tr>
            <th>Name</th>
            <th>Value</th>
        </tr>
        <tr>
            <td>Red</td>
            <td>ff0000</td>
        </tr>
    </table>
</div>
```

Cut Down on Comments

I'm sure you've seen many examples of HTML comments strewn throughout web sites. They are in this format:

```
<!-- comment goes here -->
```

Often, they are used to note the beginning and end of particular tags or sections of the page. While this may be useful when trying to establish which server-generated code is doing what to your front-end output, most development environments and built-in browser development tools allow you to locate the starting and ending points of blocks and sections of content, so this usage of comments is somewhat redundant.

Including large numbers of comments within your HTML means the end users must download more markup data to their browser across the network before they have a page displayed that they can interact with. I recommend steering clear of HTML comments, with the following exceptions:

- Where the use of particular markup might seem odd to another developer viewing your code at a later date. A comment can provide an explanation and avoid confusion.

- Where it causes a particular browser to have a certain, specific behavior. This is the case with conditional comments in IE, which we will look at next.

Use Conditional Comments for IE

As of IE version 5 and above (Windows-only), Microsoft added a very useful feature called *conditional comments*. The idea is that if a developer needs to write code to specifically target a particular version of IE, or for IE itself, this can be done by a specially formatted comment tag, rather than by using JavaScript or server-side browser detection. To all other browsers, the contents of the tag appear as a standard comment, so they are ignored.

Here is an example of a conditional comment targeting IE version 6 and above:

```
<!--[if gte IE 6]>
    <p>You are browsing with Internet Explorer version 6 or above.</p>
<![endif]-->
```

The following includes a conditional comment targeting IE users only:

```
<!--[if IE]>
    <p>You are using Internet Explorer browser.</p>
<![endif]-->
```

And, as a final example, this conditional comment targets versions of IE older than version 7:

```
<!--[if lt IE 7]>
    <p>You are using a version of Internet Explorer older than version 7.</p>
<![endif]-->
```

Within conditional comments, lt denotes less than, gt means greater than, lte means less than or equal to, and gte means greater than or equal to.

This technique really comes into play with regard to importing external style sheets. Consider the following code, which would sit within the <head> block of an XHTML document. It conditionally loads an external style sheet for IE 6 users,

```
<link rel="stylesheet" href="master.css" type="text/css" />
<!--[if IE 6]>
    <link rel="stylesheet" href="master.ie6.css" type="text/css" />
<![endif]-->
```

When they read in this code, most web browsers see a reference to a single style sheet, master.css, followed by a comment (between the <!-- and --> comment markers), which they ignore. IE 6 is the exception. Because it identifies the opening of a conditional comment block that specifies that the containing code should be read by only that specific version of IE, it chooses to read and parse the code within that comment.

This allows developers to maintain their master style sheet for all standards-compliant web browsers. But, for those instances where specific versions of IE just won't play ball, they can include a reference to a smaller style sheet containing style fixes to only those elements that are out of whack. In the future, when IE version 6 is a distant memory, developers need only delete the conditional comment and the code within it to remove any version-specific code or styles from their site.

Set the <html> Tag Correctly

After the DTD declaration in every HTML document comes the `<html>` tag, wrapped around the rest of the document's contents.

For HTML documents, this can be left as just the tag without any attributes specified, but in the case of XHTML, certain attributes must be included. Take a look at this example from an XHTML document:

```
<html xmlns="http://www.w3.org/1999/xhtml" xml:lang="en-GB" lang="en-GB" dir="ltr">
```

This example has the following components:

`xmlns`: This attribute defines the namespace for custom tags within the document (this is required, although it is rarely used in real-world applications at present).

`xml:lang` and `lang`: These attributes specify the language, such as en for English (and often including the region locale, such as en-GB for Great Britain) of the entire document. Where the language of specific content changes in the document, such as when using the French expression *c'est la vie*, this text must be marked up with a tag surrounding it. In many cases, you would use a `<span>` tag, setting the `xml:lang` and `lang` attributes for this element. In the preceding example, this attribute's value would be fr-FR.

`dir`: This specifies the text direction of the content within the document. For most Western languages, this value will be ltr (left to right). However, if the text direction changes within the content, you should note this by setting the `dir` attribute on a tag surrounding that content. The only other possible value is rtl (right to left).

Specify the Content Type

It is advisable to specify to the browser or user agent the content type of the document, in case it is incapable of reading this directly from the file itself, as it reduces assumptions and ensures that the content is readable in the form it was written. Use the `<meta>` tag within the `<head>` part of the HTML file to do this, as in this example:

```
<meta http-equiv="Content-Type" content="text/html; charset=utf-8" />
```

In this line of code, the browser is told that the content type is in the UTF-8 character set. This particular character set is very flexible, in that most worldwide characters can be inserted directly into your document without the need for conversion to HTML entity codes. This is especially useful for characters outside the standard English alphabet.

Set the Page Title

The `<title>` tag is an essential part of any document. It needs to be a single heading that describes the document in as few words as possible. It is used as the text for the link to your page within search engine results, and is displayed at the top of the window within your browser.

With this in mind, you might decide to reveal some other information in your page title about the location of the page within the site structure, to provide some context for those who have stumbled across your page through a Google search. The following format seems sensible enough to portray this information while being readable and fairly succinct:

```
<title>Page title - Section name - Site name</title>
```

The *Page title* in this example will almost always match up with the main title of the page, usually contained within the `<h1>` tag of the document. Of course, you can use whichever separator you like between the values; the order is the essential part.

It is sensible to ensure that each distinct page in your site has a unique page title within its section, so that duplicate results with the same name do not appear in search engine results or on a site map.

Separate Presentation, Content, and Behavior

It is important to separate the content of a document from the code needed to apply its design and layout. This level of separation allows you to make style changes easily, without needing to alter the markup. You can even swap out the entire layout of the web site for another layout fairly simply, without affecting its content.

You should avoid using inline styles within your markup (set with the `style` attribute of many tags), as this makes maintenance of your pages incredibly difficult. Developers should know to look within style sheet files for everything involving style and layout, and HTML documents for everything regarding content. The two should never be intermingled. You should also keep all your JavaScript code outside the HTML document.

Instead, within your HTML, reference style sheets through the use of the `<link>` tag. Reference JavaScript code with the `<script>` tag. Adding `class` and `id` attributes to tags within your HTML should be the only method for providing the connections between these files; `style` attributes and JavaScript on-method handlers should not be mingled with your content.

It is possible to reference style sheet files according to the device on which you want those styles to be displayed. For example, you will probably want to include separate style sheets for the printer and the screen, as in this example:

```
<link rel="stylesheet" href="master.css" media="screen" />
<link rel="stylesheet" href="master-print.css" media="print" />
```

Where the `media` attribute is specified on a `<link>` tag, the printer will read a style sheet only when that attribute contains the `print` value, and the screen will read a style sheet only when this attribute contains a value of `screen`. This allows you to style your content differently depending on the presentation media. For example, on the printer, you probably need little more than the basic content of the page. You could create styles that hide the navigation, header, and footer of your page, leaving only the main body of content, which is usually what most people printing your page want to read when they are away from their browser.

Add a Wrapper Element to the Whole Document

Within the <body> tag of your pages, you often will want to add certain layout styles to the whole page. You will soon discover that applying these styles to the <body> tag alone is not sufficient for all the positioning and layout you wish to perform. As a solution, I recommend that you add a "wrapper" element, usually a <div> tag, around the page content, and place the extra layout styles within this element, rather than using the <body> tag itself.

A <div> tag merely defines a block of content and adds no extra meaning to the content within. Use the id attribute to set an appropriate name for this element to which you can hook the CSS styles, like this:

```
<body>
    <div id="page">
        ...
    </div>
</body>
```

If your design is really simple, you may be able to get away with just using the <body> tag. However, consider adding a wrapper element anyway, since you never know how your design may change in future.

Help CSS and JavaScript Target Individual Pages

A practice I advocate is to add a unique id attribute to the <body> tag on each page in your site. Suppose that you have generic styles created for a multipage web site, and you wish to target one specific style slightly differently on a particular page. In this case, you will need to create an exception to the rule. If each page on the site has a unique id attribute, you can create a style that targets just this one page over all others.

Imagine you wish all paragraph text in your site to appear with black text on a white background, but on your home page, you want it to be inverted: white text on a black background. The home page will have a unique id attribute, like this:

```
<body id="homepage">
```

and the styles for the paragraph text will look something like this:

```
p {
    background:white;
    color:black;
}

#homepage p {
    background:black;
    color:white;
}
```

In addition, by using the id attribute in this way, you can easily get a reference to a specific page with JavaScript code, using the document.getElementById method:

```
var homepage = document.getElementById("homepage");
```

Name Your ID and Class Attributes Consistently

You should wrap each logical section or block of the body copy in its own `<div>` tag using sensible, contextual values for their `id` attributes. Certain elements are common across most pages and sites, including the navigation, header, and footer. These types of elements should be kept consistent across pages and projects, where possible, to aid with future maintenance. This allows developers to recognize elements, even when working with unfamiliar pages.

Consider using `id` attribute values along the lines of the following:

```
<div id="header">
<div id="content">
<div id="aside">
<div id="footer">
<div id="navigation">
```

You should name your `id` or `class` attribute values according to the type of content they enclose, rather than any style they use. For example, this form:

```
<p class="error">
```

is better than this one:

```
<p class="red-text">
```

■**Tip** Using a hyphen (-) to separate words in `id` and `class` attribute values makes them easier to read.

Labeling your `class` attributes with content-related information means that when your site designers alter specific parts of the page, you won't need to change your markup; only your style sheet will need modification. It also means that the HTML document stands alone as a description of only the content within, rather than any external file, style, or code.

Order Your Content Correctly

Getting the order of the content within your document correct is just as important as ensuring that it is marked up with the correct tags. Remember that you need to make sure that when the page is read aloud, the most important page content—the main body or subject of the page—is read first, and the less important content—such as navigation links and copyright information—is read last. Screen reader software vocalizes the content of the document strictly in source code order, which means what comes first in your markup is read aloud first.

So that users of screen readers get the content in the most meaningful way, you should organize the `<body>` content of your markup in the following order:

- Page title
- Short list of links that jumps the reader straight to content further down in the page (in-page links)
- Main body content

- Aside content (sidebar, related content, or context-sensitive links)
- Main navigation
- Footer and copyright information

You can use CSS to alter the visual layout of the page so that it matches designs that you must work with. This is explained in the "Accessibility Guidelines for Styles" section later on in this chapter.

Separate Foreground Images from Backgrounds

It is important to make a distinction between those images on your page that are directly related to the content and those that relate to the layout or template of the site.

Images that are directly relevant to the content of the page—figures, charts, pictures of your pets, and so on—should be marked up using the `<img>` tag, as you might expect. All other images, including company logos and icons, should be referenced using background images within your style sheet files. This provides another way to distinguish page layout from relevant page content.

Ask yourself, "If I printed out only the body content of this page, would this image be out of place, or is it contextually relevant to the content?" In practice, you will find that the majority of image files will be referenced from within CSS and not be marked up with the `<img>` tag.

In those instances where you do use `<img>` tags, remember to use the `alt` attribute to describe the content of the image for those users who are unable to view images in their browser for whatever reason. If the image is complex, such as a graph or chart, it might need a more detailed explanation. In this case, consider using the `longdesc` attribute to point to the URL of a page that contains an in-depth description of the information conveyed by the image.

Use Tables Properly

Up until a few years ago, it was common practice to position page components using HTML `<table>` tags. The `<table>` tag should be used only to represent tabular data, and never for positioning content on the page; CSS is more than up to the task of positioning content and providing page layout.

There are many ways you can add extra semantic information to tabular data, all of which aid accessibility to the information contained within the table, and so are worth implementing. In a nutshell, these are as follows:

- Use the `<caption>` tag after your opening `<table>` tag to add a caption to the table. Remember that you can always use style sheets to hide the contents of this tag if you don't want them displayed, but it is wise to add as much semantic data as possible to your pages.
- Use the `summary` attribute of the `<table>` tag to provide a brief overview of the contents of the table and what it aims to represent. This attribute can be read aloud to summarize the table's contents.

- Group the header, body, and footer sections of the table together using the `<thead>`, `<tbody>`, and `<tfoot>` tags. Be aware that these must be placed in a specific order: `<thead>` and `<tfoot>` first, followed by `<tbody>`. This allows the browser to display the header and footer rows of the table while the rest of the content may still be loading.

- Use the `<th>` tag to mark up header cells and `<td>` for actual data.

- Give each header cell a unique `id` attribute value. Then, for each data cell, assign its `headers` attribute value to be a comma-separated list of the `id` values of the associated header cells.

The following is an example of a table using all of these markup techniques:

```
<table summary="Table showing that the average age of students in this course is 26">
    <caption>Table of students registered for this course with their ages</caption>
    <thead>
        <tr>
            <th id="student-name">Student name</th>
            <th id="age">Age</th>
        </tr>
    </thead>
    <tfoot>
        <tr>
            <th id="average-age">Average age</th>
            <td headers="age, average-age">26</td>
        </tr>
    </tfoot>
    <tbody>
        <tr>
            <td headers="student-name">John Lewis</td>
            <td headers="age">24</td>
        </tr>
        ...
        <tr>
            <td headers="student-name">Peter Jones</td>
            <td headers="age">28</td>
        </tr>
    </tbody>
</table>
```

Improve Your Forms

You should group logically related sections of a form together using the `<fieldset>` tag, with each containing one `<legend>` tag to provide a header for that particular grouping of fields within the form. For example, a credit card application form may contain sections for personal information, credit history, and bank details. In this case, the form could be created with three `<fieldset>` tags with `<legend>` tags of Personal information, Credit history, and Bank details, respectively, as follows:

```
<form method="get" action="/">
    <fieldset>
        <legend>Personal information</legend>
        ...
    </fieldset>

    <fieldset>
        <legend>Credit history</legend>
        ...
    </fieldset>

    <fieldset>
        <legend>Bank details</legend>
        ...
    </fieldset>

    <input type="submit" value="Save" />
</form>
```

Make sure that each field within your form that has an associated text label has that label marked up with the <label> tag. This tag takes a for attribute, which you should set to the same value as the id tag you set on the associated field. The default browser behavior in this case is to make the <label> tag clickable, bringing the focus of the form into the associated field, and allowing the user to interact with that form field when the label is selected. To allow for more scope of applying style rules to form fields and their associated labels, add a <div> wrapper tag around each field, which lets you target the fields through style sheets and set spacing and other visual properties. Here is an example:

```
<div class="field">
    <label for="first-name">First name</label>
    <input type="text" id="first-name" name="first-name" />
</div>
```

Pay special attention to the text used within the <legend> and <label> tags within a <fieldset>. When these field labels are read aloud by certain screen reader software, the text within the <legend> tag is prefixed to the text in the <label> tags to provide extra context to the listener. You must ensure that when this is read aloud, it makes sense to the listener.

Avoid Using Frames

You should avoid using framesets at all cost. They make the content and layout of a site difficult to maintain, are a pain to use on small-screen devices (such as mobile phones), and make navigating around content difficult for end users who do not use a mouse as their primary form of input to their computer.

Inline frames (using the <iframe> tag) should be used sparingly, if at all. They can be confusing to the end user and lack the inherent accessible nature of a single-page HTML document.

Accessibility Guidelines for Web Content

If you are not familiar with the Web Content Accessibility Guidelines (WCAG), read these W3C recommendations at `http://www.w3.org/TR/WCAG20/`. These guidelines denote three different levels of accessibility compliance of a web page: A, AA, and AAA, where AAA is the most accessible content.

The accessibility guidelines relate not only to technology, but also to creative design, copy writing, and information architecture, which together provide the total experience for the end user. AAA compliance is the holy grail of any web site developer and should always be strived for. However, AA compliance is usually achievable and is a happy medium for developers who are impeded by time or design constraints. Following the guidelines in this chapter will get you well on the way to providing the most accessible experience you can through technology, but you must be aware of how different users interact with web pages, so I encourage you to read the WCAG document.

Don't Be Fooled by Access Keys

Once touted as a fantastic addition to web pages, access keys are keyboard shortcuts that allow users to jump to certain content on the page or to external pages. However, modern thinking has reasoned their use away, and you should avoid using access keys.

Keyboard shortcuts are very useful to end users who do not use a mouse. In fact, those users often have their own shortcuts set up within their operating system. Unfortunately, access keys often conflict with user-defined keyboard shortcuts. Users will find it confusing when they think they are using their own shortcut, but are actually using the access key shortcut instead, or vice versa.

Access keys can also be confusing because different sites typically use different keys to perform the same action. This means that the end users must become familiar with a different set of shortcuts for each web site visited. This is not expected in the world of computer software, where certain keyboard shortcuts usually perform the same action, regardless of the program.

One of the golden rules of accessibility is to reduce confusion among end users. So, we must regard access keys as nice in theory, but bad in practice.

Don't Be Fooled by Tab Indexes

Another so-called accessibility addition that you should steer clear of is tab indexes. These set the order that links, form fields, and so on become active as the user presses the Tab key on the keyboard. Unfortunately, it is not possible to simply add a tab index to a single field. If you specify a tab index for one element, it must be specified for every element; otherwise, you cannot maintain control over the tab order. The daunting task of maintainability and its limited impact on accessibility makes this a write-off.

A better solution is to ensure your document is well structured, with important content toward the top of the page, and to specify links and form fields in the source code in the order that you wish for them to be tabbed. You can then use style sheets to position these elements on the screen in the desired location or order for visual effect.

Don't Rely on Plug-Ins

By definition, a browser plug-in is not inherently accessible. Since it is not part of the browser itself, the presence of any plug-in must never be assumed. If the end user does not have a particular plug-in, such as Adobe's Flash Player, alternative content should be provided, as explained earlier in this chapter.

It is not wise to wrap an entire web page within a Flash movie, as is so often the case on the Web. The content within the movie remains inaccessible to users of certain browsers and those without the plug-in, and is invisible to most search engines. Instead, consider the use of Flash components on your page—perhaps a movie trailer displayed within a Flash movie container or a special creative treatment to a navigation bar. Then ensure that those users without the plug-in are able to access the content in an alternative way. For example, you might include a transcription of the movie trailer or a plain navigation bar without creative treatment. In this way, you are creating beautiful, smart web pages without sacrificing accessibility.

Add Extra Semantics Where You Can

Some open standards are emerging for adding extra meaning to certain blocks of content within the document markup. One such standard is known as *microformats*. Microformats are blocks of HTML that represent things like people, events, tags, and so on in web pages. They are readable by humans and machines, and entail little more than assigning certain values to certain attributes.

The hCard microformat, for example, is used to mark up address card information, similar to the vCard format, which is a commonly used for exchanging address information between computer software. The following is an example of using the hCard microformat to mark up a name, web site URL, and mobile telephone number:

```
<div class="vcard">
    <a class="url fn" href="http://www.denodell.com/">
        Den Odell
    </a>
    <span class="tel">
        <span class="type">Mobile</span>
        <span class="value">+441234567890</span>
    </span>
</div>
```

The actual tags used are unimportant. Rather, it is the attribute names that are detected by software built to recognize them, including some existing web browsers. Style sheet rules can be used to hide any of the pieces of content that you do not want displayed on your page and will leave them as the pure semantic data within the markup.

Tip Other microformats exist for marking up calendar events (hCalendar), content reviews (hReview), and more. New microformats are being recommended as this book is being written. Follow the progress and see more examples online at http://microformats.org/.

Formatting Best Practice: CSS

As a developer, you have most likely opened a style sheet file that someone else worked on and thought to yourself, "How am I meant to understand this?" Once you separate all layout styles from the markup of the document, you will notice just how many style definitions make up a single page or site!

Because of the sheer number of style definitions required to lay out a page, it soon becomes cumbersome to maintain the layout without sticking to some sensible guidelines for structuring CSS files and styles.

Regarding Pixel-Perfect Reproduction of Designs

As developers, we should always strive to build pages that match the creative designs we are working from as pixel perfectly as possible. However, sometimes the effort required for this pixel-perfect consistency is not worth the visual gain that comes from it.

Consider form fields, for example. I have lost track of the number of creative designs I have worked from that showed `<select>` drop-down boxes with custom-designed handles (the *handle* is the downward-pointing arrow on the edge of the box). Those of us who have attempted to style these boxes in the past—and believe me, I have tried—have discovered the extreme variations between browsers.

It does appear that the more modern the browser, the more control we have over the native controls. That doesn't help the majority of us, however. Many of us are still required to support older browsers such as IE 6, however arcane their form controls may appear.

The solution is to take a best-effort approach. For those browsers that can support it, offer the custom-styled form controls. For older browsers that don't render the required results, it's necessary to be pragmatic.

All major browsers allow you to style the background color, text color, font, and line height (although the height specification can give different results in different browsers, so some experimentation is needed). Not all browsers allow you to specify a border style or color, or to customize the appearance of a drop-down box handle. You should ensure your client is aware of this fact in advance. Otherwise, you will need to adjust the designs accordingly to achieve an identical appearance across different browsers.

From experience, and a healthy dose of common sense, we know that most end users run only one browser on their machine. Furthermore, most users are not examining the design elements. Typically, they will not spot a border on a `<select>` box that doesn't match the other form fields on the page. End users are mostly concerned with whether they can get the information they want from your page quickly.

The following are a couple of rules of thumb for where to draw the line with cross-browser variations using the same CSS:

- You may exclude certain design aspects of the page if the development time required to build the support in the first place is unreasonable for the visual gain produced.

- You may exclude certain design aspects of the page if the maintenance tasks required to make changes to the code base in the future to support the layout would be too cumbersome to expect of any developer.

W3C CSS Standards

CSS 1.0 was recommended by the W3C to developers back in 1996. Its support is virtually universal in about 99% of the browsers in common use today.

CSS 2.1 is the current recommendation, and while it is not universally supported in all browsers (currently limited to the Firefox 3, Safari 3, IE 8, Opera 9.5, and Google Chrome versions of the most common browsers), partial support can be found in that same 99% of browsers. Support exists for CSS positioning (also referred to as CSS-P before CSS 2.1 reached recommendation) to place elements on the page at absolute locations with reference to the top-left corner of the browser window, and at relative locations with respect to the element in which they are contained.

Currently seeking recommendation is CSS 3 (though it has been in this stage for a long time, as suggestions keep being made for additions). The best CSS 3 support so far can be found in Safari 3, but recent releases of both Firefox and Opera have increasing levels of support. Don't be afraid to use CSS 2.1 and CSS 3 style rules, as long as you ensure you can adequately represent your design in as many browsers as possible.

Guidelines for Style Sheets

By following CSS best practices, you can achieve the main goals of making your web pages fully accessible and your code easy to maintain. The guidelines presented in this section will help prepare your style sheets for any changes that may be required in the future, while ensuring the needs of your end users are met.

Separate Common Style Rules

It is highly desirable to include on each page only the CSS style rules required to render that page. Having extra style rules that are not used results in extra data the browser must download and interpret before it knows to dismiss that data. However, two things must be kept in mind: maintainability and an understanding of how the browser works.

Consider a web site dedicated to up-to-the-minute sports scores, which is made up of four pages. The home page describes the purpose of the site to the visitor and provides links to the other pages. The other pages include one with the sports scores, a news update page, and a frequently asked questions (FAQ) page. According to the guideline, the only style rules on each page would be those required to render that specific page.

Now consider how these web pages might look on the screen. Most web sites have components that exist across every page, such as a header section with the site logo and navigation and a footer with copyright information. Also, most site designs are based on a layout template. so each page fits the same rough dimensions and adopts a grid layout specified by the designer. Think of the maintenance nightmare of having to update the header, footer, and general page layout if their styles were duplicated in each of the four style sheet files for the site's four pages. A more sensible approach is needed to ensure maintainability and avoid style rule duplication.

All major web browsers seek to give the end user the fastest and most pleasurable web-browsing experience they are able to offer, and they adopt many approaches in order to do that. One such approach is called *caching*, which involves storing a copy of all the HTML, images, style sheets, JavaScript files, and other static assets requested to display the web page locally on the end user's hard disk. This means that when the users click the web browser's back button or revisit a page, the browser only needs to look on the hard disk to retrieve the data required to display the page. This avoids downloading these assets again over the comparatively slow Internet connection, so the page is displayed much faster than before.

In simple cases, an image—the site logo, for example—is downloaded once when the user visits the home page. Provided that each page is pointing to the same image file on the web server, and that image has not been updated in the meantime, the web browser will take that image from its cache on the hard disk, rather than waste time downloading it again. We can take this same principle and apply it to style sheets.

Let's say you have one style sheet for your web site that contains only the styles for the general page layout and common components that appear across all pages. You include a reference to this same file on each of your pages. The web browser will download this file once, when the end user first visits a page on the web site (usually the home page), and thereafter on subsequent page visits, the browser will use the file already downloaded. This speeds up the rendering of pages, as time isn't spent downloading more files than are necessary. This has the added benefit of keeping all the page styles common to the entire site together in one file, so you no longer have style rule duplication across your pages.

You can lay out the page-specific style rules in single files of their own, so each page will reference two external style sheets: one common to the site and one unique to the page.

Understand Cascade and Specificity

Two important terms used when discussing style sheets are *cascade* and *specificity*. Cascading (the letter *C* in the acronym CSS) is used to describe how styles are applied in an additive fashion. Specificity describes the specific levels of instance at which a particular style is applied to the page.

The most sensible way to organize your style rules is to start off writing generic styles and increase the specificity of your styles as you progress. Often, the more generic your styles, the more efficient your style sheet files can be. Try to avoid overspecifying a style rule. There is no need to list every tag, ID, or class applied to the element you are styling—keep things short and simple.

As an example, consider an HTML page with the following markup for the <body> tag:

```
<body>
    <div id="page">
        <div id="header">
            <h1>My Page Title</h1>
        </div>
        ...
    </div>
</body>
```

Rather than specifying the following to apply styles to the heading tag:

```
body #page #header h1 {
}
```

specify something simpler:

```
#header h1 {
}
```

Since you know that all `id` attribute values within HTML must be unique, there can be only one element on the page with the `id` value of `header`, so specifying its parent elements in the style rule adds redundancy. You do not need to specify the `body` tag selector either, since the only tags you are able to apply styles to are within the `<body>` tag, by definition. Also, in the preceding new style rule, you are able to keep `header` as a distinct component of the page that is not restricted by its parent element. If you choose to move the `<div id="header">` tag around the markup and place it within a different parent element, you know the style rule will apply to it in the same way.

Let's consider another example. Suppose you want two paragraphs of text to appear in the same font, and differ only in their size and color. Here's the HTML:

```
<body>
    <div id="page">
        <p>The quick, brown fox jumped over the lazy dog.</p>
        <div class="alternative">
            <p>The five boxing wizards jump quickly.</p>
        </div>
    </div>
</body>
```

Now check out the style rules:

```
#page p {
    font-family: Verdana, Arial, Helvetica, sans-serif;
    font-size: 1.3em;
    color: #000;
}


#page div.alternative p {
    color: #f00;
    font-size: 1em;
}
```

The styles described in the most generic style rule, the former of the two rules in the preceding code, will be applied to all paragraph tags within the `<div id="page">` tag. The latter style rules are applied to the more specific paragraph tags within the `<div class="alternative">` tag. This additive effect is what we call *cascade*.

Also of interest is the `!important` keyword, which can be added to the end of any style to force that rule to take precedence over any other rules at a more specific level. You could add this keyword to the preceding example, like this:

```
#page p {
    font-family: Verdana, Arial, Helvetica, sans-serif;
    font-size: 1.3em;
    color: #000!important;
}


#page div.alternative p {
    color: #f00;
    font-size: 1em;
}
```

Since the color of the more generic style has been marked as !important, its style will take precedence over a more specific instance of that style. In this case, the color #000 is applied to all paragraph text within the sample page.

In many cases, the usage of the !important keyword to enforce incorrect precedence is wrong, and is the sign of a poorly architected style sheet. Needing to return to the style sheet file later to figure out why the styles specified are not being applied is not worth the time or headache. Consider refactoring your styles if you find yourself needing to use the !important keyword, so the correct rules are applied to the desired elements. In some cases, this may mean adding a little extra markup to the page to ensure the styles can be applied in the correct way. But this is better than having a poorly structured style sheet with confusing style rules.

Think About the Printer

When building the style sheets for a site, most developers neglect the printer, though rarely deliberately. It is important to know what does and what does not get printed when your users click that print button on their browser's toolbar. There are three items you need to consider:

Wide content: Content wider than the width of a printed page is usually chopped off—not printed at all. Some browsers allow scaling of content to fit the printed page, but this can result in text that's very difficult to read, depending on the width of your site layout.

Background images and colors: Since you should be including as foreground images only those graphics that directly relate to that page's content, all other images (such as logos) should be background images. In many cases, all the images on the page will actually be background images, specified within external CSS style sheet files. Most browsers will not print those background images and colors. This was a smart move on the part of the browser vendors to save ink and print only what's necessary: the textual content of the page. As noted earlier, in most cases, users print a web page to read its main body content—whether it's a train timetable, book review, or bank statement. Rarely will a site visitor want to print the page exactly as it appears on screen. For those who do, there are often hidden preference settings within the browser to enable the printing of background images and colors, but these options are rarely switched on by default.

Text color: Most users in an office environment will have access to a laser printer only, which will often print in black and white. Most home users will have an inkjet printer capable of full-color, photo-quality printing. Consider the lowest common denominator and test print your pages on a black-and-white printer, if you have access to one, or by choosing to print on your inkjet printer with black ink only. Text color also comes into play when you consider background images. Suppose your web page has white text on a dark background. Since that background color won't print, you will be left with white text printed on your crisp, white paper. Of course, the printer has no white ink to print with, so the user actually gets a blank page!

A printout of a web page usually shows large chunks of blank space where background images and colors once were, often with some content chopped off the page and some light-colored text missing entirely. This is hardly what the users want to see on their printed pages.

You don't want to be responsible for user frustration, so you should get around these limitations by specifying a style sheet that will be read only by the printer, using this markup:

```
<link rel="stylesheet" href="master-print.css" media="print" />
```

Within this print-only style sheet, you will want to minimize the whitespace that would appear on the printed page, removing unnecessary components, and ensure that no content is chopped off or hidden in the final printed article. For example, you can remove the navigation by applying the following style rule:

```
#navigation {
    display: none;
}
```

You may want to specify a font color, such as black, to override all other text colors on the page. This can be achieved with the following style rule:

```
* {
    color:#000!important;
}
```

This applies the color black (in hexadecimal notation, black is #000000 or, in shorthand, #000) to all elements on the page (the * wildcard is used to target all elements on the page). Note the use of the keyword !important at the end of the style rule. As I noted earlier, this is a dangerous keyword to use, as it enforces this style's importance over any other style in the document. However, it is very useful in a printer style sheet, as allows you to override the font color of any element on the page, as specified by a master style sheet, without needing to consider its level of specificity.

Format Your Style Rules

One tried-and-tested layout for style rules that demonstrates good legibility is shown in the following example:

```
.module-heading,
.module-subheading {
    background: #333;
    color: #f00;
    float: left; /* inline comment */
}
```

In this style rule, multiple style selectors are used to apply this style rule to page elements with two different CSS classes. Rather than putting the style definitions on the same line, which could be confusing, the style selectors are placed on separate lines. The style rule is opened at the end of the line following the last CSS class name and closed on a separate line after all the style rules. The style rules themselves are indented one tab stop with respect to the style definitions themselves. A space appears between the colon character after each style property name and its respective value.

Each style property exists on its own line, and each line is terminated with a semicolon. If you need to supply a comment to associate with any style rule to aid future development or maintenance, this comment should follow the semicolon on the same line as the rule itself. For consistency in your style rules, you may choose to order your style property names alphabetically, according to the type of style property (text, color, layout, and so on), or by any other grouping that is suitable for your application.

Apply Multiple Class Names to a Single Page Element

As mentioned earlier in this chapter, CSS class names specified within your HTML markup should describe the information that the element's content represents, rather than how that content should be displayed.

You may wish to apply multiple class names to the same element, to avoid duplicating your style rules. Within your markup, this can be achieved simply by separating each CSS class with the space character, as in this example:

```
<div class="article main-article">
    <p>Hello, world.</p>
</div>
```

Style rules written for both `article` and `main-article` classes will be applied to the `<div>` tag, from left to right, so styles specified within the `main-article` style rule will take precedence over those within the `article` style rule.

If you need to apply a special style to elements that contain multiple classes in this way, the following CSS selector syntax will allow you to do just that:

```
div.article.main-article p {
    color: #0f0;
}
```

This style rule applies to `<p>` tags whose parent tag is `<div class="article main-article">`. Note the lack of a space character between the CSS class names.

Reset the Browser's Default Styles

By default, a web browser will have its own set of default style rules to apply to a page without styles. This will include font face, size, line height, and color, as well as padding and margins to differing degrees on different elements and tags.

To provide a level playing field for your own styles, I recommend that you reset the browser's default styles. This passes the precise control over each element to your own style sheets, providing more consistency across different browsers.

At its very simplest, the following style rule levels all margin and padding applied to all page elements down to zero, ready for you to specify your own margin and padding spacing individually for each element that requires it in your style rules:

```
* {
    margin: 0;
    padding: 0;
}
```

CSS style guru Eric Meyer provides a very comprehensive reset style sheet that completely eradicates cross-browser differences between the default style rules (http://meyerweb.com/eric/tools/css/reset/). Its current incarnation is shown in Listing 1-1.

Listing 1-1. *Eric Meyer's Universal Cross-Browser Style Reset*

```css
/* v1.0 | 20080212 */
html, body, div, span, applet, object, iframe,
h1, h2, h3, h4, h5, h6, p, blockquote, pre,
a, abbr, acronym, address, big, cite, code,
del, dfn, em, font, img, ins, kbd, q, s, samp,
small, strike, strong, sub, sup, tt, var,
b, u, i, center,
dl, dt, dd, ol, ul, li,
fieldset, form, label, legend,
table, caption, tbody, tfoot, thead, tr, th, td {
    margin: 0;
    padding: 0;
    border: 0;
    outline: 0;
    font-size: 100%;
    vertical-align: baseline;
    background: transparent;
}

body {
    line-height: 1;
}

ol, ul {
    list-style: none;
}

blockquote, q {
    quotes: none;
}

blockquote:before, blockquote:after,
q:before, q:after {
    content: '';
    content: none;
}

/* remember to define focus styles! */
:focus {
    outline: 0;
}
```

```
/* remember to highlight inserts somehow! */
ins {
    text-decoration: none;
}

del {
    text-decoration: line-through;
}

/* tables still need cellspacing="0" in the mark-up */
table {
    border-collapse: collapse;
    border-spacing: 0;
}
```

Eric Meyer has spent a lot of time researching and testing CSS support in each major browser, and his reset style is the much-appreciated fruit of this labor.

Whether you choose to use the simple margin/padding reset code shown at the beginning of this section, Eric Meyer's full reset-the-heck-out-of-everything code shown in Listing 1-1, or one of the other alternatives you can find through a quick search of the Web, you should specify these reset styles at the very start of your main site CSS file, before you apply any other style rules.

Master Shorthand Style Rules

Certain styles can be combined or shortened and, where possible, you should use these versions to reduce the size of your CSS files and save on the volume of data downloaded across the wire from the web server to the browser.

As a simple example, certain margin and padding values on an element could either be specified the long-winded way:

```
p {
    margin-top: 5px;
    margin-right: 7px;
    margin-bottom: 5px;
    margin-left: 7px;
    padding-top: 6px;
    padding-right: 3px;
    padding-bottom: 6px;
    padding-left: 3px;
}
```

or in shorthand:

```
p {
    margin: 5px 7px 5px 7px;
    padding: 6px 3px 6px 3px;
}
```

Note that the order of the shorthand values for `margin`, `padding`, and `border` is always as follows:

- Top
- Right
- Bottom
- Left

In the case where the values for `margin-top` and `margin-bottom` are identical, and the values for `margin-left` and `margin-right` are also identical, further shorthand notation may apply, like so:

```
p {
    margin: 5px 7px; /* 5px top and bottom, 7px left and right */
    padding: 6px 3px;
}
```

Other styles—such as `font`, `color`, and `background`—also have their own form of shorthand notation. Chapter 4, which focuses on improving performance in CSS files, provides more details about the shorthand for these styles.

Accessibility Guidelines for Styles

By now, you know that one of our primary concerns as web developers is accessibility—ensuring our content is available to everyone, regardless of browser, device, or input method. Primarily, the focus is on ensuring semantic markup, as discussed earlier in this chapter, but you must ensure that your style sheets back up the principle. Users with displays of different sizes and resolutions should be able to view your page content in a clear manner.

Hide Content from CSS-Capable Browsers

You can use style sheets to visually hide the contents of a particular tag within your markup if you do not want them displayed on the screen. Recall the movie review site example earlier in this chapter, where you wanted to ensure the text was in your HTML, so that if the content were read aloud or read without any style sheets applied, the user would understand the rating the reviewer had assigned to that movie. Now it's time to apply your CSS. You want to show an image representing the equivalent four-out-of-five star rating, rather than show that text.

Hiding text in this way should be accomplished using the `text-indent` style property, choosing a value that positions the text off the left edge of the browser viewport so that it is no longer visible, as follows:

```
div#hide-me {
    text-indent: -9999px;
}
```

Using any other style property for hiding the text has the unfortunate side effect of rendering the text unreadable through the popular JAWS screen reader software, manufactured by Freedom Scientific (http://www.freedomscientific.com/).

Move Content Blocks to Maintain Correct Markup Source Order

Earlier in this chapter, you learned that the order of blocks of content within your markup should be such that when the page is read aloud, the most relevant page content comes first, and secondary content, including navigation and copyright information, comes last. Of course, this order may not suit the visual appearance of your site, where you most likely wish to have your navigation links appear above the main body of content.

If you have two block elements in sequence within your markup and would rather have the latter content appear in the browser before the former, you can use the style property float to reorder those two blocks of content. Look at the following snippet of HTML code:

```
<div id="body">
    ...
</div>

<div id="navigation">
    ...
</div>
```

By default, the `<div id="body">` tag would appear before the `<div id="navigation">` tag, but you can reverse this order with the float style property, as follows:

```
#body {
    float: right;
}

#navigation {
    float: left;
}
```

You may also wish to consider using combinations of absolute and relative positioning to relocate content blocks around the page to achieve the layout you need.

Use Relative Font Sizes

Some site visitors, who are perhaps visually impaired or simply have their screen resolution set high, may resize the base font size in their browser to view the site optimally. All the major browsers have this feature. As developers, we must consider the end user's needs in addition to the design criteria for our web pages.

To handle the possibility of font resizing, you should use relative units within your style sheets, so that as the browser's base font size changes, so too does the page text, proportionally. The em unit is one such relative unit, as is % (percent). You should absolutely not use px (pixel) or pt (point) values to specify font sizes in your style sheets, as these will not scale according to the end user's need.

To make calculation of font sizes easier when working with relative font size units, try setting the default font size on your `<body>` tag element to a size of 62.5%. At this level in default browser settings, the size of 1em becomes visually equivalent to the size of 10px. Each 0.1em increment then corresponds to a visible increase of 1px, so 1.1em is visually equivalent to 11px and 1.2em to 12px. This trick is extremely useful when working with creative designs that invariably have font sizes measured in pixels. The following are examples of sizes:

```css
body {
    font-size: 62.5%; /* resets font sizes so 1em is visually equivalent to 10px */
}

ul li {
    font-size: 1.1em; /* visually equivalent to 11px */
}

h2 {
    font-size: 1.5em; /* visually equivalent to 15px */
}
```

Comment Blocks

To aid with maintenance and to help other developers understand your style sheets, it is smart to group logically related style rules together within your style sheet files. Precede them with a comment describing the purpose of this group's styles, using a consistent notation, such as the following:

```css
/* ------------------------------------------------------------------
    Form styles

    Group of styles for displaying form controls according to
    the agreed design

*/
```

Inline comments, placed next to style rules themselves, should be included only when necessary to clarify a particular rule. For example, where a style rule has been added to deal with an edge case in a particular browser, it makes sense to note this, so that a future developer does not deem the rule unnecessary and remove it without understanding its original intention.

At the very top of each style sheet file, it may be sensible to include an opening comment section, detailing the author(s) of that file and the purpose of the style rules in the file, and listing each of the logical groups contained within the file in the order in which they occur, using a consistent format. Here is an example of the format of a comment block describing an entire style sheet file and its purpose:

```css
/* ------------------------------------------------------------------
    Filename        common.css
    Author          Den Odell me@denodell.com
    Description     Basic page layout and default styles for site

    Contents
    - Reset styles
    - Page column layout
    - Form control styles
```

```
    Color palette
    #777        Medium grey
    #aaa        Light grey
    #a3d60a     Site-wide green
--------------------------------------------------------------
*/
```

Including such a comment block allows developers to see at a glance whether the file contains the code they are seeking. In the case of your common site-wide style sheet, it may be wise to include a list of some of the key colors used across the site. Developers can then easily find these colors, and copy and paste those values if necessary.

Browser Work-Arounds

If you need to include extra styles to target specific versions of IE, you should use the conditional comments technique described earlier in this chapter to include a separate style sheet file for those styles.

Caution Steer clear of hacks that involve setting style values that are out of the ordinary or use combinations of backslashes, comments, and other odd characters to confuse and bewilder certain browsers. If you cannot avoid the use of a particular hack, be sure to include a clear comment as to why you have chosen to leave it in and what purpose it serves, to warn other developers who may view that style sheet file in future.

When using PNG-24 images in IE 6 or earlier, transparent portions of the image files appear in gray/light blue, rather than as transparent. Unfortunately, Microsoft did not introduce support for transparencies in this file type until the release of IE 7. However, you can use a work-around that enables simple PNG-24 images to display as background or foreground images on the page.

Let's say that in your main style sheet, you have the following style rule defined:

```
#header {
    background:url(my-image.png) no-repeat;
}
```

In your IE 6-specific style sheet file, which you have referenced using conditional comments, you would include something like the following style rule:

```
#header {
    background: transparent none;
    filter:progid:DXImageTransform.Microsoft.AlphaImageLoader(src='my-image.png', ➥
        sizingMethod='scale');
}
```

This IE 6-specific style rule hides the background image specified in the original style sheet and instead uses a Microsoft-specific DirectX filter to reference the same image file. This filter is able to display the transparent portions of the image correctly and places it where the background image once sat. There are several limitations with this technique, however, including a lack of support for background positioning and repeating, so use it with so me caution.

Localization Considerations

One of the most important pieces of future-proofing for a web site is to consider that the site may need to be viewable in alternate languages or in country- or region-specific versions.

Not only will the text content of the web site be different, but there will most likely be some alteration to at least one portion of your style sheets. For example, you may need to replace an image file that contains text embedded in a certain language within it, or some other region-specific style, which could even mean altering the text direction for certain alphabets.

To aid this future-proofing, from the outset, you should aim to include all region-agnostic styles within your main style sheet files and to include a separate style sheet file to provide the locale-specific style rules that override the main style sheet on a per-locale basis. In this way, it becomes easy to add support for new languages and locales, as it is simply a case of creating a new style sheet file from the existing region-specific file and making substitutions to those styles to apply to the new region and/or language.

Structuring Your Folders, Files, and Assets

A simple but expandable folder structure provides a good foundation for the addition of future content and assets, without making the task of maintenance more of a burden to the developer. The following sections provide some guidelines for structuring your folders, files, and assets.

Readable URLs

You should create folders that correlate to the site map of your project, so that HTML pages and server-side scripts are stored in folders that cause their URLs to be sensible, readable, and meaningful. Often, the default or index page within each folder can be assigned within the web server configuration so that URLs can be requested by folder name only, and the index file is loaded by default.

You should also attempt to reflect the hierarchy of your site map similarly with folders, so that URLs read as hierarchy structures also. Some search engines may use text in the URL, as well as page contents, as search criteria.

For example, this URL:

```
http://www.mywebsite.com/news/
```

is neater, readable, and more memorable than this one:

```
http://www.mywebsite.com/news.php
```

Also, the sections of the URL should reflect the site map and a sensible hierarchical structure, such as in the following example:

```
http://www.mywebsite.com/music/rock/
```

File and Folder Naming

When naming folders and files, you should use lowercase alphanumeric characters, with each word separated by a hyphen character for legibility. Steer clear of using characters other than English letters, numbers, or hyphens. When referencing these folders and files from code, make sure the casing is consistently lowercase, as certain web server operating systems, including Unix, Linux, and Mac OS X, are case-sensitive. Also, never use the space character or characters reserved for URLs, including the ampersand, hash character, or the question mark, for naming folders or files, or you may find these cannot be referenced consistently from different web browsers.

One requirement that crops up time and time again is to provide your end users with site content localized into their language. It can be incredibly disruptive to perform this localization task after you have built your site, as it may require you to rewrite or refactor your HTML, CSS, and JavaScript files to support it. You should group together assets that relate to a specific region, language, or locale into their own folders, named after the locale (specified, for example, as language and location, such as en-us for US English). Store nonlocale-specific assets at the same level as this folder structure.

■Tip Consider the use of XML files, a content management server, or server-side resource files to provide localized content directly into script-generated markup. This will make maintenance tasks simpler than editing copies of static HTML pages.

File Encoding

The UTF-8 encoding type should be used for all text-based files, as this allows the direct use of extended characters and non-English character sets within the files, without the need for special control characters and ASCII codes.

In practice, it is a lot easier to create files in UTF-8 format from the outset, rather than to translate them later. If you need to convert a file from another encoding format to UTF-8, make a backup of the existing file and use your development environment's file properties dialog box to set the format of the document to the appropriate encoding type. This may affect the encoding of certain characters already within the file, so use the backup file to copy and paste the characters from the backup to the newly UTF-8 encoded file.

In some cases, the byte-order mark (BOM) at the beginning of a UTF-8 encoded file can cause havoc with server-side technologies such as PHP. When encoding files that are to be processed by such technologies, ensure the BOM is removed using the development environment's file properties dialog box, if this option exists.

Organizing Assets

Consider whether placing all static asset files (style sheets, images, scripts, audio, and video), excluding HTML, within a common folder might be worthwhile. This logically separates client-side code from the structure of the site and its content, avoiding clutter at the root level of the site's document tree. The following directory structure is an example of one that follows this approach, and has also been created with localization in mind:

```
\assets
    \images
        \en-gb
        \fr-fr
    \scripts
        \third-party
    \styles
        \en-gb
        \fr-fr
    \flash
    \documents
        \en-gb
        \fr-fr
    \video
        \en-gb
        \fr-fr
    \audio
        \en-gb
        \fr-fr
```

Image Guidelines

Group together contextually related images within folders with meaningful names, to make them easier to find. These names may correlate to the site map of the project or to their content or usage on the page.

Choose the image format that gives the lowest file size, while still retaining the best quality. Use compression carefully. The desired result is an image practically indistinguishable from the original to the human eye at a distance of about 0.5 meter (about 1.5 feet) from the screen.

The PNG file format often results in smaller file sizes for certain types of images. PNG is a lossless format and allows alpha transparencies for web browsers that provide support for that feature (unfortunately, IE 6 does not, by default, but you can try applying the work-around described earlier in this chapter). However, many image manipulation programs include extra gamma information in the image file. Unfortunately, this gamma information is not interpreted in a similar way across browsers, meaning that odd image artifacts and colors may appear. Fortunately, several tools exist to remove this gamma information from PNG files, without compromising the quality of the final image, which has the added benefit of reducing the file size of the image (since extra information is removed). Smush it (http://www.smushit.com/) is one such web-based tool for removing this extra information.

See Chapter 4 for more details on selecting the best image format for the most faithful reproduction of graphics, while ensuring the smallest possible file size.

Multimedia Guidelines

The ubiquitous Adobe Flash Player plug-in should be used to display video until all browsers include their own built-in codecs. Supply a download link to the displayed movie file, preferably in multiple formats, so users without the Flash plug-in may download the movie file for offline viewing.

Use the MP3 storage type for all audio, and harness Adobe's Flash Player to present it to the end user. A download link to the MP3 file should be supplied for users without the Flash plug-in.

Chapter 7 provides more details about including multimedia components in your pages.

Setting Up Your Development Environment

It's also important to consider how you will work on your projects, whether you are working alone or as part of a team. In this section, we'll look at which tools you can leverage to write your files, store your files, and test your pages in a modern, effective way.

Writing Your Files: Integrated Development Environments

Gone are the days of using Notepad for Windows or TextEdit for Mac OS X for writing client-side code for the Web. Modern web sites require a lot of code spread out over multiple files and folders, so an effective way of navigating these folders and editing these files is needed. Desktop application developers have long used integrated development environments (IDEs) to write, maintain, and debug their code. Now the time is right for web developers to follow suit. Each IDE is slightly different, and it really is a matter of personal taste which you find best for your own needs.

One IDE gaining a lot of popularity in the web development community, and my personal favorite, is Aptana Studio (http://www.aptana.com/). This IDE is built upon Eclipse, one of the more popular and well-established development environments for Java developers. It allows you to store project files together; supports syntax highlighting of HTML, CSS, and JavaScript files; and even contains a built-in web server for testing your code without needing to deploy to a separate web hosting infrastructure. Files can be synchronized between your computer and an FTP or SFTP server, and Aptana ensures that files aren't overwritten when they shouldn't be when performing a sync. The same plug-in architecture found in Eclipse is supported, so the multitude of extensions and add-ons already developed for that IDE are available for use within Aptana, making it more than just a basic package.

Other IDEs that are popular among developers include the following;

- Notepad++ (http://notepad-plus.sourceforge.net/) for Windows systems
- Microsoft Visual Web Developer (http://www.microsoft.com/express/vwd/) for Windows systems
- TextMate (http://macromates.com/) for Mac OS X systems
- Coda (http://www.panic.com/coda/) for Mac OS X systems
- Adobe Dreamweaver (http://www.adobe.com/products/dreamweaver/) for both Windows and Mac OS X systems

Investigate these IDEs, try them out, and find which works best for you.

■**Caution** Be wary of any IDE that attempts to write code for you automatically. As a developer, you need to be confident of your own skills and consciously aware of all code that is added to your project.

Storing Your Files: Version Control Systems

One of the guidelines I proposed earlier in this chapter is to regularly purge your folder structure and files for content that is no longer relevant or needed. The result is a tidy, pruned project holding only the code that's needed for the site you are building. This is all well and good, but what if you accidentally delete some code or files you later need? This is where version control systems come into play.

Version control systems store revisions and backups of your files and folders, allowing you to step back in time and recover lost code. Such systems also manage team collaboration, so more than one developer can work on the same file at the same time. The version control system manages the merging of the changes made by each developer into a single file or central storage location for the code.

Subversion (`http://subversion.tigris.org/`) is a popular, open source version control system used in personal and professional development environments. You set up the server part of the system on a web server available via a URL, and the developers use a Subversion client tool to access that web server, taking a local copy of the code to their computer to work on it there. Making a change to a file is as simple as editing the file. When the developers are comfortable that they have completed the feature they were working on, they then "commit" their code back to the server, which manages any merging of files and creation of backup copies.

Subversion appears to be surprisingly simple for developers to use, which is probably why it has been so quickly adopted in the relatively short time it has been around. Of course, the lack of any price tag helps make it accessible to personal users as well as professionals.

You don't need to set up your own server if you want to take advantage of Subversion. Several companies offer services to store your code online, safely backed up each and every time you make a change. One such company is Beanstalk (`http://beanstalkapp.com/`), which offers different pricing models depending on your needs, but also provides a limited free storage plan (up to 20MB at the time of writing), which may be sufficient if you are working on a relatively small project. Google has its own Subversion hosting system known as Google Code (`http://code.google.com/hosting/`), which is free and also contains a wiki and bug-tracking system. Another open source online storage repository is GitHub (`http://github.com/`), which offers various pricing solutions, including a free service for smaller projects. This service uses the GIT technology, rather than Subversion, but the two version control systems are actually very similar in structure and setup.

Once again, investigate these systems and see which one might work best for you. Remember that if you do not use a version control system for your projects, large or small, you run the risk of losing valuable code at any time.

Testing Your Pages: Browsers and Development Tools

Now that you've decided which IDE and version control system you're going to use to work on your files, you need to consider your testing setup. Testing and code validation are vitally important to your work as a professional web developer. You need to make sure that the sites you build work in all the major desktop web browsers (currently IE 6, 7, and 8; Firefox 2 and 3; Opera 9.5 and up; Safari 3 and up; and Google Chrome) and as many mobile devices you can lay your hands on. Of course, the guidelines I've endorsed in this chapter should mean that your sites work in all of these and more. But the only way to know for sure and to iron out subtle differences in HTML, CSS, and JavaScript implementations is to test everything you write thoroughly in as many different browsers and systems as possible.

Be sure you've installed copies of all the web browsers you can on your machine. Some browsers don't support the running of multiple versions on the same machine, so you may want to consider using virtual machine technology to run a secondary copy of your operating system within memory. For Windows users, Microsoft Virtual PC (http://www.microsoft.com/windows/products/winfamily/virtualpc/) is the ideal choice. It is free, and Microsoft even provides regularly updated machine images preinstalled with different versions of IE via the web site, to aid your testing. For Mac OS X users, VMware (http://www.vmware.com/) and Parallels (http://www.parallels.com/) are your best options.

If you are unable to run such virtualization systems, you might be able to use the services of a browser testing web site, such as BrowserShots (http://www.browsershots.org/), which run a URL you supply through various web browsers on different machines and relay the screen grab of the results to you for your comparison. This alternative is certainly not ideal, but it's a good backup or secondary option.

Different browsers have different development tools available for you to prod and poke within the HTML, CSS, and JavaScript output of your pages. Some such tools even allow you to make changes to your code on the fly and see the results immediately. The gold standard is the Firebug plug-in for Mozilla's Firefox (http://getfirebug.com/). I've never met a web developer who hasn't sworn by it for investigating which styles have been applied to their page elements and what the values of variables in their JavaScript are at any given time. When errors occur on your page, the Firebug console points these out to you, and shows on which line numbers in your code these errors occurred. If you're debugging JavaScript errors, you can see the list of function calls that occurred before the error took place, which can help you track down the error.

The Internet Explorer Developer Toolbar plug-in is available for IE 6 and 7. This tool pales in comparison to Firebug, but it does allow you to see which styles are applied to which page elements. IE 8 has its own built-in developer tools, which sit somewhere between those of the Developer Toolbar and Firebug. For debugging JavaScript issues within IE, Microsoft's Visual Web Developer IDE is a very useful tool. It is able to hook onto the internal processes that run IE on the Windows machine. When a JavaScript error occurs, Visual Web Developer allows you to see a full list of all the actions and code called prior to the error taking place, including links to where that error occurred. This is helpful for probing variable values and debugging the issue.

Opera, Safari, and Google Chrome have their own built-in developer tools. Most of these do not seem to be fully feature-complete at the time of writing, but they are shaping up to be about as useful as Firebug.

You should download and learn how to use each browser and its associated development tools, so when those elusive browser-specific bugs rear their heads, you are able to quickly and effectively track down the source of the problem and nip it in the bud.

One last word about testing: don't leave it until the last moment. The projects that consistently deliver on time without developer misery are those that have been tested in many different browsers from the get-go and all the way through the development process, to ensure the final product is the best, most compatible web site possible.

Summary

This chapter discussed the importance of using tried-and-tested current ideas, known as best practices, and how to use discernment when selecting which guidelines to apply to your own projects. We have gone through HTML, CSS, file structures, and development environments, reviewing smart, modern, and effective techniques for writing and maintaining code. You now know that the whole purpose behind using these best practices is to ensure the pages you create are fully accessible by anyone, regardless of browser, device, or input method. You also want to make sure that the code you write can be easily read, understood, and updated in the future.

The next chapter guides you through JavaScript best practices. It covers how to structure your client-side code in such a way that it is similarly easy to read, understand, and update, regardless of the size of the code base. This will help you to build effective RIAs, based on solid, scalable code rules.

CHAPTER 2

JavaScript for Rich Internet Applications

In the previous chapter, I explained how to assemble a solid foundation for your web site code, including making your pages fully accessible and operational without requiring any front-end technology except HTML. I explained that the other components that make up your site—the style sheets, images, plug-ins, and so on—are layers built on your HTML foundation to apply visual layout and design to your pages, and provide a more natural experience for your site visitors.

In this chapter, the focus is on JavaScript, which we use in our pages to simplify tasks for our end users, provide reactions to their actions, and attempt to make their time on the Web a gentler and user-friendlier experience. You're going to build on your existing knowledge of this language throughout this chapter to discover how to structure your code in a scalable, flexible, and maintainable way; use object-oriented programming principles; and overcome cross-browser implementation differences. You'll then discover techniques to help you build RIAs and, finally, learn how to write automated tests for your code to make it more robust.

This is going to be a fairly theoretical chapter, but it is full of useful and important information, so let's get to it!

Coding Style Guidelines

As a web developer, you can simplify your day-to-day coding experience by structuring and organizing your JavaScript code in a consistent manner, writing code to solve your problem or meet your goal, without overcomplicating its appearance. By following some guidelines, you can make your code cleaner, clearer, more manageable, better understood, better documented, and easier to read.

Use Consistent Formatting

As you saw in the previous chapter, the hallmark of legible code—be it HTML, CSS, or JavaScript—is consistent formatting. The contents of JavaScript functions, for example, should be indented one tab space with respect to the function name and enclosing braces. You should end each statement with a semicolon character, and each statement should exist on its own line to ensure good legibility, as in the following example:

```
function myFunction() {
    alert("Hello, world");
    return true;
}
```

Similarly, the contents of logical blocks and loops should also be indented. As a rule of thumb, the contents of a set of opening and closing braces ({ and }) should be indented with respect to these braces, as in this example:

```
if (x == y) {
    alert("We have a match!");
} else {
    alert("We have a problem!");
}
```

However, you may want to use extra indentation where it makes the code easier to read, as in the case statements in the following code:

```
switch (prompt("What is your favorite fruit?", "banana")) {
    case "banana":
        alert("Well done. Bananas are full of potassium.");
        break;
    case "mango":
        alert("Exotic and tasty!");
        break;
    default:
        alert("That's not to my taste, but keep it up to get your 5-a-day.");
        break;
}
```

Use Braces and Brackets

Braces ({}) and brackets (()) are used throughout JavaScript to delineate blocks of code and reduce confusion within long statements. You should use them whenever possible to minimize potential defects and increase legibility, both of which will aid any future code maintenance.

The following example shows a JavaScript routine where braces and brackets have been removed in order to shorten the code.

```
var result = 0;
if (confirm("Would you like to do some math?"))
    result = 10 / 2 * 100 % 30;
alert("OK, the result is: " + result);
```

This is perfectly valid syntax within the language, however it makes the logic slightly harder to follow.

The following form is less confusing and therefore a wholly more stable, legible, and maintainable code routine.

```
var result = 0;
if (confirm("Would you like to do some math?")) {
    result = ((10 / 2) * 100) % 30;
}
alert("OK, the result is: " + result);
```

Notice that with this format, you can be sure when the `alert` statement will execute. And you can see how much more understandable math routines become when using brackets to group operations together.

Add Meaning with Letter Casing

A few simple rules for letter casing in variable and function names will enable you to tell at a glance how they are used within your code. The following are a few common guidelines for casing that you would be wise to follow in your own code:

- Begin most variable and function names with a lowercase letter.

- Begin object constructor names with an uppercase letter. (Object constructors are discussed in the "Objects, Classes, and Constructors" section later in the chapter.)

- Use *camel case*, where each new word begins with an uppercase letter and all other characters are lowercase, to mark the start of new words.

- Use all uppercase characters to denote constants—values that should never change throughout the life of code.

The following code shows examples of each of these types of casing:

```
// Object constructor - see later in the chapter for what this means
var Calendar = function() {

    // Uppercase for constants
    var DAYS_IN_ONE_WEEK = 7;

    // Lowercase character to start variable or function name
    var count;
    function add() {
    }

    // Camel casing for new words in variable and function names
    var currentDate;
    function doSomethingWithCurrentDate() {
    }
}
```

Use Descriptive Variable and Function Names

Choosing appropriate names for your variables and functions is one of the fundamentals of an easy-to-understand code base. Name your variables and functions so they indicate their use and purpose. Don't be afraid to use lengthier names if they get across the message.

Imagine you saw your code with only its variable and function names, without any logic or values. Could you understand the purpose of each at a glance? If not, it's time to start renaming. Here are some examples of descriptive variable and function names:

```
var currentDate;
function setCurrentDate() {
}
var userName;
function updateUserName() {
}
```

You should also avoid the use of so-called *magic numbers*, which are numbers used in calculations that seem to have appeared from nowhere. This example shows magic numbers in action:

```
var daysInAYear = 52 * 7; // With some thinking, you can figure it out
var  seatsOnThePlane = 25 * 6; // But what does this really mean?
```

Where did all the numbers come from, and what do they mean? You should aim to reduce all confusion in your code. Spell it out, so a developer won't need to stare at each line of code to understand it. The following version adds definitions for the number constants used in the previous example.

```
var WEEKS_IN_A_YEAR = 52;
var DAYS_IN_A_WEEK = 7;
var daysInAYear = WEEKS_IN_A_YEAR * DAYS_IN_A_WEEK; // Forget leap years

var SEAT_ROWS_ON_PLANE = 25;
var SEATS_PER_ROW = 6;
var seatsOnThePlane = SEAT_ROWS_ON_PLANE * SEATS_PER_ROW; // Ah, clarity!
```

Notice how much clearer everything suddenly becomes.

Maintain Short Function Blocks

A function should do one thing and do it well. Try to avoid combining unrelated code into one function, as in this example:

```
function feedbackOnUsersFavoriteFruit() {
    var favoriteFruit = prompt("What is your favorite fruit?", "None");
    var score = 0;
    switch (favoriteFruit.toLowerCase()) {
        case "banana":
            score = 6;
            break;
        case "apple":
            score = 4;
            break;
        default:
            break;
    }
```

```
    if (score > 5) {
        alert("You picked one of my favorites too!");
    } else if (score > 0) {
        alert("Credit for choosing a fruit, at least!");
    } else {
        alert("Not sure about your choice of fruit!");
    }
}
```

The simpler each function is, the easier it is to test and debug. If your function needs to do many logically different operations in succession, separate the one large function into several smaller functions to perform each task individually, as in this example:

```
function getFavoriteFruit() {
    return  prompt("What is your favorite fruit?", "None");
}

function getFruitScore(fruit) {
    var score = 0;
    switch (favoriteFruit.toLowerCase()) {
        case "banana":
            score = 6;
            break;
        case "apple":
            score = 4;
            break;
        default:
            break;
    }
    return score;
}

function getMessageByScore(score) {
    var message = "";
    if (score > 5) {
        message = "You picked one of my favorites too!";
    } else if (score > 0) {
        message = "Credit for choosing a fruit, at least!";
    } else {
        message = "Not sure about your choice of fruit!";
    }
    return message;
}

function feedbackOnUsersFavoriteFruit() { // The old function name
    var favoriteFruit = getFavoriteFruit();
    var score = getFruitScore(favoriteFruit);
    alert(getMessageByScore(score));
}
```

As far as possible, each function should do one logical action, taking an input and producing an output, as necessary.

Use Comments As Documentation with ScriptDoc

Rather than including many inline comments next to your code, ensure that your variables and functions are named accurately, and that your code blocks are short and self-explanatory. Littering your code with many inline comments reduces the chance that any of them will actually be read.

You should document each function you write by providing a comment block before the function that defines what the function does, its expected inputs, and the kind of output it produces, as well as some example uses. This type of comment block has the following advantages:

- It ensures all developers understand what a function is (and isn't) supposed to do.

- It helps you determine when a function is performing too many actions, as discussed in the previous section. If the function's description is particularly complicated, this indicates it should be separated into several smaller functions.

- It helps define the sort of testing you could perform on that function, by noting which ranges or types of input the function should be able to accept.

- It provides visual separation within your code.

You should use the open ScriptDoc format (http://www.scriptdoc.org/) to document your code. This format has been designed so it can be used regardless of programming language. Since the format and structure are predefined, you can use software such as Aptana Studio (http://www.aptana.com/) to automatically produce documentation in a readable style from specially formatted comment blocks within your code.

The following example shows how to document what an entire JavaScript file does. The comment should exist as the very first thing in the JavaScript file, so developers will be able to understand the purpose of the functions contained in the file.

```
/**
 * @projectDescription This file contains code to perform date object manipulation
 *
 * @author Den Odell me@denodell.com
 * @version 1.0
 */
```

Here is an example of how to document a function within a file using the ScriptDoc format:

```
/**
 * Takes a number and squares it, rounding the result to the nearest integer
 *
 * Examples:
 *     square(2.5); => 6
 *     square(2); => 4
 *
```

```
 * @param {Float} number The number to be squared
 * @return {Integer} Returns the rounded square of the input
 */

function square(number) {
    return Math.round(number * number);
}
```

I encourage you to familiarize yourself with the specification given on the ScriptDoc web site, and the specific options to use to describe and document your functions appropriately. Using it will vastly improve the understanding of your code and can provide useful documentation to provide to other developers who might wish to work on your code in the future.

Mark Remaining Tasks with TODO

A useful habit to get into while coding is to mark sections of your code that are not complete with a comment containing the word TODO, like this:

```
function checkPasswordStrength(password) {
    // TODO: Complete this function, checking the strength of the supplied password
    return true;
}
```

This allows you to later search your code base for this word, and quickly locate any areas that require completion.

Professional JavaScript Programming

Now that we've reviewed some basic guidelines for formatting, documentation, and clarity in your JavaScript files, let's look at some JavaScript coding principles. Professionals follow these practices to make their JavaScript robust, scalable, and built on a solid understanding of the problem they are trying to solve.

Avoid Solving Nonexistent Problems

When you write JavaScript code, write only the code you need to solve the problem at hand. For example, suppose you wish to write some JavaScript code that allows the users of your site to log in to their profile page, dynamically refreshing part of the page when they provide successful credentials. To solve this problem, you do not need to write code that will refresh any piece of content on any page in your site—at least not until that becomes a requirement or the solution to a new problem.

Your code can be completed in less time by following this guideline, as you build only the exact code to do the job, rather than attempting to build generic, overcomplicated code that is often less reliable in practice.

Later, when you need to solve a different problem and you think that some code you have written already could be reworked to do the job, that would be the time to rewrite it.

Use the Document Object Model

As an extension to the JavaScript language, the W3C recommended the Document Object Model (DOM), which standardizes the way that web developers interact with elements within the HTML of their rendered pages. Methods were added to the language to locate page elements by their id attributes or their tag names, allowing for dynamic manipulation of their attributes, CSS style properties, and even the removal or addition of entire elements.

The DOM recommendation defines everything that exists within an HTML page to be known by the generic name *node*. Five types of nodes can exist within a page, as follows, all of which are JavaScript representations of page components:

- *Document node*: Represents the topmost node of the HTML page, effectively mapping to the <html> element.

- *Element node*: Every HTML tag on the page is represented as an element node.

- *Attribute node*: Every attribute of a tag, such as the attribute href related to an <a> tag, is represented as an attribute node. Each attribute is always associated with an element node.

- *Text node*: The text between opening and closing tags, such as the text between <p> and </p>, is represented as a text node. Each text node is associated with an element node.

- *Comment node*: An HTML comment is represented as a comment node.

Each element node may contain other element nodes within it, known as *child nodes*. The <html> element has two child nodes, <head> and <body>, according to the structure represented within XHTML.

The following example shows the HTML <body> element with two child nodes beneath it:

```
<body>
    <h1>My Page Title</h1>
    <img id="chart-image" src="my-chart.jpg" alt="My chart" />
</body>
```

The first child node (which represents the <h1> tag) has a text node beneath it, containing the text My Page Title. Note that the text within an element is not considered part of the element itself, but rather a child node of it.

The second child node of the <body> tag is another element node (representing the <img> tag) containing two attribute nodes (representing the values stored in src and alt). From the point of view of the <h1> tag, the <body> tag is known as its *parent node*, and the <img> tag is know as its *sibling*, since they exist at the same level within the document hierarchy.

Element nodes can be found directly within a document by using one of two methods, both of which are demonstrated in the following example:

```
// Returns an element node representing the tag with an id attribute chart-image
var img = document.getElementById("chart-image");

// Returns an array of element nodes, all of which are <body> tags
var bodyTag = document.getElementByTagName("body");

// Returns the element with id attribute chart-image within the first <body> tag
var img = bodyTags[0].getElementById("chart-image");
```

■**Note** Two new element location methods are available in some browsers but are not yet ubiquitous. These methods are `querySelectorAll()`, which locates element nodes based on CSS 3 selectors, and `getElementsByClassName()`, which locates element nodes based on CSS class names.

Once you've located an element, chances are you'll want to do something with it. Maybe you want to alter its text or any of its attributes; maybe you want to remove the element from the page completely, or add a new element before, after, or within it. The DOM provides methods to handle all of these cases.

Dynamically Alter CSS Properties

Reading and altering CSS style properties is as simple as using the style object on the element you have located. The following demonstrates how to read the color CSS property and alter the margin-left CSS property.

```
var navigationEleemnt = document.getElementById("navigation");
if (navigationElement.style.color == "black") {
    navigationElement.style.marginLeft = "50px";
}
```

■**Note** CSS style property names that use hyphens to divide words in the name are referred to within JavaScript using camel casing instead.

Manipulate Elements and Their Contents

The simplest, and in many browsers the quickest, way to set the content of an element through the DOM is to use the innerHTML property of the element. This property represents the HTML code of everything within the element as a string, which can be read out or set to whatever you want. Here's an example of how to read and set the innerHTML value of an element:

```
var pTag = document.getElementsByTagName("p")[0]; // First <p> tag on page
alert(pTag.innerHTML); // Outputs current HTML string contents of tag
pTag.innerHTML = "<b>New HTML contents!</b>"; // Rewrite the tag's HTML
alert(pTag.innerHTML); // Outputs "<b>New HTML contents!</b>" and the ➡
    tag's contents on the page are now in bold text
```

Although this is quick and easy, there is a risk of introducing errors, such as causing rendering bugs by setting HTML that is not properly closed. The most robust way to manipulate elements is to use built-in DOM node-manipulation methods, which will always add HTML code to the page with the correct formatting according to the current DOCTYPE of the page.

The following example demonstrates creating a new element node using the createElement() method. We can insert this new element into the page using the appendChild() method, which creates a new horizontal rule element and appends it to the end of the list of nodes contained within the <body> tag. It will show up at the bottom of the HTML page.

```
var horizontalRule = document.createElement("hr"); // In memory only, for now
var bodyTag = document.getElementsByTagName("body")[0];
bodyTag.appendChild(horizontalRule); // Make the <hr> tag appear on the page
```

In the converse fashion, removing an element from the page is as simple as calling the removeChild() method on the parent element of the element you want to remove, as follows:

```
var horizontalRule = document.getElementsByTagName("hr")[0];
// The <hr> tag above must be a direct child of the <body> tag
var bodyTag = document.getElementsByTagName("body")[0];
bodyTag.removeChild(horizontalRule); // The element disappears from the page
```

I've shown you just a few of the DOM methods. I recommend that you become familiar with the DOM. It is the unified way for accessing your page contents through JavaScript. Mozilla maintains a useful online resource with plenty of examples and explanations at https://developer.mozilla.org/en/Gecko_DOM_Reference.

Don't Mix JavaScript and HTML

As I noted in the previous chapter, you should never put JavaScript code inline with your HTML code. If you find yourself using attributes such as onclick, onmouseover, and so on within HTML, stop right now! Locate elements using the DOM methods available for doing so, and apply your code to these. This separates your behavioral code from your content, and allows you to make changes to each without affecting the other in a drastic way.

Some browsers do not support JavaScript. Some users prefer to switch it off. Some users are working in closed environments where JavaScript is disabled as a matter of course. These users shouldn't need to download all the JavaScript code for the page they are accessing, as this makes the page size larger without providing any benefit to them.

You should aim to include all JavaScript code within external files, referenced via <script> tags within your HTML code, so users without JavaScript download only the content they need, and other browsers download the file via the referenced URL. This also allows the browser to locally cache the external file, so that if multiple pages reference that file, it is downloaded only once and loaded from the local copy on every subsequent request.

Separate Style from Code

You'll find that sometimes you want to affect certain style properties of elements on your page from your JavaScript. Perhaps you want to show or hide a portion of the page, or apply a new color scheme to certain elements when a user performs an action. As far as you can, separate style rules out into CSS, and then use the DOM to switch the CSS class name being used on the element you wish to change; the browser will then handle the change in style properties for you. In this way, you create looser connections between the display style and the behavioral code.

By allowing the CSS file to be responsible for the design and layout, and the JavaScript to take care of the interactions and behaviors, you know in which file to look to make changes to either. You can also create a whole new design using CSS, without needing to alter your HTML or JavaScript code.

Exceptions to this rule apply when you need to dynamically alter certain properties by amounts you cannot know ahead of time, such as changing the width of a component to match the distance the mouse has moved from an initial position. In this case, there would be too many possible values to code every option within CSS. Instead, only the width property should be altered through JavaScript, and all other styling associated with the same element should be performed within your CSS files.

Chain Function Calls

Chaining refers to executing methods on the results of other methods, saving redundant lines of code. The following example demonstrates this by executing several methods in turn, each acting on the result of the previous call. The final value returned is the result of the final method in the chain.

```
// Gets the width of the element with id horizontal-rule within the <body> tag
var hrTagWidth = document.getElementsByTagName("body")[0] ➥
    .getElementById("horizontal-rule").style.width;
```

Write Bulletproof Code

When writing your code, certain method calls may not always return the values you rely upon in the rest of your code. If this is the case, you'll end up with JavaScript errors, and your code will stop executing. Professional JavaScript developers check that the values returned from such methods are in the required format before performing further operations on them.

The following example shows this practice in action, where an element is found using the DOM.

```
var horizontalRule = document.getElementById("horizontal-rule");
if (horizontalRule) { // If the element exists, then...
    horizontalRule.parentNode.removeChild(horizontalRule); // ...remove the node
}
```

This code checks that the element actually exists—that its value is not null or undefined. If you were to perform operations on an element that is later removed from the HTML, an error would occur, and code execution would stop.

Handle Fatal Exception Errors Gracefully

A useful feature of the JavaScript language, like many others, is the ability to wrap groups of statements that you have reason to suspect might cause an exception—the kind of error that forces your code to stop executing—within a try/catch code block in order to handle the error in a graceful manner. The code within the try section will execute; the code in the catch section will execute only if the try section code causes an error to occur. If no error occurs, the code in the catch section is ignored. Here is an example of a try/catch structure that alerts the user to an error in code execution when it occurs, without this exception causing JavaScript code execution to cease.

```
try {
    // The following code is not valid and would normally cause an exception
    document.getElementById("horizontal-rule").propertyName.toString();
} catch (error) {
    alert("An error occurred.");
)
```

Notice how the catch block exposes a variable, which I've named error. This variable contains information about the error that occurred. In the following code, I attempt to find out the type of error that occurred so I can provide a more useful message to the end user or developer.

```
try {
    // varx is not in the language, so a SyntaxError exception will be thrown
    varx x = 0;
} catch (error) {
    // There are six basic exception types, all described here
    if (error instanceOf TypeError) {
        // A variable used was not of the expected type
    } else if (error instanceOf SyntaxError) {
        alert(error.message); // Output the message describing the exception
    } else if (error instanceOf RangeError) {
        // A numeric variable has exceeded its allowed range
    } else if (error instanceOf EvalError) {
        // The eval() JavaScript function was used incorrectly
    } else if (error instanceOf ReferenceError) {
        // An invalid reference was used
    } else if (error instanceOf URIError) {
        // The encodeURI() or decodeURI() functions were used incorrectly
    }
}
```

Define Custom Exceptions

In addition to catching and handling the built-in JavaScript exceptions, you can define your own type of exceptions, which you can force to occur at any time in your code. The following example demonstrates how to define and raise a custom error in specific circumstances.

```
// Define a new type of error
var domObjectNotFoundException = new Error("DOM object not found");

function getDOMObjectById(id) {
    var domObject = document.getElementById(id);
    if (!domObject) {
        // Throw an exception of our custom error type if the DOM object ➡
            doesn't exist
        throw domObjectNotFoundException;
    }
```

```
    return domObject;
}

try {
    // Assume we're trying to act upon an element that does not exist
    getDOMObjectById("this-id-is-not-on-the-page").style.width = "100px";
} catch (error) {
    if (error instanceOf domObjectNotFoundException) {
        alert(error.message); // Outputs "DOM object not found!"
    } else {
        // Catch different type of error
    }
}
```

And Finally . . .

As an extension to the familiar try/catch block structure, you can add an extra block denoted by the finally keyword. The finally keyword allows you to add an extra set of statements to execute, regardless of whether or not an exception occurred, in order to structure related code together. In the following example, the final alert statement is called, regardless of whether the DOM object was found.

```
try {
    getDOMObjectById("this-id-is-not-on-the-page").style.width = "100px";
} catch (error) {
    alert(error.message);
} finally {
    alert("That's all, folks!");
}
```

Code with Localization in Mind

Localization is one of the more common requirements given to RIAs that have already been built. Imagine you've built a large dynamic web application, only to find out you need to restructure all your code in order to be able to localize the text strings used throughout.

Separate your text strings into variables, and include these all together in one place within your code. This allows you to simply override their values at a later stage, if needed. Using this approach will save you valuable time at a later stage when you need to add regional-specific text strings to your JavaScript code.

You could consider moving these variables to a separate file—perhaps one for each language—so the HTML page can choose to reference the language-specific file it needs, and the rest of the application uses these variables as normal. This off-loads the language selection to the HTML page, which seems like a sensible choice, since there will be language-specific text in the content already.

Object-Oriented JavaScript

JavaScript coding has come a long way since its humble beginnings and has reached the point where many front-end web developers find themselves writing complex code in a manner not dissimilar to that of traditional software engineers. Over time, developers have sought to minimize errors, increase code reuse, and ease understanding of their code by applying some of the same object-oriented principles as those used by traditional programmers.

By grouping related code together into reusable components, or *objects*, each with its own variables and functions, you promote code reuse and provide a layer of abstraction that will help you and your fellow developers to understand your code better. Gone are the days of your JavaScript files being long lists of functions that show little interrelation to each other and are difficult to navigate.

■**Caution** JavaScript was not designed as an object-oriented programming language, and to think of it as such can lead to some confusion. Some of the principles of object-oriented code design do apply, but not all. Read this section carefully if you are familiar with the use of these principles in other languages, so you understand the differences.

This section will help get you in the habit of writing JavaScript code using object-oriented principles and techniques, just as the professionals do.

Objects, Classes, and Constructors

Two important concepts of object-oriented programming are objects and classes. You're now going to discover what these mean and how they relate to the JavaScript language.

What Is an Object?

An *object* is a special type of data that contains functions and variables. JavaScript contains several built-in core objects, including Math, Array, and String. These provide a set of functions to perform actions on certain types of data. The following shows some examples of calling the methods of these objects.

```
alert(Math.round(9.9)); // Outputs '10'
var cityList = new Array("New York", "London", "Stockholm");
var sortedCityList = cityList.sort(); // "London", "New York", "Stockholm"
alert(sortedCityList.join()); // Outputs "London, New York, Stockholm" as a string
```

Notice how you can access the method within the object by using a dot (.) between the object's name and the name of the method you're calling.

What Is a Class?

A *class* is a definition of an object. It is never used itself within code, except as a basis for creating objects. Defining a class in JavaScript is as simple as writing a function. The following example shows two ways to define a class using the function keyword.

```
function EmailMessage() { // Defines a class with the name EmailMessage
}

var EmailMessage = function() { // Different way of defining the same class
}
```

Both of these are valid forms for defining classes. Use whichever form you prefer in your code.

Objects As Instances of Classes

Look again at the example of using objects:

```
alert(Math.round(9.9));
var cityList = new Array("New York", "London", "Stockholm");
var sortedCityList = cityList.sort();
alert(sortedCityList.join());
```

Observe the difference between the usage of the Math object and the Array object. Notice that the Math object can be used as is, but the Array object needs the new keyword before it. The Array object defines a template of array list-related functions, which makes it a class, according to our previous definition.

To create something from a class that is usable within your code, you use the new keyword, which creates an *instance* of that class. Essentially, this allows you to create one or many objects that each contain all the functions and variables defined within the class, without interfering with each other. The following shows a few examples of creating objects as instances of classes.

```
var oceans = new Array("Atlantic", "Pacific", "Indian", "Arctic", "Antarctic");
var myMessage = new EmailMessage(); // Using the class defined previously
var anotherMessage = new EmailMessage(); // Independent of myMessage, above
```

Constructors

A *constructor* is optional code that can be executed at the instant an object is created from a class, using the new keyword. In JavaScript, this is performed as simply as adding code to the function that defines the class, as follows:

```
var EmailMessage = function() {
    // Action that should be performed when the class is instantiated
    alert("New message created.");
}

var myMessage = new EmailMessage(); // Outputs "New message created."
var anotherMessage = new EmailMessage(); // Outputs "New message created."
```

Just as normal functions within the JavaScript language can be passed parameters that the function can use internally, so can class constructors. Here is a class constructor that takes one parameter:

```
var EmailMessage = function(message) {
    alert(message);
}

// Outputs "Return to sender"
var myMessage = new EmailMessage("Return to sender");
```

Properties

In object-oriented terminology, a *property* is a variable stored within an object. Properties are defined within the class, using the this keyword, and are then available to each object instantiated from that class. The following example shows how to define properties within a class and how to access those properties from object instances.

```
var EmailMessage = function() {
    this.subject = ""; // Use the this keyword to assign a property to a class
}

var myMessage = new EmailMessage();
myMessage.subject = "Check this out..."; // Assign a value to the property

var anotherMessage = new EmailMessage();
anotherMessage.subject = "Have you seen this before?";

alert(myMessage.subject); // Outputs "Check this out..."
alert(anotherMessage.subject); // Outputs "Have you seen this before?"
```

You use the this keyword within the class to refer to the scope of the instantiated object, as discussed in a little more detail shortly.

Methods

While properties define variables associated with a class or object, methods define executable functions available to all object instances. The following example demonstrates how to add a method to a class and how to execute it from within an object instantiated from that class.

```
var EmailMessage = function(subject) {
    this.subject = subject;
    this.send = function() {
        alert("Message '" + this.subject + "' sent!");
    }
}

var myMessage = new EmailMessage("Dear John...");
myMessage.send(); // Outputs "Message 'Dear John...' sent!"
```

The prototype Keyword

Another way to assign properties and methods to a class, outside the class definition itself, is by using the `prototype` keyword against the class name after it has been defined. Here's how to add properties and methods to a class in this way:

```
var EmailMessage = function(subject) {
    this.subject = subject;
}

EmailMessage.prototype.from = ""; // Dynamically assign new property to class
EmailMessage.prototype.send = function() { // Dynamically assign new method
    alert("Message from " + this.from + " sent!"); // 'this' still behaves as normal
}

var myMessage = new EmailMessage("My new website");
myMessage.from = "me@denodell.com";
myMessage.send(); // Outputs "Message from me@denodell.com sent!"
```

As well as allowing you to add extra properties and methods to the class after it has been defined, you can use the `prototype` keyword to assign new properties and methods to objects already created from those classes. This allows you to dynamically add new functionality to object instances that already exist. The following example demonstrates this principal.

```
var EmailMessage = function(subject) {
    this.subject = subject;
}

// Instantiate an object from the EmailMessage class
var myMessage = new EmailMessage("Coming to visit...");

// Add a new method to the class
EmailMessage.prototype.send = function() {
    alert("Message sent!");
}

// The new method exists on an object created before the method was added!
myMessage.send(); // Outputs "Message sent!"
```

Singletons

A singleton is a class that will only ever have a single instance in your code, such as the `Math` object that exists within the JavaScript language itself. You cannot create new instances of this object, though it does contain properties and methods you can take advantage of in your code. Listing 2-1 demonstrates how to create a singleton.

Listing 2-1. *Creating a Singleton*

```
var User = function() {
    this.username = "";
    this.password = "";
    this.login = function() {
        return true;
    }
}

// Create an instance of the User class, storing it in the same variable used to
// define the class initially. The original class has now been removed from the
// code, leaving only the single object instance of it
User = new User();

// Example method call on the single instance of User
User.login();

// Example of a self-instantiating class
var Inbox = new function() {
    this.messageCount = 0;
    this.refresh = function() {
        return true;
    }
}();
// The new keyword and braces force the function to immediately execute,
// meaning the Inbox variable now contains the single object instance,
// not the class

// Example method call on the single instance of Inbox
Inbox.refresh();
```

Now you are familiar with creating classes with properties and methods. Let's move on to an important aspect of object-oriented programming: inheritance.

Inheritance: Creating New Classes from Existing Ones

Inheritance allows you to create classes derived from other classes in order to specialize that class in some way. The original class is known as the *parent*, and the new class derived from it is known as the *child*.

Inheritance in JavaScript is performed using the prototype keyword, once again. After definition of the child class, you assign the parent class to the child's prototype, which has the outcome of making the parent's properties and methods immediately available to the child. The child class can then override or extend any of the parent's methods or properties, as it requires. Listing 2-2 shows how basic inheritance is performed using JavaScript.

Listing 2-2. *Basic Inheritance in JavaScript*

```
var EmailMessage = function(subject) {
    this.subject = subject;
    this.send = function() {
        alert("Message '" + this.subject + "' sent!");
    }
}

// Create a new, empty class
var EventInvitation = function() {};

// Inherit properties and methods from the EmailMessage class
EventInvitation.prototype = new EmailMessage();

// EventInvitation thinks it is the EmailMessage class, so correct this...
EventInvitation.prototype.constructor = EventInvitation;

// Define the subject for all instances of the EventInvitation class
EventInvitation.prototype.subject = "You are cordially invited to...";

// Create an instance of the EventInvitation class
var myEventInvitation = new EventInvitation();

// Outputs "Message 'You are cordially invited to...' sent!"
myEventInvitation.send();
```

Encapsulation: Each Class Doing What It Does Best

When using inheritance to create variations or specializations of existing classes, all the properties and methods of the parent class are available to the child. You do not need to declare or define anything extra within the child class to be able to use properties and methods of the parent. This is termed *encapsulation.* The child class needs to contain definitions only for the properties and methods that are in addition to those of the parent.

Polymorphism: Redefining Inherited Properties and Methods

You have seen that, when creating a new child class that inherits from a parent class, the child has available all the properties and methods from the parent. Now suppose that you want your child class to contain a method with the same name as that of the parent, and to execute the code within that method in your child, instead of using the method from the parent. This is known as *polymorphism*. Listing 2-3 demonstrates polymorphism, where the child class contains a method with the same name as the parent class from which it was inherited.

Listing 2-3. *Polymorphism in Action: Replacing the Method of a Parent Class*

```
var EmailMessage = function(subject) {
    this.subject = subject;
    this.send = function() {
        alert("Email message sent!");
    }
}


// Inherit EventInvitation class from EmailMessage
var EventInvitation = function() {};
EventInvitation.prototype = new EmailMessage("You are cordially invited to...");
EventInvitation.prototype.constructor = EventInvitation;

// Override the inherited send method
EventInvitation.prototype.send = function() {
    alert("Event invitation sent!");
}

var myEmailMessage = new EmailMessage("A new email coming your way.");
var myEventInvitation = new EventInvitation();

myEmailMessage.send(); // Outputs "Email message sent!"
myEventInvitation.send(); // Outputs "Event invitation sent!"
```

Now suppose that you want to override a method in a child class so that it executes extra code in addition to that of the method in the parent class. So, instead of replacing a parent's method, you wish to extend it in some way, while still using the same method name provided by the parent. Listing 2-4 demonstrates this principle.

■ **Caution** Any methods or properties you wish to extend as demonstrated in Listing 2-4 must be declared in the parent class using the `prototype` keyword; otherwise, they cannot be located from within the child class.

Listing 2-4. *Polymorphism in Action: Extending the Method of a Parent Class*

```
var EmailMessage = function(subject) {
    this.subject = subject;
}

// We wish to be able to extend this method later,
// so it must be declared using the prototype keyword
EmailMessage.prototype.send = function() {
    alert("Email message sent!");
}
```

```
// Inherit EventInvitation class from EmailMessage
var EventInvitation = function() {};
EventInvitation.prototype = new EmailMessage("You are cordially invited to...");
EventInvitation.constructor.prototype = EventInvitation;

// Override the inherited send method
EventInvitation.prototype.send = function() {
    // Add code to the EventInvitation send method
    alert("Event invitation sent!");

    // Find and execute the send method from the EmailMessage class
    // this.constructor.prototype refers to the EmailMessage class
    this.constructor.prototype.send.call(this);
}

var myEmailMessage = new EmailMessage("A new email coming your way.");
var myEventInvitation = new EventInvitation();

// Outputs "Email message sent!"
myEmailMessage.send();

// Outputs "Event invitation sent!" followed by "Email message sent!"
myEventInvitation.send();
```

The this Keyword

A fundamental part of building any object-based RIA is understanding the this keyword within JavaScript. You have seen it used in this chapter's code examples, when associating properties and methods with classes and when calling parent class methods from within child classes. Knowing how to properly use this powerful keyword will improve your coding skills and give you a better handle on the JavaScript language itself.

The this keyword refers to the owner of the function it is contained within. If it occurs within a method as part of a class, it refers to the class itself, or rather the object instance of the class created when your code is executing. Out of the context of a class, this usually refers to the global window object of the page. Take a look at Listing 2-5, which shows a few examples of the this keyword in action, based around a single function being used in different contexts.

Listing 2-5. *The this Keyword in Action*

```
var showSubject = function() {
    // Output the subject property with the same owner as this function
    alert(this.subject);
}

// Outputs "undefined" since the this keyword refers to the global window object
// which has no variable named subject
showSubject();
```

```javascript
// Set the a global subject property
this.subject = "Global subject";

// Outputs "Global subject" now that the property has been set
showSubject();

// Define the EmailMessage class
var EmailMessage = function(subject) {
    this.subject = subject;
}

// Copy and assign the showSubject function to the EmailMessage class,
// making the EmailMessage class the owner of the function.
// Note the lack of braces after the function, which copies the code of the
// function rather than executing it straightaway
EmailMessage.prototype.showSubject = showSubject;

// Create a new instance of the class
var myEmailMessage = new EmailMessage("I am the subject.");

// Outputs "I am the subject.", since the owner of the function is the class
myEmailMessage.showSubject();

// Outputs "Global subject" just to demonstrate that this has not been lost
showSubject();

// Now let's add another method to the class, calling showSubject differently
EmailMessage.prototype.outputSubject = function() {
    showSubject();
}

// Outputs "Global subject" since this method calls the function
// that is associated with the window object
myEmailMessage.outputSubject();
```

If you wish to call a function or method and ensure that the this keyword refers to a different object than the one it would normally refer to, two functions allow you to do this: apply and call. The difference between the two in implementation terms is very minor. apply expects any arguments you are passing to the function to be supplied as an array, whereas call does not. Listing 2-6 shows these two functions in action, altering the value of the this keyword in a set of reusable functions.

Listing 2-6. *Using apply and call to Alter the Value of the this Keyword*

```javascript
var showSubject = function() {
    alert(this.subject);
}
```

```
var setSubjectAndFrom = function(subject, from) {
    this.subject = subject;
    this.from = from;
}

// Executed against the global window object
showSubject(); // Outputs "undefined"
setSubjectAndFrom("Global subject", "me@denodell.com");
showSubject(); // Outputs "Global subject"

// Create EmailMessage class
var EmailMessage = function() {
    this.subject = "";
    this.from = "";
};

// Instantiate class
var myEmailMessage = new EmailMessage();

// Execute setSubjectAndFrom function, forcing the this keyword within the function
// to refer to myEmailMessage instead of the window object. Parameters are
// passed in series after the object to apply as the owner, setting the subject to
// "New subject" and the from property to "den@denodell.com"
setSubjectAndFrom.call(myEmailMessage, "New subject", "den@denodell.com");

// As a demonstration, we will do the same thing now using apply instead of call;
// apply expects an array of arguments, unlike call.
// You can use either apply or call in your code
setSubjectAndFrom.apply(myEmailMessage, [ "New subject", "den@denodell.com" ]);

// Outputs "New subject"
showSubject.call(myEmailMessage);
```

Access to Properties and Methods

Most programming languages allow you to define the level of access a particular property or method within an object has within the scope of the entire application. All of the properties and methods for classes created in the examples so far have been publicly available, which is to say that they can be accessed from anywhere within the code base. Creating a new instance of a class allows read and write access to any property within the instance, and allows any of the methods to be executed.

But what if you were creating a property or method for a class that you wanted to be available only internally within the class, termed *private*? Or suppose you wanted read-only access to a private property from outside the class definition; you might say this is a *privileged* property.

■**Caution** Don't confuse the terms *public*, *private*, and *privileged* here with similar names in other languages. In this context, we are discussing only access to properties and methods within classes from outside that class.

The different types of access to properties of a class are demonstrated in Listing 2-7.

Listing 2-7. *Restricting Access to Properties and Methods of a Class*

```javascript
var EmailMessage = function(subject) {
    // Publicly accessible properties and methods
    this.subject = subject;
    this.send = function() {
        alert("Message sent!");
    }

    // Private properties and methods.
    // Use of var instead of the this keyword to set a property means that the
    // scope of that variable is restricted to the function it sits inside of and is
    // not accessible externally
    var messageHeaders = "";
    var addEncryption = function() {
        // TODO: Add encryption method
        return true;
    }

    // Protecting a property, making it read-only from outside of the class
    // achieved by creating a private property and a public method
    var messageSize = 1024;
    this.getMessageSize = function() {
        alert(messageSize);
    }
}

var myEmailMessage = new EmailMessage("Save these dates...");

alert(myEmailMessage.subject); // Outputs "Save these dates..."
myEmailMessage.send(); // Outputs "Message sent!"

// Outputs "undefined" as messageHeaders is not a publicly visible property
alert(myEmailMessage.messageHeaders);

// Causes an exception to occur since the method does not exist
try {
    myEmailMessage.addEncryption();
} catch (e) {
    alert("Method does not exist publicly!");
}
```

```
// Outputs "undefined" since messageSize is not accessible outside of the class
alert(myEmailMessage.messageSize);

// Outputs "1024", the value of the private messageSize variable
myEmailMessage.getMessageSize();
```

Object Literals and JavaScript Object Notation

An *object literal* within the JavaScript language is essentially a list or grouping of any number of property names and their associated values. Object literal values can be strings, integer numbers, floating-point numbers, Boolean values, arrays, functions, or even other object literals, denoted in a particular format.

The format for object literals is commonly known as JavaScript Object Notation (JSON). The start and end of an object literal are denoted by curly braces: { and }. Each item in the list within the braces is separated by a comma, and each name is separated from its value by a colon.

Object literals are used within the language to group together related properties and methods in a similar way to a class. However, an object literal only ever has one instance, and it is not possible to execute any code statements at the point of its creation, as you could with a class definition. Listing 2-8 shows an object literal with values of many different types.

Listing 2-8. *Object Literal with Many Types of Values*

```
var earth = {
    name: "Terra Firma", // String
    planet: true, // Boolean
    moons: 1, // Integer (whole) number
    diameter: 12756.36, // Floating point number (decimal)
    oceans: ["Atlantic", "Pacific", "Indian", "Arctic", "Antarctic"], // Array
    poles: { // A nested object literal
        north: "Arctic",
        south: "Antarctic"
    },
    setDiameter: function(diameter) { // Function
        this.diameter = diameter; // The this keyword refers to the earth variable
    }
}

// Dot notation is used to access properties of the object
alert(earth.diameter); // Outputs "12756.36"
earth.setDiameter(12756.37);
alert(earth.diameter); // Outputs "12756.37"
```

You can use object literals to create singletons, provided that you do not need to execute any specific code when that singleton is instantiated.

Using Object Literals When Creating Classes

The object literal notation can be used together with the `prototype` keyword to set the definition of a class, as follows:

```
var EmailMessage = function() {};
EmailMessage.prototype = {
    subject: "",
    from: "",
    send: function() {
        alert("Message sent!");
    }
}
var myEmailMessage = new EmailMessage();

// Properties and methods are accessed as normal
myEmailMessage.subject = "Come over for a party...";
```

The limitation with this format is that you may need to write extra code to initialize the properties within the class.

Using Object Literals As Inputs to Functions

When you are writing a function that requires several arguments, you should consider accepting an object literal as the input to such a function. This allows you to replace all arguments with a single one; values can be extracted from the single argument using dot notation. Using object literals in this way often results in code that is easier to read and understand, since each property value in an object literal is named, providing context to the arguments supplied to the function.

Listing 2-9 demonstrates two functions that are identical in behavior, but one accepts multiple arguments and the other accepts just a single argument.

Listing 2-9. *Object Literal As an Input to a Function*

```
// Using multiple arguments in a specific order
var sendEmail = function(to, from, subject, body) {
    alert("Message '" + subject + "' from '" + from + "' sent to '" + to + "'!");
}
// Arguments must be in the correct order when calling the function.
// Outputs "Message 'Dinner this week?' from 'me@denodell.com' sent to
// 'you@denodell.com'!"
sendEmail("you@denodell.com", "me@denodell.com", "Dinner this week?", ➥
    "Do you want to come over for dinner this week? Let me know.");

// Same function, but a single object literal argument containing named properties
var sendEmail = function(message) {
    alert("Message '" + message.subject + "' from '" + message.from + "' sent ➥
        to '" + message.to + "'!");
}
```

```
// One object literal argument with named property values in no specific order
// Outputs "Message 'Dinner this week?' from 'me@denodell.com" sent to
// 'you@denodell.com'!"
sendEmail({
    from: 'me@denodell.com',
    to: 'you@denodell.com',
    subject: 'Dinner this week?',
    body: 'Do you want to come over for dinner this week? Let me know.'
});
```

Creating Namespaces and Hierarchies

Creating too many variables within the global window object is commonly referred to as *polluting the global scope*. This practice is dangerous, since you may define a variable that is also used by a third-party script you may be running on your site. JavaScript does not give you a warning when a variable is being overwritten in this way, so you may be relying on values that have been overwritten outside your control.

The solution to this problem is to create a single variable in the global scope that acts as an object literal or singleton, containing all the code for your application. This is known as a *namespace* in many programming languages. You are able to create other object literals or singletons within this global object to maintain a hierarchy of namespaces, grouping related code together. Here is an example of a namespace hierarchy:

```
var MyCompany = new function(){
    this.MyClient = { // Object literal
        WebMail: function() { // Constructor
            alert("Creating WebMail application...");
        }
    };
}(); // Create MyCompany as a singleton

// Now you can access the hierarchy through dot notation.
// Outputs "Creating WebMail application..."
var myWebMail = new MyCompany.MyClient.WebMail();
```

Libraries and Frameworks

Several open source JavaScript libraries have been written in recent years to simplify the development of dynamic web pages and RIAs. Primarily, they exist to smooth out inconsistencies between different browsers' implementation of JavaScript and to help developers write fewer lines of code to achieve their goals.

Unfortunately, browsers differ in their support for certain aspects of JavaScript—not all browsers support the same actions using the same methods. Some of the key points of variation include the following:

- Handling events that occur when the user interacts with the page
- Loading remote content from a web server

- Detecting when the DOM has been initialized and is ready to use

- Determining which CSS styles are applied to a particular element

JavaScript libraries iron out these differences by plugging missing functionality and fixing improper implementations.

Additionally, many JavaScript libraries include extra utility methods to simplify common tasks, such as locating page elements by using CSS 3 selector notation. Many libraries are also starting to add support for appealing effect transitions, smoothing the appearance as one style adapts into another on the page.

■**Tip** A guide to the CSS 3 selector notation can be found at `http://www.w3.org/TR/css3-selectors/` `#selectors`. Bear in mind that the list of selectors is still a work in progress at present.

You should use a JavaScript library when building RIAs. You will not be able to survive without the cross-browser smoothing over, and the extra utility methods will help you code more efficiently.

Selecting a Library

Several open source JavaScript libraries are available. Currently, some of the most popular libraries include jQuery (`http://jquery.com/`), Dojo (`http://www.dojotoolkit.org/`), Prototype (`http://www.prototypejs.org/`), MooTools (`http://mootools.net/`), Yahoo! User Interface Library (`http://developer.yahoo.com/yui/`), and Ext JS (`http://extjs.com/`). A number of these libraries have a multitude of third-party plug-ins that support extra functionality.

When investigating and selecting a JavaScript library, consider the following criteria:

Avoids extending JavaScript objects: Choose a library that does not rely heavily on extending native JavaScript objects, such as `Function`, `String`, `Array`, and so on. If you discover a library that allows you to call methods or alter properties on such objects that are not part of the JavaScript language, be very wary. Future additions to the language could break these methods and properties, and other third-party JavaScript libraries could overwrite the same methods in a different way.

Is well documented: Choose a library that is well documented and has a multitude of test cases that are run before new releases to the library are made available.

Has an active community: Choose a library that has an active community of developers and users. It is more likely that any problems you encounter will have been solved before. And, if not, there's a better chance that your problem will be addressed and any necessary changes to the library made as a result.

Does not have memory leaks: Choose a library that does not leak memory. This goes back to the test cases mentioned previously.

Is small and efficient: Choose a library that is not large and bloated. Small does not necessarily mean better, but it does mean that the users of your code have less JavaScript to download before they can use your site.

Has its own namespace: Choose a library that doesn't pollute the global scope. Make sure that the library sits within its own namespace.

Allows standard JavaScript syntax: Finally, choose a library that allows you to write JavaScript as it was intended to be written. Be wary of a library that forces you to spend a lot of time learning how to use its patterns, as if it were a different language entirely. Remember that you are a JavaScript programmer, not a library programmer.

Not all of these criteria are met by every library. You should research the available libraries carefully so as to make an informed decision about the library you'll come to rely upon when building your RIAs.

Building a JavaScript Library

In order to understand the kinds of problems that libraries solve, particularly regarding cross-browser compatibility, and to demonstrate the sort of library that adheres to most of the guidelines suggested in the previous section, let's go through the formation of a basic JavaScript library. This library will serve as the basis for many of the code examples used in this book.

Using the principles of object-oriented programming discussed in this chapter, let's create a class to describe our JavaScript library, naming the library simply $:

```
var $ = function() {};
```

Not only is this a valid name within the language for a function or variable name, it is actually used fairly frequently as the name to represent a JavaScript library's global namespace due to its short length (meaning shorter code). Its use originally came about from its existence in the Ruby and PHP programming languages.

Detecting When the DOM Is Available

A major bugbear of JavaScript programmers is that the DOM is sometimes not available for use at the point when an executing script needs it to be. If the script is referred to within the `<head>` section of an HTML page, it will be executed before the `<body>` of that page has loaded, meaning it will not be able to locate page elements at that time. Previously, developers would add their entire code to the `window.onload` event, meaning it would execute when the entire page—including any external images, CSS, and JavaScript files—had loaded. The more images on the page, the longer the user would wait before the script was executed.

Eventually, several browser manufacturers, together with the W3C, introduced a `DOMContentLoaded` event, which fired at the point when the page elements were loaded and could be accessed through JavaScript. This event fired before the `window.onload` event and before the external files had finished loading, meaning that developers could have their scripts executing against the DOM without needing to wait for the entire page contents to load.

Unfortunately, the `DOMContentLoaded` event is not yet implemented in all common browsers, notably IE 6, 7, and 8. To smooth over this inconsistency and provide support for this event where it exists and a work-around where it doesn't, you need to write your own method to execute your code when the DOM is ready to be used. Listing 2-10 shows one way of achieving this behavior in all browsers as part of your $ library.

Listing 2-10. *Executing Code When the DOM Is Ready for Access*

```
$.prototype.onDomReady = function(callback){ // callback should be a function
    if (document.addEventListener) {
        // If the browser supports the DOMContentLoaded event,
        // assign the callback function to execute when that event fires
        document.addEventListener("DOMContentLoaded", callback, false);
    } else {
        if(document.body && document.body.lastChild){
            // If the DOM is available for access, execute the callback function
            callback();
        } else {
            // Reexecute the current function, denoted by arguments.callee,
            // after waiting a brief nanosecond so as not to lock up the browser
            return setTimeout(arguments.callee, 0);
        }
    }
}

// Example usage

// Instantiate the $ library object as a singleton for use on a page
$ = new $();

// Outputs "The DOM is ready!" when the DOM is ready for access
$.onDomReady(function() {
    alert("The DOM is ready!");
});
```

Handling Events in the Browser

JavaScript events fire within the browser when certain actions occur, such as hyperlink clicks and form submissions, and you can write code to be executed at these points. The problem is that the way to assign functions to these events differs between IE 6 and 7 and other browsers. Not only that, but the method of establishing the page element the event occurred on and other attributes of the event, such as mouse positions, also differs between these browsers. Listing 2-11 shows how to add methods to your $ library to smooth out these inconsistencies.

Listing 2-11. *Writing Methods to Standardize Event Handling in Browsers*

```
// Add a new namespace to the $ library to hold all event-related code,
// using an object literal notation to add multiple methods at once

$.prototype.Events = {

    // The add method allows us to assign a function to execute when an
    // event of a specified type occurs on a specific element
```

```
add: function (element, eventType, callback) {
    // Store the current value of this to use within subfunctions
    var self = this;
    eventType = eventType.toLowerCase();

    if (element.addEventListener) {
        // If the W3C event listener method is available, use that
        element.addEventListener(eventType, function(e){
            // Execute callback function, passing it a standardized version of
            // the event object, e. The standardize method is defined later
            callback(self.standardize(e));
        }, false);
    } else if (element.attachEvent) {
        // Otherwise use the Internet Explorer-proprietary event handler
        element.attachEvent("on" + eventType, function() {
            // IE uses window.event to store the current event's properties
            callback(self.standardize(window.event));
        });
    }
},

// The remove method allows us to remove previously assigned code
// from an event

remove: function (element, eventType, callback) {
    eventType = eventType.toLowerCase();

    if (element.removeEventListener) {
        // If the W3C-specified method is available, use that
        element.removeEventListener(element, eventType, callback);
    } else if (element.detachEvent) {
        // Otherwise, use the Internet Explorer-specific method
        element.detachEvent("on" + eventType, callback);
    }
},

// The standardize method produces a unified set of event
// properties, regardless of the browser

standardize: function(event) {

    // These two methods, defined later, return the current position of the
    // mouse pointer, relative to the document as a whole, and relative to the
    // element the event occurred within
    var page = this.getMousePositionRelativeToDocument(event);
    var offset = this.getMousePositionOffset(event);
```

```javascript
        // Let's stop events from firing on element nodes above the current
        if (event.stopPropagation) {
            event.stopPropagation();
        } else {
            event.cancelBubble = true;
        }

        // We return an object literal containing seven properties and one method
        return {
            // The target is the element the event occurred on
            target: this.getTarget(event),

            // The relatedTarget is the element the event was listening for,
            // which can be different from the target if the event occurred on an
            // element located within the relatedTarget element in the DOM
            relatedTarget: this.getRelatedTarget(event),

            // If the event was a keyboard-related one, key returns the character
            key: this.getCharacterFromKey(event),

            // Return the x and y coordinates of the mouse pointer,
            // relative to the document
            pageX: page.x,
            pageY: page.y,

            // Return the x and y coordinates of the mouse pointer,
            // relative to the element the current event occurred on
            offsetX: offset.x,
            offsetY: offset.y,

            // The preventDefault method stops the default event of the element
            // we're acting upon from occurring. If we were listening for click
            // events on a hyperlink, for example, this method would stop the
            // link from being followed
            preventDefault: function() {
                if (event.preventDefault) {
                    event.preventDefault(); // W3C method
                } else {
                    event.returnValue = false; // Internet Explorer method
                }
            }
        };
    },

    // The getTarget method locates the element the event occurred on
```

```
getTarget: function(event) {
    // Internet Explorer value is srcElement, W3C value is target
    var target = event.srcElement || event.target;

    // Fix legacy Safari bug which reports events occurring on a text
    // node instead of an element node
    if (target.nodeType == 3) { // 3 denotes a text node
        target = target.parentNode; // Get parent node of text node
    }

    // Return the element node the event occurred on
    return target;
},

// The getCharacterFromKey method returns the character pressed when
// keyboard events occur. You should use the keypress event
// as others vary in reliability

getCharacterFromKey: function(event) {
    var character = "";
    if (event.keyCode) { // Internet Explorer
        character = String.fromCharCode(event.keyCode);
    } else if (event.which) { // W3C
        character = String.fromCharCode(event.which);
    }
    return character;
},

// The getMousePositionRelativeToDocument method returns the current
// mouse pointer position relative to the top left edge of the current page

getMousePositionRelativeToDocument: function(event) {
    var x = 0, y = 0;

    if (event.pageX) {
        // pageX gets coordinates of pointer from left of entire document
        x = event.pageX;
        y = event.pageY;
    } else if (event.clientX) {
        // clientX gets coordinates from left of current viewable area
        // so we have to add the distance the page has scrolled onto this value
        x = event.clientX + document.body.scrollLeft + ➥
            document.documentElement.scrollLeft;
        y = event.clientY + document.body.scrollTop + ➥
            document.documentElement.scrollTop;
    }
```

```
            // Return an object literal containing the x and y mouse coordinates
            return {
                x: x,
                y: y
            }
        },

        // The getMousePositionOffset method returns the distance of the mouse
        // pointer from the top left of the element the event occurred on

        getMousePositionOffset: function(event) {
            var x = 0, y = 0;

            if (event.layerX) {
                x = event.layerX;
                y = event.layerY;
            } else if (event.offsetX) {
                // Internet Explorer-proprietary
                x = event.offsetX;
                y = event.offsetY;
            }

            // Returns an object literal containing the x and y coordinates of the
            // mouse relative to the element the event fired on
            return {
                x: x,
                y: y
            }
        },

        // The getRelatedTarget method returns the element node the event was set up to
        // fire on, which can be different from the element the event actually fired on

        getRelatedTarget: function(event) {
            var relatedTarget = event.relatedTarget;
            if (event.type == "mouseover") {
                // With mouseover events, relatedTarget is not set by default
                relatedTarget = event.fromElement;
            } else if (event.type == "mouseout") {
                // With mouseout events, relatedTarget is not set by default
                relatedTarget = event.toElement;
            }
            return relatedTarget;
        }
};
```

```
// Example usage

// Instantiate the library as a singleton for use on a page
$ = new $();

// Clicking anywhere on the page will output the current coordinates
// of the mouse pointer
$.Events.add(document.body, "click", function(e) {
    alert("Mouse clicked at 'x' position " + e.pageX + " and 'y' position "+ ➥
        e.pageY);
});
```

Loading Content on Demand with Ajax

One of the fundamental parts of most RIAs is the ability to communicate directly with a web server without the need to refresh the page. This allows web applications to behave more like desktop applications, which can load and save data in the background, and update portions of the page independently of others.

Asynchronous JavaScript and XML (Ajax for short) is the name commonly given to this practice of downloading or sending content to and from a remote web server through JavaScript. Although it is mentioned in the name, the technique does not actually rely on XML-format data for communication; indeed, any type of content can be transmitted or received. The term *asynchronous* means that, while content is being loaded, the rest of your script can still execute—the code doesn't stop to wait for the content to finish loading before it continues.

Caution As a security measure, when you use the Ajax technique, browsers will allow you to access only content that is stored on the same domain as the page that is currently executing the code. Many developers work around this restriction by including a server-side script on their web server which, when passed a URL as a query string parameter, loads the contents of that URL and passes them back to the Ajax request on the page.

Don't forget that when you're writing your code, if you provide the means to perform an action or load certain content using this technique, the same action must be able to be performed using HTML alone, where it is relevant. If you are creating a web mail client, for example, you should build the application to work with HTML first, before adding JavaScript and Ajax techniques to turn this into an RIA.

Let's add some JavaScript methods to your $ library to deal with the interaction between the browser and the web server. There are several cross-browser obstacles to overcome, as explained in the comments in the code. Listing 2-12 demonstrates how to load content dynamically in a cross-browser way.

Listing 2-12. *Loading Content Dynamically Using Ajax*

```
// Define a new namespace within the $ library, called Remote, to store
// our Ajax methods

$.prototype.Remote = {

    // The getConnector method returns the base object for performing
    // dynamic browser-server communication through JavaScript

    getConnector: function() {
        var connectionObject = null;
        if (window.XMLHttpRequest) {
            // If the W3C-supported request object is available, use that
            connectionObject = new XMLHttpRequest();
        } else if (window.ActiveXObject) {
            // Otherwise, if the IE-proprietary object is available, use that
            connectionObject = new ActiveXObject('Microsoft.XMLHTTP');
        }

        // Both objects contain virtually identical properties and methods
        // so it's just a case of returning the correct one that's supported
        // within the current browser
        return connectionObject;
    },

    // The configureConnector method defines what should happen while the
    // request is taking place, and ensures that a callback method is executed
    // when the response is successfully received from the server

    configureConnector: function(connector, callback) {
        // The readystatechange event fires at different points in the life cycle
        // of the request, when loading starts, while it is continuing and
        // again when it ends
        connector.onreadystatechange = function() {

            // If the current state of the request informs us that the
            // current request has completed
            if (connector.readyState == 4) {

                // Ensure the HTTP status denotes successful download of content
                if (connector.status == 200) {

                    // Execute the callback method, passing it an object
                    // literal containing two properties, the raw text of the
```

```
                    // downloaded content and the same content in XML format,
                    // if the content requested was able to be parsed as XML.
                    // We also set its owner to be the connector in case this
                    // object is required in the callback function

                    callback.call(connector, {
                        text: connector.responseText,
                        xml: connector.responseXML
                    });
                }
            }
        }
    },

    // The load method takes an object literal containing a URL to load and a method
    // to execute once the content has been downloaded from that URL. Since the
    // Ajax technique is asynchronous, the rest of the code does not wait for the
    // content to finish downloading before continuing, hence the need to pass in
    // the method to execute once the content has downloaded in the background.

    load: function(request) {
        // Take the url from the request object literal input,
        // or use an empty string value if it doesn't exist
        var url = request.url || "";

        // Take the callback method from the request input object literal,
        // or use an empty function if it is not supplied
        var callback = request.callback || function() {};

        // Get our cross-browser connection object
        var connector = this.getConnector();

        if (connector) {
            // Configure the connector to execute the callback method once the
            // content has been successfully downloaded
            this.configureConnector(connector, callback);

            // Now actually make the request for the contents found at the URL
            connector.open("GET", url, true);
            connector.send("");
        }
    },

    // The save method performs an HTTP POST action, effectively sending content,
    // such as a form's field values, to a server-side script for processing
```

```
    save: function(request) {
        var url = request.url || "";
        var callback = request.callback || function() {};

        // The data variable is a string of URL-encoded name-value pairs to send to
        // the server in the following format:
        // "parameter1=value1&parameter2=value2&..."
        var data = request.data || "";

        var connector = this.getConnector();
        if (connector) {
            this.configureConnector(connector, callback);

            // Now actually send the data to script found at the URL
            connector.open("POST", url, true);
            connector.setRequestHeader("Content-type", ➥
                "application/x-www-form-urlencoded");
            connector.setRequestHeader("Content-length", data.length);
            connector.setRequestHeader("Connection", "close");
            connector.send(data);
        }
    }
}

// Example usage

// Instantiate the library as a singleton
$ = new $();

// Load the contents of the URL index.html from the root of the web server
$.Remote.load({
    url: "/index.html",
    callback: function(response) {
        // Get the plain text contents of the file
        var text = response.text;

        // If the HTML file was written in XHTML format, it would be available
        // in XML format through the response.xml property
        var xml = response.xml;

        // Output the contents of the index.html file as plain text
        alert(text);
    }
});
```

```
// Send some data to a server-side script at the URL process-form.php
$.Remote.save({
    url: "/process.form.php",
    data: "name=Den&surname=Odell",
    callback: function(response) {
        // Output the server-side script's response to the form submission
        alert(response.text);
    }
});
```

The Ajax technique is data-format agnostic, so the data sent and received should be in a format that makes is easy for you to actually do something with it in your code. From experience, we know that XML parsing through JavaScript is rather slow, and so JSON provides a lighter alternative, both in terms of data size and the speed at which it can be converted into a meaningful native format for JavaScript to use. Since JSON is inherently just a JavaScript object, it is incredibly simple to parse into a usable object. In most cases, it is possible to represent XML data in JSON format using fewer characters.

In some cases, you may wish the server to return HTML so that, instead of parsing with JavaScript, you can simply insert that content into the DOM. XHTML provides a great format for this. When dynamically inserting HTML into the page through JavaScript, all the necessary CSS styles on the page will be applied as expected to the new markup, This means that you do not need to do anything further to achieve the required look of the page when adding content dynamically to a page using Ajax.

Using Utility Functions

Many JavaScript libraries contain a handful of useful methods that allow developers to save time and write shorter, more efficient code within their own routines. Listing 2-13 adds a few string-manipulation methods and a method that allows you to merge together two object literals (which is not built into the language as it stands) to your $ JavaScript library.

Listing 2-13. *Adding Utility Methods to the $ Library*

```
// Add the Utils namespace to hold a set of useful, reusable methods

$.prototype.Utils = {

    // The mergeObjects method copies all the property values of one object
    // literal into another, replacing any properties that already exist, and
    // adding any that don't

    mergeObjects: function(original, newObject) {
        for (var key in newObject){
            // for ... in ... loops expose unwanted properties such as prototype
            // and constructor, among others. Using the hasOwnProperty
            // native method allows us to only allow real properties to pass
```

```
        if (newObject.hasOwnProperty(key)) {
            // Loop through every item in the new object literal,
            // getting the value of that item in the original object and
            // the equivalent value in the original object, if it exists
            var newPropertyValue = newObject[key];
            var originalPropertyValue = original[key];
        }

        // Set the value in the original object to the equivalent value from the
        // new object, except if the property's value is an object type, in
        // which case call this method again recursively, in order to copy every
        // value within that object literal also
        original[key] = (originalPropertyValue && ➡
            typeof newPropertyValue == 'object' && ➡
            typeof originalPropertyValue == 'object') ? ➡
            this.mergeObjects(originalPropertyValue, newPropertyValue) : ➡
            newPropertyValue;
    }

    // Return the original object, with all properties copied over from
    // the new object
    return original;
},

// The replaceText method takes a text string containing placeholder values and
// replaces those placeholders with actual values passed in through the values
// object literal.
// For example: "You have {count} messages in the {folderName} folder"
// Each placeholder, marked with braces - { } - will be replaced with the
// actual value from the values object literal, the properties count and
// folderName will be sought in this case

replaceText: function(text, values) {
    for (var key in values) {
        if (values.hasOwnProperty(key)) {
            // Loop through all properties in the value object literal
            if (typeof values[key] == undefined) { // Code defensively
                values[key] = "";
            }

            // Replace the property name wrapped in braces from the text
            // string with the actual value of that property. The regular
            // expression ensures that multiple occurrences are replaced
            text = text.replace(new RegExp("{" + key +"}", "g"), values[key]);
        }
    }
```

```javascript
        // Return the text with all placeholder values replaced with real ones
        return text;
    },

    // The toCamelCase method takes a hyphenated value and converts it into
    // a camel case equivalent, e.g., margin-left becomes marginLeft. Hyphens
    // are removed, and each word after the first begins with a capital letter

    toCamelCase: function(hyphenatedValue) {
        var result = hyphenatedValue.replace(/-\D/g, function(character) {
            return character.charAt(1).toUpperCase();
        });
        return result;
    },

    // The toHyphens method performs the opposite conversion, taking a camel
    // case string and converting it into a hyphenated one.
    // e.g., marginLeft becomes margin-left

    toHyphens: function(camelCaseValue) {
        var result = camelCaseValue.replace(/[A-Z]/g, function(character) {
          return ('-' + character.charAt(0).toLowerCase());
        });
        return result;
    }
};

// Example usage on a page

// Instantiate the library as a singleton
$ = new $();

// Combine two object literals
var creature = {
    face: 1,
    arms: 2,
    legs: 2
};

var animal = {
    legs: 4,
    chicken: true
};

// Resulting object literal becomes...
// {
//      face: 1,
//      arms: 2,
```

```
//      legs: 4,
//      chicken: true
// }
creature = $.Utils.mergeObjects(creature, animal);

// Outputs "You have 3 messages waiting in your inbox.";
$.Utils.replaceText("You have {count} messages waiting in your {folder}.", {
    count: 3,
    folder: "inbox"
});

// Outputs "fontFamily"
alert($.Utils.toCamelCase("font-family"));

// Outputs "font-family"
alert($.Utils.toHyphens("fontFamily"));
```

Handling CSS and Styles

So far, we've looked into how to deal with handling events and dynamically loading content in a cross-browser way. Both techniques are essential for building RIAs. In addition to these, most developers require the ability to discover which styles are applied to a particular element, and require the ability to add and remove CSS class names from elements to alter styles in a dynamic way within their application. Listing 2-14 shows how to perform these actions in a cross-browser manner and add them to your $ library.

Listing 2-14. *Adding CSS Style-Related Methods to the $ Library*

```
// Define the CSS namespace within the $ library to store style-related methods

$.prototype.CSS = {

    // The getAppliedStyle method returns the current value of a specific
    // CSS style property on a particular element

    getAppliedStyle: function(element, styleName) {
        var style = "";

        if (window.getComputedStyle) {
            // W3C-specific method. Expects a style property with hyphens
            style = element.ownerDocument.defaultView.getComputedStyle( ➥
                element, null).getPropertyValue($.Utils.toHyphens(styleName));
        } else if (element.currentStyle) {
            // Internet Explorer-specific method. Expects style property names
            // in camel case
            style = element.currentStyle[$.Utils.toCamelCase(styleName)];
        }
```

```javascript
        // Return the value of the style property found
        return style;
    },

    // The getArrayOfClassNames method is a utility method which returns an
    // array of all the CSS class names assigned to a particular element.
    // Multiple class names are separated by a space character

    getArrayOfClassNames: function(element) {
        var classNames = [];
        if (element.className) {
            // If the element has a CSS class specified, create an array
            classNames = element.className.split(' ');
        }
        return classNames;
    },

    // The addClass method adds a new CSS class of a given name to a
    // particular element

    addClass: function(element, className) {
        // Get a list of the current CSS class names applied to the element
        var classNames = this.getArrayOfClassNames(element);

        // Add the new class name to the list
        classNames.push(className);

        // Convert the list in space-separated string and assign to the element
        element.className = classNames.join(' ');
    },

    // The removeClass method removes a given CSS class name from
    // a given element

    removeClass: function(element, className) {
        var classNames = this.getArrayOfClassNames(element);

        // Create a new array for storing all the final CSS class names in
        var resultingClassNames = [];

        for (var index = 0; index < classNames.length; index++) {
            // Loop through every class name in the list
            if (className != classNames[index]) {
                // Add the class name to the new list if it isn't the one specified
                resultingClassNames.push(classNames[index]);
            }
        }
```

```
        // Convert the new list into a space-separated string and assign it
        element.className = resultingClassNames.join(" ");
},


// The hasClass method returns true if a given class name exists on a
// specific element, false otherwise

hasClass: function(element, className) {
    // Assume by default that the class name is not applied to the element
    var isClassNamePresent = false;

    var classNames = this.getArrayOfClassNames(element);
    for (var index = 0; index < classNames.length; index++) {
        // Loop through each CSS class name applied to this element
        if (className == classNames[index]) {
            // If the specific class name is found, set the return value to true
            isClassNamePresent = true;
        }
    }

    // Return true or false, depending on if the specified class name was found
    return isClassNamePresent;
},


// The getPosition method returns the x and y coordinates of the top-left
// position of a page element within the current page, along with the
// current width and height of that element

getPosition: function(element) {
    var x = 0, y = 0;

    var elementBackup = element;

    if (element.offsetParent) {
        // The offsetLeft and offsetTop properties get the position of the
        // element with respect to its parent node. To get the position with
        // respect to the page itself, we need to go up the tree, adding the
        // offsets together each time until we reach the node at the top of
        // the document, by which point, we'll have coordinates for the
        // position of the element in the page
        do {
            x += element.offsetLeft;
            y += element.offsetTop;

            // Deliberately using = to force the loop to execute on the next
            // parent node in the page hierarchy
        } while (element = element.offsetParent)
    }
```

```
        // Return an object literal with the x and y coordinates of the element,
        // along with the actual width and height of the element
        return {
            x: x,
            y: y,
            height: elementBackup.offsetHeight,
            width: elementBackup.offsetWidth
        }
    }
};

// Example usage on a page

// Instantiate the library as a singleton
$ = new $();

// Locate the first <hr> element within the page
var horizontalRule = document.getElementsByTagName("hr")[0];

// Output the current width of the <hr> element
alert($.CSS.getAppliedStyle(horizontalRule, "width"));

// Add the hide CSS class to the <hr> element
$.CSS.addClass(horizontalRule, "hide");

// Remove the hide CSS class from the <hr> element
$.CSS.removeClass(horizontalRule, "hide");

// Outputs true if the hide CSS class exists on the <hr> element
alert($.CSS.hasClass(horizontalRule, "hide"));

// Outputs the x and y coordinates of the <hr> element
var position = $.CSS.getPosition(horizontalRule)
alert("The element is at 'x' position '" + position.x + "' and 'y' position '" + ➥
    position.y + "'. It also has a width of '" + position.width + "' and a height ➥
    of '" + position.height + "'");
```

Locating Elements Within the Page

You already know how to use the methods getElementById() and getElementsByTagName() to locate elements within the DOM, but what if you want to locate a group of tags that share the same CSS class name, for example? A reusable method to provide this kind of DOM element location could be incredibly useful. Listing 2-15 shows how to perform this kind of element location and make it reusable by adding it to your $ library.

Listing 2-15. *Adding Methods for Locating Elements Within the DOM to the $ Library*

```
// Add a new Elements namespace to the $ library

$.prototype.Elements = {

    // The getElementsByClassName method returns an array of DOM elements
    // which all have the same given CSS class name applied. To improve the speed
    // of the method, an optional contextElement can be supplied which restricts the
    // search to only those child nodes within that element in the node hierarchy

    getElementsByClassName: function(className, contextElement){
        var allElements = null;
        if (contextElement) {
            // Get an array of all elements within the contextElement
            // The * wildcard value returns all tags
            allElements = contextElement.getElementsByTagName("*");
        } else {
            // Get an array of all elements, if no contextElement was supplied
            allElements = document.getElementsByTagName("*");
        }

        var results = [];
        for (var elementIndex = 0; elementIndex < allElements.length; ➥
                elementIndex++) {
            // Loop through every element found
            var element = allElements[elementIndex];

            // If the element has the specified class, add that element to
            // the output array
            if ($.CSS.hasClass(element, className)) {
                results.push(element);
            }
        }

        // Return the list of elements that contain the specific CSS class name
        return results;
    }
}
```

Completing the Library

Before you can actually use your $ library class, it must be instantiated into a singleton object. Let's put all this code together into one file named $.js and add the code shown in Listing 2-16 to the very end of the file. Then you will be able to reference this file externally from your HTML page, allowing you to use its methods to ensure your code works across the different browsers.

Listing 2-16. *Instantiating the $ Library*

```
// Instantiate the $ library as a singleton right at the end of the file,
// ready to use on a page which references the $.js file

$ = new $();
```

Throughout the rest of this book, the $ library will be used as the basis for many of the code examples.

You will find the same functionality exists with virtually all other JavaScript libraries, so feel free to use any library you prefer within your own code. Remember to use the criteria explained at the beginning of this section to select a library that will provide the best results and support.

Building RIAs

Throughout this chapter, you have been introduced to the building blocks that will work together to enable you to build your own RIAs.

When beginning work on an RIA, you should define the classes and objects that represent the major concepts within your application. Any concept that is repeatable should be created as a class, and any concept that exists only once in the system should be created as an object literal or a singleton. Use the concept of namespaces to group logically related code together, much as you did when building the $ JavaScript library in the previous section.

Structuring the Application

Let's take a web mail client as an example, and come up with the high-level concepts that represent the entire system. The primary concept within any e-mail client is that of the mail message. A mail message should represent, at the very least, the sender and recipient(s) of the message, the subject, message body, and any file attachments. The actions that can be performed on a mail message primarily include composing, sending, and deleting.

When creating a new e-mail message within your code, you might want to be able to prepopulate the values of the message, if you're creating a message on behalf of the user. Alternatively, you might want to take input from the user to compose the message.

You can form the bare-bones structure for this class using this information, as shown in Listing 2-17. Notice how you provide default values in case any input values are missing and, if no input values are passed to the class when instantiated, you force the compose() method to fire.

Listing 2-17. *The Bare-Bones Structure of an E-Mail Message Class*

```
var EmailMessage = function(input){
    this.from = input.from || "";
    this.to = input.to || []; // Array of recipients
    this.subject = input.subject || "";
    this.body = input.body || "";
    this.attachments = input.attachments || []; // Array of attachment URLs
    this.compose = function() {
```

```
            // TODO: Bring up an email composition form, populating the object
            // instance with the data entered
        };
        this.send = function() {
            // TODO: Send the message data to a server-side mail sender
            // script using Ajax
        };
        this.remove = function() {
            // TODO: Delete the message
        };

        // If the input attribute is not supplied, force the compose method to fire
        if (!input) {
            this.compose();
        }
    }
}

// Example usage on a page

// Create an object representing a populated email message
var myEmailMessage = new EmailMessage({
    from: "me@denodell.com",
    to: ["test@denodell.com"],
    subject: "Test message.",
    body: "This is a test message. Please ignore."
    // We don't supply attachments so the default value will be used instead
});

// Create a new empty message, which will force the compose method to fire
var emptyEmailMessage = new EmailMessage();
```

Now you have the basic class in place that represents the primary data structure of the application. Next, let's introduce one more class structure to represent a folder, which can contain one or many messages and one or many subfolders. Each folder must have the ability to add new messages into its structure. Listing 2-18 shows the code to represent a folder class.

Listing 2-18. *A Folder Class Structure*

```
var Folder = function(input) {
    this.name = input.name || "";
    this.folders = input.folders || []; // Array of instances of the Folder class
    this.messages = input.messages || []; // Array of EmailMessage instances
    this.addMessage(message) = function() {
        this.messages.push(message);
    },
```

```
        this.removeMessage(message) = function() {
            // TODO: Remove the message from the folder
        },
        this.listMessages = function() {
            // TODO: Display a list of the messages in this folder
        }
}

// Example usage on a page

// Create a new Inbox folder
var inbox = new Folder({
    name: "Inbox"
});

// Create a new message
var myEmailMessage = new EmailMessage({
    from: "me@denodell.com",
    to: ["test@denodell.com"],
    subject: "Test message.",
    body: "This is a test message. Please ignore."
});

// Add the new message to the inbox folder
inbox.addMessage(myEmailMessage);
```

In addition, you need a singleton to represent the entire web mail client application. This singleton should contain the list of top-level folders, be able to load the folders and messages stored on a web server, and be able to initialize the application using these, as shown in Listing 2-19.

Listing 2-19. *Singleton Representing a Web Mail Client Application*

```
var WebMail = new function() {
    this.folders = [];
    this.loadFolders = function() {
        // TODO: Load list of folders via Ajax from the server and populate Folder
        // object instances from this information
    };
    this.loadMessagesIntoFolders = function() {
        // TODO: Load list of messages via Ajax from the server, create EmailMessage
        // object instances and populate the folder instances with these messages
    };

    // Initialize the data, loading messages into folders, ready for use
    this.folders = this.loadFolders();
    this.loadMessagesIntoFolders();
```

```
    // Initialize the user interface. When the user clicks the create-mail-button
    // element, a new EmailMessage is created, which launches the new mail
    // composition form automatically
    $.Events.add(document.getElementById("create-mail-button"), ➥
            "click", function() {
        new EmailMessage();
    });
}();
```

So far, you have defined structures to hold folders and messages within your web mail system, which are essentially the data-related components of the application. But a web mail client needs to allow the users to create and manage these structures via their browser using an intuitive user interface. You need to build that interface using HTML and CSS, and then use JavaScript to listen for user interaction with any page components and execute code based on the actions taken. Remember that you need to make the application work first and foremost when JavaScript is switched off in the browser, so be sure this is all in place before adding any JavaScript code.

If the user clicks a Create Message button, for example, you could execute the code to create a new instance of the EmailMessage class, which would display the form on the page in order to create a new message. You would handle your code as follows:

- All code related to the data storage and user interface of e-mail message-specific data should be handled within the EmailMessage class.

- All code related to the data and user interface of folder-specific data should be handled within the Folder class.

- All code related to the user interface of the application itself should be stored within the singleton representing the application as a whole.

With this level of separation, you should find it easier to maintain your code base as it grows larger. When problems surface, you should be able to locate their sources quickly.

Managing Two Sets of HTML

You will be building the HTML of your RIA to function correctly when JavaScript is unavailable. So how can your user interface dynamically present forms and other HTML code, which are stored within separate files? You have two options available to help you achieve this.

Maintain two sets of HTML code: You will have one set for the HTML-only application and another for the JavaScript application. You can store the HTML for the JavaScript application directly within the code, either in plain text or created dynamically using the DOM.

Use server-side scripting: With server-side scripting, you can maintain a single include file containing each page's or component's HTML code. Within your HTML-only application, you refer to a page that contains the header, footer, navigation, and other page elements surrounding the include file HTML. Within your JavaScript code, you use the Ajax technique to dynamically load in the include file only, giving you exactly the HTML code you need. You can then insert this code into the page in the desired location, using the DOM.

So far, we have explored building RIAs following one particular software architectural design pattern, or code organization technique: using a singleton to pull together the objects and classes to create a user interface that is incredibly powerful and scalable. Now let's look at a couple other patterns,

Using Design Patterns

Along with the Singleton pattern, two other patterns can be used to construct and assemble your code: the Model-View-Controller pattern and the Observer pattern.

The Model-View-Controller Pattern

The Model-View-Controller (MVC) software architecture pattern divides an application into three logically separate groupings:

- The *model*, which contains code related to data storage and manipulation
- The *view*, which contains code related to building and managing the user interface
- The *controller*, which acts as a bridge, containing code to connect the model and view together through an event-based mechanism

The controller links together the model and view, both of which are agnostic of each other—completely stand-alone. Figure 2-1 illustrates the logical division of the MVC software pattern.

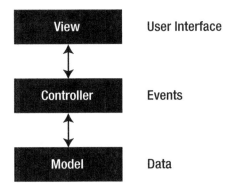

Figure 2-1. *The MVC pattern of code separation*

Listing 2-20 shows the web mail application example adapted to the MVC pattern.

Listing 2-20. *Web Mail Client Application Using the MVC Software Pattern*

```
var WebMail = new function() {

    // The Model contains only the code needed to store and manipulate the raw
    // data of the application. Our EmailMessage and Folder classes are therefore
    // defined within this code, as well as any other data storage and manipulation
    // code for the application as a whole
```

```javascript
var Model = function() {
    this.EmailMessage = function(input) {
        // TODO: Insert class definition code for EmailMessage here
    };

    this.Folder = function(input) {
        // TODO: Insert class definition code for Folder here
    };

    this.folders = [];
    this.getMessages = function(folderName) {
        // TODO: Return a list of messages within the specified folder
    }
    this.composeMessage = function() {}
    this.sendMessage = function(messageId) {}
    this.deleteMessage = function(messageId) {
        // TODO: Insert code to delete message with the specified messageId
    }
};

// The View contains only the code needed to construct the user interface and to
// wire up button events - though it does not specify what code to execute when
// those events occur, that is handled by the Controller

var View = function() {

    // Define the methods to execute when certain events occur - the code for
    // the methods is passed in from the Controller
    this.onComposeButtonClick = function() {};
    this.onSendButtonClick = function() {};
    this.onDeleteMessageButtonClick = function() {};

var self = this;

    // Wire up the HTML button events on the page
    $.Events.add(document.getElementById("compose-button"), "click", ➥
        this.onComposeButtonClick);
    $.Events.add(document.getElementById("delete-message-2"), "click", ➥
            function(e) {
        // Pass a message identifier parameter, defaulted to a value of 2
        self.onDeleteMessageButtonClick(e, 2);
    });

    // Add user interface-specific methods
    this.showComposeMailForm = function() {
        // TODO: Show the form to compose a new email
```

```
            // Wire up a new button, which we want to use to send the new email
            $.Events.add(document.getElementById("send-button"), "click", ➥
                    function(e) {
                // Pass an extra message identifier parameter, defaulted to 2
                self.onSendButtonClick(e, 2);
            });
        };

        this.updateMessageList = function(messages) {
            // TODO: Add code to remove the compose mail form from the page
        }

        this.updateMessageList(messages) {
            // TODO: Display the list of messages
        }
    }

    // The Controller contains event-based code and higher-level actions,
    // connecting the Model and the View to create the full application

    var Controller = function(model, view) {
        var composeEmail = function(e) {
            // Stop the default button click event from occurring - that would be
            // for the HTML-only version of the site, which we are overriding
            e.preventDefault();

            view.showComposeMailForm();
        };

        var sendEmail = function(e, message) {
            e.preventDefault();

            var messageId = new model.EmailMessage(message);
            model.sendMessage(messageId);
            view.hideComposeMailForm();
        };

        var deleteMessage = function(e, messageId) {
            e.preventDefault();

            model.deleteMessage();
            view.updateMessageList(model.getMessages("Inbox"));
        };
```

```
        // Connect the user instantiated events in the View to actual code
        view.onComposeButtonClick = composeEmail;
        view.onSendButtonClick = sendEmail;
        view.onDeleteMessageButtonClick = deleteMessage;
    }

    // Plug the whole MVC structure together
    new Controller(new Model(), new View());
}();
```

Don't feel too overwhelmed by this code. It may seem complicated at first, but once you get some practice building code with the MVC pattern, you will soon understand how it works and discover its inherent scalability.

The Observer Pattern

The Observer pattern is very powerful and highly scalable. I personally find it to be every bit as useful as the MVC pattern, if not more so, in my own projects.

The Observer pattern relies on two ideas: broadcasting events (the terms *publishing* and *firing* are also commonly used), and listening for events (the term *subscribing* is also commonly used). Code is grouped together into logical blocks, each of which fires its own events and listens for other events fired within the wider application. No two blocks of code are ever connected together or know about each other, which is a marked difference from the MVC pattern, where the controller knows about the model and the view.

Figure 2-2 illustrates the Observer pattern. In this case there are two code blocks, both unaware of each other, firing and listening for events within a shared event space. Theoretically, there could be an infinite number of code blocks all sharing the same, or several, event spaces.

Figure 2-2. *Observer pattern with two distinct code blocks and one event space*

Within code, you can implement the Observer pattern by creating a new class that stores a list of events, and contains methods to listen to a certain event within that list and to fire a certain event within that list. You may wish to reuse this pattern across your application in different places. Listing 2-21 shows the Observer pattern defined as a class you can use within your application. Add this listing to the $ library code you created earlier in this chapter, before the end of the file, where it is declared as a singleton.

Listing 2-21. *A Class Representing the Observer Pattern*

```
$.prototype.Observer = function() {
    // Create an array to store the events
    this.events = [];
```

```
    // The listen method listens for an event of a specific name to fire, assigning
    // a method to execute when it does
    this.listen = function(eventName, method) {
        if (typeof method == "function") {
            if (!this.events[eventName]) {
                this.events[eventName] = []
            }
            this.events[eventName].push(method);
        }
    };

    // The fire method fires an event of a specific name, executing all methods
    // that have been associated with that event in turn, passing in any optional
    // parameters that have been sent along with the request to fire
    this.fire = function(eventName, params, scope) {
        scope = scope || window;
        for (var methodIndex = 0; methodIndex < this.events[eventName].length; ➥
                methodIndex++) {
            this.events[eventName][methodIndex].call(scope, params);
        }
    }
}
```

Listing 2-22 shows the code for using the Observer pattern class within the sample web mail client application.

Listing 2-22. *Web Mail Client Application Using the Observer Pattern*

```
// We will inherit the Observer pattern later, bringing in the listen
// and fire methods to the WebMail constructor
var WebMail = function() {

    // Define an object literal constant to represent the list of different
    // events that are allowable within the application
    this.EVENT = {
        UI_READY: 0,
        MESSAGES_LOADED: 1,
        DELETE_MESSAGE: 2
    }

    // Define a code block called Data to house all data storage and manipulation
    // properties and methods. This block does not know about any others, it is
    // only aware of the list of EVENTs and listen and fire events of the WebMail
    // application, which is passed into the code block as the app input variable,
    var Data = new function(app) {
```

```javascript
    var EmailMessage = function(){
        // TODO: define EmailMessage class
    };
    var Folder = function(){
        // TODO: define Folder class
    };

    // Execute the attached function when the UI_READY event is fired
    app.listen(app.EVENT.UI_READY, function() {

        // TODO: Insert code to load messages from the server via Ajax
        // into the messages variable
        var messages = [];

        // Inform any code block listening to the MESSAGES_LOADED event
        // that the messages have been loaded from the server, passing
        // across the list of messages also
        app.fire(app.EVENT.MESSAGES_LOADED, messages);
    });

    // Execute the function when the DELETE_MESSAGE event is fired
    app.listen(app.EVENT.DELETE_MESSAGE, function(messageId) {
        // TODO: Insert code to actually delete message
    });
// This self-instantiation makes the app variable equal to the
// this keyword value, which is WebMail itself
}(this);

// Define a code block called UserInterface to house all user interface-
// related properties and methods. This block is agnostic of all others and
// knows only about the events being fired around the application
var UserInterface = new function(app) {
    // TODO: Build user interface components within the browser

    $.Events.add(document.getElementById("delete-button"), "click", ➥
            function(e) {
        // Stop the default action of the delete button within HTML
        e.preventDefault();

        // TODO: Establish the real id of the message being deleted
        var messageId = 0;

        // Inform any code block listening for the DELETE_MESSAGE event that
        // a message with the given message ID needs to be deleted
        app.fire(app.EVENT.DELETE_MESSAGE, messageId);
    });
```

```
        app.listen(app.EVENT.MESSAGES_READY, function (messages) {
            // TODO: Display the messages passed in from the event
        });

        // Inform any code block listening that the UI has been constructed
        // and is ready for use
        app.fire(app.EVENT.UI_READY);
    }(this); // Self-instantiate, as we did with Data previously
}

// Inherit the Observer pattern, adopting its listen and fire events
WebMail.prototype = new $.Observer();

// Create the WebMail application as a singleton, executing the code within
WebMail = new WebMail();
```

The code in Listing 2-22 creates a singleton representing the beginnings of a web mail client within the browser. Its data-specific code and user interface–specific code know nothing of each other. However, they both know about the list of predefined events that has been created for their use and any variables that need to be passed across with each event. The web mail application is then defined by the list of events that exist within it. These events almost invariably are named after high-level actions within the system, such as delete message or send mail, which makes the code fairly easy to read.

The two code blocks are said to be *loosely coupled*, because they both perform actions against each other's data, but are not tied to, or reliant upon, each other's code in any way. Any single code block could be removed from the system without causing any errors in the browser. This cannot be said for the MVC pattern, whose controller needs both the model and the view available at all times to operate without errors.

You can also fire and listen for events outside the application code. For example, any code within the page can listen for the WebMail.EVENT.MESSAGE_DELETE event and add its own code to execute when this event is fired within the web mail application. So, you can create smaller modules using the Observer pattern that fit together into a larger application, and the application itself may also use the Observer pattern. This makes this pattern extremely powerful, versatile, and maintainable.

Testing and Test-Driven Development

You should be testing your code as you write, pretty much line by line or function by function. Don't spend your days just writing code without testing it. Always test, and test across as many different browsers as you can, so you have confidence in your code and coding skills.

Test-driven development is a concept that has found favor among programmers. The general principle is that when you are ready to write a new function, you create just the basic shell of that function first, defining its inputs and outputs. You then write your series of test cases for that function immediately, predicting the outputs for a set of inputs. With the test cases written, you may then return to your function and write the code that then fulfils the test cases. This is a sensible approach to development, as it ensures that testing becomes a main priority and ensures that each function is robust and less prone to errors.

Testing frameworks exist to ensure that no matter what reasonable set of inputs you can provide to the functions you have written in your code base, you will get sensible outputs. By knowing that your function works in a series of predetermined conditions, you can be sure that when you use it within your code, it will work as expected.

Yahoo! has released a very useful testing framework for JavaScript called YUI Test (http://developer.yahoo.com/yui/yuitest/). YUI Test is part of the Yahoo! UI JavaScript library, but it behaves just fine if you are using another JavaScript library. It allows you to write and run effective test cases on your code, detecting and logging errors as they occur. Test cases can be grouped together into larger test suites to provide a simple way of running multiple tests in one pass. What sets this testing framework above others I have used is that it provides support for testing asynchronous method calls, which allows you to test Ajax callback methods. It also provides simulation of DOM events in most common browsers.

To use YUI Test, you first create a test page that refers to the YUI Test JavaScript file and your own JavaScript code you wish to test. Then, within a `<script>` tag on the page, you call one of the functions in your code multiple times with different inputs. You tell the test framework which outputs you are expecting for each input, and the framework logs whether the real output of the function call matched your prediction. Any output that doesn't match your prediction is flagged as an error. Listing 2-23 shows a simple test suite written to run with the YUI Test framework.

■**Note** When writing your test cases, be sure that you test "edge" cases—those conditions that might not be expected in typical use but may occur in odd circumstances, such as when input data is expected but missing.

Listing 2-23. *Basic Test Suite HTML Page Using YUI Test*

```
<!DOCTYPE html PUBLIC "-//W3C//DTD XHTML 1.0 Strict//EN" ➥
    "http://www.w3.org/TR/xhtml1/DTD/xhtml1-strict.dtd">
<html xmlns="http://www.w3.org/1999/xhtml">
    <head>
        <meta http-equiv="Content-Type" content="text/html; charset=utf-8" />
        <title>Test suite example with YUI Test</title>

        <!-- Include Yahoo! CSS and JS for the Test framework -->
        <link rel="stylesheet" type="text/css" href="http://yui.yahooapis.com/ ➥
            2.6.0/build/logger/assets/skins/sam/logger.css" />
        <link rel="stylesheet" type="text/css" href="http://yui.yahooapis.com/ ➥
            2.6.0/build/fonts/fonts-min.css" />
        <link rel="stylesheet" type="text/css" href="http://yui.yahooapis.com/ ➥
            2.6.0/build/yuitest/assets/skins/sam/yuitest.css" />
        <script type="text/javascript" src="http://yui.yahooapis.com/ ➥
            2.6.0/build/yahoo-dom-event/yahoo-dom-event.js"></script>
        <script type="text/javascript" src="http://yui.yahooapis.com/ ➥
            2.6.0/build/logger/logger-min.js"></script>
```

```
    <script type="text/javascript" src="http://yui.yahooapis.com/ ➡
        2.6.0/build/yuitest/yuitest-min.js"></script>
</head>
<body>
    <h1>Test suite example with YUI Test</h1>
    <div id="testLogger"><!-- The logging console will go here --></div>

    <script type="text/javascript">
        // This will be the function we will write our test cases for
        var squareAndRound = function(number) {
            return Math.round(number * number);
        }

      // Now, create the test case code
       YAHOO.namespace("example.yuitest");

       // Create a new test case
       YAHOO.example.yuitest.MyTestCase = new YAHOO.tool.TestCase({
           name: "My test case", // Give a name to label the test case with

           // All test case functions must begin with the test prefix
           testTen: function() {
               var Assert = YAHOO.util.Assert; // Allows you to test the value

               // Execute the function we're testing
               var result = squareAndRound(10);

               // Assert that you expect the result of the function to be 100.
               // If it is, the test passes, if not an error is logged
               Assert.areEqual(100, result);
           }

           // Insert a multitude of other test cases here to push the
           // function to the limit
       });

       // Create a new test suite and add the test case to it
       YAHOO.example.yuitest.ExampleSuite = new ➡
           YAHOO.tool.TestSuite("Example Suite");
       YAHOO.example.yuitest.ExampleSuite.add( ➡
           YAHOO.example.yuitest.MyTestCase);

       // When the DOM is ready...
       YAHOO.util.Event.onDOMReady(function (){
           // Create the logging console on the page
           var logger = new YAHOO.tool.TestLogger("testLogger");
```

```
                   // Add the test suite to the test runner's list of tasks
                   YAHOO.tool.TestRunner.add(YAHOO.example.yuitest.ExampleSuite);

                   // Run the test runner, which executes the tests and outputs the
                   // results in the logging console
                   YAHOO.tool.TestRunner.run();
                });
            </script>
        </body>
</html>
```

Figure 2-3 shows an example of the logging console that indicates how well your code is running against your test cases.

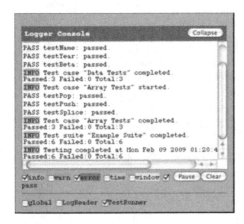

Figure 2-3. *Yahoo! UI Test framework logging console*

Using Third-Party Scripts

Reusing code that has already been written to solve the problems you are facing as an RIA developer makes good sense. You've seen it in practice already with JavaScript libraries. Similarly, allowing others to reuse code that you have written benefits the web development community in return.

Here are some guidelines for using third-party scripts in your applications:

- Check that the code has been thoroughly tested with a testing framework, such as the YUI Test framework we looked at in the previous section.

- Make sure that the script supports all the browsers that you support with your application, so you won't need to later replace the script with one that does provide all the support you need.

- Keep all third-party scripts together in a single folder, out of the way of your own scripts. Treat them as plug-ins to your application, rather than part of the core code itself.

Throughout the rest of this book, I will introduce you to several third-party scripts that should be useful to you as you seek to add extra functionality to your RIAs.

Summary

In this chapter, you have learned how to build RIAs in JavaScript using object-oriented programming principles and software architectural design patterns.

The chapter covered how to apply a clean and readable coding style, and how to use the JavaScript language in a robust way. You've seen how third-party libraries and frameworks allow you to build your code on a solid, cross-browser foundation. You've also learned how to test your code in a thorough way, to ensure no errors exist in your applications.

This marks the end of the first part of this book. Now you are ready to begin building your own RIAs. By applying the principles covered in this part, you will create a solid, accessible application, available to anyone using any web browser on any device.

In the next part of this book, you will learn how to improve the performance and responsiveness of your web applications, which will provide the best experience for your end users.

PART 2

■ ■ ■

Performance

At this point, you should have a solid grounding in HTML, CSS, and JavaScript coding, and be able to build a simple RIA using these technologies. The first part of this book covered the best practices for creating scalable, maintainable, and robust RIAs.

The second part of this book focuses on performance, efficiency, and speed. Here, you will discover techniques for ensuring that end users get a more responsive user interface, while reducing the bandwidth burden on your hosting provider.

CHAPTER 3

███

Understanding the Web Browser

The web browser acts as a facilitator—downloading, rendering, and executing your web application for your end users. The web browser has the power and potential to make simple code look like a glossy magazine article (in the case of Apple's Safari browser) or as plain text without any images or advanced abilities (in the case of the open source Lynx browser, available from `http://lynx.isc.org/`).

This chapter explains how web browsers work internally to put together the page your users see on their screen based on the code you've written. It also describes how web pages get to your browser over your network connection, and highlights a number of points of contention that can hinder performance.

Engines: The Browser's Powerhouse

Before we delve into the inner workings of the browser, you need to understand an important distinction, which is between the user interface of the web browser and the code it runs behind the scenes. Let's use the analogy of a car. The car engine determines whether you have a powerful or efficient car. The car body may look beautiful and be well designed, which is great when it's stationary, but not much use when you're trying to get from point A to point B in good time. Like a car body, a well-designed web browser user interface reflects little of its inner workings. And like the engine under the hood of the car, the behind-the-scenes code for the browser does the heavy lifting. In fact, this code is also referred to as the browser's *engine*.

The Rendering and JavaScript Engines

Most browsers are constructed internally of two main engines:

- A rendering engine (also known as a layout engine), which converts HTML and CSS to a visible page on the screen

- The JavaScript engine, which interprets the JavaScript code you have written into something that the browser can understand and execute

These internal engines are distinct from the browser's user interface. Different engines, written by different companies, organizations, and individuals, essentially distinguish how one browser displays a web page compared to another. Since the engine is separate from the user interface, it is technically possible to use the same rendering and JavaScript engines within two web browsers that look completely different from each other. The user interface can be thought of as the "skin" that surrounds the engines. In fact, some web browsers are built on the same rendering engines, as Table 3-1 attests.

Table 3-1. *Web Browsers and Their Associated Rendering Engines*

Rendering Engine	Web Browser
Trident	Microsoft Internet Explorer
Gecko	Mozilla Firefox
Presto	Opera browser
WebKit	Apple Safari (including iPhone), Google Chrome, Nokia (for mobile devices)

Table 3-2 lists the main JavaScript engines and a selection of the browsers that use those engines. Note that different combinations of rendering and JavaScript engines can be used in the same browser, as the two can be distinct from each other, demonstrated in practice by Google Chrome and Safari.

Table 3-2. *Web Browsers and Their Associated JavaScript Engines*

JavaScript Engine	Web Browser
JScript	Microsoft Internet Explorer
SpiderMonkey	Mozilla Firefox (up to and including version 3.5)
TraceMonkey	Mozilla Firefox (version 3.6)
JavaScriptCore	Apple Safari (up to and including version 3.2)
Nitro	Apple Safari (version 4)
V8	Google Chrome
Futhark	Opera

As larger and more complex JavaScript-driven RIAs are developed and made available online, browser engines need to be able to interpret them into something users can access. JavaScript engine developers are motivated to improve their software to claim theirs is the fastest and most efficient browser on the market. The actual aim of these developers is to ensure that end users experience RIAs in a way similar to their experience with desktop applications. In many ways, the browser is becoming the new operating system. Negative experiences such as long loading times, browser hangs, and slow responses to user actions are slowly becoming things of the past.

JavaScript Engine Performance Benchmarking

Let's return to our car analogy. As you might expect, not all engines are created equal. Some engines are more efficient than others; some require more resources than others (memory space, disk space, and so on); and some are faster than others. Just as figures, charts, and raw data are used to compare performance and efficiency of car models and manufacturers, so, too, are such comparisons made in the web browser world. Performance benchmark tests are commonplace, and their results are viewed with much interest by web developers.

Some controversy surrounds such comparisons, as many manufacturers choose to promote the benchmark test results that favor their product. This means that some vigilance and examination of the results are required to take in the full performance picture.

At the time of writing, four major JavaScript benchmarking test suites are in common use to compare the performance of different JavaScript engines in different browsers:

SunSpider: Created by the WebKit engine development team, SunSpider is currently the most commonly used JavaScript performance benchmarking suite. Its tests focus solely around core JavaScript functionality, such as function calls, recursion, looping, and mathematical operations. However, SunSpider also includes tests for specific applications, such as generating a tag cloud from an input in JSON format using string manipulation, decompression, and cryptography. This test suite does not contain any tests for benchmarking DOM interaction performance.

Dromaeo JavaScript test suite: This JavaScript benchmark suite was created by Mozilla developers to allow them to test their own JavaScript engines in real-world situations. It contains the tests to measure the performance of core JavaScript processing, including binary tree traversal, string and array processing, and prime number computation. This test suite does not include any DOM-specific tests.

Dromaeo DOM test suite: In addition to the core JavaScript tests, the Mozilla team created a benchmark suite for testing DOM traversal and manipulation within the browser. These tests are vitally important to RIA developers, since many web applications feature a lot of page interaction through JavaScript. The faster the DOM interaction is, the faster the perceived performance of the web application will be. Unfortunately, currently this test suite does not run correctly within IE versions 6, 7, and 8, causing a JavaScript exception error to fire partway through its execution.

V8 Benchmark Suite: This test suite was created by Google. V8 is the name of the JavaScript engine used within Google's Chrome browser. Google's developers settled on a new approach to addressing the problem of JavaScript efficiency by effectively interpreting JavaScript code down to machine-code level—the very codes that the silicon chips within your computer understand. While this makes Chrome very efficient at core JavaScript performance—and is what the V8 benchmark tests focus on exclusively—this means very little when attempting to interact with a web page through the DOM, which relies on efficient cross-communication between the JavaScript engine and the rendering engine.

As you can see, politics are involved in benchmarking. You might, for instance, suspect SunSpider of including tests that give favorable results when run in a WebKit-based browser, since the same team built both the browser and the testing tool. None of the benchmark creators claim to favor any particular browser, of course. However, it would be wise to take the results of all the benchmarking tools into consideration. Let the combined results of all four test suites influence your judgment of which is the best-performing JavaScript engine.

Each test suite can be run via the Dromaeo JavaScript performance site, at http://dromaeo.com/, which amalgamates all the benchmarking tools into a central JavaScript performance-testing hub.

Each benchmarking suite runs many different tests several times in quick succession, measuring how many tests are completed in a given time frame, and the average of the results is taken, which gives the final performance figure for each test suite for each browser. These tests tend to center on two main facets of JavaScript: raw processing power of code execution and interaction with a web page via the DOM. You can't put a performance figure on the true illustration of real-world use of JavaScript within web pages without testing both facets.

I ran several browsers through the different benchmark suites on the same test machine in near-identical circumstances so as not to give favoritism to any particular browser. Table 3-3 shows the results of those tests, along with an average of the three core JavaScript tests—V8, SunSpider, and Dromaeo JS—to provide a single set of results for comparison. Exact numbers aren't so important here, as we are looking at the relative performance differences of the browsers.

Table 3-3. *JavaScript Benchmark Test Suite Results (in Tests Run per Second)*

Browser	V8	SunSpider	Dromaeo JS	Dromaeo DOM	Core JS Average
Internet Explorer 6	0.82	5.38	5.42[*]	18.52[*]	3.87
Firefox 2.0.0.20	1.41	6.09	8.11	13.33	5.20
Google Chrome	67.95	121.04	129.32	48.75	106.10
Firefox 3.0.6	4.16	25.66	22.39	41.07	17.40
Firefox 3.5 Beta 2	3.49	56.96	33.56	51.91	31.34
Firefox 3.6 Alpha 1	2.82	79.12	38.06	82.99	40.00
Internet Explorer 7	0.96	6.02	3.70	12.12	3.56
Internet Explorer 8	1.98	18.10	49.00	24.73[*]	23.03
Safari 3.2.1	4.60	22.06	38.01	52.61	21.56
Opera 9.6.3	3.89	13.96	13.79	19.07	10.55
Safari 4 Beta	72.90	120.97	65.95	291.42	86.61

* Estimated from extrapolation of results

Figure 3-1 shows the results of Table 3-3 in a more accessible form. The combination of DOM performance and core JavaScript performance, which gives a pretty good approximation to real-world experience, is plotted on a single chart, grouped by browser. These results show that, in general, the more recent the browser, the better the JavaScript performance, in terms of both DOM access speeds and core JavaScript performance. We can also establish that IE versions 6 and 7 are among the slowest browsers of all those tested, despite these being two of the most popular browsers in the world at the time of testing. It appears from these results that RIAs experience better performance in WebKit-based browsers (Safari and Google Chrome) and Firefox. IE users suffer the worst in terms of real-world performance.

Now you have some insight into web browser engine capabilities. In the rest of this part of the book, you'll discover techniques to improve the performance and responsiveness of your RIAs.

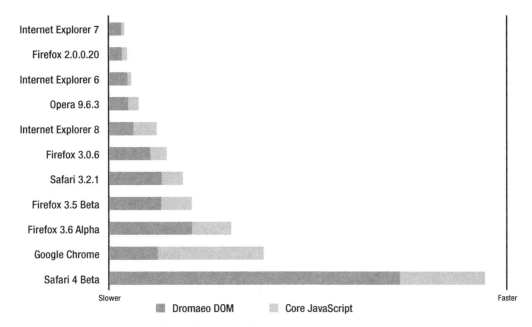

Figure 3-1. *JavaScript benchmark test results by browser*

Anatomy of a Web Page Request

Have you ever wondered what happens between the time you type a web address into your address bar and the moment a full page appears in your browser? In this section, you will learn the process involved in taking a URL and turning it into something your web browser can display.

HTTP: The Communication Standard Behind the Web

The language of communication between your browser and the destination web host is called Hypertext Transfer Protocol (HTTP). Within this language, or protocol, the browser is known as the *client* and the web host as the *server*. Messages are sent back and forth between the client and the server from the moment you follow a link or type in a new URL in your browser's address bar to the point that the page is loaded on screen. Within this language, request messages pass from the client to the server, and response messages are returned from the server to the client.

Note Preceding the web address of the current page in your browser's address bar, you will find the name of the protocol used to access that URL. In most cases, this appears as `http://`, denoting HTTP. However, if you are browsing certain web sites or pages, this might appear as `https://`, which denotes HTTPS, a secure form of HTTP for sending sensitive data. Other protocols include `ftp://` and `feed://`, for browsing File Transfer Protocol (FTP) sites and RSS news feeds, respectively.

Type `www.google.com` into your browser's address bar and let's take a look at what happens once you click the Go button.

An HTTP Request Message

When your browser makes a request for a URL, a plain text HTTP request message is created, which will be sent to the server, asking it to send back a page or file from it. Listing 3-1 shows an example of an HTTP request message.

Listing 3-1. *HTTP Request Message Example for www.google.com*

```
GET / HTTP/1.1
Host: www.google.com
User-Agent: Mozilla/5.0 (Windows; U; Windows NT 5.1; en-GB; rv:1.9.0.3) ➡
    Gecko/2008092417 Firefox/3.0.3 (.NET CLR 3.5.30729)
Accept: text/html,application/xhtml+xml,application/xml;
Accept-Language: en-gb,en;
Accept-Encoding: gzip,deflate
Accept-Charset: ISO-8859-1,utf-8;
Keep-Alive: 300
Connection: keep-alive
Cookie: PREF=ID=64637ffc707d92f4:TM=1222191214:LM=...
```

This may look a little confusing if you're not familiar with HTTP. Let's break it down and go through each *header*, or entry, in the request message so you understand what is happening. The first part of this header defines the action, or method, used for sending this request. Eight actions can be supplied within an HTTP request message, as summarized in Table 3-4. The actions GET, HEAD, OPTIONS, and TRACE merely retrieve information from the server; whereas POST, PUT, and DELETE cause changes to occur to data residing on the server.

Table 3-4. *HTTP Request Actions*

Action	Description
GET	Requests the body contents of a page at a specified URL, usually in HTML format, and nothing more. This is the most commonly used action on the Web.
POST	Sends data back to the server, where the data is included in the request message itself. This action is commonly used to send data from an HTML form back to the server for processing.

continued

Action	Description
HEAD	Same as GET, except the body of the HTML page requested will not be sent back with the response. This can be used if you need to know only the metadata that comes along with a response, rather than the response itself, or if you simply wish to prove that a resource at a particular URL actually exists.
PUT	Used to update a URL resource on the server, similar in many ways to POST, but only if the server allows it for the URL requested.
DELETE	Deletes the resource at a particular URL from the server, if the server allows it for the URL requested. You wouldn't be able to delete Google's home page, for example.
TRACE	Sends the request received by the server back to the sender. This can be used to show what servers or services located in the connection chain between the client and the server have been added, changed, or removed from the request.
OPTIONS	Returns a list of all the other actions available for use on a particular URL, such as DELETE and PUT. If you send the URL as a wildcard character (*), the response will contain a list of the actions supported by the web server software.

The sample HTTP request in Listing 3-1 begins like this:

```
GET / HTTP/1.1
```

It performs a GET request so that the server will return the HTML markup of the page being requested. The page in question is specified here as /, which denotes the root of the web site being accessed. HTTP/1.1 denotes the version number of the language used in this request.

```
Host: www.google.com
```

It's no use specifying the URL to access as / (the root), if you don't also send the domain name of the server you are trying to access in the message. The Host header of the HTTP request message states that domain name.

```
User-Agent: Mozilla/5.0 (Windows; U; Windows NT 5.1; en-GB; rv:1.9.0.3) ➥
    Gecko/2008092417 Firefox/3.0.3 (.NET CLR 3.5.30729)
```

User agent refers to the web browser or software used to access web pages. This header entry in the request message specifies not only the browser name and its version number, but also information about the operating system the browser is running within (in this example, Windows NT 5.1, which denotes Windows XP), the current locale set in the operating system (en-GB, for UK English), and any additional data the browser or operating system chooses to add. In Listing 3-1, the version of the .NET common language runtime (CLR) is included. By sending this information, the server has the option to use this information however it wants— either by storing the information in its log files for later statistical analysis or by responding with different HTML markup based on the type of browser software being used to request the data. For instance, if the server detects that the user agent is one from a mobile device, a cut-down version of a normal web site's markup, better suited for such devices, could be delivered in the response. In practice, it's best not to rely on this data, though, as it can be easily spoofed and altered.

```
Accept: text/html,application/xhtml+xml,application/xml;
```

The `Accept` header contains a list of Multipurpose Internet Mail Extensions (MIME) types that the browser accepts—meaning those types it knows how to interpret into something human-readable. The MIME type `text/html` indicates HTML, `application/xhtml+xml` indicates XHTML (though some web browsers don't recognize this type at the time of writing), and `application/xml` indicates XML content.

```
Accept-Language: en-gb,en;
```

Similar to the `Accept` header, the `Accept-Language` header tells the server the language and locale that is currently configured within the browser. The server can then decide whether to send language- or locale-specific data back to the browser, based on this information. In Listing 3-1, there are two values: `en-gb`, which denotes English language and UK locale, and as a backup, simply `en`, which denotes only the English language with no specific geographical locale. Of course, the server may choose to ignore this information if the web site being accessed has only one language version, or if the developer of the site wishes to give this choice to the user without making any assumptions.

```
Accept-Encoding: gzip,deflate
```

Specific content encoding types supported by the browser are sent with the `Accept-Encoding` header. If the server is unable to support the encoding types passed in this list, it will use its own standard encoding. However, if it is able to support one or more of these encoding types, it allows for the data to be sent to the browser compressed, safe in the knowledge that the browser will be able to support the decompression at the other end. Compression allows the same content to be represented with less data, meaning that the browser will receive the response faster.

Two different algorithms for compression are specified in Listing 3-1: `gzip` and `deflate`. Both compression algorithms give effective results, although files that are plain text—including HTML, CSS, and JavaScript files—will compress much more efficiently than binary files, such as images. This is because plain text files tend to contain a lot of whitespace characters, which can be compressed very efficiently.

```
Accept-Charset: ISO-8859-1,utf-8;
```

Character sets, which are data encodings of letters and symbols of world alphabets, that the browser understands are declared in the `Accept-Charset` request header. The ISO-8859-1 set is commonly referred to as Latin-1 and can represent most European characters, including accented letters. The UTF-8 set is more recent and is capable of storing representations of virtually all the world's languages, making it extremely versatile and highly recommended.

```
Keep-Alive: 300
```

The `Keep-Alive` header value dictates the length of time in seconds to keep the connection open between the client and server. This persistently open connection will be reused for subsequent requests and responses, instead of opening a new connection each time. By keeping the connection open, there is no need to reestablish the connection each time, which can take time and uses up network resources. The connection specified in Listing 3-1 is allowed to remain open for 300 seconds, or 5 minutes.

```
Connection: keep-alive
```

The `Connection` header specifies the preferred connection type for this request. With the HTTP/1.1 protocol, `keep-alive` is the most common connection type.

```
Cookie: PREF=ID=64637ffc707d92f4:TM=1222191214:LM=...
```

HTTP cookies are small pieces of text-based data stored on your computer. Cookies are placed by web sites you visit so that the web site might be able to store and retrieve data capable of providing you with a personalized experience. For example, you may visit http://www.google.com/ and log in to the Gmail service. The process of logging in will store a cookie on your machine with an identifier value that Google can retrieve on subsequent visits to automatically log you in.

Each HTTP request message will send any cookies that have been stored on the computer associated with the particular domain name (web site address) being accessed. In Listing 3-1, an identifier representing the user's Google login is stored in a cookie and sent to the server to automatically log the user into his account. Cookies can make life a bit more convenient for users. But they are sent with every request, so they should be kept small.

An HTTP Response Message

When the server receives the request message and processes its data, it creates an HTTP response message to contain the results. Listing 3-2 shows the server response message to the request message shown in Listing 3-1.

Listing 3-2. *HTTP Response Message Example for www.google.com*

```
HTTP/1.x 200 OK
Cache-Control: private, max-age=0
Date: Fri, 27 Mar 2009 12:42:14 GMT
Expires: -1
Content-Type: text/html; charset=UTF-8
Content-Encoding: gzip
Server: gws
Content-Length: 2520

<html><head>
... rest of HTML for Google's home page ...
</body></html>
```

Let's go through these headers one at a time, to make sure you fully understand what the browser receives from the server and how it uses this information.

```
HTTP/1.x 200 OK
```

The first header of the response from the server lets the browser client know which version of the HTTP protocol is used to format the rest of the message. In this case, any minor version number within version 1 of the specification will understand the message. After the version is a status number and short description informing the browser what the outcome of the request was, which determines the sort of data in the rest of the message. These status codes are important to understanding what is happening within the browser upon receipt of a response message, and they are described in the following section.

```
Cache-Control: private, max-age=0
```

Browsers maintain a local file cache, storing files that have recently been requested on the computer accessing them so as to avoid downloading those files again, making the experience for the end user a little more responsive. The `Cache-Control` header gives the browser certain parameters regarding the currently requested file, telling it for how long it should cache the file, for example. In this case, `private` tells the browser and any proxy server between the web server and client that the file is specific to the user requesting it, perhaps because it has been personalized for that user. Without this setting, proxy servers could send another user's customized home page to the requesting user, causing real confusion. The `max-age` property tells the browser or proxy server how long to cache the file, in seconds. In this case, a value of 0 ensures a fresh copy of the file is requested every time from the server, which is best for personalized sites such as Google's home page. Other files, such as images, CSS, and JavaScript, might ideally be sent with longer `max-age` values, ensuring they do not need to be requested on every new page request.

Note Setting `Cache-Control` to a value of `no-cache` tells the browser not to store the file in its cache, forcing it to download the same file from the server every time it is requested.

```
Date: Fri, 27 Mar 2009 12:42:14 GMT
```

The `Date` header value simply indicates the date and time the response message was sent.

```
Expires: -1
```

The `Expires` header specifies the date and time at which the file sent is considered stale (or old), and a new copy should be downloaded. A value of `-1` indicates that the content is already too old, forcing the browser to download a fresh copy from the server next time.

```
Content-Type: text/html; charset=UTF-8
```

The `Content-Type` header specifies the MIME type of the content sent in this request. `text/html` denotes that the content sent is HTML. The character set of the content, if it is text-based, can also be specified in this header.

```
Content-Encoding: gzip
```

The type of content encoding applied to the content sent in the response is indicated with the `Content-Encoding` header. The server listens for the `Accept-Encoding` request header, described earlier, and should send back content only in an encoding that is supported by the client.

```
Server: gws
```

The name of the web server software is sent to the client in the `Server` header. A value of gws indicates Google's own web server software was used to generate the response.

```
Content-Length: 2520
```

The size, in bytes, of the file contents sent with this response message is specified in the `Content-Length` header.

```
<html><head>
... rest of HTML for Google's home page ...
</body></html>
```

The final part of the response message contains the actual file contents returned from the server for the requested URL. Listing 3-1 requests an HTML page, so Listing 3-2 returns the HTML markup. If the file type requested were an image, you would see a text representation of the binary data stored within the image file requested, which would then be converted back into binary data within the client, displaying the image correctly.

HTTP Status Codes

HTTP status codes are three-digit codes that denote the server's response to the request, indicating whether it was successful or whether some other action now needs to take place within the client in order to locate the requested data successfully. Here, I will describe some of the more common status codes returned in HTTP response messages. For a full list of all HTTP status codes, see `http://en.wikipedia.org/wiki/List_of_HTTP_status_codes`.

200+ (Success)

A status code in the range 200–299 indicates that the request was received by the server, understood, and processed, and that the client should expect some kind of content to be sent with the current response message. Table 3-5 lists the common status codes in this range.

Table 3-5. *HTTP Status Codes Indicating a Successful Response*

Status Code	Description
200 OK	Successful request. The response message contains the data requested.
201 Created	A new resource was created on the server according to a POST or PUT action in the request.
204 No Content	Successful request, but there is no content at the requested URL to send back to the client.
206 Partial Content	The response message contains the partial contents of a larger request. This allows browsers to resume downloads of large files that have been interrupted due to a network failure or user cancellation of the download.

300+ (Redirection)

A status code in the range 300–399 indicates that, in order to successfully complete the request, the client must take an extra step and redirect to another URL, or not expect any content. Table 3-6 lists the common status codes in this range.

Table 3-6. *HTTP Status Codes Indicating a Redirection Is Required*

Status Code	Description
301 Moved Permanently	The requested URL has been moved, and the client should no longer attempt to use that URL, effectively blacklisting it. The client should use the URL returned in the response message for all future requests.
302 Found	The requested URL has been moved temporarily and can be accessed by the URL given in the response message. No blacklisting occurs, as it is only a temporary redirection.
304 Not Modified	The requested URL has been requested before and has not changed since the last time it was requested. The client should use a locally cached copy of the file at the requested URL instead, to conserve bandwidth and deliver the file to the end user faster.

400+ (Client Error)

An HTTP status code in the range 400–499 indicates that there was an error in the request message sent to the server, and the server was unable to return the requested file. The indication is that the fault lies with the client, not the server. Table 3-7 shows the common status codes in this range.

Table 3-7. *HTTP Status Codes Indicating an Error in the Client's Request Message*

Status Code	Description
400 Bad Request	The request message was not in the expected format and so could not be understood by the server.
401 Unauthorized	The server was expecting a username and password to be sent along with the request, to access a restricted area of the server, and these details were missing.
403 Forbidden	The server refuses to respond to the client's request. For example, this could be because the IP address of the requesting machine has been placed on a blacklist.
404 Not Found	No content could be found at the requested URL. The client is welcome to try this URL again in future, at which point a file may exist at that location.
405 Method Not Allowed	The HTTP request message specifies an action that is not permitted on the specified URL. If a request message tried to call a DELETE action on the Google home page, for example, you would receive this message.
410 Gone	Identical to 404 Not Found, except that the client should never try to access this URL again. If the client is a search engine spider, it should remove this URL from its index.
413 Request Entity Too Large	The request message is too large for the server to process. Such a status code could be returned if an HTML form posted more data to the server than it could handle.
414 Request URL Too Long	If the server maintains a limit for the acceptable size of a URL, this status code is returned when the request message contains a URL longer than this limit.

500+ (Server Error)

A status code in the range 500–599 indicates that the request sent was valid, but the request could not be successfully fulfilled due to a problem with the server. The indication is that the fault lies with the server, not the client. Table 3-8 lists the common status codes in this range.

Table 3-8. *HTTP Status Codes Indicating an Error with the Server*

Status Code	Description
500 Internal Server Error	The most common status code returned denoting a general error occurred on the server. This often arises when the requested URL is a server-side script that ran into an error while it was executing.
501 Not Implemented	The server does not understand or support the HTTP action being requested.
502 Bad Gateway	A proxy server passing messages between the client and destination server has a problem, which means the destination server cannot understand the request or cannot be certain of giving a response that will be received correctly by the client.
503 Service Unavailable	The server is not processing requests right now, perhaps because it has been overloaded with data or because of a scheduled maintenance period.
504 Gateway Timeout	A proxy server between the client and destination server is not forwarding messages between the two in a timely fashion.

How Messages Are Transmitted

Now that we've covered the language of communication messages on the Web, we need to look at how these messages are actually transmitted between the browser and the destination server. The messages need to travel from where the browser is located to where the web server is located, and back again, which could be around the world. This section explains how these messages go from their source to their destination without getting lost along the way.

IP Addresses: Phone Numbers of the Internet

Once the browser has created its HTTP request message, it needs to deliver that to the web server. So, its first task is to locate that web server. Taking our HTTP request message example from Listing 3-1, the domain name of the web server, www.google.com, needs to be converted into an Internet Protocol (IP) address before it can be located. This type of address looks like a series of numbers separated with a dot (.) character. In the case of www.google.com, this might look like 209.85.171.99. IP addresses help the browser and other Internet-connected systems find the information they need to route the message through to the destination web server. An IP address is like a phone number for the server.

In order to convert the human-readable domain name (which is also known as a *hostname*) into this sequence of numbers, your browser must connect to an online database, called a Domain Name System (DNS) or *name server*, which contains information about hostnames and their associated numerical IP addresses. A name server is useful for two primary reasons:

- Human-readable hostnames are much easier to remember than a sequence of numbers.

- The hostname and IP address can be updated independently of each other.

For example, Google could move its web server to another machine in another part of the world where the IP address would be different. Instead of having to communicate this change of address through the hostname, Google merely asks that the IP address be updated in the DNS database to point to the IP address at the new location. This makes the system transparent to the end user.

Before we delve further into how the DNS system works, it is important that you understand the different components of a URL. Using the URL www.google.com as an example, let's divide the address by the separator dots and look at each component, in turn, beginning with the last and working backward.

com: The rightmost section of any web address is called the *top-level domain*. You will have seen .net, .org, and many others used. The DNS system uses this portion of the URL first, to filter the list of addresses to only those within this top-level domain.

google: The middle part of our URL tells the DNS server to locate the google entry within its list of .com URLs. The system is effectively filtering the available URLs.

www: The first portion of the URL relates to the specific server, or subdomain, at google.com to access. Again, the list has effectively been filtered to only those servers at that domain.

Don't believe that there is only a single DNS server that is actively processing all these requests for IP addresses from every browser and Internet-connected device in the world. There are 13 root-level DNS systems in existence (each of which is structured of a cluster of servers to deal with the traffic load), though it is possible for companies or organizations to provide local copies of these to their own networks to speed up the lookup process.

Root-level DNS systems take care of the top-level domain and server portions of the URL, looking up the IP address for this level only. From that point, the request is moved to the servers at that domain—in this example, the DNS servers at google.com.

Every entry in a DNS database contains not just IP addresses, but also contact details of the owner of the domain and addresses of a couple of key servers, including ones for local name servers.

Most organizations will have, at the very least, a primary and secondary name server of their own on their network (Google has four name servers at present). In case of a problem on the first server, the request will be redirected to the second, reducing the likelihood of a lookup failure. The root-level DNS system passes the request for www.google.com/ to the local Google name servers, who then return the exact IP address for the local server named www, returning the final IP address of the destination web server.

Packets: Chunks of Data

Communication messages sent between computers on the Internet are formed of small chunks of data, called *packets*. Several packets usually make up one request.

The primary reason for sending packets of data instead of the whole data message in one shot is to reduce the effect of network problems. If a packet doesn't get delivered, it can be sent again until it is successfully received. It's not necessary to resend the entire data message. Also, for less powerful computer systems, smaller packets are easier to manage than larger ones, as they each take only a small portion of available memory to process.

Routes and Routers: The Switchboard of the Internet

Once your browser has learned the IP address of its final destination, it then needs to connect to that destination to send it the request message and wait for the response data. Devices called *routers* sit at every major traffic junction on the Internet, performing the connection and routing of data packets around the world. These devices maintain local *routing tables*, which contain information about how best to direct data packets from where they are now to a location closer to the web server until the packets reach their destination.

You can see for yourself how data is routed between your browser and the server you are trying to access using software already built into your computer. If you are a Microsoft Windows user, load the command prompt. To do this, select Start ➤ Run. In the box that appears, type cmd, and then press Enter. In the command prompt window, type the following command and press the Enter key:

```
tracert www.google.com
```

If you are an Apple Mac user, load the Terminal application from within your Applications/Utilities folder. In the window that appears, type the following command and press Enter:

```
traceroute www.google.com
```

You will see something that looks similar to the following:

```
Tracing route to www.l.google.com [64.233.183.103] ➥
    over a maximum of 30 hops:

1      6 ms     <1 ms     <1 ms   10.0.1.1
2      2 ms      5 ms      5 ms   gw1.A218.priv.bahnhof.se [85.24.240.1]
3    642 ms        *       15 ms   hsb-A218.c3750-stortorget.bahnhof.net [85.24.152.50]
4      4 ms      3 ms      4 ms   stortorget-mmo.c7600-limhamn.bahnhof.net ➥
                                  [85.24.151.29]
5      4 ms     17 ms      6 ms   c7600-limhamn.mlm-rr1.bahnhof.net [85.24.151.202]
6      4 ms     14 ms      1 ms   82.96.55.41
7     56 ms    200 ms    205 ms   v1315-r84.tc-cr1-r69.sto.se.p80.net [82.96.1.61]
8     28 ms     11 ms     15 ms   72.14.198.177
9     15 ms     10 ms     10 ms   209.85.252.186
10    33 ms     35 ms     33 ms   209.85.252.192
11    51 ms     35 ms     36 ms   66.249.95.132
12    38 ms     37 ms        *    72.14.233.79
13    39 ms     45 ms     48 ms   216.239.43.34
14       *      42 ms   3402 ms   nf-in-f103.google.com [64.233.183.103]

Trace complete.
```

This is a visual representation of a chunk of test data moving from your computer to the server at www.google.com. Within the square brackets in the first line of the response, you see the IP address found from a DNS lookup. Following that is a list of several servers, the first of which is your computer and the last the destination server at google.com. In between are the router devices that are taking that data and moving it around the world to make sure the data reaches the destination. You should be able to see that the first few entries correspond to servers owned by your Internet service provider (ISP).

You may notice that routers do not necessarily select geographically nearby locations. This is because the most efficient way of getting the data around the world may be to jump across county, country, and continental boundaries.

Loading Order of an HTML Page

Once the browser has received the response for a page request, it takes the HTML markup provided in that response and displays it. This section explains how this is performed, and the impact that repositioning certain HTML tags within a page can have on its loading time.

An HTML document contains two main sections: the head and the body, denoted by the <head> and <body> tags, respectively. Browsers will usually begin constructing the page while the data in the response message is still downloading, beginning with the <head> section before moving onto the <body>. The head section may contain any of the following tags: <style>, <link>, <script>, <meta>, <title>, and <base>.

All of these tags, with the exception of <script>, are permitted only within the <head> section and nowhere else. This rule tells you something of what the browser needs to know before it renders the <body> portion of the HTML. If you take a look at the description of each of these tags in turn, it should become obvious why this information needs to be known in advance of processing the <body> markup:

<style>: Contains CSS style definitions in order to lay out the HTML on the page in a custom design. The browser needs to know how to lay out the tags before it displays those tags on the screen, in order to prevent ugly rendering effects. Otherwise, the browser would draw tags in their default style before applying the custom style to them. This tag ensures this never has to happen.

<link>: Links to external data. When referencing an external style sheet, the browser needs to know about these links for the same reasons as it needs to know about the styles in the <style> tag. Where it applies to linking to other documents within the site, it merely represents header information, separate from the main body of the page.

<meta>: Provides data defining the content of the page but external to the page content itself. Examples include specifying keywords and descriptions of the page for use by search engine spiders. It is also possible to use this tag to perform the same action as certain HTTP response message header values—for example, to set an expiration date on the content or to specify the content type.

<title>: Specifies the title of the page. This is the text that appears in the window title of your browser, your bookmark link, search engine results, and other places.

<base>: Allows the page developer to stipulate a base URL for all links, images, and other URLs specified within the page content. For example, if the <base> tag is set to point to http://www.google.com/ and a link in the page is specified only as logo.gif, then the full URL that the browser will look for will be a combination of the two URLs: http://www.google.com/logo.gif.

Once the browser has read the <head> section and downloaded all the necessary externally linked files therein, it can get on with the job of reading and parsing the body of the HTML document sequentially, tag by tag.

Page Performance

An important aspect of page performance is how long it takes to download that page to the web browser. If you find that page is taking too long, you can try to discover what is causing it to perform poorly.

Viewing the Performance of a Page

Two tools are useful for viewing the live download times of your page and its contents:

- The most popular tool is the Firebug plug-in for Firefox. Firebug can be downloaded from `http://www.getfirebug.com/`.

- The other option is the network timeline tool in Safari 4. To enable this feature, open the browser's preferences page, click the Advanced tab, and check the "Show Develop Menu in menu bar" option. You can then access the network timeline tool by selecting Develop ➤ Show Web Inspector and selecting the Resources tab.

Both tools allow you to see how long the server took to respond to the request message, as well as the time it took to download the files.

Figure 3-2 shows visually the loading time of various components of the Google home page using the Firebug plug-in. Two vertical lines are shown in the results: the first marks the point at which the DOM became available for access through JavaScript, and the second marks the time the page, including all its external references, completed downloading. Figure 3-3 shows the loading of Google home page components using Safari's network timeline tool.

Figure 3-2. *Viewing the loading time of a page using the Firebug plug-in*

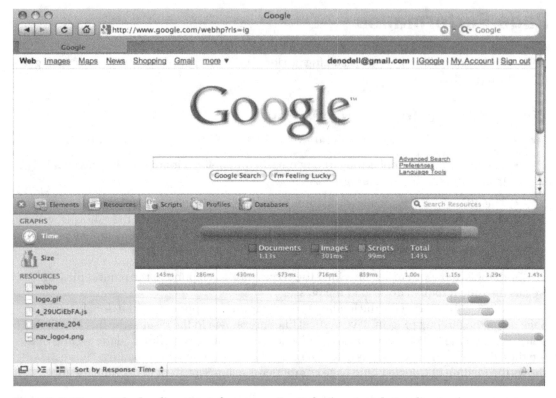

Figure 3-3. *Viewing the loading time of a page using Safari's network timeline tool*

I recommend that you install one or both of these tools to test your pages as you build them, to see where points of contention lie in the performance of your web applications.

Identifying Potential Bottlenecks in Performance

We want to believe that our browsers are always loading page requests as effectively as they can, downloading every last bit of data as fast as possible and rendering the page to the screen as each chunk of data is received. Unfortunately, this is not always the case.

In this section, I will expose some potential bottlenecks that could cause pages to load inefficiently. For now, I won't reveal any solutions or work-arounds to these deficiencies; but rest assured, I will show you how to solve as many of these as possible in the upcoming chapters.

Engine Horsepower

Earlier in this chapter, we looked at the rendering engine and JavaScript engine, which exist within web browsers to convert simple files in HTML, CSS, and JavaScript format into fully working, interactive web pages. It is no surprise that the engines in different browsers have different performance characteristics, since they are built on different underlying code.

Typically, with the release of a new version, a web browser engine's efficiency is increased, as the browser manufacturer alters its underlying code to make the resulting engine more powerful as part of the upgrade. This serves to make the performance of the current generation of most of the leading web browsers several times better than that of any previous generation. In general, the older the browser being used, the worse rendering and JavaScript performance your end user is likely to experience.

User's Upload Speeds

Most users connect to the Internet via their ISP through an asymmetrical connection. This means that the bandwidth most users have available to download data is far larger than the bandwidth they have available to upload data; both connection speeds are not identical. Bandwidth is directly proportional to the speed it takes to download or upload data.

You may wonder what data needs to be uploaded from your computer to make a web page request. In fact, each external file that is linked to from the requested page—each image, style sheet, and JavaScript file—requires that a new HTTP request message be constructed and sent to the server before it can be downloaded. If you have a large number of external files linked to from your page, regardless of the size of those files, you may find that the upload limit is reached for the user's Internet connection, and it will need to wait until previous requests are sent before sending new ones. Internet speeds are improving all the time, so this problem is decreasing, but it's worth making adjustments to your pages to reduce the problem for those on slower connections, such as mobile users.

Parallel Connection Limits

Many browsers have internal limits set on the number of simultaneous connections that can be established to each server at the same time. A page in a modern RIA, especially one with a complicated design, could have in excess of 50 external file references to load to render the full page. A limit on the number of simultaneous connections can clearly limit the speed that a page is downloaded and displayed to the user.

The HTTP 1.1 specification makes a recommendation of a simultaneous connection limit of two file downloads at a time. Opera and Safari browsers increase this limit to four. IE 8 increases it to six downloads simultaneously. These limits clearly throttle the performance of a browser. If all files could be downloaded at the same time, the page would be presented to the end user faster.

Choice of Image Format

Historically, three image formats have prevailed on the Web: GIF, JPEG, and PNG. These formats are very different from each other. By making the wrong choice when encoding your images for your pages, or opting for inefficient compression settings, it is possible to cause your image files to be larger than is necessary. Since most web pages consist of images more than any other type of file, the choice of file format should be of primary concern.

Unnecessary Content

The larger the file size, the longer the wait to download it to the browser. When constructing your markup, ensure that you aren't making reference to unnecessary style sheet or JavaScript files, or including large commented sections within your pages. By including unnecessary code, you run the risk of downloading data to the user's browser that will never be used, increasing the time taken to render the complete page.

Cache Settings

Some web developers choose to disable all caching in their web browsers so they always have the latest copy of their own files for testing. Most end users, however, leave their cache settings at the default, which usually means that the rules for deciding what gets cached and for how long lie with the response headers of the web server transmitting the content. Tweaking the server to send only content that has changed from previous similar requests ensures less data needs to be received by the browser, resulting in a faster experience for the end user.

Uncompressed Text Files and Extra Whitespace

When you structure and write your text-based HTML, style sheet, and JavaScript files, the use of whitespace can be important. Tab spacing, line breaks, character spaces, and comments are useful in making your code easier to read and understand, and simpler to maintain.

Each tab, line break, and space character is data that the browser does not need to render a page effectively. If you can remove this unnecessary data, your file sizes will be smaller and therefore faster to download.

Most browsers and servers support compression algorithms, usually `gzip` and `deflate`, which shrink the size of the data and remove all unnecessary characters at the point of transmission, and then decompress the data when it is received. Without compression, files are larger than they need to be, and page download time is adversely affected.

Summary

This chapter described the process involved in requesting a page from a web server to be sent to your web browser, turning that response into a web page, and highlighted several factors that adversely affect the speed and efficiency of this process.

In the following chapter, I will reveal how you can make drastic improvements to the performance of your web applications through specific changes to your web servers and code, giving your end users a better experience.

CHAPTER 4

■ ■ ■

Performance Tweaking

The previous chapter explained how the browser and web server communicate with each other through messages and how these messages find their way around the world to the correct destination. You saw that the performance of the different web browsers varies depending on their rendering and JavaScript engines.

In this chapter, we will look at how to make your web page come to life, ready for your visitors to use in their web browser, as quickly as possible. Studies have shown that users don't notice good performance, but they do feel hurt by poor performance. People expect their web sites to load as soon as they make a request for it. Why should we give them any less of an experience than they expect? The key here is efficiency—getting the most data downloaded to the browser in the quickest time.

Is Performance Really an Issue?

In today's world of ever-increasing communication speeds, broadband and fiber-optic connections, and ever-more powerful home computers, you might ask yourself whether we need to be efficient at all. After all, if your home broadband speed is now 4 Mbps, and last year it was 2 Mbps, then surely that web page built over 12 months ago will load twice as fast now as it did then. While there would be a performance improvement, unfortunately, this is not always proportional to the speed increase of the connection. Doubling download speed doesn't halve delivery time. To construct RIAs under this assumption neglects the bigger world communications picture and can have a negative effect for some users.

The previous chapter pointed out some bottlenecks that can prevent the most efficient delivery of a web page and its assets to the browser for display:

- Users' upload speed, which is almost always much lower than their download speed
- Parallel connection limits imposed by the web browser, which limit the amount of data that can be loaded from any one server at any one time
- File format choices for images
- Inclusion of unnecessary content
- Inefficient cache settings
- Inclusion of whitespace data in text files, which is ignored by the browser

The effect of one or any combination of these things will limit the speed at which a web page is rendered within the web browser.

Consider, for example, a 20KB HTML page, which references a 10KB CSS file, a 15KB JavaScript file, and 25 external images of 5KB each. In total, this represents 170KB of data to be downloaded to the browser. A 2 Mbps home ISP connection could feasibly download 170KB of data in around 1.5 seconds, but in real-world tests, such a page would take considerably more time to download, perhaps 3 or 4 seconds at best.

Each file needs to be requested separately, and each consists of an HTTP request message being formed by the browser, being sent to the server, and waiting for the server to execute any scripts before responding with an HTTP response message containing the data requested. This will happen 28 times in this example.

You have seen that there is a parallel connection limit imposed by the browser, which, depending on the browser, will download between two and eight files at the same time. Assuming the worst-case scenario, which is present in IE 6 and 7, after the first file—the HTML file containing the requests for all the other files—is received, files will be downloaded in up to 14 separate instances, each with the time overhead of the request/response connection, which is typically in the order of about 150 milliseconds. This will therefore add around 2 seconds to the total load time of the page in these browsers. So what seems as though it could take 1.5 seconds to reach your end users might take more than twice that time.

Performance and efficiency are therefore very relevant topics, particularly for users with restrictive browsers or slow network connections. These include browsers running on mobile devices and users with dial-up connections.

The recent rise in raw computing power supplied for mobile devices has allowed full-featured web browsers to be offered by many manufacturers. These browsers display web pages virtually identically to how they appear on desktop computers. Popular mobile browsers include Opera, IE, and specific-variations on the WebKit rendering engine, such as Safari on Apple's iPhone and Google Chrome on Google Android devices.

Although mobile devices may be able to display web sites in the same way as desktop computers, they do have some limitations. The iPhone, for example, is capable of storing in its local cache only items that are no greater than 25KB. If you have a JavaScript file included across all pages of your site, and this file is larger than 25KB, the iPhone will be forced to download that file with each page request.

Often, the smaller the device, the more limiting its memory and disk space offered to the browser cache. Files that would be downloaded and stored between multiple page requests on a desktop computer need to be downloaded with each page on a mobile device. Therefore, you need to consider efficiency for the sake of users on these devices.

Also realize that, although the number of broadband connections has surpassed those of dial-up modem connections in many countries in the Western world, in many other parts of the world, dial-up connections are still dominant. The difference between a 100KB and 1024KB web page at dial-up speeds is several seconds. You need to make your code efficient because of the many millions of users in the world who are still using dial-up connections.

Now that you understand why it's important to make your web pages lean and efficient, let's take a look at how you can go about making that happen.

Tweaking Your Web Server for Performance

There are three parts working in tandem to deliver a web site to the end user: the web server, the web browser, and the physical connection between the two. The physical connection is virtually out of your control, but, in most cases, you do have control over the other two components, so you need to tweak both to provide the best performance for your site visitors. Let's start by looking at the web server and what you can do behind the scenes to make your site load faster.

Tip For more information about the guidelines presented here, see the Yahoo! best practice guidelines for speeding up your web site, at `http://developer.yahoo.com/performance/rules.html`.

Use Separate Domain Names for External Assets

You should consider setting up a second domain name for your web application, if you intend to use HTTP cookies within your site.

Cookies—small text files saved to the user's computer—are sent to the web server with each page request, as you saw in the previous chapter. These are important for page requests, so that the web server can assemble custom HTML based on the data in the cookie. If you were logged in to a web site, a cookie might contain your login identifier, which the server could then use to show you a customized home page, for example.

You usually customize only HTML based on cookie data, but the trouble is that the data is sent with every file type request—HTML or otherwise. This means that in the vast majority of cases, the cookie data is sent by the browser and then ignored by the server. The cookie data is sent automatically by the browser based on the domain name of the site being accessed; you cannot override this behavior based on file type.

A solution is to use different domain names. By creating two separate domain names for a site, you can choose to host all images, style sheets, JavaScript files, and other external assets from one domain name, and all HTML from the other. By having the cookie data saved only to the domain that hosts the HTML files, you ensure that the cookie data is not sent to the server when requesting any other file type. This makes the data sent in the HTTP request message smaller, allowing it to reach the web server faster.

This technique is recommended only where you rely on cookie data being stored in the user's browser. In other circumstances, the extra DNS lookup, to locate the IP address of the second domain name, would actually result in worse performance for the end user, so this technique should be used carefully.

Use a Content Delivery Network

The Internet is a complicated beast—a connection of nodes in a gigantic, expanding network—and it can sometimes be difficult to believe the speed at which data is actually able to travel great distances between your computer and the remote server. Typically, however, the greater the distance your data needs to travel, the more computers and routers it must pass through to get to its destination. Each stopover on the journey can add time to the trip. The quality and type of cabling connecting these points also impact the amount of time between your browser requesting a page and the web server sending the data back in the response. This speed difference will mean that users connecting to your RIA from various locations around the world will not all be able to access the data at the same speed as each other.

Several companies have set up their own servers in numerous locations around the world and provide a service whereby your code is replicated to all those locations. This reduces the distance between your browser and the web server, improving the response time—often very noticeably. These local server installations are often referred to as *content delivery networks* (CDNs).

By hosting your files on one of these CDNs, you bring your files physically closer to the end user, resulting in a real boost in performance. Google adopts this approach extensively, and the benefits are evident by the speed at which Google sites operate. This technique is also used heavily in the hosting of video and media files, for which the immediacy of playback is important for the site owner.

Companies such as EdgeCast (`http://www.edgecast.com/`) and Akamai (`http://www.akamai.com/`) provide this service for small, medium, and large businesses. Their costs can be a little off-putting for a smaller, more personal site. Google offers a couple of options for personal users, allowing them to host certain files for free on its network. Video files can be hosted via Google's YouTube service (`http://www.youtube.com/`); small page components can be hosted via the iGoogle (`http://www.google.com/ig/`) widget hosting service; and certain popular JavaScript libraries are hosted via Google's Ajax APIs service, as described in more detail in the "Access JavaScript Libraries Through CDNs" section later in this chapter. All three solutions are free and allow you to take advantage of Google's globally distributed server network.

Send HTML to the Browser in Chunks

Most web servers aren't serving flat HTML files to their end users. Typically, the user requests a file, which causes the server to perform some action. The result of that action is the piecing together of a final HTML file, which is then sent to the user. Those actions are typically written in server-side scripting languages such as PHP, ASP.NET, or Java Server Pages (JSP).

After making a request to the server to view a page, the browser is left waiting while the server pieces together the HTML code to send back. If you could get access to some part of this resulting HTML as soon as possible, the browser could begin its work of loading in external assets, such as style sheets, while waiting for the server to send the remainder of the HTML page. This means the whole page will be ready for the end user to interact with sooner than if the browser had to wait for the entire HTML page to be sent in a single, large chunk.

As the HTML page is assembled, it is stored in a memory buffer on the server until the page assembly is complete, and then the buffer is emptied into the HTTP response message. It is possible to flush this buffer to the HTTP response stream on demand in your server-side code, which results in the HTML created up to that point being sent to the browser. If you perform this flushing of the buffer at tactical points in your page, the browser gets HTML to render sooner, and the end users have something in front of them on their screen sooner. In other words, you get an increase in performance.

One such tactical point at which to empty the memory buffer is between the end of the HTML `<head>` tag and before the start of the `<body>` tag. Since most of the hard work on the server is typically performed on elements within the body of the page, the head section is usually ready to be sent much earlier in the page-formation stage. By giving this `<head>` section to the browser early, it can then load in the style sheets and other external assets at the same time as the rest of the HTML page is being received by the browser.

The reason this is not performed by default by the server is simply that the server is not aware of when you might wish to perform the operation on your page. By executing the command at the wrong place in the page—such as midway through a tag or before a closing tag—you could potentially cause rendering bugs. Exercise some caution where you choose to use this technique, but I thoroughly recommend you employ it where possible.

Caution A known limitation exists within certain versions of IE: the browser will not display any output until it has received the first 256 bytes of page data. Flushing the buffer near the start of the page will have no performance improvement effect in this browser if there are fewer than 256 characters within the <head> section being written.

Let's look at how you can use this technique with three common languages: PHP, C#, and JSP.

Flushing the Buffer with PHP

If your server-side code is written in PHP, there is a directive you can call in your page to flush the buffer at the point of your choosing. Simply execute the following code between the end of the head section and beginning of the body section of the page:

```
</head>
    <?php flush(); ?>
<body>
```

Flushing the Buffer with ASP.NET/C#

If your server is running Microsoft's ASP.NET with the C# language, there is a directive to flush the buffer on demand. Execute the following code between the end of the head and beginning of the body section on your page:

```
</head>
    <% Response.Flush(); %>
<body>
```

Flushing the Buffer with JSP

If your server-side scripting language is JSP, there is an equivalent command to flush the buffer at the point of your choosing. Execute the following code between the end of the HTML head section and start of the body section in your page:

```
</head>
    <% response.flushBuffer(); %>
<body>
```

Customize HTTP Headers to Force Browser Caching

The topic of caching comes up many times in any discussion of performance. Once you have downloaded certain assets to the end user's browser, you don't want that browser to download those assets again on subsequent page requests or visits to the site, unless they have changed. Aside from the obvious performance advantage of taking those files directly from the user's computer, rather than downloading them again, this reduces the load on the web server, which is incredibly useful if you suddenly get an unexpected rise in traffic on a certain day (this is often called the *Digg effect*, after the popular link submission and rating site at http://www.digg.com/).

You can force the browser to hold on to copies of files it has already downloaded by sending those files along with certain header content in the web server's HTTP response. There are two headers you can take advantage of here:

- Expires: This literally tells the browser that the file downloaded is valid up until a certain date and time, so it does not need to download it again until that date.

- Cache-Control: This can be used to inform the browser, and any proxy server sitting between the web server and browser, to cache the particular file.

The Expires header value is a full date, marking the point after which any subsequent requests by the browser should go directly to the server for a fresh copy.

```
Expires: Thu, 15 Apr 2010 20:00:00 GMT
Cache-Control: Public
```

Using Cache-Control allows you to store your data closer to the end user. This means that, for example, if one user accessing the Web through a certain ISP requests your page, the data can be cached onto the proxy server so that a second user from the same ISP will be served the data from the physically closer proxy server (assuming both share the same proxy server). You have already seen that physical proximity between browser and server can impact performance, so this effect is desired, where possible.

The Cache-Control header value contains one of four possible values:

- Private: Proxy servers should not cache this file, but it can be stored in the browser's cache. This value is usually set on HTML files that contain some form of personalization to a particular user.

- Public: Shared caches, including those on proxy servers, will keep a copy of the requested file. The proxy server will then send subsequent requests to the browser, instead of needing to make a request directly from the web server. This is the ideal value to use for as many files as possible, as it results in the best performance for end users.

- No-cache: The file sent in the response should not be cached outside the current session. A fresh copy will be downloaded from the server in another session.

- No-store: The file sent in the response should never be cached. Subsequent requests in the same session will cause the server to send back a whole new copy of the page.

Ideally, you will want to set the Expires header for static components, like your JavaScript files, style sheets, and other external assets, together with a Cache-Control value of Public. Certain dynamic HTML files, or pages that return data for Ajax requests, should have their Cache-Control header values set to a more appropriate value, such as No-cache .

One trick is to set an `Expires` header for all static components to a date far in the future, in the order of a few years, so that, once downloaded, such files will never again be requested from the server, resulting in large performance boosts for subsequent page visits. Of course, you still need a way to send file updates to the end user when you make changes. This can be achieved by adding a version number to the URL of the files being requested, in the file name, domain name, or folder name. This new URL won't match any in the browser's cache, so it forces the browser to take a fresh version from the server. You then set the `Expires` header of the new file so far in the future that once it is downloaded, it is never requested from the server again.

To use this technique, create a folder or file for each release of your web application, incrementing the release version number each time you send a new code release to the server. Here, you can see the version number embedded in the file request in two different ways, which both perform the same task of requesting a totally new file:

```
/v1.0.1/assets/styles/mysite.css
/assets/styles/mysite-v1.0.1.css
```

You will discover you are able to make a large impact on performance through clever usage of this feature, which is gaining popularity and is used by many major sites, including Yahoo!

Consult the manual for your particular web server to learn how to set the `Expires` and `Cache-Control` headers for your site.

Compress the Output from the Server

Probably the single biggest web server performance improvement can be achieved by compressing your text-based content—HTML, style sheets, and JavaScript files—before it is sent to the browser, letting the browser decompress the data before displaying it. Compression involves encoding data in a different, more efficient way. In some cases, compression can reduce file sizes by up to 70% of the original. The two popular compression algorithms are known as `gzip` and `deflate`, which were mentioned in the previous chapter.

The great thing about this technique is that it is simple to enable on the server. It is supported by virtually every modern web browser. Browsers that don't support the compression technique will be sent the data uncompressed from the server instead, so data is never lost. You should enable this feature in your web server, if it is not set by default, at your earliest available opportunity. You will immediately notice its impact, and so will your end users.

Compressing data on the server does increase the server's CPU load over simply returning the file uncompressed. This is usually not enough of an increase to cause any issues, but is certainly worth being aware of if your server hardware is limited in any way.

Note Certain very old browsers tell the server that they support compressed content but actually do not. Some compression server components are smart enough not to send compressed data to these browsers. In practice, this is not enough of an issue to cause any real concern.

Let's look at how you can enable compression on three popular servers: Apache, Microsoft Internet Information Services (IIS), and Tomcat.

Enabling Compression in Apache Web Server

If you are running Apache web server version 1.3, you should install and enable the `mod_gzip` module, available online at http://sourceforge.net/projects/mod-gzip/. If you are running version 2.*x* of Apache, you should configure the `mod_deflate` module, which is included in the Apache installation. Full instructions on `mod_deflate` can be found online at http://httpd. apache.org/docs/2.0/mod/mod_deflate.html. Basic configuration is as simple as typing the following into your `apache.confd` file:

```
AddOutputFilterByType DEFLATE text/html text/plain text/xml ➡
    text/javascript text/json
```

Enabling Compression in IIS

If you are running Microsoft IIS version 7, some files are compressed by default. However, you should enable compression for all files by executing the following command from the server's command line:

```
appcmd set config -section:urlCompression /doDynamicCompression:true
```

Unfortunately, enabling `gzip` compression in Microsoft's IIS version 6 is not quite as simple. Instead of listing all the exhaustive steps here, I refer you to the following instructions for enabling this fantastic performance feature: http://www.wwwcoder.com/main/parentid/170/ site/3669/68/default.aspx.

Enabling Compression in Tomcat

Enabling the same kind of compression within Tomcat is just as simple as with other technologies. Here is the line to add to your `server.xml` file:

```
compression="on"
```

Now we've taken a look at some important changes to make to the web server to boost the speed at which content is received into the browser. Next, let's see what can be done on the front end, within the browser itself, to ensure your pages load as quickly as possible.

Tweaking HTML for Performance

Most of the improvements you can make for performance can be achieved through changes to front-end code. We'll start our discussion of front-end performance with the bare bones of every web page: the HTML to mark up your document.

You might wonder how it is possible to strip down what is already probably one of the smallest files in your application, but believe me, it's doable, and it's worthwhile. The HTML page is the key to downloading all other assets. It contains all the references to your external files for layout and behavior, so it follows that the faster your HTML loads, the less of a bottleneck it will be to the download of your other assets. In addition to this, you can make some tweaks to your HTML to take advantage of certain browser behaviors to get the page onto the screen even faster.

In Part 1 of this book, I suggested some best practices for HTML, some of which are inherently performance-friendly. These include writing well-formed XHTML to prevent the browser from having to guess where each tag ends, and referencing style sheets and JavaScript files externally using `<link href="">` and `<script src="">` tags, respectively, to take advantage of the browser's cache. Here, we'll look at some other ways to improve browser performance by making changes to your HTML content.

Shrink Your HTML File Size with HTML Tidy

When your web browser reads in your HTML file, it parses the tags contained within into internal objects, which it then applies layout and design to according to your style sheets. Note that this parsing step pays attention only to the tags within your HTML, disregarding any formatting or spacing around those tags, except within tags themselves, such as the text within a paragraph tag. Despite looking like empty space, each whitespace character—single space, tab, or line break—is represented in your HTML file as a single byte of data. Adding together all these redundant spaces for a large HTML document can reveal that anything up to around 25% of the total file size is taken up with redundant data that will effectively be ignored by the browser. If you could remove these spacing characters, you would reduce the file size, bringing the HTML file to the browser faster.

You don't want to remove the whitespace characters from the original HTML you work from, since that would make maintenance extremely difficult (you wouldn't be able to determine the nesting of tags). You want to deploy the copy of the file without the whitespaces to your live web servers, while retaining the full HTML source for development.

One tool that will automatically strip out these unnecessary whitespace characters and also the HTML comments, which are not useful to end users, is called HTML Tidy. Originally developed by Dave Raggett of the W3C organization, it is now maintained and continually improved upon by the open source community. You can just run this tool on your computer or, if you're working with other developers and have set up an automated build environment, it can be automated to run on the source HTML and overwrite the file of the same name in the resulting zip or package file for deployment. More details on this excellent tool can be found at `http://tidy.sourceforge.net/`.

Reference JavaScript Files at the End of Your HTML

Common web site development practices, and most tutorials, tell you to reference your external JavaScript files from within the `<head>` portion of your HTML documents. But you can improve the performance of your pages by referencing these files right at the end of your markup, just before the `</body>` tag.

In normal circumstances, when your web page is being loaded and rendered, the browser will download several files, such as style sheets and images, simultaneously. This is not the case when the browser encounters linked, external JavaScript files. In this case, the browser typically blocks the download of any other page component until the JavaScript code has been loaded and executed. Since JavaScript can alter the contents of a web page dynamically through the DOM, this rule is important to ensure that these manipulations occur in the order specified by the developer. It would not be acceptable for two external JavaScript files to be read in and for the second script to execute before the first if it downloaded faster.

Take a look at the following code, which shows the `<body>` contents of a simple HTML page.

```
<body>
    <h1>JavaScript content blocking test</h1>
    <img src="image1.jpg" alt="" />
    <script type="text/javascript">
        document.write((new Date()).toString());
    </script>
    <img src="image2.jpg" alt="" />
</body>
```

When a typical browser encounters this code, it begins rendering the page one tag at a time, starting with the <h1> tag. Upon encountering the <img> tag, the browser begins downloading the image file referenced and moves on to the next tag in source code order. This next tag is a <script> tag, so the browser temporarily pauses its parsing, and reads and executes the contents of that tag before resuming, moving on to loading the image referenced in the next tag.

Since JavaScript is very powerful in its ability to manipulate the layout and content of an HTML page, if the rest of the page continued to render while the script was executing, you could experience unexpected behavior based on the speed of the page download, as well as the performance of the browser's rendering and JavaScript engines. You could never guarantee that the script would execute at the same time every time you refreshed your page. It is almost essential that the browser pause its rendering of the remaining page while interpreting and executing the script in order to produce the reliable behavior you expect when writing your scripts.

Assuming you have moved all of your scripts into external files for ease of maintenance and in order to take advantage of the browser's local disk caching of those files, if you include your references to those external files in the <head> of the HTML document, the browser will pause downloading and rendering any other part of the page while it reads in and executes those scripts. Since the browser reads in the contents of the <head> tag before processing the <body> tag, this will slow down the rendering of the page for the user. Clearly, the larger the scripts, the longer the wait before the user can access the page. By simply moving your external script references to the end of your HTML files, just before the closing </body> tag, you avoid impeding the downloading and rendering of the rest of the page, thus improving the performance for your end user.

Note Some more modern browser releases no longer pause downloading other assets while waiting for JavaScript files to download, but the execution of these scripts always happens in the order specified in the HTML document.

Reduce the Number of HTTP Requests

Since the network is almost always the greatest bottleneck in web page performance, it follows that the fewer components and external files referenced from any web page, the less communication that needs to occur between the browser and the server to fetch those files. There are two primary techniques you can use to achieve the goal of reducing the number of file requests from the server: structure your project appropriately and combine files when possible.

Good Division and Structure

First and foremost, you need to make sure you have a structure to your external style sheets, scripts, and assets that ensures you have loaded on each page only the code that is necessary to render that page. You will want to group together all of your common style rules, for example, into a single style sheet file, and then have further style sheet files for any page- or component-specific style rules. The common style sheet file will be downloaded and cached the first time it is requested, and subsequent requests for that file from different pages within your site will cause the local cached copy to be used, saving on downloads on these subsequent pages

Combine Files

As a basic rule of thumb, the fewer the files, the fewer the HTTP requests, and the faster that page will render. Each file contains a header portion of its own, in addition to the HTTP header, which is hidden within the start of the file. This header portion does not typically contain much information for a text file such as an HTML file, a style sheet, or a JavaScript file, but for other types of files, it can contain a lot of extra information. For example, a photographic image file's hidden header might include copyright information and camera settings. Finding ways to combine related files will reduce the file header sizes and the number of browser/ server communication requests. This may increase the time taken to download a single file on its first request, but will reduce the amount of data downloaded overall. You might combine several separate JavaScript files into a single file, if your scripts are divided up. The same could apply to your style sheet files.

This will also reduce the amount of code within your HTML file, as you will need to reference fewer external files. If you are working with other developers and have access to an automated release-management tool, you should be able to configure that to automatically combine together all your CSS files and all your JavaScript files into two single files.

A caveat regarding this technique is that it can contradict the advice given in the previous section regarding making sure files are cacheable. You don't want to be repeatedly downloading the same code to the browser on each different page request, as this will result in more data being requested from the server than is necessary. Remember to choose the path that results in the least browser/server communication and most use of locally cached files. Typically, I will reference the following files:

- Two external style sheet files: a common site-wide file and page-specific file

- Two external JavaScript files: a JavaScript library file, to smooth out cross-browser inconsistencies and add useful utility methods, and a site-specific code file

Where you reference several third-party JavaScript files throughout your site, combine these all into one file so they are loaded from the cache after their initial download.

Don't Load Every Asset from Your Home Page

Your home page is most often the first page your visitors will see when they visit your web site. You need to make a good impression with this page, both with its layout and its performance. If it takes 10 seconds to render your home page to a usable state, visitors are unlikely to want to continue into your site, as they might believe that each page will take that long to render. Ideally, your web page should take no longer than 4 seconds to load once the server has started sending back its first response. A recent study undertaken for Akamai (http://www.akamai.com/) has shown that 75% of users would not return to a web site that took longer than 4 seconds to load, and that page load time was one of the major sources of frustration they encounter online—exactly the situation you are trying to avoid.

Typically, the home page is the most frequently visited page on a site, and usually only a fairly small percentage of users actually make it past that page into the site itself. These users may have lost interest, accidentally visited the wrong page, or, hopefully, have acquired all the information they need from the home page so don't need to delve any deeper into the site.

You may make the decision that, in order to speed up the rest of your web site, you are going to load all of the CSS and JavaScript for the entire site from the home page. These files will then be stored in the browser cache, so subsequent page requests will be faster. Unfortunately, by weighing down the site-entry page in this way, you cause a lot more data than is necessary to be downloaded, slowing down the rendering of what is the most important page on the site. Only reference what you absolutely need to on your home page, as it is the one that, above all others, needs to be perfect from a performance perspective.

Reduce Domain Name Lookups

As explained in the previous chapter, the DNS database links together the common domain names you see advertised (for example, www.google.com) with IP addresses (for example, 216.239.51.99) that Internet-connected devices use to route data from your browser, at one place on the Internet, to the web server you want to access, at another location.

Each time you, or a file referenced within your HTML, CSS, or JavaScript, makes a request for a file located on a different domain name, your browser needs to run a DNS lookup, to find the IP address of the new domain in order to access it. Each one of these lookups takes time, in the order of around 20 to 120 milliseconds. So, in a worst-case scenario, if you request files from eight different domain names, the lookups alone could potentially take 1 second to complete, which is a huge amount of time, considering you are attempting to download all your assets and have your page up and running within about 4 seconds.

Browsers will actually cache the results of a DNS lookup for a certain period of time, to aid with performance of subsequent file requests. However, the duration this cached information is valid varies among browsers. For example, in IE, this lookup is typically cached for 30 minutes. In Firefox, the lookup is cached for only 1 minute. These values are nominal, completely arbitrary, and at the discretion of the browser manufacturers.

By referencing files across several domains, you cause a performance overhead to be introduced to your page. On the other hand, in order to avoid HTTP cookies being sent with all file requests, it is advantageous to reference certain assets from a different domain than the HTML code itself. Therefore, you need to reach a compromise. A recommendation is to use no more than two to four separate domain names for file hosting. After this level, the DNS lookup overhead becomes too much of a performance burden versus the performance benefit it is intended to give.

■**Note** You could point all your file references to the resolved IP address of multiple domain names, to avoid the need for DNS lookups to be performed. This technique has the drawback of not being particularly scalable or maintainable—you would need to update all your pages if you wanted to move your server to another ISP or location. DNS provides a convenient and necessary redirection service. You update the pointer in the domain name database, rather than updating and redeploying all of your pages.

Split Components Across Domains

The HTTP 1.1 specification includes a recommendation relating to the number of simultaneous files the browser should be able to download in parallel from the same domain name: it suggests a limit of two concurrent files. Some browsers enforce this limit to the letter; some choose to allow more than two simultaneous downloads from the same domain name. Table 4-1 shows the number of simultaneous downloads permitted per domain name and total permitted simultaneous downloads within the most common browsers.

Table 4-1. *Number of Simultaneous File Downloads by Browser*

Browser	Simultaneous Downloads per Domain Name	Maximum Simultaneous Downloads
Internet Explorer 6	2	60
Internet Explorer 7	2	56
Internet Explorer 8	6	60
Firefox 2	2	24
Firefox 3	6	30
Opera 9.6	4	20
Google Chrome	6	60
Safari 3	4	60
Safari 4 Beta	4	60

You can see that the browser is limited in the number of simultaneous requests *per domain name.* So let's set up another domain, point its DNS record to the same IP address as the first domain—since the limitation is only by domain name, not by IP address—so they are both referencing the same code on the same web server.

By dividing your assets among the available domain names in this way, you are able to introduce a potentially large performance boost to your pages. Don't forget the suggested limit of two to four separate domains, to avoid the DNS lookup performance burden discussed in the previous section.

■**Tip** Your domains do not need to be top-level domains. They can be only subdomains (such as `http://assets.mydomain.com/`), which don't require you to purchase new domain names from a registrar.

Avoid Linking to Redirects

As discussed in the previous chapter, HTTP redirects commonly occur when the browser makes a request for a file that no longer exists on a web server. In this case, the web server usually accounts for this by supplying a redirect message, pointing to the new location of the requested file.

In this scenario, the browser/server communication is doubled. First, the request is made for the missing file, and the server responds with the correct location. Then the browser makes a request for the file at the correct URL, and the server responds with the contents of that file. Since one of the greatest performance bottlenecks in a web application is the communication network between the browser and server, by doubling the amount of traffic for a particular file request, you are reducing the performance of your application. In addition, most browsers do not cache the server's supplied redirect information, so if you are requesting files from, for example, `http://google.com/`, and that server redirects all traffic to `http://www.google.com/`, that redirection is going to occur for all external file references from that one page, adding a potentially large performance drain to the page load time. If you know a file's location has moved on the server, and you are accessing that file via an old URL, be sure to alter the link to point to the new location of the file.

You might be linking to a redirect without being aware of it. Many developers add links without including a trailing slash character (/) at the end, as in `http://www.google.com`. Leaving out this trailing slash character will cause many web servers to raise an HTTP redirect message, pointing to the URL including this slash character: `http://www.google.com/`. To improve the responsiveness of your links, add a trailing slash character to all your links that do not point directly to file names.

Reduce the Number of HTML Elements

The number of HTML elements on your page not only affects how long your HTML takes to download to the browser, but also the performance of your JavaScript code and the speed with which the browser's rendering engine is able to apply your CSS to your page.

Particularly burdensome on performance is the level of nesting your HTML structure uses. The more complicated and deep your nesting, the more work the browser's rendering engine must do in order to make sense of the structure. A light structure, only three or four tags deep, will give better performance compared to a deeper structure.

Each HTML element that exists in your page is represented to JavaScript through the DOM. The browser itself creates the DOM references from the elements that exist on the page, and this is organized in a hierarchical structure that matches the structure of the HTML document. The more complex the structure, or the more elements, the longer this process of generating the DOM in the browser will take, and the longer it will take to access individual elements through JavaScript.

When building your HTML, think carefully about each tag. Consider whether it needs to be there. If you are introducing it only to achieve a layout effect, you should strive to achieve the same outcome through CSS, where possible. If you are introducing dummy elements that you will later populate with JavaScript, consider creating these elements using JavaScript and injecting them onto your page via the DOM.

Don't Link to Nonexistent Files

As you've already seen, HTTP requests that don't return an intended response are wasteful; they keep the web server and the browser occupied for little benefit.

Frequently, when reviewing web site performance, I observe that requests for certain assets return HTTP 404 errors, meaning the file requested does not exist on the server. In many cases, these requested files are background images referenced from CSS classes where the image file itself has since been removed—a hangover from the development process. Since, unlike foreground images, background images can go unnoticed, they are often unintentionally left referenced within CSS files. These images are still requested by the browser, and the server responds with a 404 error.

For some web sites, the developer or web server creates a custom error page, which often matches the design and layout of the rest of the site. This is great for the users, as often such pages contain links to a page they intended to reach but typed the URL incorrectly, and it improves their experience of the web site. However, often the HTML code for an HTTP 404 error is returned, though not displayed. The browser must download the HTML for this error page for each incorrect file request. It won't be cached one time and used for each different request, as the URL for each failed asset will be different. The browser will then attempt and fail to interpret the HTML as an image, style sheet, or JavaScript file. This particular scenario will add a lot of unnecessary performance overhead. To avoid this, audit your pages, checking each and every referenced file to ensure it exists.

Don't forget the browser is able to make requests for only a limited number of files at a time. To waste this limit with requests that do not produce any worthwhile gain reduces the performance of your web application.

■**Caution** If a JavaScript file is being requested by the page that does not exist on the server, and an error page is returned by the server instead of the requested file, the browser will pause its parsing of the page while waiting for the contents of the error page to download. This exacerbates the effect of linking to nonexistent files.

Reduce the Size of HTTP Cookies

Each HTTP request message that is sent from the browser to the server contains the HTTP cookie data associated with that domain. This is so that both the client, through JavaScript, and the server, through any back-end processing, have access to this information in order to customize the site for that particular user. Obviously, this data takes up space in the request message. Since it is communicated for each file being requested, it can add a lot of extra information that is rarely used except, typically, for the page that returns the HTML document.

By ensuring that the data stored in the cookie is small, the data being sent in each HTTP request message is reduced, and the server receives the message sooner.

Consider including nothing more than a simple, unique user identifier within the HTTP cookie and storing other information within a database on the server, using the unique identifier as a key to look up this extra information.

Tweaking Your Style Sheets for Performance

You have learned that combining style rules into external style sheet files delivers the best performance, as it allows those files to be cached independently of the HTML files that reference them. Now we will look at techniques related to the contents of your style sheet files and how they can be tweaked to provide better performance within the browser.

Shrink Your CSS File Size with CSSTidy

You have already seen how whitespace characters can add to the size of your files, which are useful to developers but not browsers. Similar to the HTML Tidy tool for HTML files, the CSSTidy tool removes extra whitespace characters from CSS files. It has the added benefit of allowing you to optimize your styles where the opportunity exists to do so and to strip out comments from the CSS, which are useful only to developers, not to the browser or your end users.

CSSTidy is a command-line tool, so it can be configured to run automatically as part of an automated development/release process, should you work in an environment set up in that way. To find out more about this tool and download it, visit `http://csstidy.sourceforge.net/`.

Don't Use the @import Command

You can include a reference to an external style sheet file from within your HTML file either by using the HTML `<link>` tag or by using the `@import` directive within a style sheet file or HTML `<style>` tag, as in this example:

```
<style type="text/css">
    @import url("filename.css")
</style>
```

In many browsers, the behavior of both methods is identical. However, certain versions of IE behave in a slightly different way when using the `@import` method. They actually wait until the whole page has been read and rendered before loading and applying the external reference from the `@import` directive. For this reason, the `@import` method should be avoided. Use the `<link>` tag to associate external style sheets with your HTML files.

Speed Up Table Layouts

Rendering HTML tables is notoriously labor-intensive on the browser. There are typically four or more levels of tag nesting that, alone, take time to parse. The browser then needs to calculate the widths of each table cell, which it attempts to do intelligently based on the width of the contents of each cell in the table. This means the browser usually needs to read in the data for the entire table before it is able to render it correctly. On a slow page, where you see the HTML table loading progressively onto the page, you might observe that the layout of the table alters—some of the columns change width—as the data is still being downloaded, and settles on its final dimensions only when all the data has completed downloading.

The CSS `table-layout: fixed` style rule reduces this constant calculation and reevaluation work the browser must do to render your HTML tables. It's used as follows:

```
table {
    table-layout: fixed;
}
```

The `table-layout: fixed` rule "fixes" the table layout, which means that the rendering engine will calculate the widths of the table cells based solely on data found in the cells contained in the header row of the table. Since it does not need to do any more cell-width calculations, the time taken to render a long table is reduced.

Make sure you have set widths, through CSS style rules, for the cells in the header row of the table. These will then apply automatically to each of their associated columns in the table, regardless of the content of the cells in the rest of the table.

Avoid CSS Filters and Expressions in IE

IE introduced several new CSS properties and extra layout functionality, which are custom only to IE and not adopted by other browsers. Two such style properties are CSS filters, which allow developers to access some of Microsoft's native DirectX drawing components, and CSS expressions, which allow dynamic scripting capabilities within otherwise static style rules.

If you've ever attempted to provide handling for transparent PNG images within IE 6, where they are not natively supported, you may have come across and used one particular CSS filter, `AlphaImageLoader`:

```
.image {
    filter:progid:DXImageTransform.Microsoft.AlphaImageLoader( ➥
        src='image.png', sizingMethod='scale');
}
```

Although there is no doubt that this filter does the job, it does have some big performance drawbacks:

- While the referenced transparent PNG is being loaded, the browser actually locks up and does not continue rendering any portion of the page or download any additional assets during that time.

- You might expect the results of one filtered image to be cached as other files are, but images referenced through CSS filters are not cached. Every transparent PNG loaded in this way, whether or not it has been loaded previously, is downloaded every time the page is refreshed.

Use Shorthand Values

CSS contains many similar and related style properties for laying out box-based structures and setting the typographical nature of page text within such structures. In several circumstances, multiple style rules can be combined into a single style rule, saving on file size and improving the download time, without sacrificing maintainability or scalability. Here, we'll look at some shorthand for colors, margins, padding, borders, backgrounds, fonts, and lists.

Colors

Use hexadecimal values to specify color properties within your style rules, because these typically take up less space than most named colors and equivalent RGB notation. If you use named color values, restrict yourself to the 16 colors defined within the HTML 4.01 specification (http://www.w3.org/TR/REC-html40/types.html#h-6.5).

A hexadecimal color value is normally specified like this:

```
body {
    color: #000000;
}
```

This example sets the text color for the HTML <body> tag to black, represented as #000000 in hexadecimal. The first two characters after the hash (#) character in this color representation denote the red component of that color, the second group of two characters represents the green component, and the final two characters represent the blue component, so the format is #rrggbb.

Browsers support a shorter notation for certain hexadecimal values, where each of the two-digit hex values for each color component is identical. Typically, these are known as the *web-safe* color values. The previous style rule could be represented in this shorter form:

```
body {
    color: #000;
}
```

Table 4-2 lists a selection of colors, their equivalent hexadecimal values, and their shorthand equivalent hexadecimal value, if available.

Table 4-2. *Some Hexadecimal Color Values*

Color	Hexadecimal	Shorthand
Black	#000000	#000
Light blue	#336699	#369
Green	#00ff00	#0f0
White	#ffffff	#fff
Dark gray	#121212	
Crimson	#dc143c	

Margins and Padding

You are likely familiar with the CSS properties for margins and padding. The margin is the space around the element, and padding is the space between the element boundary box and its contents. You are also probably aware that you can apply these style rules independently to each side of an element or in one fell swoop to every side of the element.

Suppose that you want to apply a margin of 10 pixels around each of your HTML paragraph tags using CSS. You could specify this in either of the two possible ways shown in the following code excerpt:

```
p.four-rules {
    margin-top: 10px;
    margin-right: 10px;
    margin-bottom: 10px;
    margin-left: 10px;
}

p.one-rule {
    margin: 10px;
}
```

Notice how the second style rule combines four lines of code into one, without altering the result.

Now suppose that you want to apply a different margin size to each of the four different sides of the element. Here's how multiple style rules can be combined into single rules when affecting certain properties of box-based elements:

```
/* apply 10px padding to the top of the element, 5px to right, 20px to bottom
     and 0 pixels padding to the left of the element */
padding: 10px 5px 20px 0;

/* apply 10px margin to top, 5px to left and right, 15px to bottom */
margin: 10px 5px 15px;

/* apply 10px margin to top and bottom of element, 5px to left and right */
margin: 10px 5px;

/* apply 10px padding to all sides */
padding: 10px;
```

Borders

A multitude of CSS properties are available for styling borders around page elements. Put simply, a border consists of three style properties: a width, a border style (such as solid or dotted), and a color. Specific CSS style properties allow you to apply different styles to each side of an element. For example, border-top-width specifies the width of the border above the element, and border-bottom-color specifies the color to apply to the border at the bottom of the element. Using these properties for every side of the element is rather long-winded. Instead, use one of the shorthand techniques shown in the following code to apply border styles to an element.

```
/* applies 1px wide, solid black border to each side of the element */
border: 1px solid #000;

/* applies same border style to the top side of the element only */
border-top: 1px solid #000;

/* sets top border width to 2px, left and right borders to 3px and bottom to 1px */
border-width: 2px 3px 1px;
```

```
/* sets the top and bottom borders black, and left and right borders red (#f00) */
border-color: #000 #f00;
```

Backgrounds

Several CSS style properties relate to the display and positioning of backgrounds within an element:

- `background-color`: Sets the base background color of the element.
- `background-image`: Applies a background image that will sit on top of the element's background color.
- `background-repeat`: Allows you to specify whether the background image should tile within the available space, and if it should, whether that tiling should occur horizontally, vertically, or both.
- `background-attachment`: Specifies whether the background image should scroll with the page or element, or remain fixed in the position it was in when the element was first rendered.
- `background-position`: Attaches a background image to a specific location within the element, such as attached to the bottom right of the element, or located 25 pixels in from the left edge of the element.

Rather than specifying values for each of these CSS properties individually, you can specify them all simultaneously with a single background CSS shorthand property, as follows:

```
/*
    Use the following format for shorthand background properties.

    background: color image repeat attachment position;
*/

/*
    The image image1.jpg should appear from at the top-left position (0, 0) of
    the element, it should not tile in any direction and it should scroll along with
    the page as normal. Underneath the image should appear a red background,
    filling the dimensions of the element.
*/
p {
    background: #f00 url(image1.jpg) no-repeat scroll 0 0;
}
```

Fonts

A shorthand notation exists for combining font formatting style rules into a single rule. You can combine the following individual font styles:

- `font-style`: Specifies normal, italic, or oblique text style.
- `font-variant`: Specifies normal or small capital letter text style.

- `font-weight`: Specifies the thickness of the text, enabling bold or light text styles.
- `font-size`: Specifies the size of the characters within the text.
- `line-height`: Specifies the height each line of text should consume.
- `font-family`: Specifies the typeface in which to display the text.

The following shows how these separate style properties can be combined into a single style rule.

```
/*
    Use the following format for shorthand font styles. Observe the location of
    the slash (/) character, between the font size and line height attributes. Also
    note that there can be multiple font family values, separated by commas, to
    allow for backup typefaces in the case that the preferred face is not available.

    font: style variant weight size/line-height family
*/
p {
    font: italic small-caps bold 1.2em/1.8em Arial, Helvetica, sans-serif;
}
```

Lists

Unordered, bulleted list styles can also be combined into a single style rule for brevity. The following three individual style properties can be combined:

- `list-style-type`: Specifies the type of bullet to use to denote individual list items.
- `list-style-position`: Specifies where the bullet should sit in relation to the list, either in the flow of the text or separated into its own column with spacing.
- `list-style-image`: Specifies an optional image file to use to represent the bullet. If the image does not exist or is not specified, the bullet type from the `list-style-type` property is used instead.

The following shows how these styles can be combined into a single style rule for customizing unordered lists.

```
li {
    /*
    Use the following format for shorthand list styles.
    list-style: type position image;
    */
    list-style: circle inside url(mybullet.gif);
}
```

Use the CSS Sprite Technique

You're now going to discover a technique, called *CSS sprites*, that will enable you to reduce the number and size of the image files in your RIA. This will reduce the number and size of HTTP requests (as you know, one of the largest performance bottlenecks in most web sites), and often also reduces the number of style rules needed to represent those images on the page.

The CSS sprite technique involves merging visibly related image files together into a single file. It borrows from the sprite technique used in early video games graphics, and used more recently to store groups of icon images together within a single file in some computer operating systems.

Suppose that you use four separate image files, each of identical size, to represent four buttons that will control multimedia playback on your site: Play, Rewind, Forward, and Stop. Here's how you might typically reference these files using CSS to associate them with page elements:

```
/* Each button element has two classes: control and a button-specific style  */
.control {
    /* Each icon is 100 pixels square */
    width: 100px;
    height: 100px;
    /* Any text within the button element should be hidden if the button is
        displayed as an icon using CSS */
    text-indent: -10000px;
}

.play {
    background-image: url(play.png);
}

.rewind {
    background-image: url(rewind.png);
}

.forward {
    background-image: url(forward.png);
}

.stop {
    background-image: url(stop.png);
}
```

Figure 4-1 shows how you might combine these four separate images together into a single image file, using a standard graphic software package. Each individual image measures 100 pixels wide by 100 pixels tall, and the resulting image is 200 pixels wide by 200 pixels tall.

The CSS sprite technique involves specifying the 100-pixel square portion of the larger image file that contains the specific button icon you wish to display within your element. The following example demonstrates how this can be achieved using CSS style rules, shifting the background image within the dimensions of the element to display the required portion of the image.

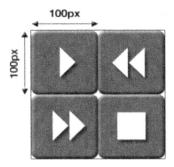

Figure 4-1. *Four related images combined into a single image file*

```
.control {
    /* Each button control element is fixed in size to 100 pixels square */
    width: 100px;
    height: 100px;
    text-indent: -10000px;
    /* Reference the single, combined image file */
    background-image: url(combined-image.png);
}

.play {
    /* Displays 100 pixels square, beginning at the top-left of the background.
        This corresponds to the Play icon in the image in Figure 4-1 */
    background-position: 0 0;
}

.rewind {
    /* Shift the background image 100 pixels to the left, so that the Rewind
        image is located at the top-left position of the element, fitting the 100
        pixel display square exactly.  */
    background-position: -100px 0;
}

.forward {
    /* Shift the background image 100 pixels upwards, so the Forward image
        is located within the top-left 100 pixel square of the element */
    background-position: 0 -100px;
}

.stop {
    /* Shift the background image 100 pixels to the left and 100 pixels
        upwards, so the Stop image is visible in the 100 pixel display square */
    background-position: -100px -100px;
}
```

By shifting the background image within the element, you are able to display the exact portion of the image you wish to appear. You have reduced four separate images into one, and added only one extra line to the CSS style rules. Since a single combined image is typically smaller than several individual images, and results in fewer HTTP requests, there is often a noticeable performance benefit to the end user with this technique.

■**Caution**   Before you start combining your entire image library together into one single combined file to use with this technique, stop and think about the context of the image files you are combining. For the sake of maintainability, consider joining together only related images, such as icons, with similar visual sizes. To ease maintenance further, use a graphics software package, such as Adobe Photoshop, which supports layers that you can utilize to reexport your sprite image file if you need to make changes to an individual image it contains.

So, the CSS sprite technique is a great performance booster. By reducing the number of HTTP requests, you are less reliant on the connection speed to the server and parallel connection limits within the browser. However, the way you combine images together will have an effect on performance. Therefore, you want to make sure to do this in the best way possible. Here are some ways to optimize CSS sprite images:

Avoid a single, behemoth sprite image file: Since you are combining smaller images into a single larger one, the resulting file size, though usually smaller than the sum of its parts, will no doubt be larger than that of any single file it replaces. Larger files take longer to download, so the users will need to wait before they see any images in their browser. The intention is to give your end users a web page that loads and displays in record time, so think carefully about your CSS sprite images. You will need to separate them into a few, carefully constructed image files, rather than a single, all-encompassing behemoth.

Use space wisely and efficiently: Huge swathes of whitespace between individual images within a sprite image are less efficient than an image with less whitespace. As with other types of files, you don't want to store extra image data that will never be used. Keep the individual images that go together to form the master sprite image as tightly packed as possible to minimize wasted space. Choose component images that are of a similar size to provide the best fit and reduce the amount of whitespace in the sprite image. You can arrange the individual images into a square grid or use a horizontally or vertically aligned sequence of images. You might think that the alignment of the images has no impact on file size, but actually, smaller file sizes are possible when images are aligned in a single horizontal row.

Consider the maintenance tasks: A single image, stored in its own file, is a lot easier to update and maintain than a group of images stored together in one single file. When editing a large sprite image, care must be taken not to alter images surrounding the individual image being edited, as such changes could pass unnoticed. If you use graphics software, such as Adobe Photoshop, which allows you to save images with separate layers and dividing grid lines, you should place each separate image into a different layer, aligned to these fixed grid lines. Keep a backup of this master file along with your images, and export your sprite image in PNG format (discussed later in this chapter) whenever an alteration is made.

Avoid Inefficient CSS Selectors

The CSS selector provides the mechanism for the browser to apply your style rules to your page. Typically, the browser will search for style rules to apply to a page element as it is created, comparing the tag name, id attribute, and class attribute of the element to the list of style rules. The browser then searches for style rules to apply based on possible inherited values from other CSS selectors in the document, and combines the results, giving precedence to more specific style rules or rules given later in the document. The browser effectively needs to perform a series of searches to locate the styles to apply to an element, and each of these searches takes a certain length of time to complete. Admittedly, these searches are over in a matter of milliseconds, but it is possible to speed up the process by writing style rules that avoid unnecessary searching.

Ensure that your CSS selector is only as long as it needs to be to apply your style rules to your elements. If you find yourself chaining a long series of tag, id, and class names together into a single selector, chances are you should be looking for a different, leaner approach.

Avoid specifying selectors that include tag names, as these typically cause the longest style rule searches to take place. Instead, filter your selectors by an appropriate id attribute located on a parent element. The search does not need to attempt to look for style rules applied to any other id attribute, thus improving the speed at which results are returned.

The following shows examples of both effective and ineffective CSS selectors, based on the style rule searching mechanism employed by most browsers.

```
/* Ineffective selectors - avoid these in your code */
table tbody tr td { ... }
#body #content #results a { ... }
form div#field label { ... }

/* More effective selectors */
#header .title { ... }
#results a { ... }
#field .label { ... }
```

Tweaking Your Images for Performance

Image files constitute the majority of all data requested from the server for most web sites. Increasingly complex designs and layouts often require complex image resources, which typically translate into larger file sizes and slower download times.

The information company Alexa (http://www.alexa.com/) provides a list of the most popular web sites in the world, based on traffic. Table 4-3 shows the top-five sites globally and the proportion of their home page data devoted to images. The YSlow extension to Mozilla's Firefox browser was used to extract this information. You can download this component from http://developer.yahoo.com/yslow/ to perform your own tests.

Being smart about the way you handle the images in your web application can make a great performance improvement, since their file sizes make up a proportionally large percentage of the page weight of most RIAs.

Table 4-3. *Proportion of Popular Sites' Home Pages Devoted to Images*

Site	Total Page Weight	Image Weight	Proportion of Weight As Images
www.yahoo.com	219.8KB	101.9KB	46.3%
www.google.com	10.1KB	7.5KB	74.3%
www.youtube.com	204.6KB	105.4KB	51.5%
www.live.com	15.2KB	9.8KB	64.5%
www.facebook.com	380.1KB	110.9KB	29.2%

Understand Image File Formats

The three major image file formats used on web pages are Graphics Interchange Format (GIF), Joint Photographic Experts Group format (JPEG), and Portable Network Graphics format (PNG). Most developers have only comparatively recently picked up on the PNG format, and its support is growing, for good reason. Let's look at the pros and cons of each of these formats, and why I recommend the PNG format.

GIF Format

The company CompuServe launched the GIF format back in 1987. It was popular on the Web because it typically produced small file sizes. Until the late 1990s, the GIF format was subject to a patent, and its use typically required a license.

GIF file sizes are small due to two main characteristics:

Color depth: The color depth of the image is only 8 bit, which means that only 256 different colors can be represented in one image file, compared to the millions of unique colors capable of being displayed on modern displays. That 256-color palette is not fixed, however, and can be selected from the full range of millions of colors. If your image uses fewer than 256 colors, only the colors actually used are saved along with the image data, reducing the size of the data stored.

Compression: The image data itself is compressed using an algorithm known as Lempel-Ziv-Welch (LZW). This type of compression does not actually remove any data from the image; rather, it represents that data in a more compressed manner. Browsers convert this compressed data back into the original image data for display, so the files can be smaller without sacrificing image quality.

This file format is very efficient for representing small icons, typically less than 16 pixels square, and simple drawings or line art. These types of images can have a restricted color palette, and the compression method is very effective for less complex images. The file format is less efficient for larger and more complex images.

When saving a GIF file, you have the option to select one of the colors in the palette to be represented as a transparent color. When such a file is then displayed within the browser, that selected color is no longer visible; instead, the contents beneath the image on the page are shown, allowing for transparencies in GIF image files. This particular technique does not work well with gradients or drop shadows, since you cannot represent different degrees of transparency—it is either on or off for a particular selected color.

The GIF image format is also capable of storing several image frames in one individual file, also holding the information about when to show those frames and for how long. This allows for a basic form of animation, where each frame is stored as a full image. You will most likely have seen these animation files used as the loading indicators for many RIAs.

GIF animations store each frame individually, which is not so efficient, especially where there are very few differences between each frame. Unfortunately, no other web image format is yet able to represent animations in all browsers, so this is the only choice for animated images, other than the use of third-party plug-ins, such as Adobe's Flash Player.

JPEG Format

For representing photographic or very complex images on the Web, JPEG (or JPG) image format is ideal. The Joint Photographic Experts Group formed in 1986 to create a file format for compressing this type of image, and the resulting format was finalized and approved as an international standard in 1994. The format is open and not subject to any patent laws.

The JPEG format is particularly suited to complex images where there are no sharp contrasts between neighboring pixels, so line drawings are not appropriate for this type of compression. Unlike GIF, JPEG is a *lossy* format. This is because, to perform the compression, data is removed from the original image and cannot be restored. The compression is not achieved by storing the existing image data in a different way, but rather by removing components from the image that typically are unnoticed by the human eye.

When saving an image in JPEG format from your graphics software, you are usually given the choice of the level of compression to apply to the resulting file. The less compression that takes place, the larger the file size will be and the more of the original image is left intact. The greater the compression, the smaller the file size but less of the original image is left intact—meaning at greater levels of compression, there is a chance that image artifacts might be visible to the eye. Choose the level of compression that allows the image to remain free of visual abnormalities, while achieving the smallest possible file size.

PNG Format

The PNG image file format was developed to improve upon the GIF file format while being open and patent-free. While this file format is the most recent of the three formats, its support is universal among modern browsers.

The PNG file format is capable of storing 24-bit image color palettes—representing more than 16 million colors in a single compressed file—and also supports alpha-channel transparent layers. This means that, rather than GIF's restrictive single-color transparency, different levels of transparency can be applied to any portion of the image independently of another.

■**Caution** Support for the PNG alpha transparency layers was not introduced by default in IE 6. Attempts to use this feature will result in a light-blue background appearing where the transparent portions of the image should be. You can get around this either by using the CSS `AlphaImageTransform` DirectX filter (but, as discussed earlier in this chapter, this has huge performance drawbacks) or by reexporting your image in a different format, such as GIF or as PNG-8 (a variant of PNG that supports single color transparencies, similar to GIF), which will reduce or remove the transparencies in the image when displayed in this browser.

Unlike JPEG, PNG is a *lossless* image format, which means that all the data from the original image is retained within the file after compression, and can be recovered at any time. The compression applied to the image uses a method similar to the GIF image file format, in that the data is simply represented in a different way, compressed using the `deflate` compression method, which can also be used to compress the HTTP response data from your web server, as discussed earlier in this chapter.

In almost all cases, PNG images are smaller in file size than their equivalent GIF counterparts (with the exception of very small images, usually less than 16 pixels square), despite being able to store and represent many more colors.

Due to its smaller file sizes, PNG is the preferred format for most images on the Web. You should use GIF only for small images, where the resultant image file will be smaller than if PNG had been used. The JPEG format should be used for complex images, such as photographs, where its compression algorithm works best, removing components from the image that would otherwise go unnoticed by the eye.

Optimize PNG Images

PNG image files contain more than just raw image data. A set of header data is also provided at the beginning of the file to describe the image contained in the rest of the file. Each set of data is known as a *chunk*. Some of the chunks are mandatory, including the color palette and image data. Many chunks are optional, such as image gamma and white balance data.

Since a PNG file needs to contain only this mandatory data, you can remove the optional data chunks from the file to reduce its size. Typically, your graphics software will save your PNG files with the optional chunks intact, so you should find a way to remove these to cut down the file size.

A command-line tool is available for most operating systems to allow you to strip the optional data chunks from your PNG files. This tool is called Pngcrush, and it's available for download from `http://pmt.sourceforge.net/pngcrush/`. You can run this tool automatically on your images as part of an automated build environment or manually on your own images, depending on your particular development setup. Conveniently, a web site called Smush it (`http://www.smushit.com/`) has been set up to make this task even easier for you. Point this web site to the URL of your own site, or upload your images to the site, and a zip file is produced of all your images, with all the unnecessary data chunks removed. The site also performs a conversion of your images from GIF and JPEG to PNG, where this would save on file size. A Mozilla Firefox browser extension is available for download from the site to allow you to apply the optimization on demand to whichever site is currently displayed in your browser window.

Don't Forget the Favicon

A favorites icon, commonly known as a *favicon*, is an image file that is located at the root of your web server and named favicon.ico, by default. It is a small (usually 16 by 16 pixels) icon that you will see displayed to the left of the URL in your browser's address bar. It is also used as the image to represent the URL when saved as a "favorite" in your browser, hence its name.

Your browser requests this type of file whenever you browse to a web site, and there is no way to turn this feature off in all browsers through code. Therefore, you should ensure that an image exists at this location to avoid having the browser receive an HTTP 404 error instead (see the discussion earlier in this chapter to discover why this is bad).

The smaller the image, the better—less than 1KB is preferable. Also, set HTTP response headers on the file to ensure it remains cached on the user's machine and is not downloaded on every visit to the site.

Tweaking Your JavaScript for Performance

Efficient JavaScript code is vital to any RIA, as it has the power to frustrate or delight your end users. With increasingly complex code comes a greater opportunity for problems to creep in, including memory leaks, performance-intensive tasks that lock up the browser, and a lack of consideration for usability and performance.

Keep in mind that JavaScript is a client-side language whose performance is directly related to the browser it is being executed within, and the power of the device on which that browser is running. With this in mind, consider using the web server to perform intensive tasks, such as constructing the initial view of your RIA, or to perform computational analysis on a large amount of data. Any operation that will cause your end users to wait an excessive amount of time for a result should be performed on the server, where possible.

In this section, we will look at how you can improve your JavaScript code, to minimize any negative performance for your server or end users. The topics covered here are not exhaustive. Since JavaScript is a large programming language, there are numerous possibilities for small and large performance tweaks to particular functions, loops, and routines. The material included here is tailored to building RIAs, so a healthy portion of the information is devoted to the performance implications of DOM and Ajax routines.

Shrink Your JavaScript File Using Dojo ShrinkSafe

Again, we return to the topic of extra information in files. JavaScript files are full of whitespace characters and (hopefully) also have plenty of comments and documentation. This information is ideal for developers who need to be able to understand the code stored inside those files, but browsers don't need any of that information—it's ignored after it's received, so there's no point in sending it.

Depending on your file, you can cut around 50% of the file size of a JavaScript file by stripping out unnecessary whitespace and comments, a process known as *minification*. You can reduce the file size further by using a process called *obfuscation*, which shortens variable and function names. But be aware that obfuscation is usually fairly risky, as it does not take into account the way in which the file being compressed is used in the context of the site where it sits.

The developers of the Dojo JavaScript library have built their own JavaScript file compressor, known as ShrinkSafe, which uses both minification and obfuscation techniques. You can download this tool from `http://shrinksafe.dojotoolkit.org/`.

ShrinkSafe works in a slightly smarter way than most obfuscators, removing the inherent risk by altering only the variable and function names of code that is not publicly accessible from outside the script. This ensures that any public API or code within that file will still work properly within the context of the site. You should use this tool to make your code as small as possible, to ensure the fastest download possible to the browser.

Access JavaScript Libraries Through CDNs

Earlier, you learned that using CDNs reduces the distance your data needs to travel over the Internet. Many JavaScript libraries, such as jQuery and Prototype, are hosted on CDNs to provide a faster response time over the network for the end users. They have the added benefit of being available in the end user's browser cache if that user has visited another site referencing the same library from the same URL.

Google is looking to be the leader in CDN JavaScript library hosting. It provides access to the following libraries and third-party JavaScript components at the time of writing:

- jQuery (plus its associated jQuery UI library)
- Prototype (plus its associated script.aculo.us UI library)
- Dojo Toolkit
- Yahoo! UI
- MooTools
- SWFObject (a useful library for embedding Adobe Flash on a page)

Each is available directly from a fixed URL as either the full, original file or as a minified version, often up to 50% smaller. The full documentation from Google on this service is available online at `http://code.google.com/apis/ajaxlibs/`.

The only drawback with accessing a file from a different domain than the one the current site is hosted on is the extra DNS lookup required to locate the IP address of the new domain name. Thankfully, this lookup time is more than made up for by the speed at which each referenced file is downloaded. The CDN allows users to receive a copy of the file from a server location physically close to their browser, ensuring network performance bottlenecks are limited.

Timing Is Everything

When JavaScript files are loaded normally, using file references within your HTML file, the browser blocks the downloading and parsing of the rest of the page until the script has downloaded and executed. This is not ideal, particularly if there is a lot of code to download. There is a way to overcome this performance bottleneck using JavaScript itself, though you must exercise caution. Scripts usually block the browser to avoid *race conditions*, where one piece of code completes before another, causing execution to occur in the wrong order. If you are going to load scripts in this way, you need a technique to have a block of JavaScript code execute once a file has completed downloading, to prevent a race condition.

Listing 4-1 shows how to load a JavaScript file on demand without blocking the browser, and how to specify some code to execute when it has completed downloading. Add this code to the $ JavaScript library you created in Chapter 2.

Listing 4-1. *Loading a JavaScript File on Demand Without Blocking the Browser*

```
$.prototype.Remote.loadScript = function(fileName, callback) {
    var scriptTag = document.createElement("script");
    scriptTag.src = fileName;

    if (callback) {
        scriptTag.onload = callback;
        scriptTag.onreadystatechange = function() {
            if (scriptTag.readyState == 4) {
                callback();
            }
        }
    }

    document.getElementsByTagName("head")[0].appendChild(scriptTag);
}

// Example usage
// Assuming an instance of the $ library exists on the page

// Loads my-script.js, then outputs "script loaded and available" when complete
$.Remote.loadScript("my-script.js", function() {
    alert("script loaded and available!");
});
```

Back in Chapter 2, I introduced you to the ability to execute JavaScript code once the DOM for the whole page has been initialized and is ready for access. This occurs before the entire page has loaded, as it considers only that the HTML has loaded, regardless of any referenced external assets, such as images. By writing your code to execute when this event fires, as shown in Listing 4-2, you enable your code to get to work sooner, cutting out extra waiting time for the end user. You can use this event to load in several JavaScript files in parallel, using the technique outlined in Listing 4-1.

Listing 4-2. *Executing Scripts As Soon As the DOM Is Ready*

```
$.onDomReady(function() {
    // This function executes as soon as the DOM is ready for access

    // Load two JavaScript files, my-script.js and my-other-script.js, simultaneously
    $.Remote.loadScript("my-script.js", function() {
        // my-script.js loaded
    });
```

```
    $.Remote.loadScript("my-other-script.js", function() {
        // my-other-script.js loaded
    });
});
```

Boost Core JavaScript Performance

By *core* JavaScript, I am referring to that part of the language that focuses on pure data processing, execution, looping, and logic, rather than the part of the language focusing on page manipulation through the DOM or the use of the Ajax technique. Here, I will propose a number of improvements you can make to your own core JavaScript code to speed up its execution time.

Use a Memoizer

A *memoizer* is a function that doubles as a storage mechanism. It saves the results of previous executions of that function routine so that future calls to the function with identical inputs will return the output from the list of stored results, instead of computing the result again. This improves the performance of functions that are called multiple times throughout your code. It is only possible to "memoize" functions that always produce the same output based on an identical set of inputs.

Listing 4-3 shows how to build a utility function that allows you to add the ability to store result values to any function, automatically returning the result of the function from its internal storage property where possible to boost performance. Add this code to the $ JavaScript library, as before.

Listing 4-3. *Using a Memoizer to Speed Up Execution Time of Repetitive Functions*

```
// memoize expects a function as an input and returns the same function
// with storage capabilities added

$.prototype.Utils.memoize = function(func) {
    return function() {
        // Add a memory object property to this function, if it does not exist
        func.memory = func.memory || {};

        // Create a key to use to store and retrieve function results within
        // the memory object property. The key should be based on a combination
        // of all the arguments passed to the function to ensure it is unique based
        // on all combinations of inputs
        arguments.join = Array.prototype.join;
        var key = arguments.join("|");

        // Does the key exist in the memory object?
        if (key in func.memory) {
            // If it does, then return the associated value to avoid recomputation
            return func.memory[key];
```

```
        } else {
            // If it doesn't, execute the associated function then save the result
            // to the memory object
            func.memory[key] = func.apply(this, arguments);

            // Return the newly saved value, the result of the function's execution
            return func.memory[key];
        }
    }
};

// Example usage
// Assuming an instance of the $ library exists on the page

// Write a function that computes the factorial of a given number
// - execute it 99999 times to exaggerate the effect of a slow-running function
var computeFactorial = function(input) {
    var result;
    for (var count = 0; count < 99999; count++) {
        result = 1;
        for (var num = 2; num <= input; num++) {
            result *= num;
        }
    }
    return result;
}

// Add memoize capability to the factorial function
computeFactorial = $.Utils.memoize(computeFactorial);

// Measure the speed of the factorial function's execution
computeFactorial(100); // Execution takes ~945 milliseconds
computeFactorial(50); // Execution takes ~506 milliseconds
computeFactorial(100); // Execution takes 0-1 milliseconds - using stored value
computeFactorial(50); // Execution takes 0-1 milliseconds - using stored value
```

Use Efficient String Concatenation

By far, the most common way of concatenating strings together into larger strings is to use the + operator, like this:

```
var outputString = "start text " + inputString + " end text";
```

When you are performing many string concatenations, such as within a code loop, the time taken to perform the full series of concatenations using the + operator adds up to a severe performance penalty, particularly in IE.

You can use an alternative technique for concatenating strings, which does not suffer the same performance penalty. This solution involves utilizing an array, as follows:

```
var myArray = [];
myArray.push('Welcome, ');
myArray.push (userName);
myArray.push(', to the site.');
myArray.join('');
```

In some cases, string concatenation performance can be improved in IE by up to 25 times by using an array in this way versus using the + operator.

Use Regular Expressions

Regular expressions provide a useful, powerful, and efficient way to perform string manipulation and pattern matching—faster than any other method. Within JavaScript, regular expressions can be defined in two different ways: as a literal or using an object constructor, as follows:

```
// Both the following regular expressions are designed to find any instance of
// a capital letter within the string being searched.
var expression = new RegExp("[A-Z]", "g"); // slow - needs to be processed first
var expression = /[A-Z]/g;  // fast - ready to use

// Outputs "_est _tring"
alert(Test String".replace(expression, "_"));
```

The RegExp object constructor takes a string and converts this into a regular expression, whereas the literal form is ready to be used without any extra processing. This makes the literal form of the regular expression the fastest way to search strings using JavaScript.

Avoid using the RegExp constructor to create a regular expression, except where you absolutely need to generate this expression dynamically. You can find a very thorough tutorial on regular expressions in JavaScript online at http://www.evolt.org/article/ Regular_Expressions_in_JavaScript/17/36435/.

Loop Faster and More Efficiently

Most JavaScript code is full of loops. Often, you will need to process arrays or iterate through object literals to perform calculations or manipulations on the data stored therein. Looping through data is a notoriously slow task in JavaScript, particular in IE 6 and 7. The following shows a typical JavaScript for loop, together with a subtly different, but incredibly more efficient, version of the same loop.

```
var myArray = [10, 20, 30, 40, 50, 60, 70, 80, 90, 100];

// The most common type of loop
for (var index = 0; index < myArray.length; index++) {
    // On every iteration through the loop, the value of myArray.length must
    // be recomputed to ensure it has not changed since the last iteration
    // - this is slow
}
```

```
// A subtly different but much faster version of the same loop
for (var index = 0, length = myArray.length; index < length; index++) {
    // The value of myArray.length is computed once and stored in a variable.
    // The value is read back from the variable on each iteration instead of being
    // recomputed - much faster!
}
```

You have two JavaScript commands at your disposal to manage your loops:

- `break` stops the current loop from executing, continuing to execute the code that follows the loop.

- `continue` stops the current iteration of the loop and moves onto the next iteration.

You can use these commands to effectively stop your loops from iterating if you have located the value you were seeking, or to skip execution of certain code blocks if they are irrelevant to the current iteration of the loop. The following shows an example of both commands.

```
var myArray = [10, 20, 30, 40, 50, 60, 70, 80, 90, 100];
for (var index = 0, length = myArray.length; index < length; index++) {
    if (myArray[index] < 50) {
        // Ignore any values in the array below 50
        // continue executes the next iteration immediately, ignoring any other code
        // within the loop
        continue;
    }

    if (myArray[index] == 90) {
        // Ignore any values in the array above 90
        // break stops the loop from iterating immediately, ignoring any other code
        // No other iterations will be performed in the loop
        break;
    }
}
```

Coming Soon: Background Web Worker Processes

The Web Hypertext Application Technology Working Group (WHATWG) is a community of developers and companies dedicated to pushing forward adoption and recommendations of new technologies on the Web. Currently, this group is busy working on a specification called Web Workers, which will allow developers to assign JavaScript code to execute in background threads, without blocking users from interacting with the browser and without blocking other code from executing.

This recommendation is in its early stages, but is being built in a preliminary form within Mozilla Firefox 3.5 and WebKit-based browsers. It is published online at http://www.whatwg. org/specs/web-workers/current-work/. When it's complete, you will be able to run code that takes a long time to execute in the background, without affecting the performance of the rest of the page. (I personally cannot wait for this recommendation to be completed and implemented in browsers—it will make core JavaScript performance issues a thing of the past!)

Improve Ajax Performance

As discussed in Chapter 2, Ajax is a staple part of most RIAs, enabling developers to retain control over their user interface in the browser, while sending and receiving data to and from the web server in the background. We have established that a major performance bottleneck in RIAs is the network connection between the browser and the web server, so you need to make all the changes you can to improve the performance and efficiency of your code to reduce this impact as much as possible.

Use JSON Format for Responses

You can use the Ajax technique to make requests for any text-based data from the server, though the technique and its underlying code does provide built-in support for XML format, converting the response from the server into an XML data structure within JavaScript where possible. The problem with this from a performance perspective is that XML parsing through JavaScript is an incredibly slow operation to perform within most browsers, so you should rule out this option when possible.

Instead, use the JSON format, introduced in Chapter 2, to encode your data. This format is hierarchical, just like XML, and represents data in name/value pairs, just like JavaScript object literals. However, it has the benefit of being incredibly lightweight, since it does not rely on opening, closing, and nesting tags to represent its hierarchical data. You are effectively able to represent the same data using less space, which means the data will be available to your web application sooner.

Since the data received will be in text format and not directly available as a JavaScript object, you need to parse the JSON-format text response into an object literal you can access with your RIA. Douglas Crockford, inventor of the JSON format, provides an open source JSON parser. This parser is available from the JSON web site (`http://www.json.org/json2.js`), and you may use it to perform this conversion from text to native object. Some browsers, including IE 8 and Firefox 3.5, provide native implementations of the JSON parser within the browser itself, speeding up parsing in those browsers.

Use JSON-P with the <script> Tag

A different approach to fetching JSON data from the server was first proposed back in 2005 by Bob Ippolito on his blog at `http://bob.pythonmac.org/`. Known as JSON with Padding, or JSON-P, the technique involves using JavaScript to dynamically create a `<script>` tag within the current page, pointing to a URL that returns data in JSON format. This allows the browser to execute the returned data as it does with any other script. Of course, JSON data is virtually identical to object literal notation, except that it is just the raw data—it is not assigned to a variable or wrapped in a function call. So, when JSON data is executed via the `<script>` tag, it is parsed by the browser but immediately disappears. If you could somehow assign this data to a variable or wrap it as the input to a function call, then you could read and manipulate it as you want.

The JSON-P technique takes exactly that approach. By passing a known query string parameter to the requested script containing the name of a function within the requesting page, the server should take the JSON data and wrap it in a call to a function of this name. The following shows how requesting a URL with or without this optional parameter should affect the JSON data returned.

```html
<!-- Make a request for a PHP script that returns JSON-format data -->
<script type="text/javascript" src="/my-json.php"></script>

<!-- Effectively produces the following code, which gets executed.
     Since the data is not assigned to a variable or used in a function call, it
     is treated as an object literal but immediately disappears -->
<script type="text/javascript">
{
    to: "den@denodell.com",
    from: "me@denodell.com",
    subject: "Dinner tonight?",
    body: "Do you feel like having dinner tonight? Call me."
}
</script>

<!-- Make a request for the same URL with an optional query string parameter -->
<script type="text/javascript" src="/my-json.php?jsonp=myFunction"></script>

<!-- Provided the PHP script knows what to do with the query string parameter,
     the JSON data is returned, wrapped in a call to the specified function name.
     The myFunction function executes and its input data is the JSON data,
     already as an object literal, so there is no need to perform any parsing -->
<script type="text/javascript">
myFunction({
    to: "den@denodell.com",
    from: "me@denodell.com",
    subject: "Dinner tonight?",
    body: "Do you feel like having dinner tonight? Call me."
});
</script>
```

When the code is executed, the function of the name specified in the query string parameter is called, and its input is the JSON data requested. This uses the browser's built-in JavaScript parser and the data is treated as an object literal; the function is executed immediately when the browser receives it.

Listing 4-4 shows how you can use the JSON-P technique to load JSON data from a given URL and make it available natively to a function, which executes once the data has been received. Add this code to the $ JavaScript library you began in Chapter 2.

Listing 4-4. *Using JSON-P*

```javascript
// The loadJSONP method mimics the existing loadScript method but allows
// the returned JSON data to be available to the callback method as an input.
// Add this method to our $ JavaScript library code.

$.prototype.Remote.loadJSONP = function(url, callback){
    // The callback function needs to exist within the global window object
    window.tempFunction = callback;
```

```
    // Append the jsonp=tempFunction query string parameter to the URL.
    // The server should wrap the returned JSON data in a call to the function
    // of the name specified in this parameter, so it is executed when
    // the data is returned
    url = url.contains("?") ? url + "&jsonp=tempFunction" : "?jsonp=tempFunction";

    // Call the existing loadScript method to place the <script> tag on the page
    this.loadScript(url);
}

// Example usage
// Assuming an instance of the $ library exists on the page

// Make a request for the file my-script.php?jsonp=tempFunction, which
// returns the JSON data wrapped in a call to the tempFunction method
$.Remote.loadJSONP("my-script.php", function(data) {
    // Outputs "object" denoting an object literal has been returned
    alert(typeof data);
});
```

■**Tip** Unlike the Ajax technique, JSON-P is not limited to requesting data on the same domain as the page making the request, since the `<script>` tag can request JavaScript files from any domain. The only requirement is that the external script returning the JSON data supports the extra query string parameter to wrap the returned data with a call to the specified function name.

Consolidate Server Requests and Responses

Instead of sending multiple requests for data in a short space of time, consider how you can alter your code to send a single request less frequently to the server, and have the server respond with a single block of data containing amalgamated responses of all the requested data. This will reduce the amount of communication between the browser and the web server, and thus improve the performance of your RIA.

In addition, where your RIA requires many updates from the server, consider using Ajax to post the data in its current state to the server, and configure your server-side script to respond with only the changes to the data that need to be made. The response should be a lot smaller than normal, easier to parse, and reduce the burden on the web server and network.

Improve DOM Performance

RIAs require updates to be made to the user interface of the page based on some kind of input, usually from the user or the server. The JavaScript DOM is required to make changes to HTML elements or CSS properties within the user interface. This is notoriously slow, particularly in older browsers, as you saw in the performance benchmark results in Chapter 3. This section presents some guidelines and code snippets designed to help improve the performance of your page interactions through JavaScript.

Minimize DOM Access

Using JavaScript to access HTML elements is a time-intensive operation, so it should be done as little as possible. If you need to access a DOM element, set it to a variable and use that variable reference throughout the rest of the code, as shown in this example:

```
// The DOM reference is located once during this routine, and referenced through
// a variable everywhere else

var menu = document.getElementById('menu');
if ($.CSS.hasClass(menu, "navigation")) {
    $.CSS.addClass(menu, "menu");
    // Outputs the current width of the menu element
    alert($.CSS.getAppliedStyle(menu, "width"));
}
```

If you need to create and add DOM elements to the page dynamically, apply all attributes and set all necessary properties before adding the new elements to the page. This way, the browser will not need to keep accessing the live DOM to make changes.

When locating page elements through the DOM, filter the DOM tree as much as possible—the less traversal, the faster the access will be. If you are searching for an element with a particular class name and you know it will exist within a certain tag, filter the node tree by this tag first to return results faster, as in this example:

```
// Locate a known element that wraps the node tree you want to traverse
var filterElement = document.getElementById("menu");

// Find all elements with a class name of selected within the filterElement.
// This is faster than traversing the entire DOM node tree of the page
var selected = $.Elements.getElementsByClassName("selected", filterElement);
```

Use DocumentFragment Objects

An often-overlooked part of the DOM specification is the ability to use DocumentFragment objects in JavaScript as a sort of mini-DOM to create, append, and manipulate elements within your code before adding the whole mini-DOM node tree onto the page in one single action. This improves performance considerably compared with the traditional method of adding each DOM element one at a time directly to the page. Here's how you can use this technique to add a set of elements to the page.

```
// Create a DocumentFragment object as an offline mini-DOM,
// which is not connected to the live DOM of the page.
var miniDOM = document.createDocumentFragment();
```

```
// Create some new DOM elements
var p = document.createElement("p");
var hr = document.createElement("hr");
var h2 = document.createElement("h2");

// Add each element to the DocumentFragment object
miniDOM.appendChild(p);
miniDOM.appendChild(hr);
miniDOM.appendChild(h2);

// Add a copy of this single DocumentFragment to the page. Making a single
// action against the live DOM means considerable performance improvement
// over multiple actions
document.body.appendChild(miniDOM.cloneNode(true));
```

Plug Memory Leaks

In most browsers, when JavaScript objects are created, memory is allocated to them on the machine or device running the code. When they are destroyed or are no longer used, that memory is reclaimed, making it available for the rest of the code to use later.

IE 6 and 7 have a memory management issue due to the fact that they have two memory managers: one for core JavaScript code and one for DOM objects. Both work perfectly by themselves, but when a circular reference occurs between them, as shown in the following example, two worlds collide, and memory leaks abound.

```
<div id="leaking"></div>

<script type="text/javascript">
    // A DOM element is assigned to a variable, which is then assigned to
    // a property of the original DOM element, creating a circular reference.
    // This causes a memory leak to occur in Internet Explorer 6 and 7.

    var leakyDiv = document.getElementById('leaking');
    document.getElementById('leaking').newProperty = leakyDiv;
</script>
```

If left untouched, these memory leaks can eventually force the browser to crash when it runs out of available memory. The memory is not even reclaimed when a page refresh occurs, so it can cause serious problems for your end users.

IE 7 introduced a work-around of sorts: when the user moves to another page or site, the memory allocated to the previous page is freed up. Unfortunately, it frees up only the memory for DOM objects that existed on the page at the point the user navigated away. If you used JavaScript to remove a few DOM elements from the page, the memory leaked due to those particular elements would never be recovered. Since it is quite common to add and remove DOM elements dynamically in web applications, memory leakage is still a big problem for RIAs in these browsers. Thankfully, there is a way to plug the leak when a page refresh occurs, by freeing up the memory using the unload event of the page, as shown in Listing 4-5.

Listing 4-5. *Plugging a Memory Leak*

```
<div id="leaking"></div>

<script type="text/javascript">
    var leakyDiv = document.getElementById('leaking');
    document.getElementById('leaking').newProperty = leakyDiv;

    $.Events.add(window, "unload", function() {
        // Remove all circular references before page is unloaded to plug the leak
        document.getElementById('leaking').newProperty = null;
    });
</script>
```

Microsoft has released the beta version of a piece of software for IE 7 called the JavaScript Memory Leak Detector, which allows you to detect memory leaks. This is a very useful tool to run while you're building your web application. It will help you to ensure you capture and plug all those memory leaks—you don't want your end users' browsers to crash because they visit your site! You can download the tool from `http://blogs.msdn.com/gpde/pages/javascript-memory-leak-detector.aspx`.

Use Event Delegates

RIAs are most often, by their nature, event-driven. They wait for events to occur, such as button clicks, mouse movements, or key presses, and execute certain code functions when they do. With DOM events, even if an event occurs on a particular element, it also bubbles up from that element and also occurs on all elements surrounding it. The following example demonstrates this behavior:

```
<body>
    <div>
        <!-- Events on the anchor tag also occur on the <div> and <body> tags -->
        <a href="/">Back to home></a>
    </div>
</body>
```

Here, a click event on the anchor `<a>` tag also fires on the surrounding elements, beginning with the inner element and bubbling outward from there to the top level of the page structure.

You may consider this behavior slightly odd, but you can use it to your advantage to provide performance improvements in the code you write to associate events with actions. Instead of creating separate event handlers for each element, write single event handlers that listen for all events of a certain type that occur throughout the entire page. You can then assign actions to occur depending on properties of the element the event occurred on, as shown in Listing 4-6. These are called event *delegates*, as they become logic blocks that delegate actions based on properties of events and page elements.

Listing 4-6. *Event Delegation*

```
<a href="/">Back to home</a>

<script type="text/javascript">
    // Listen for click events firing within the whole document
    $.Events.add(document.body, "click", function(e) {
        // e.target contains a reference to the actual element the
        // event took place on
        if (e.target.tagName.toLowerCase() == "a") {
            alert("You clicked the anchor tag");
        } else {
            alert("You clicked somewhere other than on the anchor tag");
        }
    });
</script>
```

By listening for each event type only once, on the top-level document.body element, and then identifying the element the event actually took place on, you ensure that you have only a handful of events to wire up when your page loads. This helps achieve the overall goal of reducing the time it takes before the end user is able to interact with the page.

Change Class, Not Style, When Updating CSS

Through the DOM, you are able to manipulate CSS style properties directly. Any action against a DOM element through JavaScript takes time to complete. A better solution when you need to update style properties to new, known values is to use the power of the browser's rendering engine by simply adding, removing, or swapping the class value applied to the element you wish to modify. The new styles will then be contained in style sheet files, where layout and design code belongs. This way, only one DOM manipulation would be required to add or remove whole swathes of style properties. Listing 4-7 demonstrates this technique.

Listing 4-7. *Updating Applied Class Names Instead of Individual Styles*

```
<div id="menu"></div>

<script type="text/javascript">
    $.Events.add(document.body, "click", function(e) {
        // If the user clicks on an element with an id of menu
        if (e.target.id == "menu") {
            // Toggle the menu-highlight class on that element. That class is
            // specified within the style sheet file to have a different design

            if ($.CSS.hasClass("menu-highlight")) {
                $.CSS.removeClass("menu-highlight");
```

```
            } else {
                $.CSS.addClass("menu-highlight");
            }
        };
    });
</script>
```

Duplicate Existing Nodes Rather Than Create New Ones

Creating DOM elements dynamically is a fairly common requirement in RIAs, but you pay a performance penalty each time you create an element when using the standard `document.createElement` method. Through experience, I have found that duplicating existing nodes is faster than creating new ones from scratch. If you are creating multiple elements with similar attributes, create one instance, and then use the `cloneNode` method to duplicate the element and its associated attributes for a performance boost.

Armed with this knowledge, you can add a new method to your $ JavaScript library to speed up the creation of DOM elements in certain cases, as shown in Listing 4-8.

Listing 4-8. *Creating DOM Elements Efficiently*

```
$.prototype.Elements.create = function(tagName) {
    // This method utilizes the memoizer technique
    this.memory = this.memory || {};
    if (tagName in this.memory) {
        // If we have stored an element of this tag name already, duplicate it
        return this.memory[tagName].cloneNode(true);
    } else {
        // Create a new element of the tag name and store it
        this.memory[tagName] = document.createElement(tagName);
        return this.memory[tagName].cloneNode(true);
    }
};

// Example usage
// Assuming an instance of the $ library exists on the page

// Create two elements from scratch
var newH2Tag = $.Elements.create("h2");
var newPTag = $.Elements.create("p");

// Create another element of the same type as one already created.
// Duplicates the stored element, boosting performance over creating
// the element from scratch again
var anotherH2Tag = $.Elements.create("h2"); // Uses a duplicate
```

Append Elements to the Page As HTML Strings

The correct way to add new DOM elements to your page is to use the appendChild DOM method against an existing page element. The problem with this method is that in certain older browsers, it runs fairly slowly, particularly when there are many new elements to add to the page. There is a much faster, though riskier, way of adding elements to your page: write the new elements as HTML strings and assign the string to the innerHTML property of a page element. Listing 4-9 demonstrates this technique.

Listing 4-9. *Adding Page Elements Dynamically As an HTML String*

```
<div id="container"></div>

<script type="text/javascript">
    var pageElement = document.getElementById("container");
    var newElementString = "<p>Hello, world!</p>";

    // Setting the innerHTML property of a DOM element is faster than any other
    // method for adding elements dynamically to a page
    pageElement.innerHTML = newElementString;
</script>
```

If your RIA requires you to add many elements to the page, and the DocumentFragment technique suggested earlier is not helping, you might consider using this method as a last resort.

This approach is risky is because you are able to add incorrect, invalid HTML to the page, which may cause the page layout to break. Imagine if you opened a tag in your HTML string but never closed it. So if you must use this technique, be very careful!

Summary

This chapter covered a wide range of topics related to performance. It provided many suggestions to help improve the speed of your RIAs, through tweaks made to your web server, your HTML markup, your style sheets, your images, and your JavaScript code.

Remember that your end users won't notice good performance; they will only feel the pain of poor performance. Don't give them any reason to complain. Take advantage of the wealth of information in this chapter, and give your site visitors the experience they deserve.

The next chapter deals with the different, though related, topic of perceived performance—giving the impression of a responsive application, despite what might actually be happening behind the scenes.

CHAPTER 5

■ ■ ■

Smoke and Mirrors: Perceived Responsiveness

The previous chapter covered the topic of code performance and efficiency, including many suggestions to help improve your end users' experience with your RIAs. Unfortunately, no matter how hard you try, you will not be able to reduce the amount of time required for certain actions. Ajax requests, for example, are limited by the quality of the network connection between the browser and server.

As web developers, we need to figure out how to keep our end users informed that things are occurring behind the scenes, and give them the impression that they are receiving a fast, responsive web browsing experience, despite these holdups. This chapter covers this issue of perceived responsiveness, rather than actual performance—the art of illusion and "smoke and mirrors" to provide the impression of a fast and responsive web application in those times when the browser and server just can't produce actual results quickly enough.

Providing Prompt Visual Feedback

There can be nothing more irritating than waiting for software to respond to your attempts to interact with it. If you click a button that suggests it will perform a certain action, but nothing seems to happen, you quickly become frustrated. Conversely, if you click a button and are informed immediately that the action will take some time to complete, and are given some indication of how long you will need to wait, the frustration level is significantly reduced. Providing feedback is the most important part of promoting a friendly user experience. Common sense tells us that people will prefer an interface that is friendly and responsive to one that is not.

Time It Right

Experiments show that, on average, humans tend to react to events within around 300 milliseconds; if the eye sees something it needs to react to, the brain takes about 300 milliseconds to process the input and form a reaction. This information gives us a good idea of how soon after users perform an action in the browser that they expect a response.

If your application takes more than 300 milliseconds to react after an event takes place, it will seem unnatural to most people. If you are not able to produce the final result within this time frame, you need to give some indication that you are processing their action, to avoid having users attempt to repeat the action, or simply getting frustrated and leaving the web site.

The JavaScript code in Listing 5-1 shows how to execute a function only if 300 milliseconds have passed since a user submitted a form via Ajax without receiving a response from the server. In some cases, this may be preferable to instant feedback in order to prevent any flicker, as content is added to the page and removed within 300 milliseconds. By waiting 300 milliseconds, you provide feedback only after you know the intended action has not yet completed.

Listing 5-1. *Providing a Response 300 Milliseconds After an Action*

```
$.onDomReady(function() {
    // Outputs "Please wait..." if the Ajax request does not complete
    // within 300 milliseconds

    var visualFeedback = function() {
        alert("Please wait...");
    };

    // Listen for the submit event on the first <form> tag on the current page
    $.Events.add(document.getElementsByTagName("form")[0], "submit", ➡
            function(e) {
        // Stop the default form submission from occurring
        e.preventDefault();

        // Execute the visualFeedback function after 300 milliseconds, storing a
        // reference to the timer within a variable named reaction
        var reaction = window.setTimeout(visualFeedback, 300);

        // Save the form data to the server via Ajax
        $.Remote.save({
            url: "/save-form.php",
            data: "...", // TODO: Real form data goes here
            callback: function(response) {
                // Terminate the execution of the visualFeedback function. If 300
                // milliseconds have not passed, it will not have been executed. If
                // they have, it will have executed already, providing feedback to
                // the end user
                window.clearTimer(reaction);

                // TODO: Perform actions on the Ajax response
            }
        });
    });
});
```

Use CSS Pseudo-Classes on Hyperlinks

CSS pseudo-classes allow you to provide a visual response to mouse and keyboard events that occur on hyperlinks on the page, indicating different states to the user. Listing 5-2 shows how you can use these pseudo-classes to provide a reaction to events occurring on hyperlinks within your page. For correct operation, these styles must be provided in the order shown.

Listing 5-2. *CSS Pseudo-Classes for Providing Visual Feedback on Hyperlinks*

```
a:link {
    /* Applied to unvisited links */
}

a:visited {
    /* Applied to visited links */
}

a:hover {
    /* Applied to the link currently underneath the mouse pointer */
}

a:focus {
    /* Applied to the link currently selected via the keyboard */
    /* e.g., when using the tab key to cycle through links on the page */
}

a:active {
    /* Applied to the link for a brief period while it is being selected */
}
```

Let the User Know the Form Is Being Submitted

Forms, especially those containing a lot of data, can take time to be submitted to the server. As noted in earlier chapters, most users' upload connection speed is slower than their download speed. Additionally, web servers usually need to process the data being sent before sending a response back to the client. This has been known to cause frustration to some users, who proceed to resubmit the form when they believe they have waited long enough for a response to be received.

Duplicate form submissions can cause problems on the web server, such as repeating data in a database or, in the worst case, causing credit cards to be charged multiple times. To avoid this, you can use JavaScript to provide visual feedback that lets users know that their form is being submitted, and preventing them from resubmitting the form. Listing 5-3 demonstrates this technique.

Listing 5-3. *Informing the User That the Form Is Being Submitted*

```
$.onDomReady(function() {
    // Listen for the submit event to fire within the page - this can only
    // occur on <form> tags

    $.Events.add(document.getElementsByTagName("form")[0]

        // Locate the submit button within the current form,
        // which should have a class of submit-button assigned to it
        var buttons = $.Elements.getElementsByClassName("submit-button", ➥
            e.target);

        // Code defensively
        if (buttons.length > 0) {

            // Disable the submit button so it cannot be submitted twice. This
            // visually grays out the button
            buttons[0].disabled = "disabled";

            // Set the submit button text to reflect the fact that the form is
            // now being submitted
            buttons[0].value = "Saving...";
        }
    });
});
```

Change the Mouse Pointer

One of the simplest ways you can let site visitors know that an action is taking place behind the scenes is to update the mouse pointer to indicate that the application is busy. This is just what an operating system does when you load an application or file from your hard drive, indicating that an action is occurring and could take some length of time.

Use JavaScript to set a class, such as busy, on your page's <body> tag when you begin performing an action, and remove it when the action is complete to restore the pointer to its normal state. You can then write the following CSS to set the mouse pointer to the correct state based on the class:

```
// Change the mouse pointer on every page element

body.busy,
body.busy * {
    cursor: progress;
}
```

Use a Web 2.0–Style Animated Indicator

Another approach to indicating to the user that the page, or part of the page, is busy updating for an undetermined length of time is to use the almost ubiquitous Web 2.0–style animated icon. Figure 5-1 shows an example of this indicator.

Figure 5-1. *Web 2.0–style animated loading indicator (spinner)*

For example, if you are updating only a portion of the page while posting a form back to the server via Ajax, you could center the spinner's position over that portion of the page and render any controls within that area inactive while the processing is taking place. This can be achieved by assigning an `indicator` class to a page element via JavaScript when the Ajax communication begins, and removing it once it ends. You should then use CSS to associate the indicator image to this element, as follows:

```
.indicator {
    background: url(/spinner.gif) center no-repeat;
}
```

You can browse and download a large variety of Web 2.0–style loading indicators to use with this technique from `http://www.ajaxload.info/` or `http://www.loadinfo.net/`. Customize these as necessary to fit your own web application design.

Show a Progress Bar

In some cases, you may be able to calculate how long a particular code execution is going to take or the proportion of the code that has executed as a percentage of the total. For example, if you are looping through an array of 1,000 values, you will know on each loop of the array the proportion of the array you have already processed, based on the current index and the total number of items in that array.

When you know what proportion of a particular routine has completed, you can use a progress bar–style indicator to indicate the percentage of the code execution that has taken place. Figure 5-2 shows an example of such a progress bar.

Figure 5-2. *A progress bar indicator*

In many ways, this type of progress bar is far superior to a cursor change or animated icon, as it allows the user to predict, based on how long execution has taken thus far, how long the action will take to complete. It is also a common part of the operating system user interface, so users are already used to seeing a progress bar. Giving the end users an idea of how long they will need to wait offers them the freedom to make choices based on that decision—whether they should fetch that coffee now or later, whether they have enough time to visit a different web site in a separate browser window while they wait, and so on.

Building a progress bar is as simple as creating two nested <div> elements on your page with specific class and id values:

```
<div class="progress-bar">
    <div class="progress" id="code-progress"></div>
</div>
```

Then use CSS to set the dimensions, text, and border styles of the two elements to create the bar:

```
.progress-bar {
    border: 1px solid #000;
    background: #fff;
    width: 150px;
    height: 20px;
}

.progress {
    background: #666;
    color: #000;
    text-align: right;
    height: 100%;
    width: 0%; // The default position of the bar's progress - starts at 0% complete
}
```

You then use JavaScript to dynamically update the width of the inner <div> element to the percentage of the progress of your code as it runs:

```
document.getElementById('code-progress').style.width = '70%';
```

By updating this value regularly, you can achieve a smooth progress bar effect.

Handling Long-Running Scripts

JavaScript does not run in a threaded fashion as some programming languages do; that is, most JavaScript code runs sequentially. While JavaScript is actually executing code, the browser locks up, and then becomes active again when the code is finished running. In most cases, users won't notice this happening, as scripts complete execution quickly. However, occasionally, a script will run for a sufficient length of time that users see a message dialog box in their browser. This dialog box alerts users that a script is being unresponsive and offers them the choice of terminating the script or continuing to allow it to run, as shown in Figure 5-3.

Figure 5-3. *Slow-running script dialog box*

One of our goals as web developers is to ensure our code effectively goes unnoticed by the end users. If our code is efficient and responsive enough, the users will feel as though the system is responding in a natural fashion; disturb this responsiveness, and the users will become frustrated. For this reason, you must ensure the users never see a message informing them that a script is unresponsive.

Divide Long-Running Scripts into Chunks

If you are running code that you know will take some time to execute, potentially causing this message dialog box to appear, you can restructure your JavaScript routine to break it into smaller chunks, each one calling the next after a split-second delay. The browser identifies this as several smaller scripts, rather than one longer routine, and the slow-running script dialog box is not displayed.

To take advantage of this technique, you can use the code pattern shown in Listing 5-4, adapted for JavaScript by Julien Lecomte of Yahoo! (his personal blog is at http://www. julienlecomte.net/), to divide your long-running routine into smaller chunks. Using this routine, you can update a progress bar or other visual indicator based on the current state of completion of the larger routine:

Listing 5-4. *Julien Lecomte's Code Pattern for Breaking Up Long Scripts into Smaller Blocks*

```
function myLongRoutine(progressFunction [, other arguments]) {
    // Initialize the routine's data variables here

    // The following anonymous function represents a single set of
    // operations on the data
    (function () {

        // Process or operate on the data here
```

```
        if (still data left to process) {
            // If there is still data left to process, execute the progressFunction
            // passing it the current value and total, allowing it to present this
            // information to the end user as, for example, a progress bar
            progressFunction(currentValue, total);

            // Execute the next set of operations on the data after a brief
            // pause to enable the browser to remain responsive. A value of 0
            // milliseconds is used, which ensures the briefest possible pause
            // allowed within the browser before the next operation begins.
            // arguments.callee represents the anonymous function
            window.setTimeout(arguments.callee, 0);
        }
    })(); // Begin executing the anonymous function immediately
}
```

An example usage of this technique can be seen in the sorting algorithm shown in Listing 5-5.

Listing 5-5. *A Long-Running Sort Routine Split into Smaller Code Blocks*

```
function sort(progressFunction, data) {
    var counter = 0;
    var total = 1000;
    var progressBar = document.getElementById('code-progress');

    // Create an anonymous function to encapsulate each processing
    // block of the sort algorithm
    (function() {

        // The sort algorithm itself
        for (var index = total; index < counter; index--) {
            if (data[index] < data[index - 1]) {
                var value = data[index];
                data[index] = data[index - 1];
                data[index - 1] = value;
            }
        }
        counter++;

        // Execute the progress function now this iteration has completed, to keep
        // the user informed of progress
        progressFunction(counter, total, progressBar);
```

```
        if (counter < total) {
            // If we haven't completed all iterations of the sort, execute the next
            // block after a short delay
            window.setTimeout(arguments.callee, 0);
        }
    })();
}

// The progress function simply updates a visual progress bar with an
// indication of how far through the routine the code has reached
function progress(value, total, progressBar) {
    var percentageComplete = Math.round((value / total) * 100);
    progressBar.style.width = percentageComplete + "%";
}

// Kick things off on the page once the DOM is ready to be accessed
$.onDomReady(function() {
    // Generate an array of random numbers to sort
    var data = [];
    for (var index = 0, length = 1000; index < length; index++) {
        data[i] = Math.floor(Math.random() * length);
    }

    // Execute the sort routine with this data
    sort(progress, data);
});
```

Since this technique actually interrupts the code from executing in order to keep the browser responsive, the full routine takes longer to execute than if it were to run directly. You can reduce the effect of this by running each smaller code block multiple times, instead of only a single time.

Use a Timer to Run Code Blocks Multiple Times

Running each code block of a long routine multiple times ensures there are fewer breaks. You can still make sure the browser does not lock up by introducing a timer to your code pattern. This timer will allow multiple executions of each code block until a fixed duration has been reached, at which point, it will force a break to occur. If you ensure these fixed durations do not exceed around 50 milliseconds, you continue to keep the browser responsive, but allow more code to execute without interruption. Consider it a compromise approach that keeps the code running and the user happy.

Listing 5-6 shows how the sort function of Listing 5-5 can be modified to use a timer to improve the time taken to execute a long routine.

Listing 5-6. *Improved Performance of the Sort Algorithm in Listing 5-5*

```
function sort(progressFunction, data) {
    var counter = 0;
    var total = 1000;
    var progressBar = document.getElementById('code-progress');

    (function() {
        // Store the time at the beginning of execution of this code block
        var startTime = (new Date()).getTime();

        // Store a reference to this function to call it later
        var anonFunction = arguments.callee;

        // Encapsulate the sort algorithm within a nested function so it can be
        // called multiple times within the surrounding anonymous function
        function sortAlgortihm() {
            for (var index = total; index < counter; index--) {
                if (data[index] < data[index - 1]) {
                    var value = data[index];
                    data[index] = data[index - 1];
                    data[index - 1] = value;
                }
            }
            counter++;

            // Get the current time after execution of the algorithm
            var endTime = (new Date()).getTime();

            if ((endTime - startTime) < 50) {
                // If we have been processing for less than 50 milliseconds,
                // continue sorting
                sortAlgorithm();
            } else {
                // Otherwise the duration limit has been released so force a
                // break to occur before continuing execution
                window.setTimeout(anonFunction, 0);
            }

            // Update the progress bar
            progressFunction(counter, total, progressBar);
        }

        // Start execution of the sort algorithm
        sortAlgorithm();
    })();
}
```

Anticipating Your Site Visitors' Needs

When you have included all the performance enhancements you can to your web application, and provided feedback to your users where necessary, the next step in improving the perceived performance of your web application is to attempt to anticipate your users' actions. If you have a good idea about what your end users are going to be acting upon at a particular stage of your web application flow, you can prepare for that action, loading in extra data or executing some code in advance. This way, when they take that action, they don't need to wait as long to see a result. You're not improving the actual performance of your code, but rather distributing the loading and executing of code in order to adjust the perceived responsiveness of your web application.

Preload Content

Once your page has loaded, and the user is interacting with your page, there is a lot of "dead time" in the browser, when the browser is not executing scripts, not loading data, not rendering the page—not doing anything. You can take advantage of this time to preload data or execute scripts that your users will likely need to interact with your application at a later time.

"Lazy loading" of components can help speed up the load time of your page. By loading only the content you need to display the initial view of your page, the page takes less time to be ready for your user. Nonessential components can be loaded on demand through JavaScript at predetermined times or based on some other action.

Consider what your users would need to achieve next in the flow of your web application, and use that information to determine which components and extra data you could preload and execute in advance to provide a better experience for your users.

A simple example is the web mail client, now a staple part of most online web application suites, attempting to re-create the desktop e-mail package within a browser window. The standard initial view when logging in to a web mail client is the inbox. When web mail users arrive at their inbox, they are probably going to want to open and read any unread messages. In most cases, web mail clients do not load any messages until the users click the message they wish to view. Then the message data is loaded, and the data is applied to the HTML template and placed within the page using DOM manipulation, displaying the message to the user.

By preloading unread message data once the initial view of the web application has loaded, you reduce the time for the user to see the message, which provides an instant improvement on the usual method of loading the data when the user clicks the message. Figure 5-4 shows a flowchart describing this behavior.

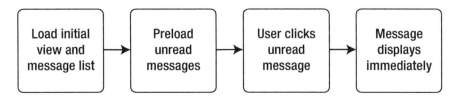

Figure 5-4. *Flow of handling unread mail messages*

Load Navigation Levels Efficiently

A common feature of many large sites is a drop-down navigation menu at the top of the page. When the users move their mouse over the top navigation, the subnavigation appears beneath it, as shown in Figure 5-5.

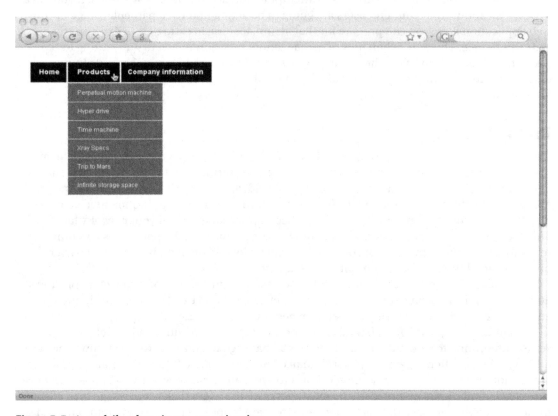

Figure 5-5. *A multilevel main page navigation*

Typically, this entire menu structure will be coded in HTML on the page in the following way:

```
<ul id="top-navigation">
    <li><a href="/">Home</a></li>
    <li>
        <a href="/products/">Products</a>
        <ul class="sub-navigation">
            <li><a href="/products/1/">Perpetual motion machine</a></li>
            ...
        </ul>
    </li>
    <li><a href="/company/">Company information</a><li>
</ul>
```

You would then use CSS to hide the `<ul class="sub-navigation">` element by default, showing it when users move their mouse over the top-level menu item by using JavaScript.

You can take advantage of the lazy loading technique by initially loading only the HTML for the top-level navigation, without any sublevel navigation, like so:

```
<ul id="top-navigation">
    <li><a href="/">Home</a></li>
    <li><a href="/products/">Products</a></li>
    <li><a href="/company/">Company information</a><li>
</ul>
```

This results in less HTML to load initially, making the web application load faster.

Now suppose that you have a larger navigation structure, with many top-level links, each containing several subnavigation items. The code to represent this would consume potentially up to half of your HTML for each page, causing the initial load time of the page to be considerably longer than you can make it using this lazy loading technique.

Since you are now loading only the top-level of this hierarchical navigation, you need to be able to load in the full navigation via an Ajax request using JavaScript, and then swap out the flat navigation with the hierarchical one at some point after the page has loaded. You have several options for when to load the full navigation:

- When the page, including all external assets and images, has finished loaded, using this code:

```
$.Events.add(window, "load", functionToLoadMenuHTML);
```

- When the HTML is accessible to the DOM, using this code:

```
$.onDomReady(functionToLoadMenuHTML);
```

- When the user moves the mouse or brings focus to the navigation

Using the third option, you delay loading until you believe the user actually wants to do something with the navigation. Rather than loading this content regardless of what the user does, you are anticipating the actual needs of the user. This behavior can be achieved using the code in Listing 5-7.

Listing 5-7. *Loading Full Navigation HTML on Interaction with a Placeholder*

```
$.onDomReady(function() {
    // Define a function to retrieve the full navigation HTML via Ajax
    var getNavigationHTML = function() {
        $.Remote.load("full-navigation.html", function(response) {
            // Set the HTML in the correct place on the page
            document.getElementById("top-navigation").innerHTML = response.text;
        });
```

```
        // Never execute this again when the mouse moves over the navigation
        $.Events.remove(document.getElementById("top-navigation"), ➥
            "mouseover", getNavigationHTML
    }

    // Execute this function when the mouse is brought over the top of the
    // navigation element
    $.Events.add(document.getElementById("top-navigation"), "mouseover", ➥
        getNavigationHTML
});
```

Catch Mouse Clicks Early

If you wish to execute some JavaScript code when the user clicks a link or button within your page, consider hooking onto the mousedown event, rather than the click event. The browser fires the click event after the mouse button has been released; the mousedown event is fired when the mouse button is pressed initially. By hooking into the mousedown event, you are able to execute your code a few valuable milliseconds sooner than when listening for the click event.

```
$.Events.add(document.body, "mousedown", function() {
    alert("I fire first!");
});

$.Events.add(document.body, "click", function() {
    alert("I am slow in comparison!");
});
```

Summary

In this chapter, you have discovered some ways to make your web site appear to be responsive, even when some actions take a while to complete. You can improve your users' experience of your site by giving them visual feedback when a more time-consuming action affects the performance of your RIA. You have seen how to use the "dead time" in your users' browser to preload and execute data that they may wish to use later on in the page's life cycle, making your web applications appear to be more responsive. Responsiveness is key to web applications, which are often attempting to replicate desktop applications within the browser.

That brings us to the end of the part of this book dealing with web application performance. Try to apply the techniques you've learned to your own web applications. You will find that your users will be really happy with the results. Happy users mean less frustration, fewer complaints, more satisfied clients, and fewer sleepless nights for you, as the developer.

The next part of the book will focus on the user interface and introduce you to several techniques for improving the presentation of your RIAs. Specifically, the next chapter will show you how to apply heading text to your pages using custom fonts that are not installed on your end users' computers.

PART 3

■ ■ ■

Presentation

So far in this book, I have shown how you can develop your code according to best practices, and how to alter that code to get the greatest performance and responsiveness from your web applications. In this, the third and final part of the book, I will take you into the realm of the user interface, introducing you to techniques and third-party reusable components that will help you to build a better-looking and better-behaving RIA. And perhaps you will be inspired to develop your own reusable components and share them with the rest of the web development community!

CHAPTER 6

■ ■ ■

Beautiful Typography

You won't be long into your career as a web developer before you discover the need to format some text in a custom or corporate font—a typeface that is not in the standard set of pre-installed fonts on your end users' computers. You will then need to decide how best to display that stylized text. This chapter presents a number of different solutions to the problem. We'll look at the pros and cons of each method with regard to ease of development and maintainability, accessibility, performance, and visual appearance.

The Challenge

Throughout this chapter, we will attempt to re-create the headings shown in Figure 6-1. The first heading in the figure uses the font Sketch Rockwell, and the second heading uses the Silom font. Neither of these fonts is guaranteed to be installed on your end users' machines. In fact, it's likely that your users won't have these fonts. Therefore, to use them in your site, you will need to represent them by means of one of the techniques covered in this chapter.

Before we get started with any coding, let's take a moment to examine exactly what constitutes a font.

Figure 6-1. *Sample page with two headings displayed in custom fonts*

The Basic Anatomy of a Font

Figure 6-2 shows the parts of a typeface and the terminology used to describe them. Working from the bottom, the *baseline* is the imaginary line upon which most of the characters sit. From the baseline, the character springs up to the *median* line, which is the line above the baseline that marks the top of most characters. The distance between the baseline and the median is the *x-hei*ght, more commonly called the *font size*.

Certain characters, including uppercase letters and lowercase *b, d, f*, among others, have portions of their character above the median line. This portion of the character that sits above the median is known as the *ascender*. Conversely, some characters, such as *g* and *j*, have a segment that sits below the baseline, known as the *descender*.

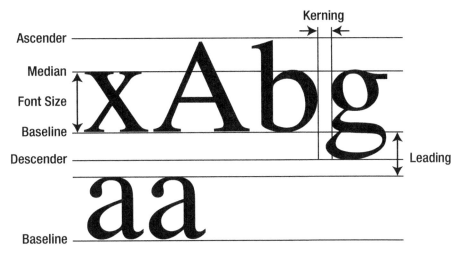

Figure 6-2. *The basic anatomy of the Times New Roman font*

The spacing between individual letters is known as *kerning*. The space between the baseline of one line and the median line of the following line is known as the *leading*, which is the spacing between lines of text.

Table 6-1 shows how this font terminology translates to CSS style properties. Note that the baseline, median, ascender, and descender positions are dictated by the typeface itself, and are not alterable through CSS. This is because to do so would severely change the appearance of the font on the page, stretching it disproportionately in any one direction.

Table 6-1. *Typeface CSS Style Properties*

Typeface Term	CSS Style Property
X-height (font size)	`font-size`
Kerning	`letter-spacing`
Leading	`line-height`[a]

a. *The* `line-height` *CSS property measures the distance between the baselines of two lines, not the baseline of one line and the median of the next line.*

Let's now take a look at some different techniques for rendering text in custom fonts onto your pages.

Using Static Images for Text

Many developers' first foray into custom fonts involves creating a flat image file of the text heading to be displayed using a graphics program, such as Adobe Photoshop. This image is then referenced as a foreground image within a tag on the page, with the text for the heading situated within the alt attribute of the <img> tag, like this:

```
<h1><img src="heading-news.png" alt="News" /></h1>
<h2><img src="heading-new-product.png" ➥
    alt="New product released: Human Teleporter" /></h2>
```

This is a quick and simple method for getting your stylized headings onto your page. However, this approach has some limitations involving maintainability and accessibility.

What if you need to change the text? You will need to re-create the image within your graphics software. If you have content that could change on a regular basis, such as the news article headings in this chapter's example (Figure 6-1), maintenance becomes a rather frequent, repetitive, and monotonous task.

Additionally, there are two issues with accessibility in this technique. One arises for users who are visually impaired and need to magnify text to read it (using extra software or their web browser's built-in zoom feature). In this case, the text size will increase but the images will not. In fact, if the images were to zoom, the pixelated nature of those image files would become more apparent, rendering them harder to read. Making text harder to read is not our goal for our end users, visually impaired or otherwise.

The second accessibility issue with this technique is the use of the alt attribute:

```
<h1><img src="heading-news.png" alt="News" /></h1>
```

If a screen reader application were to read aloud the contents of this <h1> tag, the user would hear that there is an image tag within the header and then hear its associated alt attribute value. The preferred approach is to include the same text directly within the heading tag, like this:

```
<h1>News</h1>
```

If this were read aloud, the user would hear just the header text you wish for them to hear, reducing the chance of confusion for the end user.

Similarly, search engine spiders or other remote computers accessing the content on your page would not always be able to extract the proper heading text from the markup used in the first example and, if they were, they might not assign that text as much precedence in their system as the more simplified heading of the second example. The simpler and more semantic the heading text, the more understandable it will be to your end users.

Let's take the approach of working with the more semantic HTML markup for our heading text, and use CSS to apply a background image to the heading tag, simultaneously hiding the text from view. The HTML for our headings becomes the more idealistic form:

```
<h1>News</h1>
<h2>New product released: Human Teleporter</h2>
```

And now we use CSS style rules to produce the same visual effect as using an <img> tag on the page, our stylized headings:

```
h1,
h2 {
    text-indent: -10000px; /* Hide the real text off the side of the screen */
    font-size: 1px;              /* Ensure the large font size of headers does
                                    not impact the image dimensions */
}

h1 {
    background-image: url(heading-news.png);
    width: 257px;               /* The width of the image */
    height: 65px;               /* The height of the image */
}

h2 {
    background-image: url(heading-new-product.png);
    width: 353px;               /* The width of the image */
    height: 62px;               /* The height of the image */
}
```

The result is exactly the same visual layout as before, except that we have fixed one of the previous method's accessibility disadvantages: we have removed the image tags from within the header tags and replaced them with the sole semantic text representation of each heading. This is much better. However, we still have the problem of maintainability, as updated header text will require new image files to be created. Now let's look at a more maintainable solution.

Generating Images for Text Dynamically

To remove the requirement to keep generating new image files manually whenever you need to change the text in a custom font, you can instead generate text in the required typeface dynamically. This can be done either on the server or within the browser. Let's look at the different techniques available, and their advantages and disadvantages, so you can choose the best solution to fit your application's requirements.

Using CSS to Embed Font Files Directly

Naturally, as developers, we want to use custom fonts on our page in as simple a way as possible. We want to include our text content directly within our HTML pages and use CSS to style that text in the font, color, and size of our choosing, just as we do with the built-in fonts, such as Arial, Helvetica, and Times New Roman.

The simplest approach is to specify your custom typefaces directly using CSS in the following way, in the standard format:

```
h2 {
    font-family: "Silom", monospace:
}
```

Here, we dictate that the contents of all `<h2>` heading tags should utilize the Silom font. If this font is not installed on the user's machine, it should fall back to using the default monospace font specified by the browser. (In a monospace font, all the characters occupy the same width.) Of course, not many end users will actually have the Silom font, so most browsers will display the default monospace font instead.

It is not appropriate to ask your end users to download and install custom fonts on their computer just to display your web page as it was designed. In many cases, the user may not even know how to do this, or it may not be allowed in their environment (such as in a corporate office).

CSS Web Fonts

Ideally, we need a way for the browser to load custom font files on demand when they are referenced through CSS. Interestingly, the ability to embed custom font files through CSS in this way has existed in IE since version 4, although it had been all but forgotten until recently. It regained attention with the proposal of a W3C specification known as CSS Web Fonts, which seeks to have all browser manufacturers conform to the same method of implementing this useful feature. This new recommendation, which you can read online at http://www.w3.org/TR/css3-webfonts/, allows web developers to declare new fonts for use on the page and have the associated font file load when that font name is used in the rest of the CSS style rules.

Caution CSS Web Fonts is a new W3C recommendation, and as such, is not fully implemented in all browsers. Since this technique is a W3C recommendation, once it is widely adopted by browsers, it should be considered to be the de facto standard for custom font embedding within CSS.

Take a look at the following description for the Silom font in the W3C Web Fonts format:

```
/* Declare a new font face for use within the rest of the CSS */
@font-face {

    /* Declare the name this new font will take in the CSS file */
    font-family: "Silom";

    /* Locate the font file on the server and declare that its format is the */
    /* TrueType font format */
    src: url(/assets/fonts/silom.ttf) format("truetype");
}
```

You can then reference the Silom font as you might expect within your CSS, in the same way as before:

```
h2 {
    font-family: "Silom", monospace;
}
```

Provided your browser supports the `@font-face` directive for loading external fonts in this way, you will see the Silom font in use. Browsers that do not support this technique will use the fallback font specified in the `font-family` style property—in this case, the browser's default monospace font.

Two different font formats are supported by this technique: OpenType and TrueType. OpenType is an international ISO standard and intended as a replacement for the proprietary TrueType font format, which was developed by Apple and requires licensing for its use.

Problems with Embedded Font Files

Unfortunately, browser support for the CSS Web Fonts technique is mixed at best. Firefox versions 3.5 and later support TrueType and OpenType font formats using this technique, but at the time of writing, this browser version does not have a large installed user base. The WebKit engine team has implemented this technique, and its support is available within Google Chrome 2 and Safari 3 browsers. IE versions 4 and later support the technique, but only using their proprietary Embedded OpenType (EOT) font format, a compressed and restricted version of the OpenType format.

With the EOT format, the file itself contains a list of trusted sites on which the font may be used. This restriction means that those wishing to copy and reuse a copyright-limited font file on their own web site will not be able to do so. To generate EOT fonts, you need to use Microsoft's Web Embedding Fonts Tool (WEFT), available from `http://www.microsoft.com/typography/web/embedding/weft3/weft01.htm`.

Another problem with this approach is that providing links to font files within your CSS may cause you to stumble across a legal gray area in terms of copyright. Many of your clients, corporate or otherwise, will use specific fonts for their branding, and typically, they will have paid a substantial amount to license those fonts for exclusivity. Since your CSS is publicly accessible—it must be to be usable by the browser—and is written in plain text, avid developers visiting your site may trawl through your CSS. Upon spotting a reference to an external font file, they may choose to download that font file from your server via its URL and use it, without paying for the rights to do so. This is a big copyright no-no, and most organizations do not want to allow their exclusive fonts to be inappropriately used.

Microsoft is pushing for its EOT specification to be a W3C recommendation, the main reason being that its generated font files are wrapped in a Digital Rights Management (DRM) layer. This means that the fonts can be used only by the licensed party on a list of trusted web sites embedded within the file itself. Of course, it is still possible for this type of file to be downloaded, but it cannot be used except for in the context in which it was designed, namely on the web site on which it was created to be used.

An alternative method of download restriction, known as Cross-Origin Resource Sharing, is being considered for W3C recommendation (see `http://www.w3.org/TR/cors/`), and is being implemented already by Mozilla in its Firefox browser. This is a technique that can apply to any server-requested content, not just font files. It limits the content to being delivered to the page only if the requesting domain is in a whitelist of allowed domains, maintained at the server. This access list uses new HTTP response headers, most notably the `Access-Control-Allow-Origin` header, which contains a list of domains permitted to access the requested content. For example, to allow access only to the domain `http://mydomain.com`, the following HTTP header would be added to the response:

```
Access-Control-Allow-Origin: http://mydomain.com
```

To allow access to all domains, the wildcard character can be used in place of a specific domain name:

```
Access-Control-Allow-Origin: *
```

There are two downsides to this technique as it stands:

- The font file requested would still be downloaded and cached within the browser, allowing users, if they were maliciously inclined, to take that file from their computer and upload it to their own domain, thus bypassing the access control restriction.

- Since this is still a work in progress at W3C, its browser implementation is currently too limited to be of much use. As with other standards, you won't want to use it until the technology is finalized and adopted within all the major browsers.

For now, you may wish to program your server directly to send out the font file to the requesting page only if that page is hosted on the same server. You can do this by checking domain names prior to sending the content. Unfortunately, this requires some extra processing time on the server, which could have an impact on the performance of your page, especially if applied to all external files.

Having the Server Generate Text Images

Rather than manually creating each custom-styled heading image yourself, why not rely on your web server to perform this generation dynamically on your behalf? Suppose that your server contains a script that accepts a text string as a parameter through the query string of its URL and returns an image file for inclusion on your page. The URL to create a styled header image rendering the title "News" might look something like this, where generate-image is the name of the script file generating the image:

```
http://www.myserver.com/generate-image?text=News
```

In order to make this work on your particular web server, you need to use the appropriate server-side technology and prewritten code component to download, or write your own. Now let's look at the basic scripting required for a few common server technologies: PHP, ASP.NET, and JSP.

Dynamic Image Generation in PHP

PHP provides built-in methods that allow you to generate blank canvases and to draw graphical components, including text in custom typefaces, within those canvases. The code in Listing 6-1 shows how to generate text images in PHP.

Listing 6-1. *Generating Images Containing Text in Custom Fonts Using PHP*

```
// First, we need to know the actual text we wish to represent. Assuming the text
// is being passed to this script via a query string parameter named text in the
// URL, we can extract the text to display from the URL into a variable with the
// following line of code.

$text = $_GET['text'];
```

```
// Now we that have our text, we need to know how big to create our empty canvas to
// completely encompass the rendered text in our chosen font. To establish the size
// of the bounding box surrounding our text, we can call a handy function,
// ImageTTFBBox, passing it the font size, display angle, font file location and the
// actual text we wish to represent.

$fontFilename = 'font-file-location.ttf';
$size = 24;
$angle = 0;
$boundingBox = @ImageTTFBBox($size, $angle, $fontFilename, $text);

// The variable $boundingBox is an array of points around the bounding box from
// which we can establish the width and height we require our canvas to be.

$lowerLeftCornerX = $boundingBox[0];
$lowerLeftCornerY = $boundingBox[1];
$lowerRightCornerX = $boundingBox[2];
$lowerRightCornerY = $boundingBox[3];
$upperRightCornerY = $boundingBox[5];
$width = abs($lowerRightCornerX - $lowerLeftCornerX);
$height = abs($upperRightCornerY - $lowerRightCornerY);

// Creating an empty canvas of our required dimensions is then as simple as
// calling the PHP method ImageCreate.

$image = @ImageCreate($width, $height);

// The first thing to do with our blank canvas is to set its background color. When
// we set colors, we need to separate the red, green, and blue components and
// represent them in hexadecimal. In this case, we wish to use a white background.
// Within CSS, we would specify this as #ffffff; in PHP we would specify it in the
// following format.

$background_hex['red'] = 0xFF;
$background_hex['green'] = 0xFF;
$background_hex['blue'] = 0xFF;

// To set the background color of our canvas, we use the ImageColorAllocate
// method. This method must be called for every color to be
// used within our canvas, though its first use against an image canvas always sets
// the background color, which is what it is used for here.

$background  = @ImageColorAllocate($image, $background_hex['red'], ➥
    $background_hex['green'], $background_hex['blue']);

// Now we have our empty canvas with a colored background. We move onto the
// contents of our canvas: the text. We already have the location of the font file
```

```
// to use and the size of the text. Before we write into the canvas, we need to
// also specify its color. We must specify colors in their constituent hexadecimal
// parts as with our background color, previously, and make a call to
// ImageColorAllocate to create the color reference required by other PHP
// methods later.

$color_hex['red'] = 0x00;
$color_hex['green'] = 0x00;
$color_hex['blue'] = 0x00;
$color = ImageColorAllocate($image, $color_hex['red'], $color_hex['green'], ➥
    $color_hex['blue']);

// Before we render our text into the canvas, we need to calculate the baseline
// position of our font, which will be the point at which the text is rendered from,
// as we saw in Figure 6-2, earlier in the chapter.

$top = -$lowerLeftCornerX;
$left = abs($upperRightCornerY - $lowerRightCornerY) - $lowerLeftCornerY;

// Render the text onto the canvas.

ImageTTFText($image, $size, $angle, $left, $top, $color, $fontFilename, $text);

// And finally we draw the canvas to the screen as a PNG image file using the
// ImagePNG function, first setting the correct response header to the browser,
// and finally destroying the reference to the created canvas to conserve PHP
// application memory.

header('Content-type: image/png') ;
ImagePNG($image) ;
ImageDestroy($image);
```

Assuming you save the code in Listing 6-1 to your web server root using the file name generate-image.php, you can generate images dynamically using the following image URL format within your HTML and CSS:

```
/generate-image.php?text=News
```

Dynamic Image Generation in ASP.NET (C#)

As you may be aware, the ASP.NET platform supports multiple coding languages. For the following example, I have opted to use the C# language, though it should be fairly easy to convert into other languages, as the API objects and methods are virtually identical between languages.

Create a new ASPX web form called generate-image.aspx, and then add the code in Listing 6-2 to the automatically generated code-behind file, generate-image.aspx.cs.

Listing 6-2. *Generating Images Containing Text in Custom Fonts Using C#*

```csharp
namespace CustomImage
{
    using System;
    using System.Drawing;
    using System.Drawing.Text;
    using System.Web;

    public class GenerateImage: System.Web.UI.Page
    {
        protected void Page_Load(object sender, EventArgs e)
        {
            // Extract the text we wish to display from the query string
            // parameter text.
            string text = Request.QueryString["text"];

            // Define variables for the other information we need to represent our
            // font: the font file location, its size, color, and background color
            // of the canvas we wish to display the text on top of.

            string fontFileLocation = "font-file-location.ttf";
            int size = 24;
            Color color = Color.Black;
            Color backgroundColor = Color.White;

            // Next, we create a new Bitmap object, which represents the empty
            // canvas within which we will place our text. We start with a catch-22
            // situation, however, as we want to create a canvas as large as the
            // text we wish to represent, but unfortunately we can't measure the
            // dimensions of the text without having a canvas to put the text on.
            // The way we overcome this hurdle is by starting off with a dummy
            // canvas, measuring 1 pixel by 1 pixel in size, which we will use as
            // the basis for our text measurements and then replace with the
            // real canvas later.

            Bitmap canvas = new Bitmap(1, 1);

            // Within ASP.NET, the Graphics class contains the methods we need to
            // draw and measure text that sits on the canvas. The first step before
            // using these methods is to declare an instance of the object and
            // associate it with our canvas.

            Graphics graphics = Graphics.FromImage(canvas);

            // Before writing any text, we need to define our font. ASP.NET defines
            // two types of font collections: the fonts installed on the system and
            // a private collection of fonts that can be loaded dynamically
```

```
// from a file for temporary use. It is the latter we need to use, so we
// create a new private font collection and add our font to it using the
// file location of the TrueType font we declared earlier.

PrivateFontCollection myFonts = new PrivateFontCollection();
myFonts.AddFontFile(Server.MapPath(fontFileLocation));

// Individual fonts are always associated with font families, which are
// a collection of related fonts that belong together. These families
// consist of variations of the same font, such as bold or italicized
// versions of the same font. Now we have added our font to our private
// font collection, it is stored within its family group, which has been
// defined within the font file and extracted automatically by ASP.NET.
// To get a font reference we can use in our code, we must get to it
// through its font family. We know that we have only added one font,
// which can only belong to one font family, so we can get this font
// family in code.

FontFamily myFontFamily = myFonts.Families(0);

// Now we can create a reference to the specific font within this family
// in the required size, which we choose to measure in pixels.

Font myFont = new Font(myFontFamily, size, FontStyle.Regular, ➥
    GraphicsUnit.Pixel);

// Now we have our text and a definition of our font, we need to measure
// the space that text will consume when written out to our canvas. We
// use the MeasureString method to achieve this, passing it the text to
// render and the font definition, and it gives back the width and
// height dimensions of the rendered text.

int width = Convert.ToInt32(graphics.MeasureString(text, myFont).Width);
int height = Convert.ToInt32(graphics.MeasureString( ➥
    text, myFont).Height);

// With the width and height of the rendered text established, we now
// need to re-create our canvas using these dimensions and specifying
// a color depth for the final image (24-bit RGB in this case).

canvas = new Bitmap(width, height, PixelFormat.Format24bppRgb);
graphics = Graphics.FromImage(canvas);

// We have our final canvas created, so we can start to build up what
// will be the final image. Let's start this by filling the canvas with
// our background color, which we defined earlier as white.
```

```
        graphics.Clear(backgroundColor);

        // Now, before we can write our text onto the canvas, we need to
        // generate an instance of the ASP.NET concept of a brush to paint
        // the text with. We don't want anything too fancy for now, so we'll
        // instantiate a solid color brush, using the foreground text color we
        // assigned earlier.

        SolidBrush brush = new SolidBrush(color);

        // OK, now everything is set up ready for us to paint our text onto the
        // canvas with our selected font. The following code draws the text
        // onto the canvas using our brush, starting at the top left corner of
        // the canvas area.

        int topLeftCornerX = 0;
        int topLeftCornerY = 0;
        graphics.DrawString(text, myFont, brush, topLeftCornerX, ➥
            topLeftCornerY, StringFormat.GenericTypographic);

        // We have our canvas all ready to display, so the next step is to
        // actually draw it out to the screen as a PNG-format image. Before
        // that, we first send the correct content type header to the browser
        // so it will display the data as an image, and finally we free up the
        // application memory taken up by the canvas for use by the rest
        // of the web server.

        Response.ContentType = "image/png";
        canvas.Save(Response.OutputStream, ImageFormat.Png);
        canvas.Dispose();
    }
  }
}
```

After connecting your web form to your new code-behind file, you should be able generate images dynamically in your predefined font using the following image URL format within
your HTML and CSS code:

```
/generate-image.aspx?text=News
```

Dynamic Image Generation in Java/JSP

You may have a Java-supporting web server with which you create and run JSP pages. In this
case, the procedure for dynamic text image generation is similar to that for PHP and ASP.NET:
you create an empty canvas, draw your text onto it using your specified font, and then send
that canvas to the browser with the correct content type.

Enter the code in Listing 6-3 into a new JSP file, saving it as generate-image.jsp.

Listing 6-3. *Generating Images Containing Text in Custom Fonts in JSP*

```jsp
<%
    // Let's kick things off by grabbing the value of the text parameter from the
    // query string, which we'll use as the text to render within our image.

    String text = request.getParameter("text");

    // Next, we'll declare a few variables for use later in our code, which we'll
    // use to store our font file location, the text size we wish to use and the
    // foreground and background colors for the text and canvas, respectively.

    String fontFileLocation = "font-file-location.ttf";
    float size = 24f;
    Color color = Color.BLACK;
    Color backgroundColor = Color.WHITE;

    // Now we've defined our variables, let's create an object instance to represent
    // the font we wish to use, which we'll grab from the server file system, and
    // then set our desired size.

    Font font = Font.createFont(Font.TRUETYPE_FONT, ➥
        new java.io.FileInputStream(fontFileLocation));
    font = font.deriveFont(size);

    // Before we create our canvas and draw our text onto it, we first establish how
    // large we need that canvas to be by measuring the dimensions of the text
    // drawn in our font using a temporary container to perform the measurement
    // within.

    FontRenderContext fontRenderContext = new FontRenderContext();
    TextLayout textLayout = new TextLayout(text, font, fontRenderContext);
    Rectangle2D dimensions = textLayout.getBounds();
    int width = (int)Math.ceil(dimensions.getWidth());
    int height = (int)Math.ceil(dimensions.getHeight());

    // Now we've established the width and height our canvas needs to be, we can
    // create our empty canvas, specifying a high color depth.

    BufferedImage canvas = new BufferedImage(width, height, ➥
        BufferedImage.TYPE_INT_RGB);

    // The methods we need to draw within this empty canvas are contained within
    // Java's Graphics2D class. Before we can use these methods, we must
    // associate an instance of this object with our canvas.

    Graphics2D graphics = canvas.createGraphics();
```

```
// Our next step is to fill the canvas with our background color, which is
// achieved by setting the color to be used and then creating a solid rectangle
// shape to fill the canvas with the set color.

graphics.setColor(backgroundColor);
int topLeftPositionX = 0;
int topLeftPositionY = 0;
graphics.fillRect(topLeftPositionX, topLeftPositionY, width, height);

// With our canvas filled with our background color, we can now prepare to
// write our text on top. We need to set the color and font of the text, and
// also the top and left positions of the font's baseline, the imaginary
// horizontal line upon which characters of a font are positioned, as
// described in Figure 6-2, earlier in this chapter.

graphics.setFont(font);
graphics.setColor(color);
float baseLinePositionX = (float)-dimensions.getX();
float baseLinePositionY = (float)-dimensions.getY();

// With the color, size and position set, we are finally in a position to draw
// our text onto the canvas.

graphics.drawString(text, baseLinePositionX, baseLinePositionY);

// With our canvas complete, it remains for us to output the canvas to the
// browser, first correctly setting the content type of the response and finally
// returning the application memory used by the canvas to the server for use
// elsewhere.

response.setContentType("image/png");
ServletOutputStream outputStream = response.getOutputStream();
PNGImageEncoder imageEncoder = ➥
    PNGCodec.createPNGEncoder(outputStream);
imageEncoder.encode(canvas);
graphics.dispose();
%>
```

You should now be able to dynamically generate images in your custom font using the following image URL format within your HTML and CSS:

```
/generate-image.jsp?text=News
```

Extending the Server-Script Code Routines

The three code examples in Listings 6-1, 6-2, and 6-3 demonstrate the basic structure of routines to display text within images using custom fonts. They have plenty of room for improvement. Here are some suggestions to consider if you choose to enhance these routines:

Code defensively: You will almost definitely need to add some error checking to the routine, and to make sure that the query string parameter is actually supplied. Removing assumptions in this way will improve the stability of the code.

Cache all created images: To improve performance, you should consider saving each created image canvas to disk, perhaps with a file name similar to the text being rendered. That way, when a future request is made for the same heading, you can check whether the image has already been created and exists on disk. Loading in precomputed images in this way saves a lot of processing power and time on the server.

Consider text wrapping: Some longer headings you wish to replace may not fit into the layout dimensions of the web application in your browser. In this case, you will require the ability to wrap the text at the final word break before the character limit you define.

Add text smoothing: Some graphics libraries within PHP, ASP.NET, and Java allow you to set the amount of smoothing on the text, known as the anti-aliasing effect. Smoothing your fonts will help prevent the edges of your text from appearing jagged and of poor quality.

Add other query string parameters: You may wish certain headings to appear in bold, italics, underlined, or even in different colors or using *alternative* fonts. Why not watch for extra query string parameters passed to your routine and vary your text attributes based on these parameter values? This would be far better than duplicating your code to deal with these different uses.

Generating Text in Custom Typefaces Using Flash

Adobe's Flash Player is an external browser plug-in installed on virtually all end users' browsers. Exceptions include certain mobile browsers and older browsers. Latest statistics for installed versions are available on Adobe's web site at `http://www.adobe.com/products/player_census/flashplayer/version_penetration.html`.

You must be wary of using Flash Player, or any other type of plug-in, when it is not necessary. Use it only to provide functionality that does not already exist within the browser, and even then, only if you provide suitable backup content for those users who do not have the plug-in. Using Flash Player to display headings in embedded fonts fits this role perfectly. If the plug-in isn't present, you can fall back to the same heading text in a different, though appropriate, font.

Flash supports font embedding within movie files and even allows you to specify which characters from the font set are embedded. This means that you don't need to embed every character into every movie, which can save on file size. For example, if you provide text only to an English-speaking audience, you might prevent all extended characters from being embedded within your Flash movie.

The simplest approach is to create a Flash movie containing your embedded font and a dynamic text layer. The movie would then expect to receive a variable containing the text to render passed to it from the HTML, often passed to Flash via the query string of the movie URL itself. The Flash movie would simply take the passed-in text and populate its text layer with the supplied text, which would then be rendered using the embedded font on the page.

Generating Text Using Vector Graphics

Many popular browsers have support for drawing vector graphics within the browser window. Think of vector graphics as ordinary pictures, with lines and curves making up the visual image. Instead of defining the pixels within the image, you can describe how a picture is formed from scratch from these shapes.

By being able to describe images in this way, you make such images resolution- and size-independent. Since you always know how to form an image from scratch from data that describes how the image is constructed, you can simply change a vector, such as the width, and the image will adjust to fit the new space without losing quality. This is actually how most fonts are described within their associated font files, so that resizing text does not result in a loss of quality. Drawing fonts within the browser, in the same way that they are created within font files, provides a great alternative to embedding the actual required font within your CSS, as described earlier.

The following browsers support vector graphics drawing in various forms:

- Firefox 1.5 and up
- IE 6 and up
- Opera 9 and up
- Safari 3.0 and up (including iPhone)
- Google Chrome

As you can see, this represents the majority of browsers on the market today. Using vector graphics is an extremely attractive and viable technique for rendering text in custom fonts. I will cover the topic of drawing within the browser in Chapter 11.

Using Reusable Custom Font Components

By now, you should appreciate the usefulness of a reusable script. As you would expect, ready-to-use components are available for applying custom font headings to your pages in a cross-browser-friendly manner. Developers who have been through the pain of applying the techniques discussed in this chapter, and managed to come out on the other side, have packaged their code and made it available freely for the rest of us to use in our own RIAs.

In this section, we will look at a few of the more popular prepackaged components available: Text2PNG, Scalable Inman Flash Replacement, Facelift Image Replacement, and Typeface.js. I recommend investigating each of these components, finding one that suits your needs, and giving it a try in your own web applications.

Text2PNG

By using the Text2PNG component (`http://text2png.com/`), you can replace text on your page with an image rendered with your chosen typeface. You can choose to replace specific text instances, replace the text in specific tags, or replace all text.

The Text2PNG component generates images dynamically via a web server. You are given the option to host the server-side part of the code yourself or call the code hosted on the developers' servers. If you host the code yourself, on a server running PHP version 4.3 or higher, you can use your own custom fonts, uploaded to a specific folder on the server. Otherwise, you are limited to the about 200 predefined fonts installed on the developers' servers.

Sample Text2PNG Usage

Setting up the component in your own pages is as simple as including the prewritten JavaScript code; writing your CSS to assign the fonts, colors, and sizes you wish to use; and adding a few lines of your own JavaScript to perform the image replacement on the text you choose.

To represent the headings in the example in Figure 6-1, you might write the following HTML code, where text_script.js is the supplied component JavaScript file:

```
<!DOCTYPE html PUBLIC "-//W3C//DTD XHTML 1.0 Strict//EN" ➥
    "http://www.w3.org/TR/xhtml1/DTD/xhtml1-strict.dtd">
<html xmlns="http://www.w3.org/1999/xhtml" lang="en" xml:lang="en">
    <head>
        <title>Text2PNG Example</title>
        <link rel="stylesheet" src="myExample.css" type="text/css" />
    </head>
    <body>
        <h1 id="title">News</h1>
        <h2 id="news-headline">New product released: Human Teleporter</h2>
        <p>Lorem ipsum dolor sit amet, consectetur adipiscing elit...</p>
        <script src="text_script.js" type="text/javascript"></script>
        <script src="my-example.js" type="text/javascript"></script>
    </body>
</html>
```

Within the referenced CSS file, my-example.css, specify the custom font you wish to use first, followed by the acceptable fallback fonts from the list of the default fonts available within most browsers:

```
h1 {
    font-family: 'Sketchy Rockwell', Arial, Helvetica, sans-serif;
    font-size: 1.6em;
}

h2#news-headline {
    font-family: 'Silom', Times New Roman, serif;
    font-size: 1.3em;
}
```

Within your own JavaScript file, my-example.js, you define the headings, text, or portions of the page you wish to replace with images of that text written in your custom font. Three methods are available:

- replace(): Allows you to replace the contents of a single element.
- replaceTags(): Allows you to replace the contents of all specified named tags.
- replaceAll(): Allows you to replace the content within all child elements.

Let's take a look at each in turn.

Caution Don't forget to ensure you make the calls to any JavaScript methods after the DOM is available to read through JavaScript, using the `$.onDomReady()` event of the `$` JavaScript library you started in Chapter 2. If you call these text replacement methods too early in the life cycle of the page, no text will be replaced, and you may even generate a JavaScript error within the browser, which will be shown to the end user (not acceptable!).

Replacing a Single Element

The first method at our fingertips is `replace()`, which creates a PNG image file from the entire text content of a page element. Any child elements or HTML tags within the specified tag will be removed, replaced with the image representation of the text. Using the sample HTML, you could replace the header text within the `<h2 id="news-headline">` tag using the following method call:

```
text2png.replace("news-headline");
```

This method expects to receive either a string representing the `id` attribute of the element to be replaced, as in the preceding example, or a DOM element, like this:

```
text2png.replace(document.getElementById("news-headline"));
```

Both alternatives perform the same functionality, so it is up to you which you prefer to use.

Replacing multiple specific page elements is as simple as passing extra arguments to the `replace()` method for each element you wish to replace. Let's say you wanted to replace the `<h2 id="news-headline">` element as before, and also the text within another page element, `<h1 id="title">`. This can be performed in one method call, like so:

```
text2png.replace("news-headine", "title");
```

This method will replace the text content within all the specified tags on the current page, regardless of how many of each type of tag there are. This is a quick and convenient way to perform replacement. There is no limit to the number of parameters that can be passed to this function, so you could choose to replace just the contents of a single tag or the contents of many tags.

Replacing All Content Within a Specific Named Tag

Text2PNG's built-in `replaceTags()` method performs the same type replacement as the `replace()` method, but it replaces all elements with a given tag name. Let's say that, as in the earlier HTML example, you want to replace all `<h1>` and `<h2>` header tags within your page with their text-image equivalent. To do this, simply use the `replaceTags()` method, like so:

```
text2png.replaceTags("h1", "h2");
```

This method will replace the text content within all the specified tags on the current page, regardless of how many of each type of tag there are. This is a quick and convenient way to perform replacement. There is no limit to the number of parameters that can be passed to this function, so you could choose to replace just the contents of a single tag or the contents of many tags.

Replacing the Contents of All Child Elements

The replaceAll() method provides a simple way to replace the contents of all nested HTML elements below the element passed to the method call. As an example, assume that you have a list of bullet points within your HTML document, like so:

```
<ul id="list">
    <li>Faster and more efficient</li>
    <li>Smaller and lighter</li>
    <li>Beautiful and elegant</li>
</ul>
```

To replace the text within each <li> tag with its image equivalent, use the replaceAll() method, passing it the id attribute value of the surrounding element. This way, the text within all subelements will be replaced in one go:

```
text2png.replaceAll('list');
```

This method also supports multiple parameters. For example, if you have two lists, <ul id="list"> and <ul id="other-list">, you could replace the text within both sets of child nodes with a single call to the replaceAll() method, like so:

```
text2png.replaceAll("list", "other-list");
```

Applying Extra Text Formatting with Text2PNG

The Text2PNG replace(), replaceTags(), and replaceAll() methods each accepts an optional final parameter, specified as a JSON object, that sets certain formatting properties of the resulting text image. Where possible, Text2PNG will attempt to derive the display format of the image from the CSS applied to the original text, before it is replaced. Where there is no CSS property applied, it will then attempt to establish the format from the options object passed to the method call, if that is set. If that is unavailable, default values are set internally to provide a fallback format where needed.

The following example shows how to replace all <h2> tags on the page with their text-image equivalent, applying a couple of extra formatting options in the process:

```
text2png.replaceTags("h2", {
    opacity: 50,
    bold: 1
});
```

The full list of options and CSS rules that are applied to the resulting text can be found in the documentation at the project web site (http://www.text2png.com/).

Text2PNG Appraisal

One of the first things that appealed to me about the Text2PNG component is its ability to read and assess which styles should be applied to the resulting image from the CSS applied to the text being replaced. It makes perfect sense to me that style and visual information should be stored within my CSS style definitions, whether or not I am using JavaScript to perform the replacement.

By specifying in my element's `font-family` CSS property the custom font I wish to use, along with a list of alternative fonts, I am using CSS the same way I would normally. The rare occasion may arise where my end users do not have JavaScript enabled in their browser, but happen to have the custom font I have specified installed on their computer; in that case, the font appears as I intended, and image replacement does not occur.

International languages are supported via the UTF-8 character set, provided the characters exist within the custom typeface being used. The one limitation that does exist is that only text read from left to right is supported at present, so that excludes languages like Arabic and Hebrew.

Performance is always one of my main concerns when using third-party scripts, and I am happy to report that the Text2PNG developers have left no stone unturned in this regard. The developers claim that only five HTTP requests will occur in the process of using their component, which includes everything from the initial loading of their script to the transmission of the final image back to the browser.

Only a single image is sent back to the browser, regardless of how many replacements occurred, because the script uses the CSS sprite technique (described in Chapter 4) to combine all the text to be displayed using custom fonts into a single image file. Unfortunately, the CSS sprite technique is not currently applied to IE 6 or Opera. However, the images returned to all browsers are cached both on the server and within the browser, with an expiration date set ten years into the future from the date the image was first generated.

Support for this component is provided by most browsers, from IE 6 and up, Firefox 2 and up, Safari 3 and up, and Google Chrome. Missing from the list is the Opera browser.

When JavaScript attempts to read the `font-family` style applied to a page element in Opera, only the applied font is returned to the script. Since the custom font most likely won't exist on the user's machine, Opera will return only the name of the backup font that is actually applied. Since this component requires being able to read the name of the custom font in order to ask the server to render the text within an image in that font, problems occur in Opera. Let's hope that a future Opera update addresses this issue, so its users don't lose out. That said, since this is purely a visual effect, provided a suitable backup font is available instead, displaying the same text in a custom font cannot really be described as imperative, but rather considered as "nice to have."

Scalable Inman Flash Replacement

The Scalable Inman Flash Replacement (sIFR) component, originally devised by Shaun Inman (`http://shauninman.com/`), is very popular, largely due to its flexibility, its reusability, and the speed with which it can be applied to an existing page.

This component relies on the Adobe Flash technique discussed earlier in this chapter. To use it, you must create a customized Flash movie file from a supplied template, embedding the custom font you wish to display, along with any specific extended characters needed, into the movie. With the Flash movie file created, you reference the supplied JavaScript and CSS files in your page, and then execute the specific text replacements you require via the JavaScript API made available through the developer's script.

At the time of writing, the current full release of the sIFR component is version 2.0.7, whose output Flash movie files are compatible with Flash Player version 6 (the current release of this plug-in is version 10). A separate stream of development, authorized by Shaun Inman, is now being undertaken by another developer, Mark Wubben. Currently in early beta, this version of sIFR will become version 3 of the component, compatible with Flash Player version

8 and up, giving web developers access to the many improvements to typography and text styling available in the later Flash Player versions.

Full documentation and download details for sIFR version 2 can be found at http://wiki.novemberborn.net/sifr/ and for version 3 at http://wiki.novemberborn.net/sifr3/.

Sample sIFR Usage

Let's go through an example, using the page shown earlier in Figure 6-1 as the goal, and using sIFR version 3. Including the component involves linking to the necessary style sheet and JavaScript files within your HTML file, like so:

```
<!DOCTYPE html PUBLIC "-//W3C//DTD XHTML 1.0 Strict//EN" ➥
    "http://www.w3.org/TR/xhtml1/DTD/xhtml1-strict.dtd">
<html xmlns="http://www.w3.org/1999/xhtml" lang="en" xml:lang="en">
    <head>
        <title>siFR 3 Example</title>
        <link rel="stylesheet" src="sifr.css" type="text/css" />
    </head>
    <body>
        <h1>News</h1>
        <h2 id="news-headline">New product released: Human Teleporter</h2>
        <p>Lorem ipsum dolor sit amet, consectetur adipiscing elit...</p>
        <script src="sifr.js" type="text/javascript"></script>
        <script src="sifr-config.js" type="text/javascript"></script>
    </body>
</html>
```

Assuming you have already downloaded the component, and followed the instructions to export the required fonts into custom Flash files, you must now make references to these movie files from within the script in order to use them on your page. Append a few lines to the sifr-config.js file, supplied by the component, to refer to your font-embedded Flash files:

```
var silom = {
    src: 'silom.swf'
};

var sketchyRockwell = {
    src: 'sketchy-rockwell.swf'
};
```

Note that the src attribute contains the URL of the Flash file, which is relative to the page on which it is being displayed.

The next step, before you perform any text replacement, is to load your Flash movie files into the browser. This is necessary to prevent the movie files from loading each time a replacement is made. To perform this action, append the following line to sifr-config.js:

```
sIFR.activate(silom, sketchyRockwell);
```

Now you're ready to actually perform the text replacement. This is achieved by making a call to the sIFR.replace() function, assigning your fonts to the tags or elements on the page you wish to replace:

```
sIFR.replace(sketchyRockwell, {
    selector: 'h1'
});

sIFR.replace(silom, {
    selector: 'h2'
});
```

The selector engine built into sIFR is fairly flexible. As well as separating multiple selectors using a comma to perform multiple replacements of a particular font simultaneously, you are able to select specific tags and elements using any of the following selection formats, based on CSS selectors:

- h1
- h1 > em
- h1 em
- .foo
- h1.foo
- #bar
- h1#bar
- h1#bar.foo
- #bar.foo
- .foo.baz

Now that all of your required text has been replaced, you may need to tweak the sizing, as in some cases, the sIFR component does not establish the correct font size. If necessary, edit the sifr.css file, appending the following code to the end of the file, within the @screen section:

```
.sIFR-active h1 {
    visibility: hidden;
    font-family: Verdana;
    line-height: 1em;
    font-size: 24px;
}
```

The class .sIFR-active is added to the <body> element of the page when the sIFR script initializes, so this CSS rule will be applied only if that is the case. You set the visibility property of the text to hidden so that the original page text is no longer displayed once your text replacement has occurred. The font size for display is set at the end of the rule. Remember that this style, and any other styles apart from visibility, is necessary only if there are display problems when you perform the replacement in the previous step.

Applying Extra Text Formatting with sIFR

Adobe Flash supports a subset of CSS, which allows some of the text formatting you may wish to apply to be set through your normal style sheet. The CSS class `.sIFR-root` is applied to each Flash movie and allows you to customize styles for the movie itself and its contents. Since the sIFR component, being Flash, keeps references to any child elements of the element you're replacing, these also can be styled directly within the Flash movie via CSS.

Say, for example, you are replacing a list item element, `<li>`, and that tag contains text and a nested link element, `<a>`. The link itself is also passed into the Flash movie, allowing it to continue to be clickable and also styled differently from the rest of the text. This ability alone makes this approach superior to many other text replacement methods.

By default, the customized Flash movie files support bold, italic, underlined, and normal text. Kerning and leading properties can be tweaked as necessary through JavaScript and CSS configuration. Extra text effects are possible also, either by further customizing the Flash movie file to contain those effects or by a series of filters that are present within Flash Player versions 8 and up, which sIFR makes available for configuration through JavaScript. These filters include adding a drop shadow to the text, blurring the text, adding a glow effect around the text, and many others. See the full sIFR version 3 documentation for the list of available effects and how to use them on your page.

sIFR Appraisal

The sIFR component works well for replacing a few headings on a page, and it is very flexible if you wish to use different sizes and styles. However, this component is not recommended if you need to replace more than around five or six headings on a page. At this point, performance takes a noticeable hit, as browser memory is pushed to the limit, slowing down the pages and noticeably impacting page load times.

This component is supported by IE 6 and up, Firefox 2 and up, Safari 2 and up, Google Chrome, and Opera 9.5 and up. There is the obvious requirement that the Flash Player plug-in be installed in the end user's browser. If that plug-in is not detected, no replacement occurs, and the original browser text is displayed, so you don't need to worry about the condition where JavaScript is supported but Flash is not.

Performance of this component is improving with each code release. Flash is fairly notorious for consuming large amounts of browser memory. The developers have ensured that each Flash movie exported has a low refresh rate in order to improve matters further. The Flash movie files are cached within the browser, so that they should need to be downloaded only once, and then reused freely from the cache on subsequent pages. Each movie file consumes around 50KB to 60KB of disk space by default, growing larger if extra characters are embedded within the file. The sIFR version 3 JavaScript file itself weighs in at around 32KB when minified. The combined weight of JavaScript and Flash make this one of the larger third-party text-replacement components.

This component has been around for a few years, so can be considered quite mature, stable, and well supported. Future development will focus on, among other things, the ability to piggyback the code on top of other JavaScript libraries, including jQuery and Prototype. This means that in future, there will be less code duplication, and the JavaScript for the component should become considerably lighter if you are already using one of these libraries in your code.

Again, definitely do not use this technique if you wish to replace more than a handful of headings, as the impact on performance can become rather distracting for your end users.

Facelift Image Replacement

A newer component on the block, Facelift Image Replacement (FLIR, pronounced "fleer"), has similarities with the Text2PNG component discussed earlier. Both use the server-side image generation technique, relying on a PHP server to deliver the image to the requesting web page. One noticeable difference is that with Text2PNG, you can use the developer's own server to perform the generation for free, but with FLIR, you are charged a fee for this service (admittedly, this cost is only $1 per month).

To get the component up and running on your own server requires PHP to be installed. Also, for some of the extended effects supported, it requires ImageMagick (http://www. imagemagick.org/) to be installed.

Sample FLIR Usage

Download the FLIR component from its online home at http://facelift.mawhorter.net/ and install the files on your web server. Next, copy your TrueType font files to your server and create a reference within the config-flir.php file to associate a font file with a CSS font-family value (a few examples are provided within the file to help you get started). Then set up your HTML file with references to the FLIR component's own JavaScript file and include one of your own, along with your own CSS file:

```
<!DOCTYPE html PUBLIC "-//W3C//DTD XHTML 1.0 Strict//EN" ➥
    "http://www.w3.org/TR/xhtml1/DTD/xhtml1-strict.dtd">
<html xmlns="http://www.w3.org/1999/xhtml" lang="en" xml:lang="en">
    <head>
        <title>FLIR Example</title>
        <link rel="stylesheet" src="my-example.css" type="text/css" />
    </head>
    <body>
        <h1>News</h1>
        <h2 id="news-headline">New product released: Human Teleporter</h2>
        <p>Lorem ipsum dolor sit amet, consectetur adipiscing elit...</p>
        <script src="$.js" type="text/javascript"></script>
        <script src="flir.js" type="text/javascript"></script>
        <script src="my-example.js" type="text/javascript"></script>
    </body>
</html>
```

Now configure FLIR to replace only the page elements you choose. Start this off in your own JavaScript file, my-example.js, using the following code:

```
$.onDomReady(function() {
    FLIR.init({
        path: '/path-to-flir/'
    });
    FLIR.auto();
});
```

By default, FLIR will replace all heading tags <h1> to <h5> when the FLIR.auto() method is called. However, this functionality can be overridden by passing in an array of CSS selectors corresponding to the elements you wish to replace. In this example, you could use the following to replace only the two headers you want to use custom fonts:

```
FLIR.auto(['h1', 'h2#news-headline']);
```

By default, FLIR uses the same technique as the Text2PNG component for determining which font you wish to apply to your text: it checks which font-family CSS value you have applied to the element being replaced. This font-family value is then correlated to a font file on the server using your configuration in config-flir.php, and the correct font is displayed upon replacement.

To perform single replacements, or to gain more control over the text style displayed, you can use the FLIR.replace() method, which takes an optional argument defining the text style. Here's how to perform a simple, single replacement on the <h2 id="news-headline"> tag in the HTML example:

```
FLIR.replace('h2#news-headline');
```

To set further style options for the resultant text image, you can add a FLIRStyle object as an additional argument to the FLIR.replace() method—in this case, to specify the exact font required and for the text to wrap over multiple lines:

```
FLIR.replace('h2#news-headline', new FLIRStyle({
    cFont: 'silom',
    mode: 'wrap'
}));
```

See the documentation at the FLIR web site for the full list of FLIRStyle options.

FLIR also has an architecture that supports plug-ins, and two FLIR plug-ins are currently available: FancyFonts and QuickEffects. These let you use the ImageMagick PHP component installed on the web server on your replaced text through JavaScript. More details on using these plug-ins or adding your own can be found on the component's web site.

FLIR Appraisal

As you have seen, the FLIR component is similar to the Text2PNG component. Since both use the same JavaScript technique to read the current style applied to the page elements, the same browser support exists: IE 6 and up, Firefox 2 and up, Safari 3 and up, and Google Chrome. And as with Text2PNG, there is no Opera browser support at present. Default browser text is displayed in other browsers, using the backup font-family values determined through CSS only.

The performance of this component rates slightly poorer than that of Text2PNG, as CSS sprites are not supported in FLIR; separate images are downloaded for each heading image being replaced. This means potentially several more HTTP requests and responses, reducing the speed at which the finished page is displayed. (Obviously, this component could be greatly improved with support for CSS sprite images, and that may be added in a future version.)

The ease of setup of FLIR is to be applauded. Creating direct links between custom CSS font-family typeface names and specific TrueType font files that sit on the server is painless. The default replacement mechanism, which replaces the most standard HTML heading tags, captures and simplifies the majority of developers' desires for such a component. Remember

that the easier it is to set up and use a third-party component like this, the simpler maintenance tasks on it usually are at a later stage.

The JavaScript include file that provides FLIR support to your pages weighs in at around
16KB when minified. Each image produced by the server varies in size, but should usually
weigh in at about 2KB per image, on average, which makes this component comparatively
lightweight.

FLIR is a fairly young component. That is not necessarily a problem, but it could mean
that community support will be somewhat limited until it has been around a little longer and a
few more bugs are ironed out.

Overall, this component uses some smart ideas to produce beautifully styled headers.
However, it is not as performance-friendly as it could be. Also, it requires that your web server
run PHP.

Typeface.js

The free Typeface.js component (`http://typeface.neocracy.org/`) is a fairly recent addition
to the collection of custom font text rendering tools available online. It should be considered
a work in progress for now, but shows promise for a simple component based on the vector
graphics technique described earlier in the chapter.

The font files are converted from TrueType format to a JavaScript file that describes the
various glyphs and properties of the font. This information is then converted through the
JavaScript routine into vectors that are drawn onto the page in place of the text you wish to
replace. You can convert your font files to the JavaScript format using a tool on the project's
web site.

Sample Typeface.js Usage

Let's work through the same example using the headings in Figure 6-1, as we have done
throughout this chapter. Start with the HTML:

```
<!DOCTYPE html PUBLIC "-//W3C//DTD XHTML 1.0 Strict//EN" ➥
    "http://www.w3.org/TR/xhtml1/DTD/xhtml1-strict.dtd">
<html xmlns="http://www.w3.org/1999/xhtml" lang="en" xml:lang="en">
    <head>
        <title>Typeface.js Example</title>
        <link rel="stylesheet" src="my-example.css" type="text/css" />
    </head>
    <body>
        <h1>News</h1>
        <h2 id="news-headline">New product released: Human Teleporter</h2>
        <p>Lorem ipsum dolor sit amet, consectetur adipiscing elit...</p>
        <script src="typeface-0.11.js" type="text/javascript"></script>
        <script src="sketchy-rockwell.typeface.js"➥
            type="text/javascript"></script>
        <script src="silom.typeface.js" type="text/javascript"></script>
    </body>
</html>
```

Include your own style sheet file, `my-example.css`, to define your fonts and other styles:

```
h1 {
    font-family: 'Sketchy Rockwell', Arial, Helvetica, sans-serif;
    font-size: 1.6em;
}

h2#news-headline {
    font-family: 'Silom', Times New Roman, serif;
    font-size: 1.3em;
}
```

You may be wondering why you have not included a separate JavaScript file to initialize the Typeface.js script and perform specific replacements, as you have needed to do with the other third-party components discussed in this chapter. By default, Typeface.js will replace all header tags, `<h1>` to `<h6>`, whose text has been specified through CSS to use a custom font that has been loaded through a JavaScript font description file, generated via the Typeface.js web site. Remember that vectors are resolution- and size-independent, and can be resized without losing quality. This means that all sizes of text are supported through the font representation in a single JavaScript file. If the font is described in this way, Typeface.js will replace the text with a vector-based rendering of the text in your custom font. If no custom font is specified, no replacement will occur.

Now suppose that you want to replace some text within your HTML that isn't within a header tag. You still don't need to write any JavaScript to do this, thankfully. Let's say you have the following text within a paragraph tag on your page that you wish to replace:

```
<p class="coming-soon">This product will be launched shortly!</p>
```

Set the custom font name you wish to display through the `font-family` CSS property for this element and ensure you include a reference to the JavaScript representation of that font. To tell Typeface.js to perform the replacement, simply add the CSS class name `typeface-js` to the element, like this:

```
<p class="coming-soon typeface-js">This product will be launched shortly!</p>
```

The replacement will be made once the page loads.

By enabling functionality through CSS styles, you avoid needing a separate JavaScript file to include code to perform this replacement.

Typeface.js Appraisal

Typeface.js is a newer component using a fairly advanced browser technique. The vector drawing technique is ideally suited for representing TrueType font files, which are vector definitions themselves. However, browser performance is the major issue affecting the adoption of this technique right now.

Browser support is reasonably good, including IE 6 and up, Safari 2 and up, Firefox 1.5 and up, and Google Chrome. Note that Opera is again missing from the list, for the same reasons as for the other components covered in this chapter, with the exception of sIFR.

Vector drawing performance is noticeably poor in most browsers, particularly in IE 6 and 7.

Until browser performance with vector graphics improves across the board, I suggest that text replacement with Typeface.js be limited to around five or six per page. Above this level, you risk irritating your end users.

The Typeface.js JavaScript file weighs around 10KB in its minified form, and each font definition file can be expected to weigh around 60KB to 70KB each. As this component constitutes a pretty hefty download for just a small visual change for your end users, choose wisely.

This component and a very similar one using the same technique, named Cufón (`http://wiki.github.com/sorccu/cufon/about/`), are going to be the ones to watch over the next few months and years. As browsers become more powerful, the abilities web developers can take advantage of increase, allowing us to improve the experience for our end users.

Summary

This chapter covered a number of different techniques and assessed a selection of third-party components that allow you to display text on your web pages in custom fonts not directly supported by the browser. You should now be in a position to make your own decision on which technique is best for you and your web applications. Use that technique to add beautiful typographical text to your web pages, while minimizing the impact on the performance, accessibility, and maintainability of your site. Of course, if none of these techniques or components seems right for you, don't be afraid to experiment with other techniques you invent yourself. If you create something that works, please share your experience with the rest of the web development community, so we may all benefit.

In the next chapter, we will look into the different methods and components available for displaying and controlling audio and video playback within your web applications.

CHAPTER 7

■■■

Multimedia Playback

The desire to use the Internet to broadcast audio and video to consumers has been around almost as long as the Web itself. Multimedia browser plug-ins, usually restricted to certain audio and video formats developed by certain manufacturers, and streaming servers to provide content to these plug-ins, have been around for several years. In recent times, format-specific plug-ins have been shunned by many web developers, who have opted to use the Adobe Flash Player browser plug-in, largely due to its proliferation. Flash Player boasts an installed user base of around 99% of Internet-connected browsers (according to Adobe's own statistics at `http://www.adobe.com/products/player_census/flashplayer/`) and is available for Windows, Mac, Solaris, and Linux platforms.

Flash Player is capable of displaying video and playing audio. The Flash Video (FLV) file format is most commonly used for video, and the popular MP3 format is most commonly used for audio. Version 10 of the Flash Player plug-in also provides support for H.264, a modern video-compression standard that was designed to produce smaller video files and be appropriate for mobile devices as well as desktop machines. H.264 is widely regarded as one of the best video-compression methods currently available. A brief overview of this compression format is available at the Apple web site (`http://www.apple.com/quicktime/technologies/h264/`).

This chapter begins with the important topic of how to deal with accessibility for multimedia content. Then it covers some prebuilt audio and video player components that utilize the Flash Player plug-in. Finally, we'll take a look forward to the future of native browser support for audio and video.

Handling Accessibility

One of our most important considerations as web developers is providing adequate access to our page contents, and this certainly applies to multimedia content. Your end users might be browsing via a text-based or mobile browser, or they may not have the Flash Player installed or JavaScript enabled. You need to provide these users with some relevant content in place of the video component. Similarly, for those users who have a hearing impairment or are in an environment where they are unable to listen to audio—maybe they left their headphones at home—you need to provide an alternative to the audio track.

Most third-party components use JavaScript to replace the contents of a specific tag on a web page with the required multimedia content:

```
<div id="replace-with-multimedia-component"></div>
```

This tag provides a useful location within your HTML to store extra information regarding the video or audio. It could contain metadata about the multimedia file, a description, or even a full transcription of the audio content. This information can be read by users whose browsers do not support the component, or by search engines trolling the page for their indexes. Within the replaced tag, you may also include a download link to the raw audio and video files presented using the component. This provides a backup option for users viewing your page without JavaScript or the Flash Player plug-in to be able to see and hear your multimedia content.

Another accessibility option is to add subtitles to video. Many Flash multimedia components support the display of subtitles. These subtitles can be described in a separate file, containing a transcription of the contents together with the timestamp at which the transcribed text corresponds to the audio. The W3C defines a recommendation for subtitle files, known as Timed Text, which you can read about at http://www.w3.org/AudioVideo/TT/.

Using Reusable Audio Playback Components

The vast majority of third-party multimedia components focus on video, rather than audio. However, you may need to include audio on its own, such as for a radio site or an online music shop.

Here, we'll look at one fully functional ready-to-use audio component that provides all you need to add audio playback to your web pages. Then we'll review some experiments that attempt to force the browser to play audio files without using the Flash Player.

Caution A word of warning for those keen to take advantage of playing sounds on web pages: don't overdo it! Background sounds and sound effects can have their place, but overuse or misplaced use may discourage your end users from using your application. Remember that we are not trying to irritate the users of our web applications, but rather give them a pleasurable browsing experience!

The SoundManager Component

Web developer and fervent music lover Scott Schiller has developed SoundManager, a drop-in component that utilizes version 8 of the Flash Player plug-in to expose its sound-playing ability through a JavaScript API.

To demonstrate the use of this component, let's create a sample page for an imaginary online music store selling MP3 audio tracks, as shown in Figure 7-1. In this example, you will offer the ability to play short samples of the tracks, to entice listeners to pay to download the full song. You'll use the SoundManager component to provide the audio samples when the user clicks the title of each track.

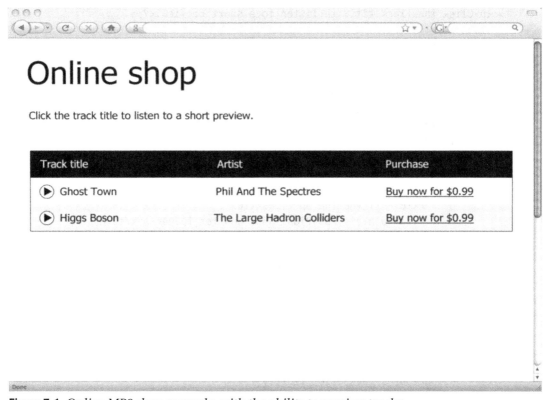

Figure 7-1. *Online MP3 shop example, with the ability to preview tracks*

To begin, visit the SoundManager project web site at `http://www.schillmania.com/projects/ soundmanager2/` and download the files for the component. The most important files are the Flash movie file, which simply exposes Flash's sound player API to JavaScript, and the JavaScript API, which you will use in your own JavaScript code to play sound files on your page.

Next, build the HTML code for the page, as shown in Listing 7-1.

Listing 7-1. *HTML Markup for the Online MP3 Store Example*

```
<!DOCTYPE html PUBLIC "-//W3C//DTD XHTML 1.0 Strict//EN"    ➡
    "http://www.w3.org/TR/xhtml1/DTD/xhtml1-strict.dtd">
<html xmlns="http://www.w3.org/1999/xhtml" lang="en" xml:lang="en">
```

```html
<head>
    <title>SoundManager Example</title>
    <link rel="stylesheet" href="my-example.css" type="text/css" />
</head>
<body>
    <h1>Online shop</h1>
    <p>Click the track title to listen to a short preview.</p>
    <table>
        <thead>
            <tr>
                <th>Track title</th>
                <th>Artist</th>
                <th>Purchase</th>
            </tr>
        </thead>
        <tbody>
            <tr>
                <td id="track1">Ghost Town</td>
                <td>Phil And The Spectres</td>
                <td><a href="/pay?id=1">Buy now for $0.99</a></td>
            </tr>
            <tr>
                <td id="track2">Higgs Boson</td>
                <td>The Large Hadron Colliders</td>
                <td><a href="/pay?id=2">Buy now for $0.99</a></td>
            </tr>
        </tbody>
    </table>

    <!-- Include our $ JavaScript library -->
    <script src="$.js" type="text/javascript"></script>

    <!-- Include the SoundManager component, which connects our page to the
         audio playback component -->
    <script src="soundmanager2.js" type="text/javascript"></script>

    <!-- Include a custom script we'll write later to play our audio files -->
    <script src="my-example.js" type="text/javascript"></script>
</body>
</html>
```

SoundManager will perform all its initializations as soon as possible after the DOM has loaded. Once initialized, SoundManager fires its onload() event, which you hook into in your code to set up your audio. Add the code shown in Listing 7-2 to a file named my-example.js.

Listing 7-2. *JavaScript Code for Online MP3 Store Example*

```
// Execute this code once the SoundManager component has initialized so that we do
// not generate any timing errors

soundManager.onload = function() {

    // Define two audio tracks we wish to play later
    var track1 = soundManager.createSound({

        // Internal identifier for this track
        id: "track-one",

        // Location of MP3 file
        url: "/track1.mp3",

        // Volume level, out of 100
        volume: 50
    });

    var track2 = soundManager.createSound({
        id: "track-two",
        url: "/track2.mp3",
        volume: 50
    });

    $.Events.add(document.getElementById("track1"), "click", function() {
        // When the user clicks the HTML element with an id of track1, the first
        // MP3 file plays
        track1.play();

        // Other SoundManager methods include: stop(), pause(), resume(),
        // setVolume(x) and mute()
    });

    $.Events.add(document.getElementById("track2"), "click", function() {
        // When the user clicks the HTML element with an id of track2, the
        // second MP3 file plays
        track2.play();
    });
}
```

This is a simple example but demonstrates the ease of use of the SoundManager component. You may wish to extend this example so that when the audio is playing, the play icon is switched to a pause icon, and when paused, the play icon reappears. Also, as it stands, it is possible to play several audio tracks simultaneously. You may choose to add some defensive coding techniques to prevent this from occurring.

The SoundManager Feature Set

The SoundManager component is feature-rich and provides everything you need to play audio tracks on your web pages. Through the JavaScript API, you are able to read many dynamically set properties of your audio, including the duration and size of the file, what proportion of it has loaded at any one time, the position within the audio that is currently being played, and whether the audio is currently playing or is paused.

You are also able to configure certain properties yourself when creating the SoundManager object, including the following:

- Whether the audio should stream (play while its loading)

- Its volume

- Its pan position in the stereo field

- Its default start position

- Whether the audio should play automatically or simply load and then wait for user interaction before playing

Each SoundManager object then exposes events that you can hook into to execute specific code when certain properties of the audio change, such as when the audio begins playing, is paused, is resumed, or finishes loading. You can even hook into an event that is called periodically while the audio is playing. For example, you could write code to update the position of a visible progress bar in your page based on the current play position of the audio.

SoundManager also exposes extra functionality to end users who have Flash Player version 9 or later installed, allowing the display of waveform and equalizer data derived from the track being playing. This means that you can provide more visual feedback to your audience, if required.

SoundManager Appraisal

The original SoundManager component has been available since 2004, and its current version since 2007. This gives a level of maturity to the product; plenty of time has been allowed for any bugs to surface and be squashed, and the component has been used on many web sites during that time.

As expected, the component will not work unless your end users are running JavaScript and have Flash Player 8 or later installed. Browser support is very good, including IE 6 and above, Firefox 1.5 and above, Safari 1.3 and above, Opera 9.5 and above, and Google Chrome.

Performance can be considered fairly good, although some older browser/machine configurations have reported a noticeable lag between executing some methods and getting a response from Flash Player. This is believed to be related to Adobe's own Flash-to-JavaScript connection interface, rather than anything the developer has specifically coded. It is most likely you will not notice any performance drawbacks, except if you choose to take advantage of the Flash Player 9–specific functionality. This additional functionality is known to place a large burden on the end user's CPU, causing the page to slow down noticeably. So, you'll want to steer clear of this functionality where possible to avoid problems.

You should be aware of a couple of known limitations with SoundManager, which are derived directly from limitations within Flash Player 8:

- The method for loading a sound file will support only the MP3 file format. I recommend using this file format anyway, but this may mean that you need to re-encode your audio to this format before you utilize this component within your pages.

- There is an issue with looping audio tracks. If you have a track that you wish to play looped, you will find a noticeable audio gap between the end of the track and before the beginning plays again. Currently, there is no work-around for this issue, so take heed.

In terms of file size, the component is fairly light. The JavaScript portion of the component weighs in at 24KB minified. If you choose to use `gzip` compression on your server, as described in Chapter 4, you will find the file effectively becomes 6KB in size when downloaded to the end user's browser. The Flash movie file that performs that actual audio playback is only 4KB, although if you wish to use the Flash Player 9–specific features, a second file is used in its place, which is 8KB.

Overall, I rate this component very highly, as it supports virtually all cases of audio playback you should ever need. You can build playback buttons within your page and have these trigger playback of the audio. You can set the volume, pan, and other settings. You may also construct a page component for feeding back to the end users the position of the playhead within the playing audio, also allowing them to seek to a new position in the audio by clicking with the mouse within the component or by pressing certain predefined keys on their keyboard.

Playing Audio Files Without Flash

Right now, browser support for playing audio natively is fairly poor. Later in this chapter, we look into the proposal for future support of native audio and video playback HTML tags. For now, let's take a look at a few experiments performed by developer Reinier Zwitserloot to allow audio playback within the browser using JavaScript alone. There's no Flash Player here, folks! He writes up his notes and shows demos at the following URL: http://www.zwitserloot.com/files/soundkit/soundcheck.html. You'll find three tests, each consisting of Play and Stop buttons to start and stop the test:

- The first test uses JavaScript to dynamically add an <iframe> on the page, pointing to an external HTML file, which contains little more than an <embed> tag linking to an uncompressed WAV audio format file.

- The second test uses JavaScript to dynamically add an <embed> tag linking to the WAV file directly in the page. Its associated Stop button removes the element from the page; clicking the Play button again adds it to the page. The DOM element exists the whole time in JavaScript and is added and removed from the page via the two buttons.

- The third test is similar to the second, except that when the Play button is clicked, a new DOM object is created each time, instead of reusing the existing object.

The results of the tests are interesting. Generally, they prove that there is not much scope for building a reusable, cross-browser component around the technique, due to the varying results in different browsers.

- In Opera, no sound is played whatsoever for any of the three tests.

- In Safari, all tests succeed in starting the audio playing; however, the first test gives a slight delay before audio feedback is heard, and the second and third tests are incapable of stopping the audio playing once started.

- Running the first test in Firefox produces the same delay before any audio is heard or stopped; however, both buttons work as expected in all three test cases in this browser.

- IE 6 refuses to play any sound using the first technique. The second test succeeds, except that clicking Play after the audio has stopped has the unexpected outcome of restarting the audio from the position where it was last stopped. The third test works as expected in IE 6.

Reinier Zwitserloot also notes that multiple sounds can play simultaneously in all browsers, aside from Opera, and that the MP3, WAV, and MIDI audio formats appear to be supported.

Ideally, developers would like to play audio within the browser natively, avoiding the need for external Flash Player components. Reiner's experiments highlight the patchy nature of this support. Toward the end of the chapter, we will look at a proposed standard for native audio playback within the browser, which is gaining some support from browser manufacturers. For now, the solution to playing audio files within the browser relies on the Flash Player plug-in.

Using Reusable Video Playback Components

Video playback within web pages is now commonplace, so knowing how to add such abilities to your own web applications is imperative. Here, we will look at two third-party reusable components that allow you to embed video files in your pages with the help of the Flash Player plug-in. As discussed earlier in the chapter, don't forget about accessibility for your users who may not have the Flash Player plug-in installed or may have JavaScript disabled. Providing backup content also gives search engine spiders something to read and index.

■**Caution** Each Flash component on your page uses up a certain proportion of your user's CPU time to run, and including multiple components on your page exacerbates this effect. Be wary of the number of Flash components you are including on your page, and don't go overboard. Remember that it may work fine on your development machine, but your end users may not be fortunate enough to have a powerful machine. Also, don't forget that the user's network speed may also have an adverse effect on the download time for each component.

To demonstrate the components, let's create a simple example. Suppose you are building a help page within a web site, which plays a video tutorial on how to install a particular product. This page provides a video playback component, with customized playback buttons and feedback controls, whose appearance is intended to match a custom design. Figure 7-2 shows the layout of the final page.

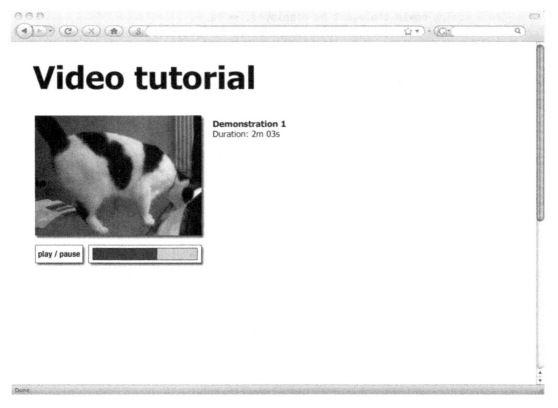

Figure 7-2. *Video tutorial page with video playback and custom controls*

Listing 7-3 shows the HTML markup for this page, which you can adjust later to suit the individual implementations.

Listing 7-3. *HTML Markup for Video Tutorial Page*

```
<!DOCTYPE html PUBLIC "-//W3C//DTD XHTML 1.0 Strict//EN"  ➡
    "http://www.w3.org/TR/xhtml1/DTD/xhtml1-strict.dtd">
<html xmlns="http://www.w3.org/1999/xhtml" lang="en" xml:lang="en">
    <head>
        <title>Video Tutorial Example</title>
        <link rel="stylesheet" href="my-example.css" type="text/css" />
    </head>
    <body>
        <h1>Video tutorial</h1>
        <h2>Demonstration 1</h2>
```

```
    <!-- JavaScript will be used to replace the following tag with the video
         playback component -->
    <div id="movie">
        <p>The movie could not be displayed. ➥
        <a href="movie.mp4">Download the movie to your computer.</a></p>
    </div>

    <!-- Placeholder element which we will populate with video playback
         controls using JavaScript later -->
    <div id="controls"></div>

    <!-- Include the $ JavaScript library -->
    <script src="$.js" type="text/javascript"></script>

    <!-- Include a custom script we'll write later to initialize the video
         playback controls -->
    <script src="build-controls.js" type="text/javascript"></script>

    <!-- Include a custom script we'll write later to display the video -->
    <script src="my-example.js" type="text/javascript"></script>
  </body>
</html>
```

Notice that the HTML code is rather sparse. You have not included the video playback controls on the page itself, but instead will construct them through JavaScript and add them to the page. This makes the page less confusing to those users without a JavaScript-capable browser. If the movie is capable of being displayed in the browser, you'll add the controls; if not, the users will see the video title and a link to download the video file to their computer for offline viewing. The HTML code, therefore, is the only code needed for non-JavaScript users.

Listing 7-4 shows the code for the build-controls.js JavaScript file included within the HTML page in Listing 7-3, which you will use to construct the video controls to add to the page.

Listing 7-4. *JavaScript to Add Playback Controls to the Video Tutorial Page*

```
$.onDomReady(function() {
    // Create duration control, <p id="duration">, insert after <h2> tag

    var durationControl = $.Elements.create("p");
    p.id = "duration";
    durationControl.insertAfter(document.getElementsByTagName("h2")[0]);

    // Create play / pause control element, <div id="play-pause">, insert within
    // the <div id="controls"> tag
```

```
    var playPauseControl = $.Elements.create("div");
    playPauseControl.id = "play-pause";
    playPauseControl.innerHTML = "play / pause";
    document.getElementById("controls").appendChild(playPauseControl);

    // Create playhead control, <div id="playhead"><div id="playhead-position">
    // </div></div>, insert within <div id="controls"> element on the page

    var playheadControl = $.Elements.create("div");
    playheadControl.id = "playhead";
    var playheadPositionControl = $.Elements.create("div");
    playheadPositionControl.id = "playhead-position";
    playheadControl.appendChild(playheadPositionControl);
    document.getElementById("controls").appendChild(playheadControl);
});
```

Now that you have added your new controls to the page through JavaScript, you need to set your CSS in the my-example.css file, referenced from the HTML page in Listing 7-3. Note that the playhead controls you created through JavaScript in Listing 7-4 are produced by the following HTML code on the page:

```
<div id="playhead">
    <div id="playhead-position"></div>
</div>
```

Use CSS to style this to behave like a progress bar, as detailed in Chapter 5.

With the bare bones of the sample page constructed, you're ready to use reusable components to embed video files on your page and to connect the controls on your page to handle playback of the video file. We'll look at two different Adobe Flash Player–based reusable components: YouTube Chromeless Player and JW FLV Player.

YouTube Chromeless Player

By far, the most popular video upload and sharing web site is the Google-owned YouTube site (http://www.youtube.com/). Hosting your video files on Google's distributed CDN through this service often gives you better performance than hosting it yourself, as you discovered back in Chapter 4.

It has always been possible to embed the standard YouTube player in your own sites, but Google has recently made available a new version of the player for developers. This version, known as the YouTube Chromeless Player, has all the default playback controls removed, leaving only the video itself. This allows you to create your own custom controls to manipulate a YouTube video through an exposed JavaScript API. Figure 7-3 shows an example of the YouTube Chromeless Player with custom controls.

■ **Note** The *chrome* of an application is defined as the controls and other elements surrounding the main point of interest. *Chromeless*, in this case, denotes that there are no controls around the video itself.

Figure 7-3. *YouTube Chromeless Player on a page with custom HTML controls*

The requirements for using the Chromeless Player are Flash Player version 8 or higher, and, naturally, JavaScript. The full reference for the YouTube Chromeless Player is available at `http://code.google.com/intl/en/apis/youtube/chromeless_player_reference.html`.

In contrast to most third-party components, which contain all the code they require wrapped in their JavaScript API, the YouTube Chromeless Player does not include code for actually placing the Flash movie component into your page. Instead, Google recommends the use of a third-party JavaScript component called SWFObject, conveniently also hosted on its CDN.

The SWFObject Component

SWFObject is a JavaScript component that allows you to embed Flash movie files in your pages. It also provides the ability to detect the currently installed version of the Flash Player plug-in, allowing you to embed movie files that require a certain version of the player only if it exists within the user's browser. It also overcomes an annoying licensing restriction in IE, where Flash content must first be clicked before it will play.

You can download the SWFObject component from its project home page at `http://code.google.com/p/swfobject/`. The component is also hosted directly by Google at `http://ajax.googleapis.com/ajax/libs/swfobject/2.1/swfobject.js`. At the time of writing, the current version of the component is 2.1.

Using the SWFObject component to embed a Flash file in your page is very similar to using any other third-party component. First, include the JavaScript API of the component, either within the <head> tag or at the bottom of the HTML, before the end of the <body> tag:

```
<script type="text/javascript" ➥
    src=" http://ajax.googleapis.com/ajax/libs/swfobject/2.1/swfobject.js" />
```

Embedding a Flash movie file in your page is as simple as referencing the following JavaScript code from your HTML page:

```
// Specify the URL of the Flash movie to display
var movieURL = "my-movie.swf";

// Specify which tag to replace on the HTML page. In this case, a tag with an id
// attribute value of movie will be replaced
var tagIDToReplace = "movie";

// Specify the dimensions of the Flash movie - 320px x 240px
var width = 320;
var height = 240;

// Specify which version of Flash is required to display this movie. Users with
// older versions of the plug-in will not see the Flash movie and the HTML
// tag will not be replaced
var flashVersionRequired = "8";
var expressInstallURL = null; // You can safely ignore this

// Specify any variables to pass to the Flash movie
var flashVars = {}; // Again, this can be ignored

// Specify parameters for the Flash movie
var parameters = {

    // Allows communication between Flash and JavaScript
    allowScriptAccess: "always"
};

// Specify some attributes for the resulting HTML tag, which embeds the
// Flash movie on the page
var attributes = {
    id: "flash-movie"
};

// Embed the Flash movie on the page
swfobject.embedSWF(movieURL, tagIDToReplace, width, height, ➥
    flashVersionRequired, expressInstallURL, flashVars, parameters, attributes);
```

The SWFObject JavaScript code weighs in at 12KB, when minified, and works well in nearly every JavaScript-enabled, Flash-supporting browser in the wild.

Now that you've seen how to take advantage of the SWFObject component to embed any Flash movie file in your page, let's see how to implement the YouTube Chromeless Player with the help of this component.

YouTube Chromeless Player Implementation

The YouTube Chromeless Player consists of two Flash movie files:

- `apiplayer.swf`: Contains the actual functionality for playing video files.

- `cl.swf`: Supplies a wrapper for the first Flash file, providing security restrictions and exposing the player's API functions for access through JavaScript. The URL for accessing this wrapper Flash file directly is `http://www.youtube.com/apiplayer?enablejsapi=1`.

To implement the YouTube Chromeless Player for the sample page, add a reference to the SWFObject JavaScript library file toward the end of the code in Listing 7-3, and then add the code in Listing 7-5 to `my-example.js`, the JavaScript file referenced within Listing 7-3. This adds video playback functionality to your page and connects your page controls to control playback of your movie file.

Listing 7-5. *Displaying a Video Tutorial Using the YouTube Chromeless Player*

```
$.onDomReady(function() {
    // To include the player onto our page, we simply use
    // SWFObject to embed the YouTube player onto our page

    var movieURL = "http://www.youtube.com/apiplayer?enablejsapi=1";
    var tagIDToReplace = "movie";
    var width = 320;
    var height = 240;
    var flashVersionRequired = "8";
    var expressInstallURL = null;
    var flashVars = null;
    var parameters = {
        allowScriptAccess: "always"
    };
    var attributes = {
        id: "flash-movie"
    };

    // Actually embed the video player onto the page
    swfobject.embedSWF(movieURL, tagIDToReplace, width, height, ➥
        flashVersionRequired, expressInstallURL, flashVars, parameters, attributes);
```

```
// Now we have the player embedded within our page, we
// need to point it to the video file we wish to play. As
// you may imagine, we can only link to videos hosted via
// the YouTube service itself. We load the video based
// on the unique identifier assigned to each movie using
// the player's loadVideoById() method. When the YouTube
// player is ready to be interacted with, it calls a
// function with the specific name onYouTubePlayerReady.
// We hook into this event by adding our own
// initialization code to a function of that name.

function onYouTubePlayerReady() {

    // We created the element with id of flash-movie with SWFObject earlier
    var youTubePlayer = document.getElementById("flash-movie");
    // This is the unique YouTube identifier for the video we wish to display
    var videoID = "u1zgFlCw8Aw";
    // Start the video at the beginning
    var startTime = 0;
    // Load the video into the player
    youTubePlayer.loadVideoById(videoID, startTime);

    // Let's wire up the controls on our page to the video
    // player. Let's start with the play/pause button. When
    // this button is pressed, we want to start playing the video if it
    // is paused and pause it if it is already playing. The
    // playVideo() and pauseVideo() methods of the YouTube
    // JavaScript API are quite self-explanatory. We just
    // need to detect whether the video is playing to
    // switch our logic. The way we do this is to use the
    // getPlayerState() method, which returns a number
    // representing the current state of the player,
    // whether the movie is playing, paused, buffering, etc.

    var playPauseControl = document.getElementById("play-pause");
    $.Events.add(playPauseControl, "click", function() {
        var playingState = 1;
        var pausedState = 2;
        var currentPlayerState = youTubePlayer.getPlayerState();
        if (currentPlayerState == playingState) {
            youTubePlayer.pauseVideo();
        } else if (currentPlayerState == pausedState) {
            youTubePlayer.playVideo();
        }
    });
```

```
        // Now we are able to play and pause the movie to our
        // heart's content. Let's display the duration of the
        // movie, which we show next to the video on our
        // example page. This information is not made
        // available to us until the video's associative
        // metadata has been loaded, which, according to
        // Google, occurs just after the video begins playing.
        // We'll write our code, therefore, to wait for the
        // video to start playing and, when it does, get the
        // duration value and write it to the browser. We can
        // listen for the player state change event and write
        // code to update the duration value on the page when
        // the event fires.

        youTubePlayer.addEventListener("onStateChange", function(newState) {
            var playingState = 1;
            if (newState == playingState) {

                // If the video is now playing, get the
                // duration of the movie, make it more user-
                // friendly, and display it on the page
                var durationField = document.getElementById("duration");
                var durationInSeconds = youTubePlayer.getDuration();
                var durationInMinutes = durationInSeconds / 60;
                var durationFullMinutes = Math.ceil(durationInMinutes);
                var durationRemainder = durationInMinutes ➡
                - Math.floor(durationInMinutes);
                var durationRemainderInSeconds = durationRemainder * 60;
                var durationText = "Duration: " + durationFullMinutes + "m " ➡
                    + durationRemainderInSeconds + "s";
                durationField.innerHTML = durationText;
            }
        });

        // Now we need to connect up our playhead control so
        // we can show our users the progress of playback
        // through the movie, using the technique for progress
        // controls presented in Chapter 5

        // Execute this routine on an interval, once a second
        window.setInterval(function() {
```

```
        // Calculate the current playback position in the
        // movie as a percentage of the total duration
        var playheadPosition = document.getElementById("playhead-position");
        var currentPlaybackPositionInSeconds = youTubePlayer.getCurrentTime();
        var durationInSeconds = youTubePlayer.getDuration();
        var playbackPositionAsPercentage = (currentPlaybackPositionInSeconds ➥
            / durationInSeconds) * 100;

        // Update the width of the progress bar to reflect this percentage
        playheadPosition.style.width = playbackPositionAsPercentage + "%";
    }, 1000); // Executed once every 1000 milliseconds = 1 second
  }
});
```

You have now created the video tutorial page, displaying a video from the YouTube service and interacting with it through custom-built page controls. The full JavaScript API includes extra functionality that was not required in this example. You can find more details about this API in the documentation, at `http://code.google.com/intl/en/apis/youtube/js_api_reference.html`.

YouTube Chromeless Player Appraisal

Google's YouTube Chromeless Player provides a simple and useful way to customize the design of YouTube-uploaded video playback to suit the design of your site. The fact that the video clips, JavaScript API, and Flash movie wrapper are linked to directly from Google's servers mean performance is pretty snappy. Also, the company has the ability to dynamically update the software to fix bugs and add new features, without you needing to make any changes to your code. The size of the files downloaded to the browser to support the player is refreshingly small.

The most obvious limitation is that your movie files need to reside within YouTube, which you may not deem appropriate, depending on the type of content you wish to present. The YouTube logo appears as an overlay on top of the playing movie clip, which, again, you may deem inappropriate or distracting. The JavaScript API is also fairly basic, providing only the bare bones of what is needed to control playback of the video.

In short, as long as you don't mind hosting your videos via YouTube and require just the basics for playback, Google's Chromeless Player is probably your best choice for embedded video playback on your site.

JW FLV Player

Developer Jeroen Wijering's Flash Video (FLV format) reusable video player component, currently in its fourth version, is a well-established, well-documented, and well-used third-party component for embedding videos in your web pages. Check out the project home page at `http://www.longtailvideo.com/players/jw-flv-player/` and download the component files to your computer.

JW FLV Player Implementation

Similar to the YouTube Chromeless Player, the JW FLV Player has its JavaScript API supplied to the page via Flash Player. Also, you need to embed this Flash file in the page using SWFObject, as discussed earlier.

To implement JW FLV Player for the sample page, first, add the SWFObject library to Listing 7-3, before the end of the <body> tag:

```
<script type="text/javascript" ➥
    src=" http://ajax.googleapis.com/ajax/libs/swfobject/2.1/swfobject.js" />
```

Next, within the my-example.js file, embed the JW FLV Player in your page, using the code in Listing 7-6.

Listing 7-6. *Video Tutorial Page Using JW FLV Media Player*

```
$.onDomReady(function() {
    // The JW FLV Player is represented as player.swf,
    // downloaded from the project web site
    var movieURL = "player.swf";
    var tagIDToReplace = "movie";
    var width = 320;
    var height = 240;
    var flashVersionRequired = "8";
    var expressInstallURL = null;

    // Specify the video file we wish to display, and
    // instruct the player to begin playing immediately
    // without displaying the player's default controls
    // within the Flash movie
    var flashVars = {
        file: "my-video.flv",
        autostart: "true",
        controlbar: "none",
        icons: "false"
    };
    var parameters = {
        allowScriptAccess: "always"
    };
    var attributes = {
        id: "flash-movie"
    };

    // Embed the media player onto the page
    swfobject.embedSWF(movieURL, tagIDToReplace, width, height, ➥
        flashVersionRequired, expressInstallURL, flashVars, parameters, attributes);
```

```
    // Once the player has initialized, it calls a
    // function on the page named playerReady. We write
    // our code to connect up our controls by adding our
    // code into a function of this name

    function playerReady(playerInstance) {

        // playerInstance is an object representing the
        // media player on the page. Its id represents the
        // id of the page element within HTML
        var myJWPlayer = document.getElementById(playerInstance["id"]);
        var playPauseControl = document.getElementById("play-pause");
        $.Events.add(playPauseControl, "click", function() {
            // When the user clicks the play/pause button,
            // send the PLAY event to the player, which
            // toggles its playback mode between play and pause
            myJWPlayer.sendEvent("PLAY");
        });

        // The player allows us to write code to hook onto
        // certain events that get fired from within the
        // Flash component itself.

        // Here, we assign the function named setDuration,
        // which we define later, to be called when the
        // LOADED event is fired by the component - which
        // happens when the video file has loaded - which
        // we will use to populate our duration element on the page
        myJWPlayer.addModelListener("LOADED", "setDuration");

        // The setPlayheadPosition function, defined
        // later, will be called when the TIME event fires
        // within the player component - this occurs at a
        // fixed interval, once every 100 milliseconds -
        // and we can use this to update our progress bar
        myJWPlayer.addModelListener("TIME", "setPlayheadPosition");
    }
});

// The setDuration method will be called by the Flash
// component when the video file has loaded, passing it an
// object literal containing the id of the player on the
// page that fired the event
function setDuration(options) {
    var durationField = document.getElementById("duration");
```

```
        // Find the player component using the id passed to this function
        var myJWPlayer = document.getElementById(options.id);

        // Get the current status of the player component and
        // establish from this the duration of the video file
        var durationInSeconds = myJWPlayer.getConfig().duration;

        // Make the duration more user-friendly
        var durationInMinutes = durationInSeconds / 60;
        var durationFullMinutes = Math.ceil(durationInMinutes);
        var durationRemainder = durationInMinutes ➥
            - Math.floor(durationInMinutes);
        var durationRemainderInSeconds = durationRemainder * 60;
        var durationText = "Duration: " + durationFullMinutes + "m " ➥
            + durationRemainderInSeconds + "s";

        // Output the duration to the element on the page
        durationField.innerHTML = durationText;
    }

// The setPlayheadPosition method will be called by the
// Flash component once every 100 milliseconds, passing it
// an object literal containing the current position of
// playback within the video and the total duration of the
// video
function setPlayheadPosition(options) {
    var playheadPosition = document.getElementById("playhead-position");

    // Get the current position of playback within the
    // video as a percentage of the total duration
    var currentPlaybackPositionInSeconds = options.position;
    var durationInSeconds = options.duration;
    var playbackPositionAsPercentage = (currentPlaybackPositionInSeconds ➥
        / durationInSeconds) * 100;

    // Move the progress bar on the page to the correct
    // position based on the percentage calculated
    // previously
    playheadPosition.style.width = playbackPositionAsPercentage + "%";
}
```

And there you have it—your video tutorial page is now ready for use, with the JW FLV Player embedded and all controls wired up and functioning correctly, as per the example shown earlier in Figure 7-2.

JW FLV Player Feature Set

The JW FLV Player offers several extra features that were not included in the example:

Playlist support: The JW FLV Player supports playlist files, specified in XML format. You can specify an external file that contains the details of a list of movie files you wish to display within your player, and the player will play each in turn. The playlist can be accessed through the API also, if you wish to present the list of all videos in your own custom control. You may even load in a playlist file dynamically, which could be very useful in a web application scenario where you do not wish to refresh the whole page to load in a new set of video files to present to your users.

Progressive download: A standard movie file hosted on any web server will progressively download and play; that is, the movie will download partially, and playback will begin before the whole movie has finished downloading. The rest of the movie will then download in the background while playing.

HTTP streaming: The JW FLV Player also supports HTTP streaming. This requires you to write a little extra code to run on the server side. With this feature, the end user can jump straight into any position of the video, regardless of whether it has downloaded to the local computer. Details of how to implement this feature on your own server are provided on the JW FLV Player project home page.

Accessibility support: As noted earlier, accessibility for your web applications is an important subject, especially in the realm of multimedia. The JW FLV Player supports closed captions (subtitles) and closed audio description, which is an extra audio track provided to give guidance to the visually impaired as to actions in the scene not discernible using the standard audio track alone. Subtitles are described using the W3C's Timed Text format, which is XML-based and describes the subtitle text to display, its start time, and its end time.

Plug-in support: If the JW FLV Player component does not perform everything you need it to, its architecture supports the ability to add plug-ins to provide extra functionality. Plug-ins can also be accessed through JavaScript using the API, which makes it very appealing for developers who find the player lacking in specific areas.

In addition to these features, the developers are consistently adding new ones. You will want to keep up-to-date with changes made to this component, which aims to be a one-stop solution for all your video playback needs.

JW FLV Player Appraisal

The JW FLV Player is an incredibly feature-rich, stable, and mature component that will allow you to embed videos and video playlists in your web applications with ease. It's your best choice if you need to do more than simply embed a single YouTube movie into your page.

The component is free to use in nonprofit sites, but for commercial use, you need to purchase a commercial license. The license cost is quite low and well worth the investment. There is also a premium option, which allows you to use the component on up to 50 different sites and web applications.

In terms of file size, the Flash component, which contains and exposes the JavaScript API also, weighs in at 44KB. This makes it heavier than the YouTube Chromeless Player, so choose which component to use carefully.

Browser compatibility is very good. Provided the Flash Player plug-in is installed on the end user's browser, this component should work without any difficulty.

The Future: Audio and Video in HTML 5

At the time of writing, the new HTML 5 recommendation is still in its draft stage. However, this hasn't stopped browser manufacturers from cherry-picking some of the more interesting features for inclusion in their browsers to gain some leverage over the competition. One of the areas of great interest being addressed in HTML 5 is in the realm of native audio and video playback within the browser, without reliance on JavaScript, Flash, or any other external plug-in.

■**Note** Other additions to the HTML 5 set in this update of the specification include drawing graphics directly onto the page, allowing offline storage of web application data (in case the user's Internet connection drops but you still wish to continue running your RIA), element drag-and-drop, browser history management, and live document editing (to allow developers to build native rich-text document editors).

The \<audio\> and \<video\> Tags

Implementation of native audio and video support is based around two new proposed HTML tags: \<audio\> and \<video\>. Placing content within these tags provides a useful mechanism for displaying alternative content to those browsers unable to support these tags. The ability to provide backup content when a feature is unsupported applies to HTML 5 in general.

Let's take a look at how to use the \<video\> tag. The \<audio\> tag is quite similar. Following is the HTML 5 code for displaying a video file natively within the browser:

```
<video id="my-video" src="/my-video.mp4" type="video/mp4" autoplay="true">
    Sorry, your browser does not support the ability to play video files natively.
</video>
```

The \<video\> tag takes a number of optional attributes:

- src: Source URL of the video file.

- type: MIME type of the video file to display.

- autoplay: Boolean setting that determines whether to play the video file automatically as soon as the page has loaded.

- `width` and `height`: Set the dimensions of the movie.
- `controls`: Boolean setting that determines whether to show the browser's default controls (play, pause, and so on) or to switch them off.
- `loop`: Boolean setting that determines whether the movie should play again from the start upon completion.
- `poster`: Image file URL to display while the video file is loading. This should typically be a still frame taken from the movie itself to provide a teaser for end users before they choose to play the movie. After playback has occurred, the `poster` frame is not shown again until the page is refreshed.

Since the tag may contain other content and page elements to provide as a backup, you could feasibly consider providing your Adobe Flash–based video playback through a tag embedded within the `<video>` tag, as in the following example:

```
<video id="my-video" src="/my-video.mp4" type="video/mp4" autoplay="true">
    <div id="my-backup-video">
        <p>Sorry, your browser is unable to display our video file, but you may ➡
        <a href="/myVideo.mp4">download the file to your computer</a> ➡
        to watch it instead.</p>
    </div>
</video>
```

Through JavaScript, you would then determine whether the API exists to support the `<video>` tag. If not, you would load in the video file through your Flash-based component as usual. This way, preference is given to the native browser method of displaying videos, falling back to Flash Player if that does not exist, and falling further back to a download link, as in the preceding code example, if that backup component is not supported or JavaScript is disabled. This approach provides good accessibility.

JavaScript API

A JavaScript API is added with HTML 5, along with support for these tags. This API allows you to control playback through JavaScript, or to design and build your own controls to manipulate playback and feedback properties of the playing audio or video.

The methods available are similar to those provided with the third-party multimedia components we have looked at in this chapter, such as `play()`, `pause()`, and `load()`. There is also a series of dynamic attributes, set by the playing file, which allow you to discover the current play position, the size and duration of the media, and other information you can use as feedback to your users.

Completing the API is a set of events, each of which you can hook into through JavaScript. These fire in response to certain occurrences, such as the starting and stopping of playback. There is even an event that triggers periodically during playback to allow for the updating of any user interface component you have developed to show the playback position to the end user.

Current Adoption Level

At present, support for the `<audio>` and `<video>` tags is available in a limited fashion in Safari 3.1 and up, Google Chrome, Opera 9.5 and up (video playback only, not audio), and Firefox 3.5 and up. While this does not constitute the vast majority of installed browsers by market share, it does provide a useful test bed for the tags and their associative JavaScript API. This gives developers a chance to iron out the bugs and implementation details before adoption becomes more widespread.

A point of contention among these early adopters has been the audio and video file format and the codecs supported. Each manufacturer has its own preference as to which is the best format and is seeking to force that to be the adopted standard. The standards body would like to settle on an open source codec, but this seems to be disputed by some manufacturers who believe their own codec to be superior. As it stands, you will find that different formats are supported through the use of these tags in different browsers, so it is too early to use them widely. You can read the latest progress online at `http://www.whatwg.org/specs/web-apps/current-work/`.

Summary

This chapter reviewed a few third-party audio and video player components, which make use of Adobe's Flash Player browser plug-in. You've seen how you can utilize these components in your own web pages to play and manipulate multimedia files. We have also taken a look into the future of browser support for native audio and video playback. You should now be in a position to implement multimedia playback in your own pages, building your own controls on the page and controlling playback of the media from those controls via JavaScript APIs exposed through each of the third-party components.

In the next chapter, we will look at customizing form controls in your pages using JavaScript, providing some more user-friendly interfaces for the completion of forms than the native HTML controls.

CHAPTER 8

■■■

Form Controls

Forms often make up a major part of any web application. A form might encourage users to submit feedback, provide search functionality, let users add information to an online database, and so on. With a form, you are inviting your end users to give some kind of information back to you in order to get something back themselves. Forms are some of the most interactive parts of the web site. They also can be the parts that most regularly frustrate users. Building and laying out forms and form fields correctly are absolutely paramount to your applications.

This chapter guides you through customization of existing HTML form fields and shows you how to add new types of controls. You'll see how to construct forms that are more understandable and visually pleasing for your end users.

Customizing Existing Form Controls

The wide variety of form fields available within HTML allow you to collect pretty much all the information you require from your users in order to perform some process or provide some functionality within your site. You are probably used to using CSS to style your form fields, and you may have noticed that certain form controls do not respond to certain styles. For example, attempting to change the border style of a `<select>` drop-down element has different effects in different browsers—some apply the style; others ignore it.

Some problems exist with styling because form fields used in browsers are typically taken directly from the equivalent form fields present within the operating system. Such controls are usually changeable only by making alterations to the operating system's theme or style. Over time, browser manufacturers have bowed to pressure and attempted to give developers more control over styling such controls. Unfortunately, support is patchy among browsers, so making style changes to controls such as `<select>` boxes may not have the same effect in each browser.

In short, some niggles persist when styling certain controls. Here, we confront these head-on and look at a few solutions—using CSS and occasionally some JavaScript—that work in as many browsers as possible. Let's get started with form buttons.

Buttons

You probably use buttons on a daily basis when browsing the Web, clicking them to save some data you've typed into a form, delete an entry from a database, send an e-mail message through a web mail client, and so on.

Buttons are typically rendered to the page using the tags `<input type="submit">`, `<input type="reset">`, `<input type="button">`, and `<input type="image">`. The first three of these button types are rendered using the operating system's or browser's default style. The intention is to provide some design consistency between the page and the operating system or browser's user interface. The `<input type="image">` button type renders an image located at a specified URL and submits the form it lies within when the user selects that image.

Button Style Customization

CSS support for the `submit`, `reset`, and `button` input types in browsers has been a little patchy in the past. For example, early versions of Safari didn't support the alteration of the default style at all. But things have settled since then, and virtually all browsers now support full CSS styling. However, even today, it is still tricky to match the exact positioning of text within the button in all the different browsers.

A common design for buttons in many RIAs uses rounded corners and shadows, as shown in Figure 8-1. Suppose that you want adjust this type of button so that its size depends on the size of the text it contains. This way, if users resize the text in their browser, the text within the customized button will also resize, without losing the style you have applied to its background, which is great for accessibility.

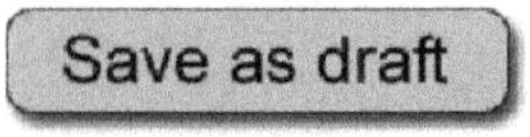

Save as draft

Figure 8-1. *Customized submit button*

To build this control in a way that allows you to resize each button horizontally depending on the amount of text contained within it, you need to add an extra element around the `<input>` element:

```
<div class="button">
    <input type="submit" value="Save as draft" />
</div>
```

Then you can use the CSS `background-position` property, in combination with a very wide image, as shown in Figure 8-2, as the background for both elements. You'll show a portion of the left side of the image as the background for the outer element, and the right side of the image as the background for the `<input>` element itself.

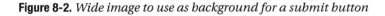

Figure 8-2. *Wide image to use as background for a submit button*

The CSS to produce this customized submit button using the preceding HTML and wide image looks like this:

```
.button {
    /* pin background to the top-left of the outer element */
    background: url(button-bg.png) top left no-repeat;
```

```
    /* force 14px of the left side of the background to show */
    padding-left: 14px;

    /* force the element to alter its width to fit its contents, no more */
    float: left;

    /* height of the background image */
    height: 50px;
}

.button input {
    /* pin background to the top-right of the input element */
    background: url(button-bg.png) top right no-repeat;

    /* 23px of rounded corner + shadow at right of image */
    /* 9px of shadow height at bottom of image */
    padding: 0 23px 9px 0;

    font-size: 1.7em; /* the em unit allows the text to be resized by the user */
    height: 50px; /* height of the background image */
    overflow: visible; /* fixes an odd rendering bug in IE */
    border: 0; /* removes the default border around the input element */
    margin: 0; /* removes the default margin around the input element */
}
```

You see that you can remove the default style of a button element and change it to suit the design and layout of your own pages, while still using browser text for the button itself.

An Alternative to Image-Type Form Buttons

You know that the `<input type="image">` element allows you to specify an image URL and use that image as a form button. Suppose that you have several such images used throughout your site. In that case, it would more efficient to use the CSS sprite technique, introduced back in Chapter 4. You could combine all these separate images into one single file, and use CSS class names to select the correct portion of the sprite image to display within the page element. Figure 8-3 shows an example of a sprite image of four custom buttons: OK, Cancel, Back, and Forward.

Figure 8-3. *CSS sprite containing four images to use as buttons*

An additional improvement is to use an `<input type="submit">` tag, instead of `<input type="image">`. This way, if the user's browser does not support CSS or it has been manually disabled for whatever reason, a standard submit button will appear on the page instead—the principle of progressive enhancement in action.

Let's walk through how to use this technique. You need two HTML elements for each button: the <input> tag itself and a wrapper tag, which could feasibly be any block-level element. In this case, you will use a <div> tag. Here's the HTML:

```
<div class="sprite ok">
    <input type="submit" value="OK" />
</div>

<div class="sprite cancel">
    <input type="submit" value="Cancel" />
</div>

<div class="sprite back">
    <input type="submit" value="Back" />
</div>

<div class="sprite forward">
    <input type="submit" value="Forward" />
</div>
```

Notice that each button has a different CSS class on the outer element and the value of the button itself is set correctly. This provides those without a CSS-capable browser access to a standard submit button instead.

Now, you need to write the CSS to produce the results you want. Let's start with the class sprite, which is set on each of the wrapper elements:

```
.sprite {
    background-image: url(button-sprite.png);
    background-repeat: no-repeat;
    width: 85px;
    height: 39px;
    overflow: hidden;
}
```

Here, you set the background image to be your sprite image, and you tell it not to repeat itself if given the chance. You force the width and height to match the dimensions of one of the button images within the sprite, and not the dimensions of the whole sprite image itself. Finally, you set the overflow property to hidden, which means that any content that extends outside the boundary marked by the width and height of this element will be cropped off and not displayed. The reason for setting this final property will become more evident in a moment.

Next, set the background position for each button to represent the correct button within each element, as follows:

```
.sprite.ok {
    background-position: 0 0;
}
```

```
.sprite.cancel {
    background-position: -85px 0;
}

.sprite.back {
    background-position: 0 -39px;
}

.sprite.forward {
    background-position: -85px -39px;
}
```

Finally, now that you've sorted out the display of the correct button, you need to apply some CSS treatment to the <input> tag to hide its text content but still allow it to be selectable:

```
.sprite input {
    padding: 0;
    margin: 0;
    border: 0;
    background: transparent;
    display: block;
    height: 39px;
    font-size: 0;
    text-align: right;
    width: 500px;
}
```

This starts out by simply resetting the margin, padding, and border properties. The values for these properties make sure that the background is transparent to show through the image of the button underneath, and force the height of the element to match that of the image so the whole thing is selectable.

The last three lines of this style are employed to make sure that the element's default text does not display on top of the image of the button. You take advantage of the fact that any portion of this element larger than that of the surrounding element will be cropped off and not displayed—thanks to the overflow: hidden style property on the outer element. All you need to do is make the <input> element considerably wider than the wrapper element and align the text, which you make as small as possible so it takes up less space, to the right of the element. This means the text sits within the portion of the element hidden from display, and leaves you with the button looking the way you intended in all browsers.

Text Fields

The humble text field accepts data in many different formats. It is by far the most common form field in the HTML set. Because this type of field is so flexible, one concern is having some control over what the user enters. In some cases, you should use a little gray matter, along with a little JavaScript, to ensure that the correct data is input. For example, you may want to restrict the field to accept only numbers or accept only the characters that are allowable within an e-mail address. We'll look at enforcing both of these types of restrictions.

A Numbers-Only Text Field

This example demonstrates how to style a text field that, provided JavaScript is available, will not accept any input other than numbers. Let's start by creating a new `<input type="text">` element and assigning it a class of `numerical`:

```
<form action="get" action="/" id="form">
    <input type="text" class="numerical" />
    <input type="submit" value="save" />
</form>
```

Now you can write your JavaScript to apply to only elements with this specific class:

```
$.onDomReady(function() {
    // Listen for keypress events within the form
    $.Events.add(document.getElementById("form"), "keypress", ➡
            function(e) {
        // Was the key pressed within a field with a class of numerical
        if (e.target.className == "numerical") {

            // The following regular expression matches everything not numeric
            if (e.key.match(/[^0-9]/g)) {

                // Cancel the keypress event if a number key was not pressed
                e.preventDefault();
            }
        }
    });
});
```

This JavaScript code will wait until the DOM is ready to be accessed, and then start listening for `keypress` events that occur within the scope of the `<form>` tag on the page. If one of these events occurs on an element with a class of `numerical`—in this case, the text field—then you use a regular expression to see if the key that was pressed is a number. If it is not a number, you prevent it from being written into the field by effectively halting the browser event in its tracks. If the key pressed maps to a number, then there's no problem; the event is allowed to proceed, and the character is written into the field.

By changing the regular expression used in this routine, you can limit which characters are allowed within the field. Let's see how that works with another kind of text field.

An E-Mail Address Field

Suppose that you have a field whose class is set to `email` and you want to restrict which characters can be entered into this field to those permitted within e-mail addresses. The HTML looks like this:

```
<input type="text" class="email" />
```

You can simply amend the code shown the previous section to cope with this case.

```
$.onDomReady(function() {
    $.Events.add(document.getElementById("form"), "keypress", ➥
            function(e) {
        switch(e.target.className) {
            case "numerical":
                if (e.key.match(/[^0-9]/g)) {
                    e.preventDefault();
                }
                break;

            case "email":
                // The following regular expression matches all characters not
                // permitted within an email address
                if (e.key.match(/[^a-zA-Z0-9@!#$%&'*+-\/=?^_{}~.]+/g)) {
                    e.preventDefault();
                }
                break;
        }
    });
});
```

As you can see, this slice of code is virtually identical to the JavaScript in the previous section, except that it uses a different regular expression. Now you are canceling the keypress event for every character that is not within the list of characters allowed within an e-mail address. You can use this approach to add new restrictions. Just use the appropriate regular expression to match the type of restriction you wish to impose.

Don't forget that some users will not have JavaScript enabled in their browsers. For these users, you must add appropriate server-side validation, so that values sent back to the server are not saved if they contain characters that would otherwise have been restricted through JavaScript.

File Upload Controls

The file upload control is fairly unique in HTML, in that it typically adds two linked form controls to the page: a text field and a button. The exception is within the Safari browser, where the text field is replaced with a text label; the file name is not editable in this case.

So, the file upload control usually consists of two distinctly different form elements added through one tag, and the two cannot be separated. Applying a design to this control using CSS is particularly difficult, because the same styles are applied to both elements. For example, styling the button with a custom image using CSS alone is not straightforward.

Thankfully, there is a technique that enables you to apply custom styles to the file upload control. The downside is that the text field portion of the control is effectively removed—it's replaced with a text label, as in Safari. Personally, I find this a perfectly acceptable limitation, as not many users actually type file locations directly into a field. Most prefer to browse to the proper file location.

Here, I'll show you how to construct your own file upload control using this technique, based on the design depicted in Figure 8-4.

Figure 8-4. *A customized file upload control*

In the HTML for the control, you wrap your file upload field in a `<div>` tag and add another `<div>` element next to the upload field, which you'll use to represent the file name of the selected text using JavaScript. In fact, since you need to use JavaScript to display the value in the text label dynamically, it makes sense that the whole customized control will be applied only if JavaScript is enabled. Other users should see the default browser style upload field. Here's the HTML to achieve this design:

```
<form method="post" action="/" id="form" enctype="multipart/form-data">
    <div class="file" id="uploader">
        <input type="file" id="file-upload" />
        <div class="file-label"></div>
    </div>

    <input type="submit" value="Save" />
</form>
```

In order to ensure the CSS for this control is applied only when JavaScript is enabled, you'll use JavaScript to dynamically add a new class of active to the `<div class="file" id="uploader">` element:

```
$.CSS.addClass(document.getElementById("uploader"), "active");
```

Then write all your CSS to hang from this new class name:

```
div.file.active {
    position: relative;
    background: url(file-upload.png) top left no-repeat;
    /* dimensions of background image */
    width: 288px;
    height: 39px;
}

div.file.active .file-label {
    /* position above background */
    position: absolute;
    top: 0;
    left: 10px;
    /* only consume the width of the text label part of the image */
    width: 175px;
    height: 100%;
    overflow: hidden;
    z-index: 1;
    font-size: 1.4em;
    /* ensure text is accurately positioned, vertically centered */
    line-height: 31px;
}
```

```
div.file.active input {
    position: absolute;
    /* make the file input transparent in Firefox */
    -moz-opacity: 0;
    /* apply transparency in IE 8 */
    -ms-filter:"progid:DXImageTransform.Microsoft.Alpha(Opacity=0)";
    /* apply transparency in IE 7 and below */
    filter: alpha(opacity=0);
    /* apply transparency in other capable browsers, e.g., Safari, Opera */
    opacity: 0;
    /* position transparent file input above background and file label */
    z-index: 2;
    /* if this border is not set, Opera does not apply the transparency */
    border: 0;
    /* fill the available space marked by the outer wrapper element */
    width: 100%;
    height: 100%;
}
```

Figure 8-5 shows how these style rules are applied to the elements in three stages, starting with the native file upload control and ending with the final customized control:

- First, you set the image that represents the whole file upload control as the background image of the wrapper element and set its size to match the dimensions of the image.

- Then, you position the file label so it sits in a layer above the background and style its text (stage two of Figure 8-5).

- Finally, you apply some style rules to the native file upload control, making it transparent so that the user can see straight through to the background image and file label underneath, but still allowing the element itself to be clickable (stage three of Figure 8-5).

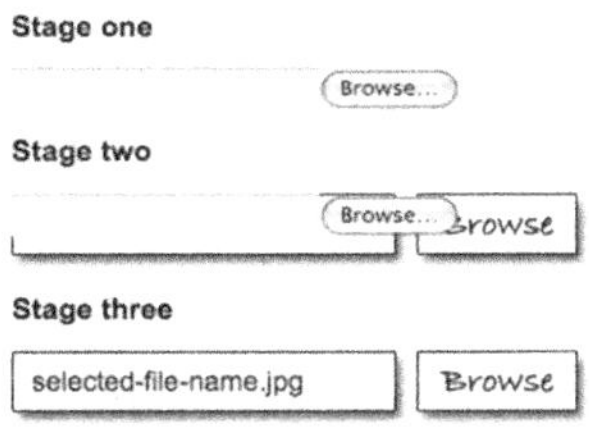

Figure 8-5. *The three stages of customizing a file upload control*

This is a pretty spectacular phenomenon, which actually works well across all modern browsers. Since setting transparency using the CSS 3 opacity property is not currently possible across all browsers, you must adopt each browser's own implementation in a set of rules to target each of the modern browser's opacity setting ability. With the control now invisible, you position it so that it sits above the background and the file label, and ensure it consumes the full width and height of the wrapper element.

All that remains is to write the JavaScript code to apply the CSS class active to the wrapper element and ensure that the text label is updated when the user selects a file using the control.

```
$.onDomReady(function() {
    // Find all the fields with class file within the <form> tag with id of form
    var fileUploadFields = $.Elements.getElementsByClassName("file", ➥
        document.getElementById("form"));
    for (var index, length = fileUploadFields.length; index < length; index++) {
        var fileUpload = fileUploadFields[index];
        // Add the class active to the file upload fields
        $.CSS.addClass(fileUpload, "active");
    }

    // We'll call the setFileLabel function when certain browser events fire
    var setFileLabel = function(e) {
        if (e.target.type == "file") {
            // Find the nearest text label to display the file name within
            var fileLabel = $.Elements.getElementsByClassName( ➥
                "file-label", e.target.parentNode)[0];
            // Get the file name from the upload field
            var file = e.target.value;

            // Display only 19 characters of text within the file name label
            var numberOfChars = 19;
            if (file.length > numberOfChars) {
                // Truncate the file name if it's longer than 19 characters
                file = file.substr(0, 4) + " ... " + ➥
                file.substr(file.length - numberOfChars + 4, file.length)
            }
            // Write the file name to the label element
            fileLabel.innerHTML = file;
        }
    }

    // Listen for change events on the control and set the label text
    $.Events.add(document.getElementById("file-upload"), "change", ➥
        setFileLabel);

    // Listen for mouseout events on the control and set the label text - used for
    // Internet Explorer which does not fire the change event when it should
    $.Events.add(document.getElementById("file-upload"), "mouseout", ➥
        setFileLabel);
});
```

This script is in two parts. The first part finds all the <div class="file"> elements within the form and applies the CSS class active to them. This allows the CSS rules you wrote earlier to be applied to these elements. The second part of the code listens for change and mouseout events to occur within the upload field and calls a method when these events are fired. This method takes the file name from the upload field and populates the text label with its value, truncating it if it's too long to fit in the available space.

To be listening for the change event might not seem surprising to you, since you want to know when the value in the upload field is changed. However, using the mouseout event might seem a little strange. The problem is that some older browsers do not fire the change event when a file is selected, but instead fire the mouseout event. Therefore, you need to listen for both events to ensure a proper cross-browser implementation.

Adding New Types of Form Controls

The standard HTML form controls are often more than enough to deal with getting data from your users into your application. However, in some cases, you may want to use some more intuitive controls or controls that are present within the operating system but not exposed through HTML. The good news is that, with a little JavaScript and the occasional dab of Flash, you can build almost any kind of custom user interface for your forms.

The way you perform this awesome feat is by hiding fields that already exist within your form, and then providing a new interface for altering the values within those fields. When the user interacts with your new controls, you update the hidden fields behind the scenes. This ensures that all the data is sent to the server through HTML form fields in the usual way, and you reduce the risk of errors or missing data.

In this section, you will see how to use this technique to build two types of form controls that are not native to HTML. Later in this chapter, I'll introduce some third-party reusable form control components.

A Calendar Widget for Date Selection

A standard HTML form may allow date selection by means of a text box whose contents are validated against a certain format for date entry, such as in the form *DD-MM-YYYY*. Alternatively, the form may present a group of three select boxes—one each for the day, month, and year, respectively—and the user is asked to pick the appropriate value from each to select the required date.

Wouldn't it be more intuitive to supply the user with a familiar calendar interface for selecting a date? Such widgets can be found on many hotel and flight booking web sites today. Some are implemented well, but some leave a lot to be desired.

For example, many existing calendar widgets require users to click a calendar icon to launch a pop-up calendar, or it may be simply presented to them when they click the usual date selection fields on the page. Although it saves on page space within the site's layout, this mechanism can frustrate end users. Some calendar widgets require the user to click a certain button to close them, rather than closing automatically when the user interacts with other fields. Some pop up their calendars inappropriately over other controls on the page, rendering those controls inaccessible.

A little thought and consideration about how your users might wish to interact with your controls can pay huge dividends. Remember that you are trying to give a pleasurable, almost unnoticeable, user experience. Any causes of frustration for end users must be avoided. With that in mind, let's see how to construct a more intuitive control: a reusable calendar widget, containing all the logic and HTML required.

The sample calendar control will be connected to three <select> tags, but the interface will look like Figure 8-6. Before looking at the code for this control, let's define how it should behave:

- Page developers can style and position the calendar as appropriate to the design of their site.

- The control can be instantiated at a time of the page developer's choosing.

- Multiple instances can exist on the same page and will not interfere with each other.

- Month and day names should be localizable but default to English.

- Page developers can hook into events that occur within the calendar widget and extract useful information from it. For example, the developer may wish to know when a new date is selected, and what that new date is.

Figure 8-6. *Custom calendar form control connected to three <select> boxes*

In order to create a widget object that can be instantiated, you need to use a constructor class. As explained in Chapter 2, in object-oriented programming, a class is like a definition of how your code should behave. An object is a specific instance of that class, where each object created is independent of the other objects, but they all share the capabilities of the class from which they were instantiated.

Internally, our widget will contain code related to its presence in the browser: HTML rendering and the wiring up of user events, such as mouse clicks. Also contained in the widget will be code related to maintaining the current state of the calendar and calculations involving dates and months. You want to keep this logical separation of data and display code, ensuring that there is no crossover between the two.

The Observer pattern (introduced in Chapter 2) provides a useful way of maintaining this distinction. You have a section of code related to data storage and manipulation. When this code performs an action that the display might like to know about, it fires an event of a predetermined name.

You tell your display-related code to listen for when certain events are fired. When they are, code can be executed within the display, taking any relevant data that has been passed to the event and using it to alter the display. The same technique applies the other way around. For example, when the user clicks to change the selected date, the data-storage code needs to know about this. The data-storage code listens for an event fired by this click. The value of the new date can be passed along with the event, and the data-storage code can be updated as appropriate.

This pattern allows for two or more distinct blocks of code to coexist within the same system, without messy cross-references between the two. A single method acts as the mediator, defining a list of permitted events and allowing each code block to fire or listen to any of those events in the system.

Creating Utility Methods for Dates

To manipulate and format native JavaScript Date objects into more user-friendly displays, you need some new utility methods. Let's make these methods reusable by adding them to the $ JavaScript library you started in Chapter 2. Listing 8-1 shows the utility methods you'll use to make the calendar widget easier to work with. Add this code to the library before it is instantiated as a singleton on its last line.

Listing 8-1. *Extending the $ JavaScript Library with Utility Methods for Dates*

```
// Add the padZero method to the Utils namespace. This method returns the string
// form of a number passed to it. If the number is less than 10, an extra 0 is
// added to the beginning of the resulting string
$.prototype.Utils.padZero = function(number) {
    return (number < 10 ? "0" : "") + number.toString();
}


// Create a new namespace called Date for holding all date-specific utility methods
$.prototype.Date = {

    // The copy method duplicates a Date object and returns the copy. Typically,
    // Dates are passed around in JavaScript as references to a single object, so
    // normal variable copying is not possible - each copy would always point as
    // a reference to the same object. This method creates a new Date object,
    // taking the exact date and time from the existing object
    copy: function(date) {
        var newDate = new Date();
        newDate.setTime(date.valueOf());
        return newDate;
    },

    // The add method takes an existing Date object and adds a specified number of
    // days, months and years to that object, returning the resulting Date object
    add: function(date, options) {
        // The options object literal contains three properties - day, month and
        // year - representing the number of each to add to the input Date object
        var daysToAdd = options.day || 0;
        var monthsToAdd = options.month || 0;
        var yearsToAdd = options.year || 0;

        // Create a new Date object and add the days, months and years
        // specified to it
        var date = this.copy(date);
```

```
        var initialDay = date.getDate();
        var initialMonth = date.getMonth();
        var initialYear = date.getFullYear();
        date.setFullYear(initialYear + yearsToAdd);
        date.setMonth(initialMonth + monthsToAdd);
        date.setDate(initialDay + daysToAdd);

        // Return the resulting Date object
        return date;
    },

    // The matchDay method returns true if the two Date objects passed to it have
    // the same day number - i.e., inputs of 28 May and 28 June would return true
    // since the day number is the same for each
    matchDay: function(date1, date2) {
        return date1.getDate() == date2.getDate();
    },

    // The matchMonth method returns true if both Date objects passed to it occur
    // within the same month and same year as each other
    matchMonth: function(date1, date2) {
        return ((date1.getMonth() == date2.getMonth()) && (date1.getFullYear() == ➥
            date2.getFullYear()));
    },

    // The match method returns true or false depending on whether the two Date
    // objects input represent identical dates
    match: function(date1, date2) {
        return this.matchDay(date1, date2) && this.matchMonth(date1, date2);
    },

    // The format method returns a date as a user-friendly formatted string
    format: function(date, formatDefinition, dayName, monthName) {
        var d = date.getDate(); // Single or double digit day
        var dd = $.Utils.padZero(d); // Double digit day
        var dddd = dayName; // Day name
        var ddd = dddd.substr(0, 3); // Short day name
        var m = date.getMonth(); // Single or double digit month
        var mm = $.Utils.padZero(m); // Double digit month
        var mmmm = monthName; // Full month name
        var mmm = mmmm.substr(0, 3); // Short month name
        var yy = $.Utils.padZero(date.getYear()); // Two digit year
        var yyyy = date.getFullYear(); // Four digit year
        var tttt = date.getTime(); // Date represented as time
```

```
        return $.Utils.replaceText(formatDefinition, {
            d: d,
            dd: dd,
            ddd: ddd,
            dddd: dddd,
            m: m,
            mm: mm,
            mmm: mmm,
            mmmm: mmmm,
            yy: yy,
            yyyy: yyyy,
            tttt: tttt
        })
    },

    // The getStartOfFirstWeekInMonthSquare method returns the Date object
    // representing the first day of a month square. This is usually a day before
    // the first of the month, which occurs on a Sunday in JavaScript, allowing a
    // calendar to display dates that fit into a neat date square, including dates
    // that occur in the previous month
    getStartOfFirstWeekInMonthSquare: function(date) {
        date = this.copy(date);
        date.setDate(1); // First day in month
        date.setDate(1 - date.getDay()); // Go back to Sunday at start of week
        return date;
    },

    // The getEndOfWeekInMonthSquare method returns the last date that would fit
    // into a neat month square around the month represented in the date
    // input parameter
    getEndOfWeekInMonthSquare: function(date, weeksInSquare) {
        var DAYS_IN_WEEK = 7;

        date = this.copy(date);
        date.setDate(1);
        date = this.add(date, {
            month: 1
        });

        // Go back to the last day of the month
        date.setDate(date.getDate() - 1);
```

```
            // Look forward to last day of month square
            var numberOfDaysToEndOfWeek = (DAYS_IN_WEEK - 1) - date.getDay();
            date = this.add(date, {
                day: numberOfDaysToEndOfWeek
            });

            return date;
        }
    }
```

Building the Calendar

Listing 8-2 shows how to build the calendar control using the Observer pattern, the utility
methods in Listing 8-1, and two completely separate code blocks: one for data manipulation
and storage, and one for the user interface and interaction code. Save this code in a file named
calendar.js.

Listing 8-2. *A Calendar Custom Form Control*

```
// Create the constructor that will represent our calendar form control. The inputs
// are contained within the options object literal, which should contain
// three properties:
// - destinationElement: the DOM element on the page within which to insert
//       the calendar form control
// - selectedDate: a JavaScript Date object representing the default selected date
//       on the calendar
// - strings: an object literal containing text strings to allow for localization of
//       the calendar form control, including day and month names and text for
//       'previous' and 'next' button labels to change the currently displayed month

var Calendar = function(options) {

    // Store the list of events supported by the calendar, according to the
    // Observer pattern
    this.eventType = {

        // The INITIALIZE event will be fired once the calendar is instantiated
        INITIALIZE: 0,

        // The READY event will be fired once the currently selected date has been
        // established after instantiation
        READY: 1,

        // The HTML_RENDERED event will be fired as soon as the calendar control is
        // rendered onto the page
        HTML_RENDERED: 2,
```

```
    // The INCREMENT_DISPLAY_MONTH event will be fired when the users indicate
    // they wish to display the next month forward from the currently
    // displayed month
    INCREMENT_DISPLAY_MONTH: 3,

    // The DECREMENT_DISPLAY_MONTH event will be fired when the users indicate
    // they wish to display the previous month before the currently
    // displayed month
    DECREMENT_DISPLAY_MONTH: 4,

    // The MONTH_CHANGED event will be fired once the currently displayed month
    // value has been changed, so that the UI can be updated to
    // reflect the new month
    MONTH_CHANGED: 5,

    // The DATE_SELECTED event will be fired when the users indicate they
    // wish to select a new date from the calendar control. The new date value
    // is passed along with the event
    DATE_SELECTED: 6
}

// The initialize self-instantiating function creates instances of the two code
// blocks in the system and fires the first event of the system, the INITIALIZE
// event, to kick off proceedings
var initialize = function(options) {

    // Data storage and manipulation code will be represented by the Data code
    // block, defined later. We instantiate the code block but do not need to
    // assign it to a variable here, since it is completely self-contained.
    new this.Data(options, this);

    // User interface and interaction code will be represented within the UI
    // code block, also defined later
    new this.UI(options, this);

    // Now that the code blocks and event list have been initialized, fire the
    // INITIALIZE event. The Data and UI code blocks can listen for this event
    // and act appropriately to initialize their own code
    this.fire(this.eventType.INITIALIZE);
}.call(this, options);
}

// Add support for the Observer pattern's listen and fire events to the calendar
Calendar.prototype = new $.Observer;

// The Data code block is a constructor and contains code to store and manipulate
// data within the calendar, primarily representing the currently selected date and
```

```
// the currently displayed month on the calendar control. When it is instantiated,
// the object literal's inputs to the calendar are passed in, along with a reference
// to the parent object, the Calendar class, from which the code block can utilize
// the events list and Observer methods listen and fire.
Calendar.prototype.Data = function(options, thisCalendar) {

    // Store three properties representing the master Calendar instance that
    // instantiated Data, the currently selected date, and the currently
    // displayed month
    this.thisCalendar = this;
    this.selectedDate = null;
    this.displayMonth = null;

    // We create getter and setter methods to protect these properties and ensure
    // sensible data gets written to them

    // The getDisplayMonth method returns a copy of the JavaScript Date object that
    // represents the currently displayed month within the control
    this.getDisplayMonth = function() {
        return $.Date.copy(this.displayMonth);
    }

    // The setDisplayMonth method sets the currently displayed month to the passed
    // in month, if it exists, or sets it to the current date if it is not supplied
    this.setDisplayMonth = function(date) {
        this.displayMonth = $.Date.copy(date) || new Date();
        // We only care about the month, not the specific day for this variable. Set
        // the day to the 1st of the month to avoid any problems jumping
        // between months
        this.displayMonth.setDate(1);

        // Allow chaining of method calls by returning this
        return this;
    }

    // The getSelectedDate method returns a copy of the JavaScript Date object
    // representing the currently selected date on the calendar
    this.getSelectedDate = function() {
        return $.Date.copy(this.selectedDate);
    }

    // The setSelectedDate method sets the currently selected date to the value
    // passed into the method, if one is provided. If it is not, the current date is
    // used instead
    this.setSelectedDate = function(date) {
        this.selectedDate = $.Date.copy(date) || new Date();
        return this;
    }
```

```
// The getCalendarInstance method returns the reference to the master Calendar
// instance that instantiated the Data code block. We need this to be able to
// access the Observer pattern methods and events list used in the whole system
this.getCalendarInstance = function() {
    return this.thisCalendar;
}

// The setCalendarInstance method sets the current Calendar object instance to
// the value passed into the method. If a value is not passed in, we use the
// current object scope instead
this.setCalendarInstance = function(thisCalendar) {
    this.thisCalendar = thisCalendar || this;
    return this;
}

// With the getters and setters complete, we define our methods to manipulate
// the dates as required by the system

// The incrementDisplayMonth method adds one month to the displayMonth property,
// then fires the MONTH_CHANGED event to notify the entire calendar control
// that the value has changed, in case the code needs to react to this event
this.incrementDisplayMonth = function() {
    this.setDisplayMonth($.Date.add(this.getDisplayMonth(), {
        month: 1
    }));

    var thisCalendar = this.getCalendarInstance();
    var eventType = thisCalendar.eventType;

    // Pass the new display month and currently selected date to any code block
    // in the calendar control listening for the MONTH_CHANGED event
    thisCalendar.fire(eventType.MONTH_CHANGED, {
        displayMonth: this.getDisplayMonth(),
        selectedDate: this.getSelectedDate()
    });
}

// The decrementDisplayMonth method subtracts one month from the displayMonth
// property,then fires the MONTH_CHANGED event to notify other code blocks that
// the display month has been altered
this.decrementDisplayMonth = function() {
    this.setDisplayMonth($.Date.add(this.getDisplayMonth(), {
        month: -1
    }));

    var thisCalendar = this.getCalendarInstance();
    var eventType = thisCalendar.eventType;
```

```
            thisCalendar.fire(eventType.MONTH_CHANGED, {
                displayMonth: this.getDisplayMonth(),
                selectedDate: this.getSelectedDate()
            });
        }

        // The addObservers method assigns functions to execute when certain events
        // are fired within the calendar control, either by the current code block or
        // by others
        this.addObservers = function() {
            var self = this;
            var thisCalendar = this.getCalendarInstance();
            var eventType = thisCalendar.eventType;

            // Listen for the INITIALIZE event being fired, then fire the READY event
            // immediately, passing it the current month to display and the currently
            // selected date. The master Calendar instance will fire the INITIALIZE
            // event once it has instantiated this code block
            thisCalendar.listen(eventType.INITIALIZE, function() {
                thisCalendar.fire(eventType.READY, {
                    displayMonth: self.getDisplayMonth(),
                    selectedDate: self.getSelectedDate()
                });
            });

            // Listen for the INCREMENT_DISPLAY_MONTH event to fire, and increment the
            // date stored in the displayMonth property accordingly when it is fired
            thisCalendar.listen(eventType.INCREMENT_DISPLAY_MONTH, function() {
                self.incrementDisplayMonth();
            });

            // Listen for the DECREMENT_DISPLAY_MONTH event to fire, and decrement the
            // displayMonth date property when it occurs
            thisCalendar.listen(eventType.DECREMENT_DISPLAY_MONTH, function(){
                self.decrementDisplayMonth();
            });

            // Listen for the DATE_SELECTED event and store the passed in JavaScript
            // Date object as the newly selected date and update the displayMonth
            // property according to the month of the newly selected date
            thisCalendar.listen(eventType.DATE_SELECTED, function(selectedDate) {
                self.setSelectedDate(selectedDate);
                self.setDisplayMonth(selectedDate);
            });

            return this;
        };
```

```
        // Initialize the Data code block, storing the passed in properties and
        // beginning to listen for events fired in the system
        var initialize = function(options, thisCalendar){
            this
                .setCalendarInstance(thisCalendar)
                .setSelectedDate(options.selectedDate)
                .setDisplayMonth(options.selectedDate)
                .addObservers();
        }.call(this, options, thisCalendar);
    };


// The UI code block is a constructor and contains code to display and allow
// interaction with the visible calendar control on the page. This code block is
// completely separate from the Data code block defined previously, but relies
// on the same set of events being fired within the control, according to
// the Observer pattern
Calendar.prototype.UI = function(options, thisCalendar) {

    // Define three properties for this code block: a reference to the master
    // Calendar instance, which will instantiate this code block, the destination
    // DOM element to place the calendar control within, and an object literal
    // containing the text strings to use for day and month names, along with
    // the text for 'previous' and 'next' buttons
    this.thisCalendar = this;
    this.destinationElement = $.Elements.create("div");
    this.strings = {
        days: ["Sunday", "Monday", "Tuesday", "Wednesday", "Thursday", "Friday", ➥
            "Saturday"],
        months: ["January", "February", "March", "April", "May", "June", "July", ➥
            "August", "September", "October", "November", "December"],
        previous: 'Previous',
        next: 'Next'
    }

    // We now declare a series of getter and setter methods to protect access to
    // these properties, ensuring they always have real values contained within them

    this.getCalendarInstance = function() {
        return this.thisCalendar;
    }

    this.setCalendarInstance = function(thisCalendar) {
        this.thisCalendar = thisCalendar || this;
        return this;
    }
```

```
// The getDestinationElement method returns the destinationElement property
this.getDestinationElement = function() {
    return this.destinationElement;
}

// The setDestinationElement method sets the destinationElement property to the
// passed in value, or creates a new element from scratch if one is not supplied
this.setDestinationElement = function(element) {
    this.destinationElement = element || $.Elements.create("div");
    return this;
}

// The getLanguageStrings method returns the strings property for use
// within the calendar
this.getLanguageStrings = function() {
    return this.strings;
}

// The setLanguageStrings method combines a supplied object literal with the
// current strings object literal property, overriding existing values with
// those supplied with an identical property name
this.setLanguageStrings = function(languageStrings) {
    this.strings = $.Utils.mergeObjects(this.strings, languageStrings);
    return this;
}

// The getDayNameByDay method expects a number representing the day of the week
// (0 = Sunday, 6 = Saturday) and returns, from the strings object literal, the
// day name that corresponds with that weekday
this.getDayNameByDay = function(day) {
    return this.getLanguageStrings().days[day];
}

// The getDayName method returns the weekday name for a supplied JavaScript Date
// object, using the strings object literal property
this.getDayName = function(date) {
    return this.getDayNameByDay(date.getDay());
}

// The getMonthNameByMonth method expects a number representing a month
// (0 = January, 11 = December) and returns the name of the month corresponding
// to that month from the strings object literal property
this.getMonthNameByMonth = function(month) {
    return this.getLanguageStrings().months[month];
}

// The getMonthName method returns the month name for a supplied JavaScript Date
// object, using the names stored in the strings object literal property
```

```
this.getMonthName = function(date) {
    return this.getMonthNameByMonth(date.getMonth());
}

// The applyStyle method sets a class on the destinationElement to allow us to
// use CSS to style the calendar control correctly
this.applyStyle = function() {
    $.CSS.addClass(this.getDestinationElement(), "cal-container");
    return this;
}

// The getHeadingElement method returns a DOM element displaying the month
// and year of the currently displayed month for inclusion at the top of the
// calendar control
this.getHeadingElement = function(displayMonth) {

    // Create a paragraph tag and format the currently displayed month by its
    // full month name and year
    var p = $.Elements.create("p");
    p.innerHTML = $.Date.format(displayMonth, "{mmmm} {yyyy}", "", ➥
        this.getMonthName(displayMonth));

    // Return this new paragraph tag. It will be added to the control at
    // a later stage
    return p;
}

// The getMonthNavigatorElement creates and returns the DOM elements that will
// allow the user to navigate forward and backward through the months in order
// to select a different date
this.getMonthNavigatorElement = function() {

    // Create an ordered list element to contain the previous and next buttons
    // within two list items
    var ul = $.Elements.create("ul");

    // Create the list item and link, which will act as the previous button to
    // take the user's calendar view back one month without selecting a
    // new date on the calendar itself
    var liPrevious = $.Elements.create("li");
    liPrevious.className = "cal-previous";
    var aPrevious = $.Elements.create("a");
    aPrevious.className = "cal-btn-previous";
    aPrevious.title = this.getLanguageStrings().previous;
    aPrevious.innerHTML = this.getLanguageStrings().previous;
    liPrevious.appendChild(aPrevious);
```

```
        // Create the list item and link, which will act as the next button to take
        // the user forward one month
        var liNext = $.Elements.create("li");
        liNext.className = "cal-next";
        var aNext = $.Elements.create("a");
        aNext.className = "cal-btn-next";
        aNext.title = this.getLanguageStrings().next;
        aNext.innerHTML = this.getLanguageStrings().next;
        liNext.appendChild(aNext);

        ul.appendChild(liPrevious);
        ul.appendChild(liNext);

        // Return the list item representing this month navigator. It will be added
        // to the calendar control later
        return ul;
    }

    // The getCalendarElement method creates the actual calendar element as
    // a <table> tag
    this.getCalendarElement = function(displayMonth, selectedDate) {
        var DAYS_IN_WEEK = 7;

        // No month can cross more than 6 weeks, so we'll render all months with
        // 6 weeks. We will display dates that fall outside the current date using a
        // different style to differentiate them from the current month but still
        // allow them to be selectable, giving the user the chance to select dates
        // that are not in the current month but fall a few days either side
        var WEEKS_TO_SHOW = 6;

        // Get the first day to display in this 6-week month block
        var dateDisplay = $.Date.getStartOfFirstWeekInMonthSquare(displayMonth);

        // Create a <table> element to house the calendar
        var table = $.Elements.create("table");
        table.cellpadding = "0";

        // Create the header cells for the table, which will display the name of
        // each day of the week
        var thead = $.Elements.create("thead");
        var tr = $.Elements.create("tr");
        for (var day = 0, totalDays = DAYS_IN_WEEK; day < totalDays; day++) {
            var th = $.Elements.create("th");

            // Format the title attribute to be the full name of the day of the week
            th.title = $.Date.format(new Date(), "{dddd}", ➥
                this.getDayNameByDay(day), "");
```

```
    // Format the displayed text to be the shortened form of the weekday
    // name, to save on space
    th.innerHTML = $.Date.format(new Date(), "{ddd}", ➡
        this.getDayNameByDay(day), "");
    tr.appendChild(th);
}
thead.appendChild(tr);

// Create the cells representing each day of the 6-week month block
var tbody = $.Elements.create("tbody");

// Loop through the weeks on display
for (var week = 0, totalWeeks = WEEKS_TO_SHOW; week < totalWeeks; week++) {

    // Each week is represented by a row in the table
    var tr = $.Elements.create("tr");

    // Loop through the days in each week
    for (var day = 0, totalDays = DAYS_IN_WEEK; day < totalDays; day++) {

        // Establish if the current date in the loop exists within the
        // currently displayed month
        var isCurrentDisplayedMonth = $.Date.matchMonth(displayMonth, ➡
            dateDisplay);

        // Establish if the current date in the loop matches the
        // currently selected date
        var isSelectedDate = $.Date.match(selectedDate, dateDisplay);

        // Represent the current date in the loop as a table cell with
        // a link inside
        var td = $.Elements.create("td");

        // The title attribute of the table cell contains the full date,
        // e.g., Thursday 14 May 2009
        td.title = $.Date.format(dateDisplay, "{dddd} {d} {mmmm} {yyyy}", ➡
            this.getDayName(dateDisplay), this.getMonthName(dateDisplay));

        // Set the class of the table cell correctly, denoting if the
        // current date is selected or if it is in the current
        // month or one of the neighboring months
        td.className = isSelectedDate ? (isCurrentDisplayedMonth ? ➡
            "cal-selected-date" : "cal-different-month ➡
            cal-selected-date") : (isCurrentDisplayedMonth ? ➡
            "cal-current-month" :"cal-different-month");

        // Create a link element to display the date within
        var a = $.Elements.create("a");
```

```
        // Set the class of the link element
        a.className = $.Date.format(dateDisplay, "cal-btn-day day-{d}", ➥
            this.getDayName(dateDisplay), this.getMonthName(dateDisplay));

        // Create a new custom attribute to store the current date as a
        // string representing the JavaScript Date object - this is so that
        // we can retrieve the date again later
        a.setAttribute("datetime", $.Date.format(dateDisplay, "{tttt}", ➥
            this.getDayName(dateDisplay), this.getMonthName(dateDisplay)));

        // Set the text within the link to display the date number of
        // the current date
        a.innerHTML = $.Date.format(dateDisplay, "{d}", ➥
            this.getDayName(dateDisplay), this.getMonthName(dateDisplay));

        // Add the link to the table cell and table cell to the table row
        td.appendChild(a);
        tr.appendChild(td);

        // Increment the date in the loop by one day for the next iteration
        dateDisplay = $.Date.add(dateDisplay, {
            day: 1
        });
    }

    // Add the table row to the <tbody> tag
    tbody.appendChild(tr);
}

// Add the header and body of the table to the <table> element itself
table.appendChild(thead);
table.appendChild(tbody);

// Return the fully populated <table> element for adding to the
// calendar control
return table;
}

// The render method constructs the calendar control from supplied values for
// the currently displayed month and currently selected date, then adds it to
// the page within the specified DOM element
this.render = function(dates) {
    var displayMonth = dates.displayMonth;
    var selectedDate = dates.selectedDate;
```

```
        // Use DocumentFragment objects for performance efficiency,
        // as described in Chapter 4
        var miniDOM = document.createDocumentFragment();
        miniDOM.appendChild(this.getHeadingElement(displayMonth));
        miniDOM.appendChild(this.getMonthNavigatorElement());
        miniDOM.appendChild(this.getCalendarElement(displayMonth, selectedDate));

        // Clear out any elements already within the DOM element container
        this.destinationElement.innerHTML = "";

        // Add the calendar control to the page
        this.getDestinationElement().appendChild(miniDOM.cloneNode(true));

        return this;
}

// The wireUpUserEvents method listens for mouse clicks occurring within
// the calendar control
this.wireUpUserEvents = function() {
    var self = this;

    $.Events.add(this.getDestinationElement(), "click", function(e) {
        // Stop the default click action of the element being selected
        e.preventDefault();

        // Execute the clickEvent method whenever the user selects something
        // within the calendar control
        self.clickEvent(e);
    });
}

// The clickEvent method is fired when the user clicks within the calendar
// control and is used to either select a different month to be
// displayed or to select a new date from the calendar
this.clickEvent = function(e) {
    var thisCalendar = this.getCalendarInstance();
    var eventType = thisCalendar.eventType;

    // Based on which element was clicked, we will fire calendar-wide
    // events using the Observer pattern
    if ($.CSS.hasClass(e.target, "cal-btn-previous")) {

        // If the user clicks the previous button in the month navigator,
        // then fire the DECREMENT_DISPLAY_MONTH event - we define
        // the behavior of that event later
        thisCalendar.fire(eventType.DECREMENT_DISPLAY_MONTH);
    } else if ($.CSS.hasClass(e.target, "cal-btn-next")) {
```

```
            // If the user clicks the next button in the month navigator, fire the
            // INCREMENT_DISPLAY_MONTH event
            thisCalendar.fire(eventType.INCREMENT_DISPLAY_MONTH);
        } else if ($.CSS.hasClass(e.target, "cal-btn-day")) {

            // If the user clicks a specific date within the calendar, we extract
            // the date from the datetime attribute we stored previously, then
            // fire the DATE_SELECTED event, passing it the selected
            // date as a JavaScript Date object
            var newlySelectedDate = new Date();
            newlySelectedDate.setTime(e.target.getAttribute("datetime"));
            thisCalendar.fire(eventType.DATE_SELECTED, newlySelectedDate);
        }
    }


    // The addObservers method assigns methods to fire when certain events fire in
    // the control, according to the Observer pattern
    this.addObservers = function() {
        var self = this;
        var thisCalendar = this.getCalendarInstance();
        var eventType = this.getCalendarInstance().eventType;

        // Listen for the READY event, which passes across the current month to
        // display and the currently selected date, and use this data to render the
        // calendar control on the page. Once rendered, fire the
        // HTML_RENDERED event
        thisCalendar.listen(eventType.READY, function(dates) {
            self.render(dates);
            thisCalendar.fire(eventType.HTML_RENDERED);
        });

        // Listen for the HTML_RENDERED event and set the appropriate class for
        // applying the correct styling to the calendar control. Also, connect up
        // browser events to detect when buttons and dates are selected
        // within the control
        thisCalendar.listen(eventType.HTML_RENDERED, function() {
            self.applyStyle();
            self.wireUpUserEvents();
        });

        // Listen for the MONTH_CHANGED event and re-render the control using the
        // new display and selected dates
        thisCalendar.listen(eventType.MONTH_CHANGED, function(dates) {
            self.render(dates);
        });
```

```
        // Listen for the DATE_SELECTED event, re-rendering the control using
        // the currently selected date. The display date will be set to the same as
        // the selected date so that, when selected, the selected month becomes
        // the month currently displayed - useful if the user clicks on one of the
        // dates that lies just outside the current month within the control
        thisCalendar.listen(eventType.DATE_SELECTED, function(selectedDate) {
            self.render({
                displayMonth: selectedDate,
                selectedDate: selectedDate
            });
        });

        return this;
    }

    // The initialize self-instantiating function stores the relevant values passed
    // in and begins listening for events fired within the control, according to
    // the Observer pattern
    var initialize = function(options, thisCalendar) {
        this
            .setCalendarInstance(thisCalendar)
            .setDestinationElement(options.destinationElement)
            .setLanguageStrings(options.strings)
            .addObservers();

        return this;
    }(options, thisCalendar);
};
```

Testing the Calendar Control

Now let's create a simple HTML page to put your new calendar control to the test. The code in Listing 8-3 defines an HTML page containing three <select> boxes to represent day, month, and year inputs in a <form>. You'll connect your calendar control to these three controls, as shown earlier in Figure 8-6.

Listing 8-3. *HTML Page Containing a Custom Calendar Control*

```
<!DOCTYPE html PUBLIC "-//W3C//DTD XHTML 1.0 Strict//EN" ➥
    "http://www.w3.org/TR/xhtml1/DTD/xhtml1-strict.dtd">
<html xmlns="http://www.w3.org/1999/xhtml" lang="en" xml:lang="en">
    <head>
        <meta http-equiv="Content-Type" content="text/html; charset=utf-8" />
        <title>Calendar example</title>
        <!-- Define and reference your own style sheet file here -->
        <link rel="stylesheet" href="calendar.css" type="text/css" />
    </head>
```

```
<body>
    <form method="post" action="/">
        <div id="select-boxes">
            <select name="day" id="day">
                <option value="1">1</option>
                <!-- Fill in the missing option values here -->
                <option value="31">31</option>
            </select>

            <select name="month" id="month">
                <option value="0">January</option>
                <!-- Fill in the missing option values here -->
                <option value="11">December</option>
            </select>

            <select name="year" id="year">
                <option value="2000">2000</option>
                <!-- Fill in the missing option values here -->
                <option value="2009">2009</option>
            </select>
        </div>

        <div id="calendar"></div>
        <div>
            <input type="submit" value="Save" />
        </div>
    </form>

    <!-- Reference the $ JavaScript library, complete with the additions
         we made earlier -->
    <script type="text/javascript" src="$.js"></script>

    <!-- Reference the file containing our calendar control constructor -->
    <script type="text/javascript" src="calendar.js"></script>

    <!-- The code to place the calendar onto the page and connect it to the
         existing HTML controls. You should place this within an external file
         in a real web application instead of in page -->
    <script type="text/javascript">
        $.onDomReady(function() {

            // Get references to the three <select> boxes representing the
            // selected date
            var dayField = document.getElementById('day');
            var monthField = document.getElementById('month');
            var yearField = document.getElementById('year');
```

```javascript
// Instantiate a calendar control, placing it in the
// <div id="calendar"> tag on the page and using
// the currently selected date from the <select> boxes.
// For fun, let's localize the calendar control into Spanish,
// so we pass the text in by means of the strings
// object literal property
var calendar = new Calendar({
    destinationElement: document.getElementById('calendar'),
    strings: {
        days: ["domingo", "lunes", "martes", "miércoles", ➡
            "jueves", "viernes", "sábado"],
        months: ["enero", "febrero", "marzo", "abril", "mayo", ➡
            "junio", "julio", "agosto", "septiembre", "octubre", ➡
            "noviembre", "diciembre"],
        previous: "anterior",
        next: "siguiente"
    },
    selectedDate: (function() {

        // Get the currently selected date from the <select> boxes
        // and pass it to the calendar control as a JavaScript
        // Date object
        var day = dayField.options[ ➡
            dayField.options.selectedIndex].value;
        var month = monthField.options[ ➡
            monthField.options.selectedIndex].value;
        var year = yearField.options[ ➡
            yearField.options.selectedIndex].value;
        return new Date(year, month, day);
    }())
});

// Use the Observer pattern nature of the calendar control to listen
// for the DATE_SELECTED event to fire from within the calendar
// control. This event fires when a new date is selected on the
// calendar and passes to any listening function the newly
// selected date as a JavaScript Date object
calendar.listen(calendar.eventType.DATE_SELECTED, ➡
        function(selectedDate) {

    // Establish the day, month, and year from the newly selected
    // date and select the appropriate options in each <select>
    // box on the page. When the HTML form is saved, the
    // selected date will therefore be saved as it now exists
    // within existing HTML form controls
    var day = selectedDate.getDate();
```

```
                    var month = selectedDate.getMonth();
                    var year = selectedDate.getFullYear();
                    for (var index = 0, length = dayField.options.length; ➡
                            index < length; index++) {
                        if (dayField.options[index].value == day) {
                            dayField.options[index].selected = "selected";
                        }
                    }
                    for (var index = 0, length = monthField.options.length; ➡
                            index < length; index++) {
                        if (monthField.options[index].value == month) {
                            monthField.options[index].selected = "selected";
                        }
                    }
                    for (var index = 0, length = yearField.options.length; ➡
                            index < length; index++) {
                        if (yearField.options[index].value == year) {
                            yearField.options[index].selected = "selected";
                        }
                    }
                });

                // When the user changes the selected options within the <select>
                // boxes, we want to reflect this on the calendar control. To do
                // this we first create a JavaScript Date object based on the newly
                // selected form field values, then fire the DATE_SELECTED event
                // within the calendar, passing the control the new Date object.
                // The display will then be updated by the code within the control
                // listening for this event to be fired
                function selectDateOnCalendar(e) {
                    var day = dayField.options[ ➡
                        dayField.options.selectedIndex].value;
                    var month = monthField.options[ ➡
                        monthField.options.selectedIndex].value;
                    var year = yearField.options[ ➡
                        yearField.options.selectedIndex].value;
                    calendar.fire(calendar.eventType.DATE_SELECTED, ➡
                        new Date(year, month, day));
                }

                $.Events.add(dayField, "change", selectDateOnCalendar);
                $.Events.add(monthField, "change", selectDateOnCalendar);
                $.Events.add(yearField, "change", selectDateOnCalendar);
            });
        </script>
    </body>
</html>
```

As an extension of this example, you could put two calendar widgets on a page, and code them so that selecting a date in one forces the other to change. To achieve this, you would listen for events fired within the first calendar instance and use that to fire events on the second.

The Observer pattern is versatile and will support a virtually limitless number of calendar widgets on one page, all of which could be associated with each other. Feel free to experiment. Pull the code apart to see what it does. Try listening to and firing events of your own, and observe the outcome.

Slider Control

Another useful control you may want to add to your forms is a slider. This type of control can provide a more visually descriptive method for selecting values than from a list. It's appropriate in cases where the values increment by equal amounts and lie within a fixed range.

To demonstrate how to build a slider control for a form, we'll walk through creating the slider shown in Figure 8-7. Above this slider is a `<select>` box that serves as a volume-level selector as part of a multimedia playback page. This list has 11 entries, representing values from 0 to 100 in steps of 10, where 0 is denoted by the Mute option and 100 is denoted by the Max option.

Figure 8-7. *A slider and connected <select> box representing a volume control*

The slider control beneath the `<select>` box provides an alternative means to set the volume level. The user can click and drag the triangular handle element left and right along the control, and the handle will snap to the positions immediately beneath the values displayed along the top of the control. When the user releases the mouse button, you take the selected value and update the `<select>` box to match it. Conversely, if the user selects a value from the drop-down box, the slider should update to the correct position.

Building the Slider

Similar to how you constructed the calendar widget in the previous section, you will use the Observer pattern for the slider control. You will create two completely separate code blocks: one for managing and manipulating the data and one for managing the displayed widget on the page. These will be connected to each other only through the published events, managed by the main slider control constructor. Listing 8-4 shows the code for this slider control. Save this code in a file named `slider.js`.

Listing 8-4. *A Custom Slider Form Control*

```
// We start by declaring the Slider class which represents the slider control, as we
// did with the Calendar control, previously

var Slider = function(options) {
```

```
        // Declare the event types that define the slider's behavior
        this.eventType = {

            // The INITIALIZE event kicks everything off and is fired after all the code
            // blocks are instantiated
            INITIALIZE: 0,

            // The READY event is fired when the data has been initialized and is ready
            // to be rendered to the page
            READY: 1,

            // The HTML_RENDERED event is fired once the control has been
            // rendered to the page
            HTML_RENDERED: 2,

            // The HANDLE_MOVED event is fired when the user has dragged
            // the control's handle
            HANDLE_MOVED: 3,

            // The VALUE_CHANGED event is fired when the slider's value has been altered
            VALUE_CHANGED: 4,

            // The MOVE event is fired when the code wishes to update the position of
            // the slider to represent a new value
            MOVE: 5
        }

        // The initialize self-instantiating function instantiates the two code blocks:
        // Data, which represents the data storage and manipulation code, and UI,
        // which represents the control on the page and its interactions with the user
        var initialize = function(options) {
            new this.Data(options, this);
            new this.UI(options, this);

            // Once the code blocks are instantiated, we fire the INITIALIZE event
            this.fire(this.eventType.INITIALIZE);

            return this;
        }.call(this, options);
    }

// Inherit the Observer pattern's listen and fire events
Slider.prototype = new $.Observer;

// The Data code block represents the data storage and manipulation part of the
// slider control's code base
Slider.prototype.Data = function(options, thisSlider){
```

```
// Store a reference to the master slider object instance in order to refer to
// its events list, and declare a property to store an array of possible values
// represented on the slider and a property to store the currently selected
// index within that array of values
this.thisSlider = this;
this.values = [];
this.selectedIndex = 0;

// A series of getters and setters provide a means for the rest of the code to
// access the stored data properties safely
this.getSliderInstance = function() {
    return this.thisSlider;
}

this.setSliderInstance = function(thisSlider) {
    this.thisSlider = thisSlider || this;
    return this;
}

this.getValues = function() {
    return this.values;
}

this.setValues = function(values) {
    this.values = values || this.getValues();
    return this;
}

this.getSelectedIndex = function() {
    return this.selectedIndex;
}

this.setSelectedIndex = function(newIndex) {
    this.selectedIndex = newIndex || this.getSelectedIndex();
    return this;
}

// The getIndexByPercentage method provides a useful way of establishing
// the index in the array of slider values that is represented by the position to
// which the slider handle has been dragged within the control, specified as a
// percentage. If the handle is dragged to the far left, the first index of the
// array would be returned; if dragged to the far right, the last index would
// be returned
this.getIndexByPercentage = function(percentage) {
    var values = this.getValues();
    var index = Math.round((percentage / 100) * (values.length - 1));
    return index;
}
```

```
// The getPercentageByIndex method returns the percentage position through
// the slider where the handle should be located, based on a specific index of the
// array of values. An index of 0 would return 0 percent. The final index
// of the array would represent 100 percent.
this.getPercentageByIndex = function(index) {
    var values = this.getValues();
    var percentage = ((index / (values.length - 1)) * 100);
    return percentage;
}


// The getValueByPercentage locates the value represented within the array
// of values for a given percentage position of the handle through the
// slider control
this.getValueByPercentage = function(percentage) {
    var values = this.getValues();
    var index = this.getIndexByPercentage(percentage);
    return values[index];
}


// The addObservers method listens for events fired within the slider control
// and reacts to them
this.addObservers = function() {
    var self = this;
    var thisSlider = this.getSliderInstance();
    var eventType = thisSlider.eventType;

    // Listen for the INITIALIZE event and immediately fire the READY event,
    // passing it the array of values to represent on the control and the
    // selected index within that array of the currently selected item
    thisSlider.listen(eventType.INITIALIZE, function() {
        thisSlider.fire(eventType.READY, {
            values: self.getValues(),
            index: self.getSelectedIndex()
        });
    });

    // Listen for the HANDLE_MOVED event, which receives the current percentage
    // position of the handle through the control. Fire the VALUE_CHANGED event,
    // passing it the array of values and the index within that array that
    // should be represented at the position of the handle
    thisSlider.listen(eventType.HANDLE_MOVED, function(percentage) {
        thisSlider.fire(eventType.VALUE_CHANGED, {
            values: self.getValues(),
            index: self.getIndexByPercentage(percentage)
        });
    });
```

```
        // Listen for the MOVE event, which receives the new index position to move
        // the control to. Fire the VALUE_CHANGED event, passing it the array of
        // values and the new index within that array so that the UI can be updated
        thisSlider.listen(eventType.MOVE, function(index) {
            thisSlider.fire(eventType.VALUE_CHANGED, {
                values: self.getValues(),
                index: index
            });
        });

        // Listen for the VALUE_CHANGED event, setting the selected index from the
        // value passed to the event
        thisSlider.listen(eventType.VALUE_CHANGED, function(results) {
            self.setSelectedIndex(results.index);
        });

        return this;
    };

    // Initialize the Data code block within the slider control by setting its
    // default values and begin to listen for events fired in the system
    var initialize = function(options, thisSlider){
        this
            .setSliderInstance(thisSlider)
            .setValues(options.values)
            .setSelectedIndex(options.selectedIndex)
            .addObservers();

        return this;
    }.call(this, options, thisSlider);
}

// The UI code block contains the code necessary to render the slider control to the
// page and provide user interaction with that control
Slider.prototype.UI = function(options, thisSlider){

    // Define the UI-related properties for the slider control, including a
    // reference to the master Slider object instance to connect to its events,
    // a reference to the DOM element to place the control within on the page,
    // and references to the handle element, its container, and the labels to
    // display beneath the handle
    this.thisSlider = this;
    this.destinationElement = null;
    this.handleElement = null;
    this.handleRangeElement = null;
    this.valueLabelsElement = null;
```

```
    // Create getter and setter methods to protect the values in the properties
    this.getSliderInstance = function() {
        return this.thisSlider;
    }

    this.setSliderInstance = function(thisSlider) {
        this.thisSlider = thisSlider || this;
        return this;
    }

    this.getDestinationElement = function() {
        return this.destinationElement;
    }

    this.setDestinationElement = function(destinationElement) {
        this.destinationElement = destinationElement || $.Elements.create("div");
        return this;
    }

    this.getHandleElement = function() {
        return this.handleElement;
    }

    this.setHandleElement = function(handleElement) {
        this.handleElement = handleElement || $.Elements.create("div");
        return this;
    }

    this.getHandleRangeElement = function() {
        return this.handleRangeElement;
    }

    this.setHandleRangeElement = function(handleRangeElement) {
        this.handleRangeElement = handleRangeElement || $.Elements.create("div");
        return this;
    }

    this.getValueLabelsElement = function() {
        return this.valueLabelsElement;
    }

    this.setValueLabelsElement = function(valueLabelsElement) {
        this.valueLabelsElement = valueLabelsElement || $.Elements.create("div");
        return this;
    }
```

```javascript
// The generateSliderElement method generates a DOM object containing the
// elements required to render a slider control on the page
this.generateSliderElement = function(values) {

    // Create a single container element within which to place all
    // other elements
    var container = $.Elements.create("div");

    // Create an element to store the set of value labels associated with the
    // array of possible data values represented within the slider control
    var valueLabels = $.Elements.create("div");
    valueLabels.className = "value-labels";

    // Loop through the array of values passed to this method, creating a
    // DOM element for each one containing the text value to show on the
    // slider control's label row
    for (var index = 0, length = values.length; index < length; index++) {
        var valueLabel = $.Elements.create("div");
        valueLabel.className = "value-label";
        valueLabel.innerHTML = values[index];
        valueLabels.appendChild(valueLabel);
    }

    // Add the valueLabels element, complete with the value labels within, to
    // the container DOM element
    container.appendChild(valueLabels);

    // Create a DOM element to use as the handle for the user to drag to select
    // values along the slider control
    var handle = $.Elements.create("div");
    handle.className = "handle";

    // Create a DOM element to use as a container for the handle, allowing us to
    // later use CSS to restrict how far the handle can be moved within
    // the slider
    var handleRange = $.Elements.create("div");
    handleRange.className = "handle-range";

    // Add the handle to its container element
    handleRange.appendChild(handle);

    // Add the handle container to the container element surrounding the
    // whole slider control
    container.appendChild(handleRange);
```

```
        // Return the single DOM element containing the slider's HTML elements
        return container;
    }

    // The render method draws the slider component onto the page within the
    // specified page element
    this.render = function(values) {
        var thisSlider = this.getSliderInstance();
        var eventType = thisSlider.eventType;

        // Get the DOM elements for the slider control and add them to the page
        var documentFragment = document.createDocumentFragment();
        documentFragment.appendChild(this.generateSliderElement(values));
        this.getDestinationElement().appendChild(documentFragment.cloneNode(true));

        // Fire the HTML_RENDERED event now that the control is on the page
        thisSlider.fire(eventType.HTML_RENDERED);

        return this;
    }

    // The applyStyle method adds a class name to the page element to allow the
    // slider control to be styled in the appropriate way
    this.applyStyle = function() {
        $.CSS.addClass(this.getDestinationElement(), "slider");

        // To ensure that the handle is always displayed within the handle range
        // container element, we specify the handle to use absolute positioning
        // relative to its container element. This ensures the slider should work
        // in the case where the CSS style rule for this has been neglected
        this.getHandleRangeElement().style.position = "relative";
        this.getHandleElement().style.position = "absolute";

        return this;
    }

    // The positionLabels method sets the position of the value label elements along
    // the width of the slider control from left to right, filling all available
    // space
    this.positionLabels = function() {

        // Find the width of the container element, encompassing the
        // individual labels
        var labelContainerWidth = parseInt($.CSS.getAppliedStyle( ➥
            this.getValueLabelsElement(), "width"));
```

```
// Get an array of all the label value elements in the slider control
var labels = $.Elements.getElementsByClassName("value-label", ➥
    this.getDestinationElement());

// Make a pretty good estimate of the width of each of the value elements
var defaultWidth = Math.round(labelContainerWidth / labels.length);

// Loop through each label element
for (var index = 0, length = labels.length; index < length; index++) {

    // Ensure each label uses absolute positioning or it will not
    // display correctly
    labels[index].style.position = "absolute";

    // Try to get the actual width of each label element based on the
    // text within it
    var width = parseInt($.CSS.getAppliedStyle(labels[ ➥
        labelIndex], "width"));

    // Sometimes, Internet Explorer does not return a width in this way.
    // If no value is returned, use the estimated width calculated
    // earlier instead
    if (isNaN(width)) {
        width = defaultWidth;
    }

    // We want to center the label text around the position we're trying
    // to find, so we need to calculate half the width of the label in order
    // to shift it that distance to the left of the central point - making
    // the text appear centered
    var halfWidth = Math.round(width / 2);
    var proportionThroughSlider = labelIndex / (labels.length - 1);
    var position = (Math.round(proportionThroughSlider * ➥
        labelContainerWidth) - halfWidth);

    // Position this label element correctly using CSS
    labels[labelIndex].style.width = width + "px";
    labels[labelIndex].style.left = position + "px";
}

// We need to set the label wrapper element's CSS positioning to relative,
// so that the label elements display correctly within it
this.getValueLabelsElement().style.position = "relative";

return this;
}
```

```
    // The setHandlePositionByPercentage method positions the handle within its
    // container element based on the supplied percentage value
    this.setHandlePositionByPercentage = function(percentage) {
        this.getHandleElement().style.left = percentage + "%";
        return this;
    }


    // The setHandlePosition moves the handle element to the position represented by
    // the selected index and data value array passed to it. If the selected index
    // is 0, the handle is moved all the way to the left. If the selected index is
    // the last in the array, the handle is moved all the way to the right
    this.setHandlePosition = function(data) {
        var percentage = (data.index / (data.values.length - 1)) * 100;
        this.setHandlePositionByPercentage(percentage);

        return this;
    };


    // The wireUpUserEvents method provides the user interactions with the
    // slider control, allowing the handle to be dragged to a new position
    this.wireUpUserEvents = function() {
        var self = this;

        // Execute methods when the mouse is pressed down on the handle, and
        // released and moved anywhere on the page
        $.Events.add(this.getHandleElement(), "mousedown", function(e) {
            self.onMouseDown(e);
        });

        $.Events.add(document.body, "mouseup", function(e) {
            self.onMouseUp(e);
        });

        $.Events.add(document.body, "mousemove", function(e) {
            self.onMouseMove(e);
        });
    }


    // Define a value to store whether the mouse button is currently
    // depressed - only gets set if the initial button press occurred over
    // the handle element
    this.mouseButtonHeldDown = false;


    // Executed when the mouse is pressed down on the handle element
    this.onMouseDown = function(e) {
```

```
    // Prevent the default mouse down action on the handle element
    e.preventDefault();

    // Denote that the mouse button is now held down on the handle
    this.mouseButtonHeldDown = true;
}

// Executed when the mouse button is lifted up anywhere on the page
this.onMouseUp = function(e) {

    // Signify that the mouse button is no longer being held down
    this.mouseButtonHeldDown = false;
}

// Executed when the mouse is being moved anywhere on the page
this.onMouseMove = function(e) {

    // If the mouse button is still being held down on the handle and the mouse
    // is being moved, this can be considered a drag of the handle, so execute
    // a new onDrag method
    if (this.mouseButtonHeldDown) {
        this.onDrag(e);
    }
}

// The onDrag method allows the slider handle to be moved horizontally within
// its container, updating the selected value within the control when it is
// moved to a new position
this.onDrag = function(e) {
    var thisSlider = this.getSliderInstance();
    var eventType = thisSlider.eventType;

    // Get the width of the handle's container element
    var handleHolderWidth = parseInt($.CSS.getAppliedStyle( ➥
        this.getHandleRangeElement(), "width"));

    // Get the current x-position of the mouse
    var mouseX = e.pageX;

    // Get the current x-position of the handle's container element
    var elementWrapperX = parseInt($.CSS.getPosition( ➥
        this.getHandleRangeElement()).x);

    // Calculate the difference between these two values, which represents the
    // distance in pixels of the current handle position from the leftmost point
    // of the container element
    var distanceFromLeft = mouseX - elementWrapperX;
```

```
        // Restrict dragging of the handle to within the confines of the
        // container element
        if (distanceFromLeft >= 0 && distanceFromLeft <= handleHolderWidth) {

            // Calculate the percentage position the handle lies within
            // its container
            var percentage = Math.round((distanceFromLeft / handleHolderWidth) * ➥
                100);

            // Fire the HANDLE_MOVED event, passing it the new percentage position
            // of the handle
            thisSlider.fire(eventType.HANDLE_MOVED, percentage);
        }
    }

    // The addObservers method listens for events fired within the slider control as
    // a whole and acts upon them to update the UI of the control
    this.addObservers = function(){
        var self = this;
        var thisSlider = this.getSliderInstance();
        var eventType = thisSlider.eventType;

        // Listen for the READY event to fire, which passes across the data values
        // and selected index, and use these to render the control and set the
        // initial position of the handle
        thisSlider.listen(eventType.READY, function(data) {
            self.render(data.values);
            self.setHandlePosition(data);
        });

        // Listen for the HTML_RENDERED event to fire, and use it to locate and
        // store references to some of the new controls added. Position the labels
        // within the control and set up the controls for user interaction within
        // the browser
        thisSlider.listen(eventType.HTML_RENDERED, function(){
            var destinationElement = self.getDestinationElement();

            self
                .setHandleElement($.Elements.getElementsByClassName("handle", ➥
                    self.getDestinationElement())[0])
                .setHandleRangeElement($.Elements.getElementsByClassName( ➥
                    "handle-range", self.getDestinationElement())[0])
                .setValueLabelsElement($.Elements.getElementsByClassName( ➥
                    "value-labels", self.getDestinationElement())[0])
                .applyStyle()
                .positionLabels()
                .wireUpUserEvents();
        });
```

```
            // Listen for the VALUE_CHANGED event to fire and update the handle position
            // to snap to the appropriate position based on the newly selected
            // data value
            thisSlider.listen(eventType.VALUE_CHANGED, function(data){
                self.setHandlePosition(data);
            });

            return this;
        };

        // Initialize the UI data block, setting the default properties and begin
        // listening for events
        var initialize = function(){
            this
                .setSliderInstance(thisSlider)
                .setDestinationElement(options.destinationElement)
                .addObservers();
        }.call(this, options, thisSlider)
    }
```

Testing the Slider Control

Now you can put your slider widget to work within a real HTML form. The code in Listing 8-5 shows an HTML page containing a `<select>` box with a fixed set of values representing the volume control, as shown earlier in Figure 8-7.

Listing 8-5. *An HTML Page Containing a Slider Control*

```html
<!DOCTYPE html PUBLIC "-//W3C//DTD XHTML 1.0 Strict//EN" ➥
    "http://www.w3.org/TR/xhtml1/DTD/xhtml1-strict.dtd">
<html xmlns="http://www.w3.org/1999/xhtml" lang="en" xml:lang="en">
    <head>
        <meta http-equiv="Content-Type" content="text/html; charset=utf-8" />
        <title>Slider example</title>

        <!-- Reference your own set of style rules for the slider control -->
        <link rel="stylesheet" href="slider.css" type="text/css" />
    </head>

    <body>
        <h1>Slider example</h1>
        <form method="post" action="/">
            <div id="volume-control">
                <label for="volume">Select volume level</label>

                <!-- Create the element to associate with the slider control -->
                <select name="volume" id="volume">
                    <option value="0">Mute</option>
```

```
                    <option value="10">1</option>
                    <option value="20">2</option>
                    <option value="30" selected="selected">3</option>
                    <option value="40">4</option>
                    <option value="50">5</option>
                    <option value="60">6</option>
                    <option value="70">7</option>
                    <option value="80">8</option>
                    <option value="90">9</option>
                    <option value="100">Max</option>
                </select>
            </div>

            <!-- Create an element to place the slider control within -->
            <div id="volume-slider"></div>
            <div>
                <input type="submit" value="Save" />
            </div>
        </form>

        <!-- Include a reference to the $ JavaScript library -->
        <script type="text/javascript" src="$.js"></script>

        <!-- Include a reference to the Slider component class -->
        <script type="text/javascript" src="slider.js"></script>

        <!-- The following script adds the slider control to the page and associates
             it with the <select> box on the page. In a real web application, this
             code should be placed within an external file and referenced here
             instead. It is included here for simplicity -->
        <script type="text/javascript">
            $.onDomReady(function() {

                // Get a reference to the <select> box we wish to use as the basis
                // for the slider control
                var volumeSelectBox = document.getElementById("volume");

                // Create a new instance of our slider control, placing the element
                // within the appropriate tag on the page and using the option
                // values from the <select> element as the slider's data values,
                // setting the default position of the slider to the currently
                // selected value in the <select> box
                var slider = new Slider({
                    destinationElement: document.getElementById("volume-slider"),
                    values: (function() {
```

```
                    // Create and return an array of data values taken from the
                    // options in the <select> box we are representing
                    // as a slider
                    var values = [];
                    for (var index = 0, length = ➡
                            volumeSelectBox.options.length; ➡
                            index < length; index++) {
                        values.push(volumeSelectBox.options[index].text);
                    }
                    return values;
                })(),
                selectedIndex: volumeSelectBox.options.selectedIndex
            });

            // Listen for the VALUE_CHANGED event to fire within the slider
            // instance, setting the selected option in the <select> box list to
            // match the newly selected value on the slider control. This allows
            // the value to be saved with the rest of the HTML form as the
            // slider value is represented within a real HTML form field element
            slider.listen(slider.eventType.VALUE_CHANGED, function(result) {
                volumeSelectBox.options[result.index].selected = true;
            });

            // Listen for changes to the selected option within the <select>
            // box, updating the slider position when the user selects a new
            // value using the drop down list instead of the slider
            // control. This keeps both controls in sync with each other
            $.Events.add(volumeSelectBox, "change", function() {
                slider.fire(slider.eventType.MOVE, ➡
                    volumeSelectBox.options.selectedIndex);
            });
        });
    </script>
    </body>
</html>
```

That's it! You've built a slider widget and connected it to a form control to provide a more intuitive way for your end users to interact with your forms, while ensuring that data gets sent back to the server in the correct format.

A drawback of this slider widget is that users without a mouse are unable to interact with the slider handle, and must use the <select> box above the slider to change the volume value. In Chapter 12, which is devoted to the topic of accessibility in RIAs, you will learn how to tackle this kind of problem by allowing users to interact with such controls using the keyboard.

You can apply the same techniques you used to construct the sample calendar and slider widgets to building your own custom form controls to offer your end users a more intuitive experience. Try to stick to building widgets that are simple to use. You might design controls that mimic those that people will already be familiar with from the operating system, but that are not exposed as part of HTML. You could also use ideas from the real world that translate well to the Web. Remember that this is a task in improving user experience, rather than demonstrating your JavaScript skills. That said, if you think you have a killer idea, don't hesitate to give it a shot, even if it isn't easy to create. If it works, share it with the rest of the web development community to promote the principle of reusable code. Don't forget to document your code and write unit tests to ensure you don't accidentally break your code with a future update.

Using Reusable Form Components

As with other areas of web development, some developers have already done the hard work of creating custom form controls, and they have made the results available as reusable components. Here, we'll look at two such components that provide functionality that is not present by default through HTML (though most web developers probably wish they were): SWFUpload for multiple file uploads and Tiny MCE for rich text editing.

SWFUpload: Multiple File Uploads with Progress Bars

The HTML file upload control works well for uploading small, single files. As you might expect, the selected file isn't sent to the server until the form is submitted, along with the rest of the data in the form. This could be a problem if the user has selected a large file that the server might reject for being too large or in a file format it was not expecting. Also, for larger files, there is no progress indicator when the form is submitted—no way of letting the users know how long they need to wait to discover if the form submission was successful. A preferred solution would do the following:

- Allow users to select one or many files

- Have those files begin sending themselves to the server before the rest of the form has been completed, if the page developer specifies this

- Show a progress indicator to give users an idea of how long they will need to wait for their file to upload

Fortunately, such solutions exist.

Adobe's Flash Player is an incredibly versatile browser plug-in that has a very strong presence on the Web, supported by a large installation base. Along with the many other Flash Player uses discussed throughout this part of the book, this plug-in supports a method for uploading files to a server. Not only that, but it is also able to report the upload progress and queue up multiple files to be sent in one shot.

Many smart Flash developers have written reusable components to expose this functionality for JavaScript developers to use on their pages. A quick Google search will reveal versions coded to work with several of the popular JavaScript libraries, such as jQuery (jQuery Transmit at `http://code.google.com/p/jquery-transmit/`) and MooTools (FancyUpload at `http://digitarald.de/project/fancyupload/`). Most of these components have virtually identical JavaScript APIs, which makes porting between them a fairly simple task.

■**Caution** You should ensure that any file upload component you choose has been updated to work with Flash Player version 10. An important security change was introduced in this version of Flash. This version requires the Browse file selection button to be contained within the Flash movie, and not on the page itself.

In this section, we'll look at a file upload component that can be run stand-alone, without requiring another JavaScript library. This component is called SWFUpload, and you can find the project home page at http://www.swfupload.org/. Download the latest release, and let's get started building a simple example form to demonstrate its abilities.

SWFUpload Sample Usage

Listing 8-6 shows a simple HTML page containing all the necessary form fields and elements to support the SWFUpload component.

Listing 8-6. *HTML Page Demonstrating the SWFUpload Component*

```
<!DOCTYPE html PUBLIC "-//W3C//DTD XHTML 1.0 Strict//EN" ➥
    "http://www.w3.org/TR/xhtml1/DTD/xhtml1-strict.dtd">
<html xmlns="http://www.w3.org/1999/xhtml" lang="en" xml:lang="en">
    <head>
        <meta http-equiv="Content-Type" content="text/html; charset=utf-8" />
        <title>Multiple file upload example</title>
        <link rel="stylesheet" href="upload.css" type="text/css" />
    </head>

    <body>
        <h1>Multiple file uploads example</h1>

        <!-- Forms with file upload fields must use the multipart/form-data encoding
            type when sending the data to the server for processing -->
        <form method="post" action="/" id="form" enctype="multipart/form-data">
            <fieldset>
                <legend>Files to upload</legend>

                <label for="make-multiple">Select files</label>

                <!-- Include a real file upload control, in case JavaScript
                    is disabled -->
                <input type="file" id="make-multiple" />

                <!-- Create an element to hold the Browse button in the Flash
                    component. The button to launch the file selection dialog
                    using Flash must itself be in Flash. Adobe considers it
                    a security risk otherwise -->
                <span id="browse-button"></span>
```

```
                    <!-- Create an element to reflect the current upload progress
                         back to the user -->
                    <div id="upload-progress"></div>
                </fieldset>
            </form>

            <!-- Reference the $ JavaScript library -->
            <script type="text/javascript" src="$.js"></script>

            <!-- Load the SWFObject API -->
            <script type="text/javascript" src="swfupload.js"></script>

            <!-- Configure our page. This code block should be contained within
                 an external file within a real web application. It is provided here
                 for simplicity -->
            <script type="text/javascript">

                // Define the settings to initialize the SWFObject component with
                var settings = {

                    // Locate the Flash file that provides the upload functionality
                    flash_url : "swfupload.swf",

                    // Specify the URL to upload the file to on the server - relative to
                    // the location of the Flash file
                    upload_url: "upload.php",

                    // Show debug information in the browser - useful for development
                    debug: true,

                    // Image file to use for the Browse button - relative to the
                    // location of the Flash file
                    button_image_url: "browse.png",

                    // Dimensions of the Browse button
                    button_width: "85",
                    button_height: "39",

                    // DOM element id to populate with the Browse button when
                    // the component initializes
                    button_placeholder_id: "browse-button",

                    // The swfupload_loaded_handler method will be called when the
                    // component has been initialized, if it has been supplied
                    swfupload_loaded_handler: function() {
```

```
                // Add a class of hide to the existing file upload control. Use
                // CSS to make the control invisible. Since the SWFUpload
                // component has successfully initialized, we no longer
                // need this control
                $.CSS.addClass(document.getElementById( ➥
                    "make-multiple"), "hide");
        }
};


// The file_queued_handler method is called by the SWFUpload component
// once a file has been selected in the file selection dialog, passing
// in an object literal containing details about that file, including
// its name, file size, and more. If multiple files are selected in the
// dialog, this method is called multiple times, once for each file.
// Here, we create an array of files to act as a file queue for
// uploading later
var queue = [];
settings.file_queued_handler = function(file) {
    queue.push(file);
}


// The upload_progress_handler event is fired regularly on a fixed time
// interval by the SWFUpload component, executing the following
// method each time. It specifies which file is currently being
// uploaded, the number of data bytes already sent to the server, and the
// total number of data bytes in the file. We use this to calculate the
// percentage complete of the file upload and reflect this within the
// HTML page while the file is being uploaded, giving our end users
// feedback on the progress of their uploads
settings.upload_progress_handler = function(file, bytesSent, ➥
        bytesTotal) {
    var percentComplete = (bytesSent / bytesTotal) * 100;
    var text = "{fileName} ({percentComplete}% complete)";

    document.getElementById("upload-progress").innerHTML = ➥
            $.Utils.replaceText(text, {
        fileName: file.name,
        percentComplete: percentComplete
    });
}


// The upload_complete_handler event is fired when a file completes
// uploading. We use this event to automatically begin upload of the
// next file in the queue. Once the last file has been uploaded, we
// submit the form on the page
```

```
            var filesCompleted = 0;
            settings.upload_complete_handler = function() {
                filesCompleted++;
                if (filesCompleted < queue.length) {
                    this.startUpload(); // Process the next in the queue
                } else if (filesCompleted == queue.length) {
                    document.getElementById("form").submit()
                }
            }
        }

        // Now that the settings for the SWFUpload control have been configured,
        // let's put it to use on our page once the DOM is ready to be accessed
        $.onDomReady(function() {

            // Apply the settings to the SWFUpload control and it's ready for
            // use on the page
            var uploader = new SWFUpload(settings);

            // Listen for the form submission event on the page
            $.Events.add(document.getElementById("form"), "submit", ➥
                    function(e) {

                // When the user attempts to submit the form, if there are files
                // waiting in the queue to be uploaded, cancel the form
                // submission and upload these files. The startUpload() method
                // of SWFUpload does exactly that. It begins upload of the first
                // file in the queue. The files then upload one by one until
                // the final file has been sent, at which point the
                // upload_complete_handler event fires and our method
                // specified earlier submits the form to the server. If there
                // are no files to be uploaded, the form will submit
                // as normal here
                if (queue.length > 0) {
                    e.preventDefault();
                    uploader.startUpload();
                }
            });
        });
    </script>
    </body>
</html>
```

This example demonstrates the use of the SWFUpload component. The page is capable of submitting multiple files for upload through a single file selection dialog box, and it shows the users a progress indicator, allowing them to infer how much longer they will need to wait for the form to be submitted.

SWFUpload Appraisal

The SWFUpload component allows you to upload multiple files, though only one simultaneously, to a server-side script, and supports cancellation of uploads at any time, all without requiring a page refresh. It allows you to restrict the file types and file size. Through a plug-in available with the component download, this component is capable of measuring the current and average upload speed of files, and allows you to relay this information to your page in order to keep your users informed. As you might expect, SWFUpload does not impose its own user interface, but rather requires that you, the page developer, build that yourself, connecting to the component through JavaScript events fired by the component. In short, the SWFUpload component provides a more elegant and user-friendlier solution for uploading multiple files or single large files than the default file upload control provided by HTML.

The component requires Flash Player version 9 or later to be installed on the end user's browser and JavaScript to be enabled. You may want to use the SWFObject component, introduced in Chapter 7, to detect through JavaScript whether the correct version of Flash Player is installed before attempting to include the component on your page.

The JavaScript file that must be included on the page weighs in at 19KB when minified. The Flash file, which exposes its capabilities to the page, is 12KB. Both are very acceptable sizes for use within a web application, and using `gzip` compression on your server will reduce these file sizes even more.

TinyMCE: Rich Text Editing

HTML's own `<textarea>` element allows users to input text in a more free-form manner than in a standard text input box, but it allows only plain text entry. You may want to provide your users with a means to input styled and formatted text, and even pictures. For example, most blog publishers would like to write text they can emphasize with bold, italics, and underline styles, and also to be able to drop images into their blog posts at specific positions. Thankfully, we are able to utilize third-party components to convert a standard `<textarea>` into a fully editable rich text area, where the content is converted into standard XHTML and saved back into the HTML form in this format. When the page is later reloaded, the content is read from XHTML and converted back into the rich text display.   ·

The forerunning component in this field is TinyMCE, which you can find at http://tinymce.moxiecode.com/. Figure 8-8 shows an example of this component on a page.

Figure 8-8. *TinyMCE rich text control displayed using the "simple" button theme*

TinyMCE Sample Usage

Implementing the TinyMCE component on your page is incredibly simple. Take a look at the HTML code in Listing 8-7, which contains a <textarea> element you can replace with the rich text component.

Listing 8-7. *Using the TinyMCE Rich Text Editor on an HTML Page*

```
<!DOCTYPE html PUBLIC "-//W3C//DTD XHTML 1.0 Strict//EN" ➥
    "http://www.w3.org/TR/xhtml1/DTD/xhtml1-strict.dtd">
<html xmlns="http://www.w3.org/1999/xhtml" lang="en" xml:lang="en">
    <head>
        <meta http-equiv="Content-Type" content="text/html; charset=utf-8" />
        <title>Rich text example</title>
    </head>

    <body>
        <h1>Rich text example</h1>
        <form method="post" action="/" id="form">
            <div>

                <!-- Create a <textarea> field we will replace with the rich text
                    editor later through JavaScript -->
                <textarea id="freetext" name="freetext"></textarea>

                <input type="submit" value="Save" />
            </div>
        </form>

        <!-- Include the TinyMCE control JavaScript file at the file path it
            installs itself by default -->
        <script type="text/javascript" ➥
            src="tinymce/jscripts/tiny_mce/tiny_mce.js"></script>

        <!-- The folllowing script would ideally be within an external file in a
            real web application. It is included in page for simplicity -->
        <script type="text/javascript">

            // Instruct TinyMCE to replace all <textarea> tags on the page with the
            // rich text editor control, using the default advanced theme button
            // set, which contains buttons for virtually all functionality provided
            // by the component. These include bold, italic, underline, and
            // strikethrough text styles; image, hyperlink, table, and list support;
            // and support for multiple levels of undo and redo in case the
            // user makes a mistake
            tinyMCE.init({
                mode : "textareas",
                theme : "advanced"
            });
```

```
            // If you only wish to replace single <textarea> instances on the page,
            // rather than all, the following code allows you to select the exact
            // elements to replace by their id attributes. The simple button set
            // theme contains controls for simple text editing and multiple levels
            // of undo, rather than the overwhelming selection of buttons in the
            // advanced theme
            //
            // tinyMCE.init({
            //      mode : "exact",
            //      elements: "freetext",
            //      theme : "simple"
            // });
        </script>
    </body>
</html>
```

TinyMCE Feature Set

The full feature list of the TinyMCE component is vast. It includes support for inserting tables, spell-checking, and selecting from a color palette. You can also customize the display and ordering of the buttons within the control.

TinyMCE has a plug-in architecture, which allows developers to add their own buttons to the editor to provide specific behaviors or to customize the way existing buttons behave. Two such plug-ins are available directly from the project home page (both have license fees):

MCImageManager: This plug-in provides a rich, graphical user interface for selecting and manipulating images through integration with a PHP or an ASP.NET back end. It supports preview thumbnails; uploading of new images; deletion of existing images; and cropping, resizing, and rotating of images.

MCFileManager: This plug-in provides a user interface for managing files on the server, hosted through a PHP or ASP.NET back end. It allows users to add, remove, and rename files.

These two plug-ins integrate together, for a full set of image and file manipulation tools that are exposable to your end users in a visually pleasing way—perfect for a content management system or blogging tool.

TinyMCE Appraisal

TinyMCE provides a clean, unobtrusive method for replacing standard <textarea> form tags within HTML with custom controls capable of rich text editing. The contents of the rich text field are converted into HTML tags, which are stored within the <textarea> itself for submission with the rest of the form. When the form is reopened for editing at a later date, these HTML tags are reconverted into rich text within the editor control.

The TinyMCE component is large—all its parts add up to 2MB of disk space. Thankfully, not all of this needs to be loaded simultaneously. The initial load is 170KB for the simple theme or 218KB for the advanced theme. No extra download is required for multiple instances of the editor on the same page.

Clearly, this is a lot of data and far surpasses the size of any other third-party component discussed in this book. The developers are aware of this and provide some server-side scripts for PHP, ASP.NET, JSP, and ColdFusion. These are gzip-style compression scripts for reducing the download time for those servers not already employing this method of compression.

In summary, the TinyMCE rich text editor is simply the best in its field; however, this comes at a price: the size of the download. My suggestion is to use the control sparingly and ensure your servers are employing gzip compression to help make the loading time shorter.

Validating Forms

No chapter on HTML forms would be complete without a mention of form validation. All form validation must be handled by a server-side script that runs after the form is submitted. However, for a better user experience, you should replicate the same validation rules applied in the back end through JavaScript before the form is submitted, so that your users do not need to wait for the server to process the script before refreshing the page to show the results of the validation.

Form validation through JavaScript should occur when the user attempts to submit the form. Field-by-field validation could be executed when focus is taken away from each field. Hooking into the submit event of the page's <form> tag allows you to specify your validation code, checking for required fields, fields in a certain format, and so on, and preventing the event from completing if validation is unsuccessful. If validation is successful, the event should be allowed to progress and the form should be submitted to the server.

Caution It is important to use the submit event of the form rather than connecting to the click event of the form's submit button. This is because there is more than one way to submit a form, including pressing the Enter key. Such cases won't be captured with the click event, so stick to the submit event of the form, and you'll be safe.

If the form contains a mixture of required and nonrequired fields, be sure to label all those that are required as such. If all fields on the form are mandatory, there is an argument for not needing to point that out explicitly. In many cases, an asterisk (*) next to the field name with a single line above the form explaining that fields marked in this way are mandatory will be sufficient for identifying required fields.

Finally, you should decide how any validation error messages should appear on the page if the form fails validation: as a list of errors in one place (either at the top or bottom of the form) or next to each relevant field on the form that failed validation. In either case, when you build the HTML code for these messages, you should use <label> tags around each individual message and use its for attribute to connect that message to the form field to which it relates. Not only is this good for accessibility, but it also means the user can simply click an error message to be taken directly to the field to which it relates, which is the common browser behavior of a <label> tag.

Summary

This chapter began by demonstrating novel ways to customize existing HTML form controls to suit the design and layout of your own web application. It then delved into building new user interfaces to replace existing HTML form fields to provide a better user experience. Next, it covered a selection of third-party JavaScript and Flash-based plug-ins, which provide extra functionality not supported by default in HTML. You should now be in a position to design forms in your web applications the way you want to, replacing existing controls where they do not provide a suitable user experience for the type of data you wish to collect.

Don't be afraid to come up with new ideas for form controls that your end users would prefer to use. If you do write anything, try to package it as reusable code and provide it to the rest of the web development community, so we may all benefit from each other's inspiration and ingenuity.

In the next chapter, we will look at how to write extra code for web applications that allow us to cope with connection drops or power failures between the browser and the web server. You'll learn how to allow for storage of data locally on the user's machine before sending it off to the server.

CHAPTER 9
■ ■ ■

Offline Storage—When the Lights Go Out

We've all been there. You've spent 20 minutes perfecting that important e-mail message in your web mail client, you're finally ready to send it—and boom!—it's not going anywhere. You try again, and still nothing. Then you realize that your network connection has dropped, so you don't have access to the Internet anymore. What do you do? At this point, many of us have attempted to copy and paste the text into a document stored on the computer itself, where it's comparatively safe. You should be able to retrieve it if you need to restart your browser or, worse still, the system crashes.

This is the problem with most RIAs: they are only as good as the reliability of the network connection and browser in which they are running. We need some way of storing important information on the user's computer or device if the network connection between the browser and the server becomes unavailable for some reason.

In this chapter, we'll investigate the methods available to us in different browsers for storing content locally. You'll see how to use a combination of these methods effectively within your own RIAs to save data, read back data, and delete data, ensuring cross-browser support.

Using Cookies to Store Data

In reality, local data storage has been available to developers since the early days of the web browser in the form of cookies. These are small text files, with an upper size limit of 4KB, which are stored on the user's computer and associated with a particular web site domain. This adds a level of security, since a site can access only the cookies associated with its domain name.

Cookies can be set by the web server and also through JavaScript in most web browsers. They are commonly used to store small items of data, such as a user's login ID or username for a certain web site to allow the user to log in automatically.

The browser manages the cookies internally and often provides a means, usually through its settings or preferences window, for users to view and delete cookies. Users can also disable cookies altogether. However, in practice, since so many web sites rely on them, including all web sites that require a user to log in, disabling cookies entirely is rarely done.

Creating Cookies

Each cookie is given a name when it is created, and any necessary text values are stored within it. When that cookie is needed, it is looked up by its name and the value is returned, provided the domain name associated with the cookie matches that of the web site executing the script.

Each cookie has an expiry date property, which defines how long the cookie should be allowed to exist before the browser erases it automatically. For many applications, the cookie will be told to expire many years from its time of creation, so the data remains on the user's machine without needing to be re-created.

For some applications, values may need to be set to last only for the duration of the user's visit to the site, This type of cookie is known as a *session cookie*, as once the browser session is ended, the cookie is deleted. A session cookie is created if an expiry date is not assigned to the cookie, meaning it will exist only for the duration of the current browsing session. Setting the expiry date of a cookie to a date that has already passed will delete the cookie from the browser permanently.

As I've mentioned, you must specify the domain name the cookie is to be associated with to provide some security. No web site hosted on another domain should be able to access the cookie. In addition to this, you can specify a path value, and the cookie will be valid only within that directory in your web site structure. Typically, this value is set to point to the root directory of the web site, so all pages can access the cookie, However, you may decide that your cookie is relevant only within a certain section of your web site; in which case, you would change the path value to point to that directory instead.

Listing 9-1 shows how to set a cookie, read back its value, and delete it through JavaScript. Add the code to your $ JavaScript library (started in Chapter 2), before the last line of the file that instantiates the library.

Listing 9-1. *Setting and Reading Cookie Values*

```
// Create a new namespace within the $ library for storage-related code
$.prototype.Storage = {}

// Create a Cookies namespace for storing cookie-related storage methods
$.prototype.Storage.Cookies = {

    // The set method sets a cookie on the local machine with the given name
    // and value
    set: function(input) {

        // Expect an object literal as an input, with name, value, expiry and
        // path properties
        var name = input.name || "";
        var value = input.value || "";

        // If an expiry date is provided, get its value as a string for setting in
        // the cookie. If no expiry date is provided, default to 10 years ahead
        var tenYearsAhead = new Date();
        tenYearsAhead.setFullYear(tenYearsAhead.getFullYear() + 10);
```

```javascript
    // Use an expiry date provided as an input or default to a date
    // 10 years in the future
    var expiry = (input.expiry ? input.expiry.toUTCString() : ➥
        tenYearsAhead.toUTCString());

    // Default to the site root directory if no path is given
    var path = input.path || "/";

    // A cookie is set as a specially formatted string. The domain will be
    // assigned automatically to the current domain of the site being accessed
    var cookieFormat = "{name}={value}; expires={expiry}; path={path}";

    // Create a new cookie by assigning the formatted string to document.cookie
    document.cookie = $.Utils.replaceText(cookieFormat, {

        // Use the escape method to ensure nonalphanumeric characters
        // are encoded and cannot break the resulting formatted cookie string
        name: escape(name),
        value: escape(value),
        expiry: expiryDate,
        path: path
    });
},

// The get method retrieves a previously stored cookie value by name
get: function(name) {
    // document.cookie is a string automatically containing all cookies valid
    // for the current domain and path of the site being accessed

    // Locate the cookie using a regular expression run against document.cookie
    var cookieFinder = new RegExp("(^|;) ?" + name + "=([^;]*)(;|$)");
    var cookie = document.cookie.match(cookieFinder);

    var value = "";
    if (cookie) {

        // If a cookie was located, take its value found using the
        // regular expression
        value = unescape(cookie[2]);
    }
    return value;
},

// The remove method deletes an existing cookie by name
remove: function(name) {
```

```
        // A cookie is removed by resetting the expiry date to any time
        // before the present
        var expiryDate = new Date();

        // Wind back the clock
        expiryDate.setTime(expiryDate.getTime() - 1);

        // Let the previously defined set method reset the cookie's expiry date,
        // deleting the cookie
        this.set({
            name: escape(name),
            expiry: expiryDate
        });
    }
}
```

Listing 9-2 provides examples of how to create, locate, and delete cookies in your own page-specific JavaScript code using the methods created in Listing 9-1.

Listing 9-2. *Creating, Locating, and Deleting Cookies Using the $ Library*

```
// Create a new cookie which will expire, by default, in 10 years
$.Storage.Cookies.set({
    name: "email",
    value: "me@denodell.com"
});

// Output the value of the cookie named "email" we created earlier.
// After a browser restart, the data will still be there
alert($.Storage.Cookies.get("email"));

// Delete the "email" cookie
$.Storage.Cookies.remove("email");

// Outputs an empty string, since the cookie no longer exists
alert($.Storage.Cookies.get("email"));
```

The Downside of Cookies

Cookies provide a simple, cross-browser way of storing small amounts of text-based data within the browser for later retrieval. They do have a downside, though.

When your browser makes a request for a page or file that resides on a certain domain, it also sends the entire contents of the cookie associated with that domain along with the request. This is by design, as it allows the web server to read the cookies stored on the user's machine and personalize the response based on its values. The more data you store in cookies, the larger these requests are going to be, up to the maximum limit of 4KB. This may not sound like a lot, but remember that the cookies are sent regardless of the content type of the file being requested. For example, if your page consists of one HTML file, two CSS files, two JavaScript files, and twenty image files, the cookie data will be sent to the server with the request for each of these files, adding a maximum of 100KB extra data (25 requests × 4KB cookie size) being sent to the web server.

You may wonder why this behavior exists at all, since it might result in excessive amounts of data being sent to the server for no reason. Unfortunately, it is the only guaranteed way to ensure that, should the server wish to use this cookie data to alter an image, script, HTML page, or some other file, it has that cookie available. This is by no means an elegant solution, but it is the simplest, and the approach taken when the HTTP specification was written to include cookie support.

Also remember that many users have an asynchronous connection, meaning their upload speed from the browser to the server is much slower than their download speed from the server to the browser. Therefore, the time taken to transmit this extra cookie data could have a big impact on performance. In Chapter 4, I explained a work-around for this technique, which involves hosting your images and external assets on a second domain, separate from the domain containing the HTML file itself. Still, sending the cookie data with every HTML request seems a little unnecessary when you consider the main goal here is to store data locally to protect against unforeseen network connection drops and unfortunate browser crashes.

Using Internet Explorer's Data Store

Microsoft introduced its own methods within IE (starting with version 5) that allow content to be stored on the user's machine from within a JavaScript web application, using what is known as the userData data store. This implementation involves using attribute nodes on a specific type of DOM element to store data, adding and removing attributes in order to add and remove data. Data is persisted by calling a save() method on the DOM element, and recalled using a load() method. These elements are added by an IE-specific userData behavior associated with the DOM element. The data store itself is actually represented internally within IE as an XML-based structure.

Microsoft imposes a base storage limit of 64KB per page within your site, and a maximum of 640KB of data per domain. Security restrictions are similar to those used within cookie storage: no domain is able to access data from another, and data can be removed after a specified time by adding an optional expiry date to the data store. Unlike cookies, however, the expiry date applies to the whole data store, not to individual pieces of data. Additionally, there is no concept of a data store that lasts only for the duration of the current session. In my opinion, the expiry date option should be ignored, allowing the data to be removed by the browser or by the user manually.

Listing 9-3 shows how to get, set, and remove data using the userData mechanism in IE. Add the code to your $ JavaScript library, before the library is instantiated at the end of its file.

Listing 9-3. *Setting, Getting, and Removing Data Using Internet Explorer's userData Mechanism*

```
// Add a UserData namespace to hold Microsoft userData-specific methods
$.prototype.Storage.UserData = {

    // Reference an element to store data within
    storageElement:null,
```

```
    // Data can be stored in different data stores by using different names. We
    // want all our data to be in one place, so we pick one name and stick with it
    dataStore: "data-store",

    // Before we can use any data, we need to initialize the DOM element
    initialize: function() {

        // Data is stored within DOM elements, so let's create one to use
        this.storageElement = $.Elements.create("span");

        // The behavior attribute is what allows the DOM element to be able to load
        // and save data to a data store
        this.storageElement.addBehavior('#default#userdata');

        // We don't want this element to be seen on the page, so hide it
        this.storageElement.style.display = 'none';

        // Add the new DOM element to the end of the page
        document.body.appendChild(this.storageElement);

        // Load any previously stored data from the data store, populating the
        // element's attributes with the data
        this.storageElement.load(this.dataStore);
    },

    // The set method saves a data value with a given name to the data store
    set: function(input) {

        // Expect an object literal as an input, containing name and value
        var name = input.name || "";
        var value = input.value || "";

        // Save the data name and value to the DOM element
        this.storageElement.setAttribute(name, value);

        // Commit the current data from the DOM element to the data store
        this.storageElement.save(this.dataStore);
    },

    // The get method returns a previously stored value from the data store from a
    // given property name
    get: function(name) {
```

```
        // Return the attribute value of the given name, or an empty string
        // if it does not exist
        return this.storageElement.getAttribute(name) || "";
    },

    // The remove method permanently removes the data name and associated
    // value from the data store
    remove: function(name) {

        // Remove the attribute of the given name from the DOM element used for
        // storing the data within
        this.storageElement.removeAttribute(name);

        // Commit the changes made to the data store so the specified data is
        // permanently removed
        this.storageElement.save(this.dataStore);
    }
}
```

Listing 9-4 shows how to create, locate, and delete data within your own page using JavaScript and the methods created in Listing 9-3.

Listing 9-4. *Creating, Locating, and Deleting userData in Internet Explorer*

```
// Initialize the userData store
$.Storage.UserData.initialize();

// Save an email address to the data store
$.Storage.UserData.set({
    name: "email",
    value: "me@denodell.com"
});

// Output the "email" value we created earlier.
// After a browser restart, the data will still be there
alert($.Storage.UserData.get("email"));

// Delete the "email" data value permanently from the data store
$.Storage.UserData.remove("email");

// Outputs an empty string since the data no longer exists
alert($.Storage.UserData.get("email"));
```

The `userData` technique provides a useful mechanism for storing larger amounts of text data offline than possible using cookies. The data is not passed with server requests, as it is with cookies, giving the benefit of permanent data storage without the overhead. This technique is supported by IE 5 and up, although IE 8 now also supports a new technique, which allows for greater storage potential, using the WHATWG Local Storage API.

Introducing the Data Storage APIs

As discussed in Chapter 7, the WHATWG organization has been active in pushing forward a recommendation for HTML 5, an update of the language relevant to the building of RIAs. Support for parts of this recommendation is already making its way into recent browser releases. Of interest to us here is a group of APIs to allow for offline storage, accessible through JavaScript. Let's take a look at each of the data storage APIs.

The Local Storage API

The first of these APIs is known as *local storage*. By default, most browsers allocate 5MB of space for data to be stored locally and shared among all sites, though this setting is user-configurable within the settings for each supported browser. This is considerably more space than if you stored data using cookies or the IE-specific `userData` mechanism. Like both of these methods, the local storage API associates the data stored with the domain the current web site is running within, providing the necessary security for the saved data.

With this API, you cannot limit access to data within different directories on the same web site, as is possible with cookies, and most important, you cannot configure an expiration date for the data. This puts the length of the existence of the data under the control of the browser and any user settings it supports to allow end users to manage the data that is being saved in their name. As with all the methods discussed so far, data can be stored only as strings.

At the time of writing, the local storage API is supported by IE 8 and up, Safari 3.1 and up, Google Chrome 2 and up, and Firefox 3.5 and up.

Listing 9-5 shows just how simple it is to implement the local storage API within your $ JavaScript library. Add this code to the library before it is instantiated at the end of the file.

Listing 9-5. *Setting, Getting, and Removing Data Using the Local Storage API*

```
// Add a LocalStorage namespace to keep local storage API code together
$.prototype.Storage.LocalStorage = {

    // The set method stores a value with a given name using the local storage API
    set: function(input) {

        // Expect an object literal as an input, containing name and value to set
        var name = input.name || "";
        var value = input.value || "";

        // Save the data using the top-level localStorage object
        localStorage.setItem(name, value);
    },
```

```
    // The get method retrieves a previously stored value by name
    get: function(name) {

        // Return an empty string if the item requested does not exist; otherwise,
        // fetch the value from the localStorage object
        return localStorage.getItem(name) || "";
    },

    // The remove method deletes a previously stored value from the
    // localStorage object
    remove: function(name) {

        // Remove the item from localStorage
        localStorage.removeItem(name);
    }
}
```

Listing 9-6 shows how you can use the methods defined in Listing 9-5 to store, retrieve, and delete data from the local computer within JavaScript on your own pages.

Listing 9-6. *Storing, Retrieving, and Removing Data Using the Local Storage API*

```
// Save an email address
$.Storage.LocalStorage.set({
    name: "email",
    value: "me@denodell.com"
});

// Output the "email" value we saved earlier.
// After a browser restart, the data will still be there
alert($.Storage.LocalStorage.get("email"));

// Delete the "email" data value permanently
$.Storage.LocalStorage.remove("email");

// Outputs an empty string since the "email" data no longer exists
alert($.Storage.LocalStorage.get("email"));
```

Mozilla's Global Storage API

Before the local storage API was defined by the WHATWG, Mozilla developers implemented its own similar, but notably different, storage API for the same purpose: to store data on the user's local computer or device. They called this *DOM storage* or *global storage*, and it provides methods for storing, retrieving, and deleting data in much the same way as the local storage API. It even has the same 5MB default data size limit. The only implementation difference between this technique and the local storage API is that the global storage object must specify which domain to store the data against, even though, for all intents and purposes, this must be the same domain on which the code is currently executing.

Listing 9-7 shows how to use Mozilla's global storage API to store, retrieve, and remove data from the local computer or device. Add this code to your $ JavaScript library before the library is instantiated at the end of its file.

Listing 9-7. *Setting, Getting, and Removing Data Using the Global Storage API*

```
// Add a GlobalStorage namespace to contain all global storage API-related
// methods
$.prototype.Storage.GlobalStorage = {
    dataStore: null,

    // The initialize method locates the data store to use if the global storage API
    // is supported in the browser
    initialize: function() {

        // The data store itself is an index of the globalStorage array, where the
        // index is always the name of the domain of the current site
        if (globalStorage) {
            this.dataStore = globalStorage[location.host];
        }
    },

    // The set method stores a value with a given name in the global storage API
    set: function(input) {
        // Expect an object literal as an input, containing name and value to set
        var name = input.name || "";
        var value = input.value || "";

        // Save the data using our data store provided by globalStorage
        this.dataStore.setItem(name, value);
    },

    // The get method retrieves a previously stored value by name
    get: function(name) {

        // Return an empty string if the item requested does not exist; otherwise,
        // locate it from the data store
        return this.dataStore.getItem(name) || "";
    },

    // The remove method permanently deletes a previously stored value by name
    // from the data store
    remove: function(name) {

        // Remove the item from the data store using the global storage API's
        // removeItem method
        this.dataStore.removeItem(name);
    }
}
```

Listing 9-8 shows how to use these methods to store, retrieve, and remove data from the local computer or device using the global storage API within JavaScript on your own pages.

Listing 9-8. *Storing, Retrieving, and Removing Data Using the Global Storage API*

```
// Initialize GlobalStorage for use
$.Storage.GlobalStorage.initialize();

// Save an email address
$.Storage.GlobalStorage.set({
    name: "email",
    value: "me@denodell.com"
});

// Output the "email" value we created earlier.
// After a browser restart, the data will still be there
alert($.Storage.GlobalStorage.get("email"));

// Delete the "email" data value permanently
$.Storage.GlobalStorage.remove("email");

// Outputs an empty string since the "email" data no longer exists
alert($.Storage.GlobalStorage.get("email"));
```

Client-Side Database Storage API

The emerging HTML 5 recommendation contains a second storage implementation API, which is more full-featured than the local storage API we looked into earlier. The client-side database storage API allows web developers to store data within a SQLite database, implemented within the browser.

Note SQLite is an open source software library that implements a database that does not require a server or any setup before it is used. Standard Structured Query Language (SQL) commands are used to communicate with the database, saving and retrieving data as necessary. Refer to the project web site (http://www.sqlite.org/lang.html) for the full list of SQL commands supported by SQLite.

By using a database to store offline data, developers can represent their data structures within a database table, rather than through text strings, which is currently the only possible cross-browser option for data storage. Databases also allow for the storage of binary data, such as image files, providing a more flexible solution for web applications that may require any type of data to be stored and retrieved at will.

Having a local database available to access through JavaScript as a standard for all browsers will take some time to achieve. At present, this API and database system are available only in Safari 3.1 on the desktop and within the Safari browser on the iPhone. Others will follow when the specification is more fully developed.

Each database is locked to the domain that created it, as a security measure. Each site may create as many databases as it requires, containing as many tables and rows as necessary. At present, in Safari 3.1, the default is 5MB of storage space for each domain. Through the browser preferences, users may choose their local database size, on a per-domain basis or a global basis (applied to all sites), from a minimum of 1MB to a maximum of 500MB.

As a performance measure, transactions and executions performed on the database are written using the SQL language and happen asynchronously. The command is executed and passed a callback function to execute once it is complete. In the meantime, the rest of the code is allowed to execute, meaning that large, complicated database transactions won't prevent the browser and the web application from reacting as normal to the end user's needs.

Listing 9-9 shows how to use the client-side database storage API to get, set, and remove text values stored within the SQLite database on the local machine. Add this code to your $ JavaScript library before the library is instantiated. Keep in mind that this is a rather limited usage, compared to all that the client-side database storage API will be able to achieve.

Listing 9-9. *Getting, Setting, and Deleting Data Using the Database Storage API*

```
// Add a DBStorage namespace to contain all client-side database storage-related
// methods
$.prototype.Storage.DBStorage = {

    // There can be multiple databases in each domain, but for this example we'll
    // define a single one to use throughout the application
    databaseName: "data_store",
    databaseDesc: "Data store",

    // Specify which SQLite database version we are using, in case future versions
    // alter methods
    sqlLiteDBVersion: "1.0",

    // 5MB of storage = 5120 bytes. This is the maximum default size of the
    // SQLite database
    FIVE_MB: 5120,

    // Define a database table name for storing our data
    tableName: "data-store",

    // Define a property to store a reference to the database
    database: null,

    // The initialize method creates the table in the database to store our name and
    // value data in, if it does not already exist. The name becomes the primary key
    initialize: function() {

        // Open the SQLite database
        this.database = openDatabase(this.databaseName, ➥
            this.sqlLiteDBVersion, this.databaseDesc, this.FIVE_MB);
```

```
    // Construct the SQL command to create a table in the database
    var command = "CREATE TABLE IF NOT EXISTS {tableName} (name ➥
        TEXT UNIQUE NOT NULL PRIMARY KEY, value TEXT NOT NULL)";
    command = $.Utils.replaceText(command, {
        tableName: this.tableName
    });

    // Execute the SQL command
    this.execute(command);
},

// The execute method executes a given SQL command against the database,
// executing an optional callback function on the command's completion,
// passing across the result of the transaction against the database to that
// callback function
execute: function(command, callback) {
    callback = callback || function() {};

    // Execute the supplied SQL command, then execute the callback function
    this.database.transaction(function(db) {
        db.executeSql(command, [], callback);
    });
},

// The get method performs a lookup against the database for the name key and
// passes the value it finds, if any, into the supplied callback function
get: function(name, callback) {

    // Generate the command to locate a value from the database by name
    var command = "SELECT value FROM {tableName} WHERE name = {name}";
    command = $.Utils.replaceText(command, {
        tableName: this.tableName,
        name: name
    });

    // Execute the SQL command
    this.execute(command, function(db, result) {
        var value = "";

        // Locate the value within the first row of the SQL data returned
        if (result.rows.length > 0) {
            value = result.rows.item(0)['value'];
        }

        // Execute the callback method, passing it the value found, if any
        callback(value);
```

```
            // Return a null value in case any calling method is expecting a
            // return value from this method - no code should expect this, but
            // just in case, we provide a return value here
            return null;
        });
    },

    // The set method stores a value by name into the database
    set: function(input) {

        // Expect an object literal as an input, containing name and value to set
        var name = input.name || "";
        var value = input.value || "";

        var self = this;

        // Check to see if a value already exists by this name in the database
        this.get(name, function(value) {

            // By default, we will insert the value into the database, so specify
            // the command to do that
            var command = "INSERT INTO {tableName} (name, value) VALUES ➥
                ({name}, {value})";

            // If a value already exists against this name in the database, perform
            // a SQL update command instead
            if (value != "") {
                command = "UPDATE {tableName} SET value = {value} WHERE ➥
                    name = {name}";
            }

            command = $.Utils.replaceText(command, {
                tableName: self.tableName,
                name: name,
                value: value
            });

            // Execute the SQL command, saving the data into the database
            this.execute(command);
        });
    },

    // The remove method deletes the name and value from the database
    remove: function(name) {
```

```
        // Generate the SQL command to remove the value from the database
        var command = "DELETE FROM {tableName} WHERE name = {name}";
        command = $.Utils.replaceText(command, {
            tableName: this.tableName,
            name: name
        });

        // Execute the command, removing the entry from the database
        this.execute(command);
    }
}
```

Listing 9-10 shows how to store, retrieve, and remove text values using a SQLite database located on the user's local computer or storage device using JavaScript within your pages. Notice how you need to use a callback function now when retrieving data. Since the database acts asynchronously, the only way to know when the data has been located is to tell the method what code to execute after that data has been found.

Listing 9-10. *Setting, Getting, and Removing Data Using the Database Storage API*

```
// Initialize the client-side database
$.Storage.DBStorage.initialize();

// Save an email address
$.Storage.DBStorage.set({
    name: "email",
    value: "me@denodell.com"
});

// Output the "email" value we created earlier.
// After a browser restart, the data will still be there
$.Storage.DBStorage.get("email", function(value) {
    alert(value);
});

// Delete the "email" data value permanently
$.Storage.DBStorage.remove("email");

// Outputs an empty string since the "email" data no longer exists
$.Storage.DBStorage.get("email", function(value) {
    alert(value);
});
```

Storing Data Using Flash Shared Objects

If your end users have Adobe's Flash Player plug-in installed (version 8 or later), another data storage technique is available. Using a specially constructed movie file, you can expose what are known as *Flash local shared objects*, commonly called *Flash cookies*, through a simple API for JavaScript to use to store data locally.

Unlike browser cookies, local shared objects allow each domain to store 100KB of data on the user's machine, and these values are not sent to the server with HTTP requests. Users are able to alter this storage amount, although many choose to leave it at the default setting. As you might expect, as a security measure, data set from one domain cannot be accessed from any other.

I have constructed the necessary Flash movie file, which is available from this book's details page at the Apress web site (http://www.apress.com/), along with the rest of the source code for this book (and also available for download from my own site at http://www.denodell. com/) for inclusion in your own RIAs. Use the SWFObject component, introduced in Chapter 7, to place the Flash movie on your pages.

The Flash movie file exposes three methods that can be called against an instance of the movie on the page: get(), set(), and remove(). Listing 9-11 shows the code to add to your $ JavaScript library to use Flash cookies. Add the code to the end of the $ library file, before it is instantiated.

Listing 9-11. *Getting, Setting, and Removing Data Using Flash Local Shared Objects*

```
// Create a Flash namespace to contain all Flash cookie-related storage methods

$.prototype.Storage.Flash = {

    // Object used to store a reference to the Flash movie element on the page
    flashComponent: null,

    // The initialize method sets the internal flashComponent object to the one
    // passed in from the page - use SWFObject to load in the movie on the page.
    // Chapter 7 shows how to use SWFObject to embed a Flash movie

    initialize: function(flashComponent) {
        this.flashComponent = flashComponent;
    },

    // The set method stores a value by name into a Flash shared object
    set: function(input) {

        // Expect an object literal as an input, containing name and value to set
        var name = input.name || "";
        var value = input.value || "";

        // Save the data using the set method within the Flash movie object
        this.flashComponent.set(name, value);
    },
```

```
    // The get method retrieves a previously stored value by name
    get: function(name) {

        // Return an empty string if the value requested does not exist
        return this.flashComponent.get(name) || "";
    },

    // The remove method deletes the value with the given name from the Flash
    // shared object
    remove: function(name) {
        this.flashComponent.remove(name);
    }
}
```

Listing 9-12 shows how to use the methods from Listing 9-11 to store, retrieve, and remove data from the local computer or device using Flash local shared objects on a page using JavaScript.

Listing 9-12. *Storing, Retrieving, and Removing Data Using Flash Local Shared Objects*

```
// Initialize the Flash shared object by referencing the DOM element on the page
// that contains the Flash storage file - you can find this file on my web site at
// http://www.denodell.com/
$.Storage.Flash.initialize(document.getElementById("flash-object"));

// Save an email address
$.Storage.Flash.set({
    name: "email",
    value: "me@denodell.com"
});

// Output the "email" value we created earlier.
// After a browser restart, the data will still be there
alert($.Storage.Flash.get("email"));

// Delete the "email" data value permanently
$.Storage.Flash.remove("email");

// Outputs an empty string since the "email" data no longer exists
alert($.Storage.Flash.get("email"));
```

Creating a Cross-Browser Local Data Storage API

So far in this chapter, you have discovered how to use several different techniques to store and retrieve text strings from the local user's computer or device. Each technique varies in the quantity of data that is permitted to be stored and in the level of support for it among different browsers. To handle local storage in your RIAs, you can set up a single API for cross-browser support, which includes all the available techniques and uses the best one available.

First, let's organize the different storage techniques in order of preference, starting with the ones that combine the largest storage space with the most standards-adopting practices and ending with the least storage space and least-preferred solution:

Local storage API: Preferred since it is becoming an established standard, is simple to use, and has fairly strong support among the latest browser releases. Provides 5MB storage by default.

Client-side database storage API: An emerging standard and, due to its versatility, would be the most preferred were it not for the fact that the specification is very much subject to change at the time of writing. Provides 5MB storage by default.

Mozilla global storage API: A good backup for those Firefox 2 and 3 users whose browsers do not yet support the local storage API but do support this very similar API. Provides 5MB storage by default.

IE's userData *mechanism*: IE versions 5 to 7 do not support any of the preferred methods so far, but do provide this mechanism for storing data locally without requiring any plug-ins. Provides 64KB storage by default.

Flash local shared objects: For those users whose browsers do not support any of the more preferred methods, the ubiquitous Flash Player plug-in can be harnessed to store data locally without relying on cookies. Provides 100KB storage by default.

Cookies: Definitely the least-preferred option. Cookie files are oppressively small, and their data gets sent with each HTTP request to the server, clogging up the connection more and more the larger the cookies become. Provides 4KB storage by default.

Using this information, you can create three universal methods—get(), set(), and remove()—which favor the most-preferred technique, moving all the way down to simple cookies when the preferred techniques are unavailable. Listing 9-13 shows a cross-browser local storage API that you can implement within your $ JavaScript library using the code given in this chapter. Notice that, since one of the techniques (the client-side database API) requires a callback function to be supplied when retrieving data, this practice needs to be adopted by the API for all techniques.

Listing 9-13. *Cross-Browser Local Data Storage API*

```
// Stores a reference to the technique's code object, set with the initialize method
$.prototype.Storage.dataStore = null;

// The initialize method selects the technique to use for local data storage. Takes
// a parameter that specifies the Flash element on the page in order to support
// Flash Shared Objects. If this parameter is not provided, Flash will not attempt
// to be used to store the data
$.prototype.Storage.initialize = function(flashElement) {

    // Work through our order of preference
    if (window.localStorage) {
```

```
        // If local storage API is available, set the dataStore to point to the
        // local storage API namespace we created earlier
        this.dataStore = $.Storage.LocalStorage;

    } else if (window.openDatabase) {

        // If the client-side database API is supported, assign the dataStore to the
        // DBStorage namespace and initialize it
        this.dataStore = $.Storage.DBStorage;
        this.dataStore.initialize();

    } else if (window.globalStorage) {

        // If the global storage API is supported, set dataStore to point to the
        // appropriate namespace
        this.dataStore = $.Storage.GlobalStorage;
        this.dataStore.initialize();

    } else if (window.ActiveXObject) {
        // If Internet Explorer's userData mechanism is present,
        // initialize that for use
        this.dataStore = $.Storage.UserData;
        this.dataStore.initialize();

    } else if (flashElement) {

        // If Flash 8 is supported, set the dataStore to use Flash Shared Objects
        this.dataStore = $.Storage.Flash;
        this.dataStore.initialize(flashElement);

    } else {

        // If all else fails, use cookies
        this.dataStore = $.Storage.Cookies;
    }
};

// The get method retrieves a previously stored value and passes it to the
// specified callback function. Because the callback technique is used in the
// client-side database API, we need to use it throughout
$.prototype.Storage.get = function(name, callback) {

    // Only one object (client-side database API) actually uses the callback
    // parameter as part of the data retrieval process. Other namespaces specified
    // in the dataStore will just ignore it
    var value = this.dataStore.get(name, callback);
```

```
    // If a value is returned (which it isn't with the client-side database API),
    // execute the callback function, passing it the value found.
    if (value && callback) {
        callback(value);
    }
};

// The set method stores a value against a specified name
$.prototype.Storage.set = function(name, value) {

    // All the different techniques accept the same inputs for setting data, so this
    // universal method is fairly simple
    this.dataStore.set(name, value);
};

// The remove method permanently deletes data by a specified name
$.prototype.Storage.remove = function(name) {

    // Each technique accepts the same inputs for removing data
    this.dataStore.remove(name);
};
```

Listing 9-14 shows how to use your new cross-browser offline data storage API to store, retrieve, and remove data from the local computer or device using JavaScript on a page.

Listing 9-14. *Getting, Setting, and Removing Data Using a Cross-Browser API*

```
// Execute the code that makes the decision about which of the various techniques
// to use within the current browser. In this case, no parameter is supplied to the
// initialize method, which means that Flash will not be used to store data
$.Storage.initialize();

// Save an email address using whichever technique was selected previously
$.Storage.set({
    name: "email",
    value: "me@denodell.com"
});

// Output the "email" value we saved earlier.
// After a browser restart, the data will still be there
$.Storage.get("email", function(value) {
    alert(value);
});

// Delete the "email" data value permanently
$.Storage.remove("email");
```

```
// Outputs an empty string since the "email" data no longer exists
$.Storage.get("email", function(value) {
    alert(value);
});
```

As you have seen in previous chapters, storing and retrieving data from local data sources is faster than accessing data from a remote web server. This is why you want to ensure that your files are cached to the browser so they need to be downloaded only once. By having your web application store the user's data within the local data store and accessing it from there, you can improve the perceived responsiveness of your application by performing the Ajax operations behind the scenes, and allowing the users to interact only with the presaved data in the data store. Then your users won't ever need to click a button to save a form via Ajax and wait for the server's response before moving on to the next part of the web application.

The cross-browser API in Listing 9-13 could be implemented in a web mail client so that new e-mail messages being composed are saved at regular intervals without user interaction. If the network connection drops, the users can carry on writing their mail, which will be stored locally as they write, until a connection to the server is restored. And if the browser crashes, the e-mail message can be resurrected—the users will not have lost their message (and their patience). Listing 9-15 shows a simple example of how to implement this behavior within an HTML page.

Listing 9-15. *Saving an E-Mail Message Being Composed into Local Storage*

```
<!DOCTYPE html PUBLIC "-//W3C//DTD XHTML 1.0 Strict//EN" ➡
    "http://www.w3.org/TR/xhtml1/DTD/xhtml1-strict.dtd">
<html xmlns="http://www.w3.org/1999/xhtml" lang="en" xml:lang="en">
    <head>
        <meta http-equiv="Content-Type" content="text/html; charset=utf-8" />
        <title>Offline email message storage example</title>
    </head>

    <body>
        <h1>Offline email message storage example</h1>

        <!-- Create a form for composing the email message -->
        <form method="post" action="/" id="compose-message">
            <div>
                <label for="to">To</label>
                <input type="text" name="to" id="to" />
            </div>

            <div>
                <label for="subject">Subject</label>
                <input type="text" name="subject" id="subject" />
            </div>
```

```
    <div>
        <label for="message-body">Message</label>
        <textarea id="message-body" name="message-body" ➥
            rows="10" cols="20"></textarea>
    </div>

    <div>
        <input type="submit" value="Save" />
    </div>
</form>

<!-- Create an element to use to place the Flash storage component later -->
<div id="flash-storage-element"></div>

<!-- Reference the $ JavaScript library -->
<script type="text/javascript" src="$.js"></script>

<!-- Reference SWFObject from Google's CDN -->
<script type="text/javascript" ➥
    src="http://ajax.googleapis.com/ajax/libs/swfobject/2.1/swfobject.js"> ➥
    </script>

<!-- The following code is included inline for simplicity. In a real web
application, it should be stored in an external file -->
<script type="text/javascript">
    $.onDomReady(function() {

        // Find this Flash offline storage component online at
        // http://www.denodell.com/
        var movieURL = "storage.swf";
        var tagIDToReplace = "flash-storage-element";
        var width = 1;
        var height = 1;
        var flashVersionRequired = "8";
        var parameters = {
            allowScriptAccess: "always"
        };
        var attributes = {
            id: "flash-storage"
        };

        swfobject.embedSWF(movieURL, tagIDToReplace, width, height, ➥
            flashVersionRequired, null, {}, parameters, attributes);

        // Initialize our offline data storage API, passing it a reference
        // to the Flash element on the page to allow storage using Flash
        $.Storage.initialize(document.getElementById("flash-storage"));
```

```
// Populate the message fields with the last saved values so that
// when the user returns to the page after a browser crash,
// the fields are prepopulated with the last saved values
// automatically for them
 $.Storage.get("to", function(value) {
    document.getElementById("to").value = value;
 });

 $.Storage.get("subject", function(value) {
    document.getElementById("subject").value = value;
 });

 $.Storage.get("message-body", function(value) {
    document.getElementById("message-body").value = value;
 });

 // Save the contents of the message being composed
 // once every 30 seconds
 var THIRTY_SECONDS = 30000; // 30 seconds = 30000 milliseconds

 var saveMessage = window.setInterval(function() {

    // Save the values of the To, Subject, and Message Body fields
    // in case of network drop or browser crash
    $.Storage.set({
        name: "to",
        value: document.getElementById("to").value
    });
    $.Storage.set({
        name: "subject",
        value: document.getElementById("subject").value
    });
    $.Storage.set({
        name: "message-body",
        value: document.getElementById("message-body").value
    });
 }, THIRTY_SECONDS);

 // When the user submits the form to save the message to the server,
 // remove the previously stored field values and stop them from
 // being saved again while the form is being submitted
 $.Events.add(document.getElementById("compose-message"), ➥
        "submit", function(e) {

    // Stop the HTML page from submitting the form so we can
    // handle the data submission via Ajax instead
    e.preventDefault();
```

```
                        // Stop saving the message field values every 30 seconds
                        window.clearInterval(saveMessage);

                        // TODO: send form field values to the server using Ajax

                        // Remove the local data now the message has been sent
                        $.Storage.remove("to");
                        $.Storage.remove("subject");
                        $.Storage.remove("message-body");

                        // TODO: change the page to display the mailbox folder contents
                    });
                });
        </script>
    </body>
</html>
```

Using a Reusable Offline Storage Component

PersistJS (http://pablotron.org/software/persist-js/) is an open source local data storage library that is being constantly updated to support newer browsers and techniques. In addition to supporting the techniques we have investigated in this chapter, this library also supports Gears.

Gears is a browser plug-in developed by Google that provides a SQLite database for offline data storage. It also offers a way to offload intensive JavaScript routines to separate worker processes on the end user's machine to boost performance. This plug-in is available for download for many browsers from http://gears.google.com/. It is built into Google's Chrome browser by default.

Summary

This chapter covered the different techniques for storing data on your user's machine through your web applications. It presented a cross-browser API for storing, retrieving, and removing data from the local data store. Using local data storage provides better user experiences because, if a network connection drops or the browser software crashes, the data is still safe. It can remain on the user's computer until it can be sent to the server, and then it can be deleted.

In the next chapter, we will investigate some advanced Ajax techniques for extracting hidden information from nontext files stored on a web server.

■ ■ ■

Binary Ajax

At this point, you should be familiar with retrieving and sending text-based data between the browser and the web server using the Ajax technique. This chapter explains how to retrieve data stored in other types of files, such as images, audio, and video, dynamically through JavaScript. This allows you to extract information stored within those files for use within your web application.

Plain Text Files vs. Binary Files

All files—whether they represent text, image, audio, or some other kind of data—are stored on a computer's file system as data according to a specified format. Computer software programs, such as Microsoft Word or Apple iTunes, load only those files that match the specific format they expect, and convert them into something more usable for the users of that software.

Computer file data is stored as a long sequence of 8-bit hexadecimal (hex) bytes, each capable of representing values from 0 to 255 in base 16 format, often represented as 0x00 to 0xFF in common hex notation. Text characters are stored in files as hex bytes within the range 0x20 to 0x7E, and computer files that contain only data bytes within this range are known as *plain text files*. HTML, style sheet, and JavaScript files are plain text files. Files containing data bytes outside that range are known as *binary files*. Images and Flash components are examples of binary files.

In order to distinguish one type of binary file from another, and to ensure the format of that file is of the expected type, each file type has its own specification, written by the individual or organization responsible for creating that data file format. This specification describes how the data is stored and formatted within that file.

Typically, a binary file will have a header section containing information describing the actual data represented within the main part of the file. In an image file, this header information might contain the width, height, and resolution of the image. In an MP3 music file, this might contain that name of the artist, track, and genre of the music stored within the file.

Reading Binary Files with Ajax

Chapter 2 presented the code required to make an Ajax request within your web application for a plain text file hosted on your web server. To demonstrate how to retrieve binary files, let's extend that code to make requests for binary files.

Note As with Ajax requests for plain text files, you are unable to request files that are hosted on servers other than the one currently running your JavaScript code.

Binary files are typically much larger than plain text files, so you will want to tell the server to return only a certain portion of the data from the file requested. You will most likely want to read the header data stored at the beginning of the file. Therefore, it makes sense to receive only the first part of the file, rather than the entire file. Fortunately, you can take advantage of the Range HTTP request header to specify how much of the file to receive. For example, the following Range header instructs the server to return only the first 1,024 bytes of the requested file:

```
Range: bytes=0-1024
```

The Range header is not supported by every web server, so before you use it, you must check to see if it is supported. This is achieved by establishing an HTTP HEAD request for the file from which you wish to read the contents. A HEAD request returns only the HTTP response headers that would accompany the requested file's contents, not the actual file contents. You then check that the Accept-Ranges HTTP response header exists and contains the value bytes, which indicates that the web server supports this feature. Once you've established this feature is supported, you can send the real HTTP GET request for the binary file, supplying the Range request header.

Listing 10-1 shows the code to add to your existing Ajax methods within your $ JavaScript library (which you started in Chapter 2) to support the connection and retrieval of data using a cross-browser Ajax connector object. Notice the similarities between requesting binary files and requesting plain text files.

Listing 10-1. *Configuring a Binary Connector*

```
// The method configureBinaryConnector takes three input parameters:
// - A cross-browser Ajax connector object
// - An optional length to specify how much data the server should
//      return, in bytes
// - A callback function to pass the downloaded binary data to

$.prototype.Remote.configureBinaryConnector = function(input) {
    // Create fallback values for each of the inputs in case they are not specified
    var connector = input.connector || this.getConnector();
    var length = input.length || -1;
    var callback = input.callback || function() {};

    // By default, Firefox will attempt to convert the binary data received into a
    // different format if it is of a known type. We will force Firefox to believe
    // the data is of an unknown type, so it does not perform any conversion on the
    // raw binary data returned by the server
```

```
if (connector.overrideMimeType) {
    connector.overrideMimeType("text/plain; charset=x-user-defined");
}


// If a length has been specified, set the HTTP Range request header to return
// only the specified amount of data from the start of the file - otherwise we
// would have to download the entire file, which would slow down any
// processing we wish to perform upon it
if (length > -1) {
    connector.setRequestHeader("Range", "bytes=0-" + length);
}


// Internet Explorer returns the binary data in the connector.responseBody
// property. Other browsers return it in the connector.responseText property
if (typeof connector.onload != "undefined") {

    // The connector.onload event handler exists within the W3C XmlHttpRequest
    // object but not Microsoft's XMLHTTP ActiveX object.
    connector.onload = function(){

        // HTTP status 200 means the file downloaded successfully in its
        // entirety, and 206 means that the portion of the file specified with
        // the HTTP Range request header was returned successfully
        if (connector.status == 200 || connector.status == 206) {

            // In those browsers that support connector.onload, the binary data
            // from the file is returned in connector.responseText
            var binaryData = connector.responseText;

            // Wrap the data in a BinaryReader object, which we will define
            // later, which will expose methods and properties for interacting
            // with the data within the binary file.
            // The this keyword refers to $.Remote
            var binaryReader = new this.BinaryReader(binaryData);

            // Execute the callback function passed into this routine, passing
            // it the new binaryReader object as a parameter
            callback(binaryReader);
        }
    }
} else {

    // The connector.onload event handler does not exist, so this should be
    // Internet Explorer - we'll use the cross-browser Ajax onreadystatechange
    // event handler instead in this case
```

```
connector.onreadystatechange = function() {
    if (connector.readyState == 4) {
        if (connector.status == 200 || connector.status == 206) {

            // The file, or part of the file requested, was returned
            // successfully. The binary data in Internet Explorer is
            // returned in the connector.responseBody property
            var binaryData = connector.responseBody;

            // Create a new instance of the BinaryReader constructor,
            // defined later, which will allow chunks of data to be looked
            // up from within the binary file as a whole.
            // The this keyword refers to $.Remote
            var binaryReader = new this.BinaryReader(binaryData);

            // Execute the callback function passed into the routine,
            // passing it the binaryReader object instance to allow the
            // callback to access the data within the file
            callback(binaryData);
        }
    }
}
```

Now you can configure your cross-browser connection object to enable you to receive the binary data. Listing 10-2 shows how you can make a request for a binary file, or part of a file, through JavaScript. Add this code to your $ JavaScript library.

■**Caution** Unfortunately, at the time of writing, the Opera browser does not return the binary data from an Ajax request in a usable form for this routine. Bear this in mind when constructing your web application around this code. All other modern browsers, including IE 6, will return the data in a usable form.

Listing 10-2. *Loading a Complete or Partial Binary File Using Ajax*

```
// The loadBinary method loads a binary file from a specified URL and executes a
// callback function, passing it the returned raw binary data. If an optional length
// parameter is specified, only a portion of the file is downloaded, up to the
// number of bytes specified in that parameter
```

```javascript
$.prototype.Remote.loadBinary = function(request) {
        var url = request.url || "";
        var length = request.length || -1;
        var callback = request.callback || function() {};

        // The this keyword here refers to the $.Remote namespace
        var self = this;

        if (length > -1) {

            // If a data length has been specified, meaning that only part of
            // the file should be downloaded, perform an HTTP HEAD request,
            // which returns only the HTTP Response headers
            self.load({
                url: url,
                type: "HEAD",
                callback: function() {

                    // Create a new Ajax connector object and open
                    // the connection
                    var connector = self.getConnector();
                    connector.open("GET", url, true);

                    // Find out if the web server supports the HTTP Range header
                    // by testing the value of the HTTP Accept-Ranges
                    // response header
                    if (this.getResponseHeader("Accept-Ranges") == "bytes") {

                        // If the web server supports the selection of ranges of
                        // data, check that the length specified does not
                        // exceed the length of all the data in the file
                        var fileLength = this.getResponseHeader( ➥
                            "Content-Length");
                        if (length > parseInt(fileLength, 10)) {
                            length = parseInt(fileLength, 10);
                        }

                        // Configure the new connector so that it specifies the
                        // length of data to retrieve from the file. This data
                        // is then passed to the callback function
                        self.configureBinaryConnector({
                            connector: connector,
                            length: length,
                            callback: callback
                        });
                    } else {
```

```
                              // The web server does not support the selection of
                              // ranges of data, so we'll leave out specifying a
                              // length when we configure the new connector,
                              // so that all the data inside the file is passed to
                              // the callback function
                              self.configureBinaryConnector({
                                  connector: connector,
                                  callback: callback
                              });
                          }

                          // Make the request for the binary file using the settings
                          // configured in the new connector object
                          connector.send("");
                      }
                  });
              } else {

                  // If no length has been specified, load the entire binary file and
                  // pass this to the callback function
                  var connector = this.getConnector();
                  connector.open("GET", url, true);
                  this.configureBinaryConnector({
                      connector: connector,
                      callback: callback
                  });
                  connector.send("");
              }
          }
      }
```

Now you're able to make requests for binary files and return the raw data from inside the file. Next, you need to be able to read the specific parts of that file that interest you. Listing 10-3 shows a new constructor you can use to read and extract specific data from the returned binary file. Add this code to your $ JavaScript library.

Listing 10-3. *Binary File Reader*

```
// Internet Explorer does not allow us to return some of the information we
// require from our binary data. To overcome this, we must write two VBScript
// (Microsoft's own scripting format) functions to the page, IEgetByte and
// IEgetLength, which we will call from our JavaScript code when needed.
// The functions are added to the page using document.writeln and are wrapped
// in an Internet Explorer conditional comment so they are not read by other
// browsers
```

```
document.writeln(
    '<!--[if IE]>' +
    '<script type="text/vbscript">\r\n' +
    '    Function IEgetByte(data, position)\r\n' +
    '        IEgetByte = AscB(MidB(data,position + 1, 1))\r\n' +
    '    End Function\r\n' +
    '    Function IEgetLength(data)\r\n' +
    '        IEgetLength = LenB(data)\r\n' +
    '    End Function\r\n' +
    '</script>' +
    '<![endif]-->'
);

// The BinaryReader constructor takes raw binary data as its input and contains
// methods to help extract data in different formats from that raw data

$.prototype.Remote.BinaryReader = function(data) {
    // Store the data input to a property of this constructor
    this.data = data;

    // The isBigEndian property denotes whether or not the binary data being
    // processed is in the standard hexadecimal format, also known as "big
    // endian" - where the number 8 would be represented within 4 bytes of data
    // as 00000008 - or in the reverse format (also known as "little endian") -
    // where the number 8 would be represented as 08000000. true indicates
    // the data is big endian, the common format
    this.isBigEndian = true;

    // Add a setter method to enable the isBigEndian property value to be
    // changed as and when needed
    this.setIsBigEndian = function(isBigEndian) {
        this.isBigEndian = isBigEndian;
    }

    // The getLength method returns the length in bytes of the binary data
    this.getLength = function() {

        // Binary data is represented as a string in all browsers except Internet
        // Explorer. Standard browsers will simply return the length property of
        // the string, IE will use the VBScript function declared earlier to
        // calculate the length of the binary data
        return (typeof this.data == "string") ? this.data.length : ➥
            IEgetLength(data);
    };
```

```
// The getByte method returns a single byte of data located at the specified
// position in bytes from the start of the data
this.getByte = function(position) {

    // Standard browsers will use the charCodeAt function to return a Unicode
    // value representing the data stored at the specified position, which is
    // then converted to a hexadecimal value. This does not work in Internet
    // Explorer, which must use its own VBScript function to extract the
    // required byte from the data
    return (typeof this.data == "string") ? ➥
        (this.data.charCodeAt(position) & 0xFF) : IEgetByte(data, position);
};

// The getChar method returns the ASCII character represented by the byte
// of data stored at the specified position
this.getChar = function(position) {
    return String.fromCharCode(this.getByte(position));
};

// The getString method returns the ASCII string represented by the data that
// begins at the specified position and continues for the specified length
this.getString = function(position, length) {

    // Create an array to store each of the characters of the string
    var chars = [];

    // Get the character stored at each byte from the specified position until
    // the specified length, and add it to the array of characters
    for (var index = position, end = position + length; index < end; index++) {
        chars.push(this.getChar(index));
    }

    // Return the array of characters joined together as a single string
    return chars.join("");
};

// The getHex method returns a string representing the hexadecimal data
// beginning at the specified position and continuing for the specified length
this.getHex = function(position, length) {

    // Create an array to store each of the individual hexadecimal strings
    var result = [];
```

```
    // Get the value of each byte and convert it to base 16 (hexadecimal),
    // then convert it to a 2-character string and add it to the output array
    for (var index = position, end = position + length; index < end; index++) {
        var newByte = this.getByte(index).toString(16).toUpperCase();
        result.push((newByte.length == 1) ? "0" + newByte : newByte);
    }

    // If the data is not stored in the standard big endian format, then reverse
    // the sequence of the array, which will provide us with little endian
    // format data
    if (!this.isBigEndian) {
        result.reverse();
    }

    // Return the array of hexadecimal characters joined together into
    // a single string
    return result.join("");
  };

  // The getNumber method executes the getHex method and converts its
  // result from a base 16 value to a standard integer number
  this.getNumber = function(position, length) {
    return parseInt(this.getHex(position, length), 16);
  };
}
```

So now you have the code you need to request binary files from the server and, using the specification of the particular type of binary file you are reading, you are able to extract the data of interest from those files. Next, let's look at how to do this with a specific type of binary file—one containing a photo.

Extracting Image Data from Photo Files

Suppose that as part of your web application, you wish to extract information from a photograph image file taken using a digital camera, such as when the photo was taken and its dimensions. Most photographs taken with digital cameras store this information in the header portion of the JPEG image file produced when taking the picture. You can use your binary Ajax file reader (Listing 10-3) to extract this information, provided you know the specification describing how the data is stored within the file. In the case of photograph files, this data is stored in the Exchangeable Image File (EXIF) format.

Before you can extract the data stored within the image file, you need to know how the data is structured within the file. This is always according to a very strict format specification, so there is no chance of the data being misrepresented or confused with a different file format.

Understanding the EXIF Format

The EXIF format describes how extra information is stored within JPEG image files. A useful description of this specification can be found online at `http://park2.wakwak.com/~tsuruzoh/Computer/Digicams/exif-e.html`.

The JPEG and EXIF Headers

A JPEG file may contain any amount of data before the EXIF data within that file begins. The beginning of the EXIF data is marked by the following data in hex notation (extra spaces added for clarity):

`FFE1 ssss 4578 6966 0000`

where *ssss* represents the size of the EXIF data block in the file as a hex number. The sequence `4578 6966` represents the string `"Exif"`.

The next point in the file marks the start of the EXIF data itself. The following 2 bytes of data in the file are either `4949` (II as a string) or `4D4D` (MM as a string). This denotes the alignment of the hex bytes in the rest of the EXIF data. If this format is specified as `MM`, the rest of the data is in the standard hex notation; for example, the number 8 would be represented in 2 bytes of hex code as `0008`. If this format is `II`, each byte sits in reverse order; for example, the number 8 would be represented as `0800`.

Following this byte-alignment indicator comes the data `002A` (`2A00` if the reverse format is being used), which is the hex representation of the number 42, but not really used for anything in particular. (Anecdotally, the number 42 was chosen because, according to author Douglas Adams, it represents the answer to the question of "life, the universe, and everything"). The following 4-byte number indicates the number of bytes from the start of the EXIF data to the actual image information data you wish to extract.

Image File Directories and Tags

EXIF image information is stored in blocks of data known as Image File Directories (IFDs). Each of these directories contains one or more tags, representing the image information data itself, matching the data structure shown in Table 10-1.

Table 10-1. *Image File Directory Structure*

Data Length	Data Type	Represents
2 bytes	Number	The number of tags represented within this directory
12 bytes × tag count	Tags	Image information data
4 bytes	Number	Distance from the start of the EXIF data to the next IFD in the sequence

Each of the tags stored within an IFD has an identical data structure, matching that shown in Table 10-2.

Table 10-2. *Image File Directory Tag Structure*

Data Length	Data Type	Represents
2 bytes	Hexadecimal	Code denoting the image data stored in this tag
2 bytes	Number	Format of the image data stored in this tag
4 bytes	Number	Length of the image data stored in this tag
4 bytes	Mixed	Image data itself if the length of the data is 4 bytes or less, or a number pointing to the location of the image data somewhere else in the file to be looked up

An example of a tag is shown here, in standard (MM) hexadecimal format (spaces added for clarity):

```
A002 0004 00000001 00000640
```

The tag A002 refers to the width of image in the current file. The format 0004 denotes that the data is represented as a 4-byte number. The length of the image data is 00000001, which denotes that there is a single 4-byte number being represented. The data itself, since it is 4 bytes of data or less, is stored within the final 4-byte sequence, 00000640. This represents the number 1,600 stored in hex format. From this tag, you have learned that the image stored in the current file has a width of 1,600 pixels. You can find a full list of the EXIF tags online at http://www.sno.phy.queensu.ca/~phil/exiftool/TagNames/EXIF.html.

Reading EXIF Data Using JavaScript

Now that you have an overview of the way data is stored in EXIF format within a JPEG image file, you can write your own constructor. Listing 10-4 shows an EXIF data reader that will convert the binary data into an object containing information about the image represented by that data. Save this code as a separate file, named exif-reader.js.

Listing 10-4. *EXIF Data Reader*

```
// The ExifData constructor takes a BinaryReader object as its only input and
// returns an object containing the image information stored within its
// binary data

var ExifReader = function(data) {

    // Create an object literal containing a selection of tag IDs stored within the
    // IFD representing the main image data
    var MainImageTags = {
        // Company name. e.g., Nikon, Motorola, Apple, etc.
        "010F": "Make",

        // Camera name. e.g., D80, iPhone, etc.
        "0110": "Model",
```

```
        // Angle of the camera when the image was taken, to the nearest 90°
        "0112": "Orientation",

        // Resolution of the x axis of the image. e.g., 72
        "011A": "XResolution",

        // Resolution of the y axis of the image. e.g., 72
        "011B": "YResolution",

        // A value representing the unit the resolution data is stored in
        "0128": "ResolutionUnit",

        // The name of the software package used to manipulate the image after it
        // was taken. e.g., Adobe Photoshop
        "0131": "Software",

        // The date and time the image was taken
        "0132": "DateTime",

        // The computer operating system used to manipulate the image after it was
        // taken. e.g., Mac OS X
        "013C": "HostComputer",

        // A value representing the location of further image data
        "8769": "ExifOffset",

        // A value representing the location of longitude and latitude data denoting
        // where on the globe the image was taken
        "8825": "GPSOffset"

        // Many more tags exist, but have been removed for brevity
    }

    // Create an object literal containing a selection of tag IDs representing
    // further image information data
    var ExtendedDataTags = {
        // The F-Stop position of the camera at the point the photo was taken.
        // e.g., F2.8
        "829D": "FNumber",

        // A value representing the color profile of the image data
        "A001": "ColorSpace",

        // The width of the image. e.g., 800
        "A002": "ImageWidth",
```

```
    // The height of the image. e.g., 600
    "A003": "ImageHeight"

    // Many more tags exist, but have been removed for brevity
}

// Create an object literal containing a selection of tag IDs representing the
// latitude and longitude position the image was taken
var GPSTags = {
    // The location in relation to the equator.
    // e.g., "N" for North, "S" for South
    "0001" : "LatitudeRef",

    // The latitude represented in degrees, minutes and seconds
    "0002" : "Latitude",

    // The location in relation to the Prime Meridian line, passing through
    // Greenwich, London. e.g., "E" for East, "W" for West
    "0003" : "LongitudeRef",

    // The longitude represented in degrees, minutes and seconds
    "0004" : "Longitude"

    // Many more tags exist, but have been removed for brevity
}

// Create an object literal to provide user-friendly text in place of those
// values that are reference values. The key of each object is the tag name
// from the lists defined above
var LookupValues = {

    // The Orientation tag data denotes a single digit from 1 to 8
    "Orientation": {
        1: "Straight On",
        2: "Straight On - Image Flipped",
        3: "180°",
        4: "180° - Image Flipped",
        5: "90° Counter-clockwise - Image Flipped",
        6: "90° Clockwise",
        7: "90° Clockwise - Image Flipped",
        8: "90° Counter-clockwise"
    },
```

```
        // The ResolutionUnit tag data denotes a single digit from 1 to 3
        "ResolutionUnit": {
            1: "No unit",
            2: "Pixels Per Inch",
            3: "Pixels Per Centimeter"
        },

        // The ColorSpace tag data is either the value 1 or the value 65535
        "ColorSpace": {
            1: "sRGB",
            65535: "Uncalibrated"
        }
    }

    // The exifPosition property stores the location within the data of the start of
    // the EXIF data. Note how we use an anonymous function to execute a routine
    // to locate this position
    this.exifPosition = function() {
        var pointer = 0;
        var length = data.getLength();

        // Loop through the binary file data, looking for the FFE1 hex value that
        // denotes the start of the EXIF data section
        while (pointer <= length) {
            if (data.getHex(pointer, 2) == "FFE1") {
                return pointer;
            }
            pointer++;
        }
    }();

    // The isExif property denotes whether there is EXIF data stored at
    // the location denoted by the exifPosition property
    this.isExif = function(position) {

        // position denotes the start of the EXIF data section. The first 4 bytes
        // of data in this section are FFE1ssss, where ssss denotes the total size
        // of the EXIF data section. The next 4 bytes should be the string "Exif",
        // followed by 2 bytes representing the number 0. If this is the case, we
        // have confirmed that this is indeed EXIF data
        var exifString = data.getString(position + 4, 4);
        var dataValue = data.getNumber(position + 8, 2);
        return (exifString == "Exif") && (dataValue == 0);
    }(this.exifPosition);
```

```
if (this.isExif) {

    // If we have confirmed that the data we are reading is in EXIF format,
    // then continue with the routine.

    // The dataStartPosition property denotes the point at which the rest of
    // the EXIF data is measured from. Any data offset values are measured
    // from this point. The point is situated after the "Exif" string and the 2
    // bytes of the number 0, located previously
    this.dataStartPosition = this.exifPosition + 10;

    // The first 2 bytes of data in this section denote the alignment of the
    // rest of the data. This data is a string with two possible values:
    // MM denotes the standard big endian data format is used, whereas
    // II denotes the reversed little endian format is being used. We use
    // this value to set the isBigEndian property of the BinaryReader object
    // instance referred to by the data object
    var byteAlign = data.getString(this.dataStartPosition, 2);
    data.setIsBigEndian((byteAlign == "MM"));

    // The next 2 bytes of data denote that IFD tag data is coming up
    var tagMark = data.getHex(this.dataStartPosition + 2, 2);

    // The next 4 bytes of data represent a number pointing to the offset
    // position of the start of the first IFD within this EXIF data
    var offsetToFirstIFD = data.getNumber(this.dataStartPosition + 4, 4);

    // Create a function we can reuse to locate tags within a particular IFD
    // and work out their values. The readIFD function takes four parameters:
    // - data: The BinaryReader object instance to read binary data from
    // - start: The start position of EXIF data
    //      (we'll pass in dataStartPosition)
    // - offset: The distance in bytes from the start position of EXIF data to
    //      the start of the IFD to be read
    // - tagSet: An object literal cross-referencing tag IDs to readable
    //      tag names
    var readIFD = function(data, start, offset, tagSet) {

        // The first 2 bytes of any IFD denote the number of tags in that IFD.
        // Each tag is 12 bytes long
        var numberOfTags = data.getNumber(start + offset, 2);

        // The last 4 bytes of any IFD denote an offset to the next
        // connected IFD
        var nextOffset = data.getNumber(start + offset + 2 + ➡
            (numberOfTags * 12), 4);
```

```javascript
// Create an object literal for storing the tag names and
// values to return
var tags = {};

// Add the location of the next IFD data to the output object literal
tags.NextOffset = nextOffset;

// Go through each tag in the directory one by one
for (var index = 0; index < numberOfTags; index++) {

    // Calculate where the tag begins. We need to account for the first
    // 2 bytes in the IFD, which denote the number of tags
    var tagStartPosition = start + offset + 2 + (index * 12);

    // The first 2 bytes of this tag denote an ID representing what the
    // data stored within this tag actually means
    var id = data.getHex(tagStartPosition, 2);

    // Look up the name relating to the tag ID from the tagSet
    // object literal
    var tagName = tagSet[id];

    if (tagName) {

        // The next 2 bytes after the tag ID denote the data format of
        // the information stored within this tag
        var format = data.getNumber(tagStartPosition + 2, 2);

        // The next 4 bytes denote the length of the tag data
        var tagDataLength = data.getNumber(tagStartPosition + 4, 4);

        // The final 4 bytes of the 12-byte tag contain either the
        // tag data itself if the length of the data is 4 bytes or less,
        // or an offset distance in bytes to the location where
        // the tag data is stored within the file
        var value = data.getNumber(tagStartPosition + 8, 4);

        // Create a temporary variable to store the tag data in
        var tagData = "";

        // Calculate the tag data value based on the format of that data
        switch (format) {

            // A format value of 2 denotes the tag data is stored
            // as a string
```

```
case 2:
    // Locate the position in the binary data file where the
    // tag data is to be found. If the tag data is longer
    // than 4 bytes, it will be found at the distance stored
    // in the value variable from the start of the EXIF
    // data. If the tag data is 4 bytes or shorter, the data
    // is located within the last 4 bytes of the tag itself
    var dataPosition = (tagDataLength > 4) ? ➥
        start + value : tagStartPosition + 8;

    // Locate the string representing the tag data.
    // According to the EXIF format, the last byte of string
    // data is always "00", so we can ignore this last byte
    tagData = data.getString(dataPosition, ➥
        tagDataLength - 1);
    break;

// A format value of 3 denotes the tag data is stored as a
// number, 2 bytes in length
case 3:

    // Find the 2-byte number stored 8 bytes in from
    // the start of the tag
    tagData = data.getNumber(tagStartPosition + 8, 2);
    break;

// A format value of 4 denotes the tag data is a
// 4-byte number
case 4:

    // In this case, we simply return the number stored in
    // the value variable that we extracted earlier
    tagData = value;
    break;

// A format value of 5 denotes the tag data is stored as a
// rational number, the result of one number divided by
// another. The first 4-byte number in an 8-byte sequence
// is the numerator, the second 4-byte number is
// the denominator
case 5:

    // Define an array to store the tag data
    var tagDataArray = [];
```

```
                            // Calculate rational numbers for as long as there is
                            // data to process
                            for (var rIndex = 0; rIndex < tagDataLength; rIndex++) {

                                // Locate the start position of the 8-byte sequence
                                // representing this rational number
                                var rationalStartPosition = value + start + ➡
                                    (8 * rIndex);

                                // The numerator is the first 4-byte number of the
                                // 8-byte data sequence
                                var numerator = data.getNumber( ➡
                                    rationalStartPosition, 4);

                                // The denominator is the second 4-byte number of
                                // the 8-byte data sequence
                                var denominator = data.getNumber( ➡
                                    rationalStartPosition + 4, 4);

                                // Add the resulting rational number to
                                // the tagDataArray
                                tagDataArray.push(numerator / denominator);
                            }

                            // Return the array of rational numbers
                            tagData = tagDataArray;
                            break;

                        // A format value of 7 denotes the tag data is of an
                        // undefined or case-specific custom type
                        case 7:

                            // Locate the position in the binary data file where the
                            // tag data is to be found
                            var dataPosition = tagDataLength > 4 ? start + ➡
                                value : tagStartPosition + 8;

                            // Return the string representation of the data
                            // stored in this tag
                            tagData = data.getString(dataPosition, tagDataLength);
                            break;

                    default:
                        break;
                }
```

```
            // Certain tag data values, such as Orientation and
            // ResolutionUnit, are stored as numbers representing
            // equivalent text values. These text values are stored
            // in the LookupValues object literal. If the current tag
            // name is found in that object literal, then replace the
            // tagData with the user-friendly text representation
            // of the current data value
            if (LookupValues[tagName]) {
                tagData = LookupValues[tagName][tagData];
            }

            // Certain tag data, such as DateTime and GPS Latitude and
            // Longitude, are not stored in user- or code-friendly formats.
            // The reformat method, defined later, reformats the tag data
            // that requires it into a better format
            tags[tagName] = reformat(tagName, tagData);
        }
    }

    // Return the tags object literal, containing the tag names and
    // their associated data in a user-friendly format
    return tags;
}

// The reformat method converts certain IFD tag data into a format that is
// more code- or user-friendly
var reformat = function(tagName, tagData){
    switch (tagName) {
        case "DateTime":

            // Tag data in the DateTime tag is stored as a string in the
            // format YYYY:MM:DD HH:MM:SS. Let's convert that string
            // to a native JavaScript Date object
            var datePart = value.split(" ")[0].split(":");
            var timePart = value.split(" ")[1].split(":");
            var year = datePart[0];

            // Months in JavaScript run from 0 - 11
            var month = datePart[1] - 1;
            var day = datePart[2];
            var hour = timePart[0];
            var minute = timePart[1];
            var second = timePart[2];
```

```
            // Replace the tagData with a JavaScript Date object
            // old representing the string-based date
            tagData = new Date(year, month, day, hour, minute, second);
            break;

    case "Latitude":
    case "Longitude":

            // Latitude and longitude data is stored as an array of three
            // values: degrees, minutes and seconds, which together refer
            // to a point on the globe. Let's take this format and convert
            // it into two others, the standard format for representing
            // geo-location data: degrees° minutes' seconds"
            // and a decimal-based format favored by Google Maps and others
            var degrees = parseFloat(value[0]);
            var minutes = parseFloat(value[1]);
            var seconds = parseFloat(value[2]);

            // The decimal format found by turning the minutes and seconds
            // from base 60 values to base 100 values and adding them to
            // the degrees
            var decimalFormat = (degrees + (minutes / 60) + ➥
                ((seconds / 60)/100));

            // Some GPS latitude and longitude tags do not represent seconds
            // separately, but rather store their minutes value as a
            // floating point number. If this is the case, we should
            // separate out the minutes and seconds values in order to
            // represent them correctly in the standard format
            if (Math.floor(minutes) < minutes) {
                seconds += (minutes - Math.floor(minutes)) * 60;
                minutes = Math.floor(minutes);
                seconds = Math.round(seconds * 100) / 100;
            }
            var standardFormat = degrees + "° " + minutes + "' " + ➥
                seconds + "\"";

            // Replace the tagData with an object literal containing both
            // standard and decimal formats representing the position on
            // the globe denoted by the original array representation
            tagData = {
                standard: standardFormat,
                decimal: decimalFormat
            }
            break;
```

```
        default:
            break;
    }

    // Return the new tagData where appropriate, or simply return the
    // original tagData if no reformatting took place
    return tagData;
}

// Create a MainImage property, containing an object literal of tag names
// and associated tag data derived from the main image information data
// section of the binary image data
this.MainImage = readIFD(data, this.dataStartPosition, offsetToFirstIFD, ➥
    MainImageTags);

if (this.MainImage.ExifOffset) {

    // If the MainImage data contains an offset pointing to the location of
    // an extended image data IFD, then read this data in addition, and
    // assign the resulting tag data to the ExtendedData property
    this.ExtendedData = readIFD(data, this.dataStartPosition, ➥
        this.MainImage.ExifOffset, ExtendedDataTags);
}

if (this.MainImage.GPSOffset) {

    // If the MainImage data contains an offset pointing to the location of
    // GPS latitude and longitude data, then read this associated IFD and
    // assign the resulting tag data to the GPSData property
    this.GPSData = readIFD(data, this.dataStartPosition, ➥
        this.MainImage.GPSOffset, GPSTags);
    }
  }
};
```

Displaying EXIF Data from a File

Let's look at a real-world example to demonstrate extracting EXIF data from an image file
loaded via the binary Ajax technique. Figure 10-1 shows an HTML page that displays the image
information data extracted from an image file included on the page with an <img> tag.

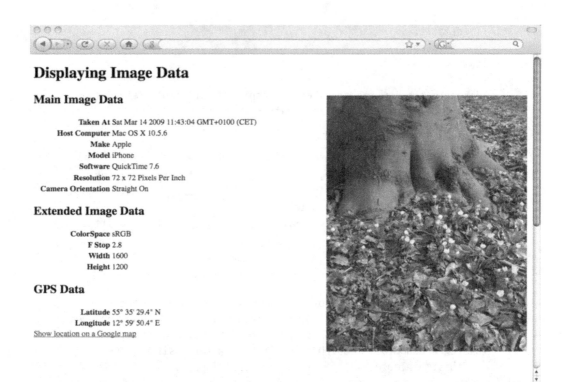

Figure 10-1. *Sample page displaying data extracted from an image file*

The HTML code for this page is shown in Listing 10-5.

Listing 10-5. *HTML Page for Displaying Image Data via Ajax*

```
<!DOCTYPE html PUBLIC "-//W3C//DTD XHTML 1.0 Strict//EN" ➥
    "http://www.w3.org/TR/xhtml1/DTD/xhtml1-strict.dtd">
<html xmlns="http://www.w3.org/1999/xhtml" xml_lang="en" lang="en">
    <head>
        <meta http-equiv="Content-Type" content="text/html; charset=utf-8" />
        <title>Displaying Image Data</title>
        <!-- Feel free to add your own style sheet -->
    </head>
    <body>
        <h1>Displaying Image Data</h1>
        <!-- Refer to the JPG photo image file you wish to extract information from
            in the following tag -->
        <img src="park.jpg" id="image" alt="" />
        <div id="output">
            <!-- We will use JavaScript to place our image information
                within this tag -->
        </div>
```

```
    <!-- Load our $ library -->
    <script type="text/javascript" src="$.js"></script>

    <!-- Load our EXIF data reader constructor -->
    <script type="text/javascript" src="exif-reader.js"></script>

    <!-- Load a JavaScript file for this page, which we will define later -->
    <script type="text/javascript" src="my-page.js"></script>
    </body>
</html>
```

The code in Listing 10-6 should be added to a file named my-page.js. This file is referenced by the HTML page (Listing 10-5) and will display the EXIF image information data on that page.

Listing 10-6. *Displaying EXIF Image Data on an HTML Page*

```
$.onDomReady(function() {

    // Wait for the DOM to become ready, then load the image file, extract its
    // information and display it on the page
    $.Remote.loadBinary({

        // Load the binary file referred to within the <img> tag on the HTML page
        url: document.getElementById("image").src,

        // Only load the first 2KB of data (2048 bytes = 2KB) from the file since
        // the header information is stored at the beginning of the file. Loading
        // too much data can cause the whole data extraction routine to
        // run a lot slower - especially in IE
        length: 2048,

        // Specify a callback function to execute once the first 2KB of the image
        // file have loaded, passing it an instance of the BinaryReader object
        callback: function(data){

            // Read the EXIF data from the binary file
            var exifData = new ExifReader(data);

            // Store the main image information in a local variable
            var mainImageData = exifData.MainImage;

            // Store the extended image information in a local variable
            var extendedData = exifData.ExtendedData;

            // Store the GPS location information in a local variable
            var gpsData = exifData.GPSData;
```

```
// Define a renderTable function, which will append a heading as an
// <h2> tag and a set of name/value pairs as rows within a <table>
// tag to a supplied DOM element
var renderTable = function(dom, headingText, fields){

    // Create a new <h2> tag, set its text to the supplied headingText
    // and add the element to the DOM object passed in
    var heading = $.Elements.create("h2");
    heading.innerHTML = headingText;
    dom.appendChild(heading);

    // Create new <table> and <tbody> tags. Internet Explorer will not
    // add <tr> table rows directly to a <table> tag. It will only do
    // this to a <tbody> tag
    var table = $.Elements.create("table");
    var tbody = $.Elements.create("tbody");

    // Loop through the name/value pairs passed in as an object literal
    for (var field in fields) {
        if (fields[field]) {

            // Create a new table header <th> tag and set its text to
            // the name portion of this name/value pair
            var th = $.Elements.create("th");
            th.innerHTML = field;

            // Create a new table cell <td> tag and set its text to the
            // value of the name/value pair
            var td = $.Elements.create("td");
            td.innerHTML = fields[field];

            // Create a new table row <tr> tag and add the table header
            // and cell tags, finally appending the row itself to the
            // <tbody> tag created earlier
            var tr = $.Elements.create("tr");
            tr.appendChild(th);
            tr.appendChild(td);
            tbody.appendChild(tr);
        }
    }

    // Append the <tbody> tag to the <table> tag and append that to the
    // DOM object passed in and return the resulting DOM object
    table.appendChild(tbody);
    dom.appendChild(table);
    return dom;
}
```

```
// Create a new DocumentFragment, as explained in Chapter 4, for
// faster DOM manipulations
var miniDOM = document.createDocumentFragment();

if (mainImageData) {
    // If the main image information data exists, then render a "Main
    // Image Data" heading and associated <table> tag containing the
    // specified name/value data pairs stored in an object literal
    miniDOM = renderTable(miniDOM, "Main Image Data", {
        "Taken At": mainImageData.DateTime,
        "Host Computer": mainImageData.HostComputer,
        "Make": mainImageData.Make,
        "Model": mainImageData.Model,
        "Software": mainImageData.Software,
        "Resolution": mainImageData.XResolution + " x " + ➥
            mainImageData.YResolution + " " + ➥
            mainImageData.ResolutionUnit,
        "Camera Orientation": mainImageData.Orientation
    });
}

if (extendedData) {
    // If the extended image information data is present, then render
    // this data onto the page
    miniDOM = renderTable(miniDOM, "Extended Image Data", {
        "ColorSpace": extendedData.ColorSpace,
        "F Stop": extendedData.FNumber,
        "Width": extendedData.ImageWidth,
        "Height": extendedData.ImageHeight
    });
}

if (gpsData) {
    // If the GPS location information data is present in the EXIF data
    // of the image file, then display this on the page
    miniDOM = renderTable(miniDOM, "GPS Data", {
        "Latitude": gpsData.Latitude.standard + " " + ➥
            gpsData.LatitudeRef,
        "Longitude": gpsData.Longitude.standard + " " + ➥
            gpsData.LongitudeRef
    });

    // In addition, create a link to Google Maps, passing the latitude
    // and longitude in the query string of the URL in decimal format
    var link = $.Elements.create("a");
    var href = [];
    href.push("http://maps.google.com/maps?z=12&q=");
```

```
        // In the decimal format, negative numbers relate to points below
        // the equator, in the southern hemisphere
        href.push(gpsData.LatitudeRef == "S" ? "-" : "");
        href.push(gpsData.Latitude.decimal);
        href.push(",");

        // In the decimal format, negative numbers relate to points to the
        // west of Greenwich, London
        href.push(gpsData.LongitudeRef == "W" ? "-" : "");
        href.push(gpsData.Longitude.decimal);
        link.href = href.join("");
        link.innerHTML = "Show location on a Google map";

        // Add this new link to the DocumentFragment object
        miniDOM.appendChild(link);
    }

    // Take the contents of the DocumentFragment and add it to the <div
    // id="output"> element on the HTML page. We only interact with the live
    // DOM once in this code, here. This provides a good performance
    // improvement over interacting with the live DOM for each element added
    document.getElementById("output").appendChild( ➥
        miniDOM.cloneNode(true));
    }
  });
});
```

Run the HTML page of Listing 10-5 from a web server to see the final result. The image data is extracted from the binary image file and displayed on the page in tabular form, as shown in Figure 10-1.

Congratulations! You are now able to read binary file data using Ajax, which should open up a whole world of extra possibilities for your own web applications.

Summary

This chapter explained how to load binary files using the Ajax technique. You have seen how to locate and extract information from these files according to a known data format specification. You took this principle and applied it to photos taken with a digital camera, allowing you to extract information about those images, such as when and where the photo was taken, from the file itself. You should now be able to apply the techniques you have learned in this chapter to extract information stored in any other type of binary files, including music and movie files, to help benefit your own RIAs.

In the next chapter, you will learn how to draw graphics dynamically within the browser based on data on your pages, without the use of <img> tags.

CHAPTER 11

Drawing in the Browser

As part of your web application, you may wish to dynamically render a chart, graph, or other visual representation of live data. Of course, you could send your data to the server and have it generate the required images, but why go to all that trouble when you can have the browser do the drawing? Methods are available to allow you to render graphic elements within current browsers by using entirely front-end code.

This chapter introduces two separate technologies available in today's browsers that make it possible to draw vector graphics in your browser: Scalable Vector Graphics and Vector Markup Language. We'll also look at a third-party cross-browser component that will allow you to draw charts, graphs, and other graphics within your own RIAs using either technology, as appropriate. Finally, you'll learn about a new HTML 5 tag for rendering graphics on your pages.

Creating Scalable Vector Graphics

As discussed in the previous chapter, standard image graphic files in GIF, JPG, and PNG format are stored as binary data. They are designed to be displayed in sizes no larger than their original version. These types of images cannot be scaled or resized larger without loss of image quality.

In contrast, vector graphics are images that can be scaled and resized without loss of image quality. This is achieved by describing the image by its constituent parts: lines, shapes, colors, gradients, and other elements that fit together to create the final graphic. Font files are an example of vector graphics. Fonts can be resized to any dimensions without loss of quality. Each time the font is resized, its appearance is recalculated based on the series of lines and shapes that make up each individual character.

Scalable Vector Graphics (SVG) is a W3C recommendation (http://www.w3.org/Graphics/SVG/) that details a specific XML format that can be used to describe two-dimensional vector graphics for display in a browser. SVG is for graphical content what XHTML is for text content. In fact, like XHTML, SVG works alongside other in-browser technologies, such as CSS and the JavaScript DOM, to allow developers to provide dynamic and interactive graphics.

SVG was developed to provide browsers and developers with native support for creating the kind of graphical content that previously was possible only by using Adobe's Flash Player plug-in. At present, SVG support is built into Firefox 1.5 and up, Safari 3 and up, Opera 9.5 and up, and Google Chrome browsers. Its use on the Web is fairly limited, mainly due its lack of support in IE and the prevalence of plug-ins such as Flash Player.

SVG data can be placed inline directly within an XHTML page or referenced as an image file, with an .svg extension, via an <img> tag on a page, just like other images. An <svg> tag surrounds the content describing the image, and acts like a canvas to contain the drawing.

Inside this canvas, you can take advantage of a myriad tags for defining the image you wish to display. Along with drawing simple shapes and lines, you can also load external image files, render text, and apply gradients to any element within the SVG canvas.

Creating SVG Image Files

First, let's look at a simple stand-alone SVG image file. Listing 11-1 shows the XML-style contents of an SVG image file, which creates a gradient, some shapes, a line, and some text. Save this code to a file named my-vector.svg and open it in a browser that supports SVG rendering. You should see the page shown in Figure 11-1.

Listing 11-1. *A Simple SVG Image File*

```
<?xml version="1.0" standalone="no"?>
<!DOCTYPE svg PUBLIC "-//W3C//DTD SVG 1.1//EN"  ➥
    "http://www.w3.org/Graphics/SVG/1.1/DTD/svg11.dtd">

<!-- We specify the custom SVG DOCTYPE shown here to add tag support -->

<!-- First, we define a canvas to draw upon, using the <svg> tag -->
<svg width="1024" height="768" version="1.1"  ➥
      xmlns="http://www.w3.org/2000/svg">

    <!-- Define a gradient. This won't be displayed yet, just defined. x1 and y1
          denote the position where the gradient will begin, and x2 and y2 denote
          where the gradient will end. The colors used and at which points along
          the gradient they change are denoted by the <stop> tags within
          the <linearGradient> tag -->
    <linearGradient id="gradient" gradientUnits="userSpaceOnUse"  ➥
        x1="0" y1="0" x2="200" y2="0">
        <stop offset="0" stop-color="#000000" />
        <stop offset="1" stop-color="#cccccc" />
    </linearGradient>

    <!-- Draw a square, beginning at the location denoted by x and y. Fill its
          contents with the gradient defined previously, referenced by its id -->
    <rect x="20" y="20" width="200" height="200" fill="url(#gradient)" />

    <!-- Draw a rectangle at position x, y with rounded corners, whose radius
          is denoted by the rx and ry attributes. Note the use of the style attribute
          which applies styles to the element as it would within XHTML -->
    <rect x="220" y="220" rx="20" ry="20" width="250" height="100"  ➥
        style="fill:#330000;"/>

    <!-- Draw a circle, with the radius denoted by the attribute r. We define a
          border around the circle using the stroke and stroke-width attributes -->
    <circle cx="350" cy="120" r="50" stroke="#336699"  ➥
        stroke-width="25" fill="#003300" />
```

```
    <!-- Draw a line from the position x1, y1 to the position x2, y2. You would
         not actually see the line until you applied a stroke-width border to it,
         which we do here by means of the style attribute on the <line> tag -->
    <line x1="20" y1="20" x2="320" y2="320"  ➥
        style="stroke:#cccccc;stroke-width:3"/>

    <!-- Write text on the canvas in a fixed size and color -->
    <g font-size="50" font-weight="bold" fill="#333333">
        <text x="200" y="460">Text Example</text>
    </g>
</svg>
```

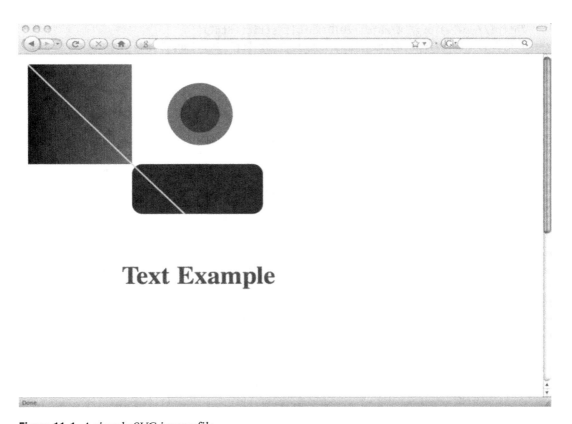

Figure 11-1. *A simple SVG image file*

Specifying SVG Within HTML

Creating separate stand-alone image files using SVG works, but this technique does not provide for dynamic rendering. By defining the images directly within your HTML pages, you're able to use the DOM for dynamic interaction with the individual elements within the canvas. Listing 11-2 shows how to describe the image of Figure 11-1 using XHTML without any external image file references.

You must save the file shown in Listing 11-2 using an .xhtml extension in order to force the browser to render the page using its XML and HTML parsers together, rather than just using its HTML parser. The XML parser contains the code necessary to render SVG, and the browser will use its XML parser only when it is absolutely sure the page contents are XML. This can be set either by specifying the file extension .xhtml or by ensuring the web server sends a MIME type of application/xhtml+xml to describe the file contents. This MIME type should actually be used to send all XHTML file contents, rather than the usual text/html MIME type for ordinary HTML documents. The only reason for not using this is that IE does not recognize this MIME type and refuses to render the page.

Listing 11-2. *A Simple SVG Image, Described Within an XHTML Page*

```
<!DOCTYPE html PUBLIC "-//W3C//DTD XHTML 1.0 Strict//EN"  ➥
    "http://www.w3.org/TR/xhtml1/DTD/xhtml1-strict.dtd">
<html xmlns="http://www.w3.org/1999/xhtml" lang="en" xml:lang="en">
    <head>
        <title>SVG Demo</title>
    </head>
    <body>
        <h1>SVG Demo</h1>
        <svg width="1024" height="768" version="1.1"  ➥
                xmlns="http://www.w3.org/2000/svg">
            <linearGradient id="gradient" gradientUnits="userSpaceOnUse"  ➥
                    x1="0" y1="0" x2="200" y2="0">
                <stop offset="0" stop-color="#000000" />
                <stop offset="1" stop-color="#cccccc" />
            </linearGradient>
            <rect x="20" y="20" width="200" height="200" fill="url(#gradient)" />
            <rect x="220" y="220" rx="20" ry="20" width="250" height="100"  ➥
                style="fill:#330000;"/>
            <circle cx="350" cy="120" r="50" stroke="#336699"  ➥
                stroke-width="25" fill="#003300" />
            <line x1="20" y1="20" x2="320" y2="320"  ➥
                style="stroke:#cccccc;stroke-width:3"/>
            <g font-size="50" font-weight="bold" fill="#333333">
                <text x="200" y="460">Text Example</text>
            </g>
        </svg>
    </body>
</html>
```

This approach is not particularly cross-browser-friendly. IE does not recognize the .xhtml file extension or the application/xhtml+xml MIME type. Even though IE does not support SVG, you still want your XHTML pages to load in that browser. Another solution is needed.

Specifying SVG Through JavaScript

Thankfully, there is a solution that allows you to write standard HTML pages but still create SVG images within your web applications, and that is to use JavaScript to dynamically add the SVG elements to the page, ensuring the browser's XML parser is used to create those elements. Listing 11-3 shows the beginnings of a representation of the image of Figure 11-1 using JavaScript to create SVG elements dynamically.

Listing 11-3. *A Simple SVG Image, Described Through JavaScript*

```
<!DOCTYPE html PUBLIC "-//W3C//DTD XHTML 1.0 Strict//EN"  ➥
    "http://www.w3.org/TR/xhtml1/DTD/xhtml1-strict.dtd">
<html xmlns="http://www.w3.org/1999/xhtml" lang="en" xml:lang="en">
    <head>
        <title>SVG Demo</title>
    </head>
    <body>
        <h1>SVG Demo</h1>

        <!-- Including script block on the page to demonstrate -
            this would normally exist in a separate JavaScript file -->
        <script type="text/javascript">

            // document.createElementNS creates a new element using a defined
            // namespace - in this case, the SVG namespace, referred to by the URL.
            // The tag created is <svg> according to the second parameter. Because
            // namespaces are a part of XHTML and XML, the element is rendered using
            // the browser's XML parser - just what we need to represent SVG
            // on our page

            var svg = document.createElementNS(  ➥
                'http://www.w3.org/2000/svg', 'svg');
            svg.setAttribute('width', '1024');
            svg.setAttribute('height', '768');

            // Dynamically create a <circle> element and add it to the previously
            // created <svg> canvas
            var circle = document.createElementNS(  ➥
                'http://www.w3.org/2000/svg', 'circle');
            circle.setAttribute('cx', '350');
            circle.setAttribute('cy', '120');
            circle.setAttribute('r', '50');
            circle.setAttribute('stroke', '#336699');
            circle.setAttribute('stroke-width', '25');
            circle.setAttribute('fill', '#003300');
            svg.appendChild(circle);
```

```
                // TODO: Represent all other vector elements here in a similar way

                // Add the <svg> tag to the page, rendering the image
                document.body.appendChild(svg);
            </script>
        </body>
</html>
```

Drawing with Vector Markup Language

Back in 1998, Microsoft submitted its own proposal for an XML-based vector graphics format, known as Vector Markup Language (VML), to the W3C for consideration as a recommendation. Since Adobe, Sun, and others were also in the process of submitting their own similar formats, the W3C decided to develop a unified format for all to use, which, in 2002, became the SVG recommendation, as discussed in the previous section. Unfortunately for web developers, Microsoft developers chose not to adopt SVG—and still have not in IE 8—and continued instead to work on and improve their VML format.

VML is supported in all releases of IE from version 5, but is not supported in any other browser. A cross-browser vector graphics library would need to support both SVG and VML to be a viable solution for developers.

VML has remarkable similarities to SVG and supports virtually identical features. The different, more succinct format of VML, however, makes its file size smaller than an equivalent representation of the same image using SVG. Interestingly, VML elements are positioned using CSS and do not require a single element surrounding them to act as a canvas. The tags can be added directly to the page in any location. Listing 11-4 shows the image in Figure 11-1 represented using VML within an HTML page.

Listing 11-4. *A Simple VML Image, Described Within an HTML Page*

```
<!DOCTYPE html PUBLIC "-//W3C//DTD XHTML 1.0 Strict//EN"  ➥
    "http://www.w3.org/TR/xhtml1/DTD/xhtml1-strict.dtd">
<html xmlns="http://www.w3.org/1999/xhtml" lang="en" xml:lang="en">
    <head>
        <title>SVG Demo</title>

        <!-- To use VML within your page, use the <style> element to switch on
            its behavior -->
        <style>v\: * {behavior:url(#default#VML); display: inline-block;}</style>

        <!-- Next, declare the VML namespace to go with the behavior -->
        <xml:namespace ns="urn:schemas-microsoft-com:vml" prefix="v" />
    </head>
    <body>
        <h1>SVG Demo</h1>
        <v:rect style='position: absolute; top: 20px; left: 20px; width: 200px;  ➥
                height: 200px' fillcolor="#000000">
```

```
            <v:fill method="linear sigma" color2="#cccccc" angle="90"  ➥
                type="gradient" />
        </v:rect>

        <v:oval style="top: 120px; left: 350px; width: 50px; height: 50px;"
            fillcolor="#003300" strokecolor="#336699" strokeweight="25px" />

        <v:line from="20px,20px" to="320px,320px" strokecolor="#cccccc"  ➥
            strokewidth="3px" />

        <!-- VML text cannot be written directly onto the page; it must be
            encompassed by another shape. Here, we create a rectangle to
            hold the text -->
        <v:rect style="top=460px; left=200px; width=500; height=100">
            <v:textbox ><span style="font-size: 50px; font-weight: bold;  ➥
                color: #333333;">Text Example</span></v:textbox>
        </v:rect>
    </body>
</html>
```

Building Dynamic Graphs with a Reusable Drawing Library

So far, you have seen how modern browsers support XML-based vector graphics, but that IE uses a different syntax than the other browsers. In order to use vector graphics within your web applications, you need a simple way of specifying your vector graphics that can be supported by the two different models. We often require JavaScript libraries to smooth out cross-browser inconsistencies, as discussed in Chapter 2. In this case, we can use Raphaël, a reusable JavaScript library built by developer Dmitry Baranovskiy.

Raphaël simplifies the creation of custom vector graphics in a cross-browser way through a single, simple JavaScript API. The library works by selecting the appropriate vector graphics drawing technique: SVG or VML, depending on the browser. You can download the library from the project home page at http://raphaeljs.com/, which also provides many examples of the component in action. The library component code weighs in at 53KB compressed.

As you have seen, every graphical object created using SVG and VML is also a DOM object, which means you can add event handlers or dynamically modify existing graphical elements, just as with any other page element.

As an example, suppose that you wish to represent a set of data to the end users of a web application using a line graph. The data is constantly changing—perhaps you are using Ajax to receive new data every 30 seconds from the server. You want to reflect the changes on the graph as the new data arrives. Figure 11-2 shows how this might look to your users. Clicking the "Get new data" link simulates the receipt of new data from the server, updating the graph. Hovering the mouse over each point on the graph highlights that point and reveals its exact value.

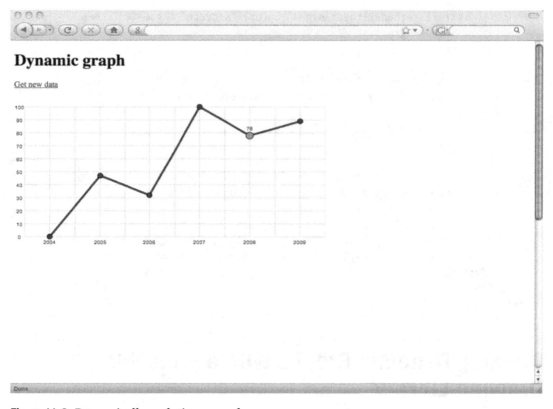

Figure 11-2. *Dynamically updating a graph*

Listing 11-5 shows how you might build the graph shown in Figure 11-2 dynamically in an HTML page, using the Raphaël JavaScript library to ensure cross-browser compatibility. First, an empty canvas is created, and then a grid is drawn and the correct x- and y-axis labels are added. Next, the data points are plotted and lines drawn between them. When the "Get new data" link is clicked, new data is generated at random, the existing lines and points are removed from the canvas, and the new data points and lines are added in their place.

Listing 11-5. *Drawing a Dynamic Graph Using the Raphaël JavaScript Library*

```
<!DOCTYPE html PUBLIC "-//W3C//DTD XHTML 1.0 Strict//EN"  ➥
    "http://www.w3.org/TR/xhtml1/DTD/xhtml1-strict.dtd">
<html xmlns="http://www.w3.org/1999/xhtml" lang="en" xml:lang="en">
    <head>
        <title>Dynamic graph</title>
        <meta http-equiv="content-type" content="text/html;charset=utf-8" />
    </head>
    <body>
        <h1>Dynamic graph</h1>

        <!-- Element we'll populate with a button later via JavaScript -->
        <p id="button"></p>
```

```
<!-- Element we'll populate with the graph later using JavaScript -->
<div id="canvas"></div>

<!-- Reference the $ JavaScript library -->
<script type="text/javascript" src="$.js"></script>

<!-- Reference the Raphaël JavaScript library -->
<script type="text/javascript" src="raphael.js"></script>

<!-- For simplicity, I include the JavaScript code to generate the graph
     within the page. You should reference it from an external file within
     your own web applications -->
<script type="text/javascript">

    // Declare a new constructor which will draw and represent our graph
    var Graph = function(input) {

        // Expected inputs include the data labels for the x axis as an
        // array, the data values themselves as an array, the width and
        // height of the canvas, and the element itself to populate with
        // the canvas
        this.labels = input.labels || [];
        this.data = input.data || [];
        this.width = input.width || 600;
        this.height = input.height || 300;
        this.element = input.element || $.Elements.create("div");

        // Create a new cross-browser canvas using Raphaël. The paper
        // property represents an object that we can execute methods on
        // later to alter and affect the new canvas
        this.paper = Raphael(this.element, this.width, this.height);

        // Establish the maximum value from the data array, rounded to the
        // nearest 100. This value will be used as the maximum point on the
        // y axis of the graph
        this.maximumDataValue = Math.ceil(Math.max.apply(Math,  ➥
            this.data) / 100) * 100;

        // The buildGrid method draws the grid onto the canvas, including
        // the axis labels, and returns the x and y coordinates of the
        // position of the actual grid (assuming spacing for the labels) and
        // the width and height of the grid itself, not counting the labels
        this.buildGrid = function() {

            // Define the height and width to allocate to the axis labels
            var xLabelHeight = 20, yLabelWidth = 20;
```

```
// Establish the x and y coordinates of the grid itself, and the
// width and height of the grid, not counting the axis labels
var x = yLabelWidth, y = 20;
var width = this.width - yLabelWidth;
var height = this.height - xLabelHeight - y;

// Calculate how many lines to draw in each direction on
// the grid
var horizLines = this.data.length * 2;
var vertLines = (this.maximumDataValue / 10);

// Draw the grid in light gray (hex color #ccc) using Raphaël
this.paper.drawGrid(x, y, width, height, horizLines, ➥
    vertLines, "#ccc");

// The drawXLabels function creates and positions the labels on
// the x axis of the graph
var drawXLabels = function() {
    for (var index = 0, length = this.data.length; ➥
            index < length; index++) {
        var x = yLabelWidth + ((index / this.data.length) ➥
            * width) + (width/(2 * this.data.length));
        var y = this.height - (xLabelHeight/2);

        // Use Raphaël to draw the label text onto the canvas
        this.paper.text(x, y, this.labels[index]).attr({
            "font": '10px "Arial"',
            stroke: "none",
            fill: "#000"
        });
    }
}.call(this);

// The drawYLabels function creates and positions the labels on
// the y axis based on the maximum data value we calculated
// earlier and rounded to the nearest 100. This allows us to
// use rounded numbers as our axis labels
var drawYLabels = function() {
    for (var index = 0, length = vertLines; index <= length; ➥
            index++) {
        var labelText = (index * this.maximumDataValue) / ➥
            vertLines;
        var labelPosition = height - (vertLines * index * ➥
            height / this.maximumDataValue) + y;
```

```
                // Use Raphaël to draw the label text onto the canvas
                this.paper.text(yLabelWidth / 2, labelPosition, ➡
                        labelText).attr({
                    "font": '10px "Arial"',
                    stroke: "none",
                    fill: "#000"
                });
            }
        }.call(this);

        // Now return the x and y coordinates of the start of the grid
        // within the canvas along with the width and height of the grid
        return {
            x: x,
            y: y,
            width: width,
            height: height
        }
    }

    // Execute the buildGrid method, storing the returned values in the
    // grid property
    this.grid = this.buildGrid();

    // The drawPath method plots the points and draws the lines onto
    // the existing grid
    this.drawPath = function() {

        // To draw a line using Raphaël, create a path and give it a
        // stroke-width value equivalent to the width for that line
        var pathAttributes = {
            stroke: "#333",
            "stroke-width": 4,
            "stroke-linejoin": "round"
        };
        this.path = this.paper.path(pathAttributes);

        // Create arrays for storing references to the points, text, and
        // shapes we're going to be drawing onto the grid
        this.points = [];
        this.text = [];
        this.rects = [];

        // Loop through each item in the data array
        for (var index = 0, length = this.data.length; index < length; ➡
                index++) {
```

```
// Calculate the x and y coordinate position of the point on
// the grid, which will represent the current data item
var x = this.grid.x + (index * (this.grid.width / ➥
    this.data.length)) + (this.grid.width / (2 * ➥
    this.data.length));
var y = this.grid.y + this.grid.height - (this.data[index] ➥
    * this.grid.height / this.maximumDataValue);

// The first data item will be represented by a point and
// will not have a line drawn to its position. All other
// data items will have lines drawn to them
if (index == 0) {
    this.path.moveTo(x, y, 10);
} else {
    this.path.lineTo(x, y, 10);
}


// The drawPoints function renders points onto the grid,
// along with a text label above each point, which is hidden
// until the user hovers the mouse over an invisible
// rectangle covering the point and a large area around it.
// This provides a larger area for the mouse interaction to
// take place, avoiding the need for the user to locate the
// smaller points on the grid in order to see the text
// label associated with that point
var drawPoints = function(){

    // Draw an invisible rectangle from the top to bottom of
    // the grid surrounding the point representing the data
    // value. The opacity value of 0 makes the rectangle
    // invisible but still present on the grid
    var rect = this.paper.rect(this.grid.x + ➥
        (this.grid.width * index / this.data.length), ➥
        this.grid.y, (this.grid.width * (index + 1) / ➥
        this.data.length), this.grid.height).attr({ ➥
        stroke: "none", fill: "#fff", opacity: 0}));

    // Add the object representing the rectangle to an array
    this.rects.push(rect);

    // Draw a point representing the data value onto the
    // grid and add it to an array of all the points
    var point = this.paper.circle(x, y, 5).attr({
        'fill': "#333"
    });
    this.points.push(point);
```

```
            // Draw a text label above the point and add it to an
            // array of labels
            var text = this.paper.text(x, y - 15,  ➡
                    this.data[index]).attr({
                "font": '10px "Arial"',
                stroke: "none",
                fill: "#000"
            });
            this.text.push(text);

            // Because the XML elements that represent each shape or
            // object within the canvas can be manipulated using
            // the standard DOM, we can use DOM methods, such as
            // insertAfter, just as with HTML elements
            text.insertAfter(dot);

            // Hide the text label by default
            text.hide();

            // We can add events to the elements created on the
            // canvas since they behave like standard HTML elements.
            // Here, we use Raphaël to dynamically alter the color
            // and size of the point created earlier, and show the
            // text label, when the user moves the mouse over the
            // invisible rectangle element surrounding the point
            rect.mouseover(function(){
                point.attr({
                    "fill": "#999",
                    "r": 7
                });
                text.show();
            });
            // When the user moves the mouse away from the rectangle
            // surrounding the point, the text is hidden once again
            // and the point is restored to its original size
            // and color
            rect.mouseout(function(){
                point.attr({
                    "fill": "#333",
                    "r": 5
                });
                text.hide();
            });
        }.call(this)
    }
}
```

```
        // Now execute the drawPath method just described
        this.drawPath();

        // The replaceData method is used to remove the vectors from the
        // grid, leaving the grid intact, so that new data can be plotted
        this.replaceData = function(data) {

            // The new data is passed as an input to the method, and the
            // existing data is replaced with that new data
            this.data = data;

            // Remove the line from the grid
            this.path.remove();

            // Remove the points from the grid, one by one
            for (var index = 0, length = this.points.length;  ➥
                    index < length; index++) {
                this.points[index].remove();
            }

            // Remove the text labels from the grid
            for (var index = 0, length = this.text.length;  ➥
                    index < length; index++) {
                this.text[index].remove();
            }

            // Remove the invisible rectangle shapes from the grid
            for (var index = 0, length = this.rects.length;  ➥
                    index < length; index++) {
                this.rects[index].remove();
            }

            // Execute the drawPath method, which draws the line, points,
            // and text labels onto the grid - this time using the new data
            this.drawPath();
        }
    }

// Instantiate the Graph constructor, passing in the data, labels, and
// DOM element to place the new graph within
var myGraph = new Graph({
    labels: [2004, 2005, 2006, 2007, 2008, 2009],
    data: [0, 47, 32, 100, 78, 89],
    element: document.getElementById("canvas")
});
```

```
        // Place a 'Get new data' button onto the page which, when clicked, will
        // generate a new set of data values at random. This is to simulate what
        // could be an Ajax call in a real-world RIA to fetch new, unknown data
        // from the server
        var getNewData = $.Elements.create("a");
        getNewData.innerHTML = "Get new data";
        document.getElementById("button").appendChild(getNewData);

        $.Events.add(getNewData, "click", function(e) {
            e.preventDefault();

            // Generate a new set of data at random, each value being in the
            // range from 0 to 100
            var data = [];
            for (var index = 0, length = 5; index < length; index++) {
                data.push(Math.round(Math.random() * 100));
            }

            // Execute the replaceData method of the Graph instance to render
            // the new set of data onto the grid
            myGraph.replaceData(data);
        });
    </script>
  </body>
</html>
```

You should familiarize yourself with the full list of features supported by this powerful JavaScript library. You can use it whenever you require the ability to display vector graphics dynamically within your own RIAs.

Using the HTML 5 <canvas> Tag

The Mac OS X Dashboard feature uses HTML, CSS, and JavaScript to generate small widgets such as clocks, calendars, weather, and stock reports. When building this feature, Apple developers introduced a new HTML tag to support the ability to dynamically create graphical components within these widgets. This tag, <canvas>, was made a recommendation by WHATWG, and support was added for the tag within Safari 2, Firefox 1.5, Google Chrome, and Opera 9.5. IE does not support this tag in any release up to version 8 (there is eternal hope that the developers will include it in the next version). As described at the end of this section, some work has been done to provide an implementation of the <canvas> tag in IE using the Flash Player plug-in.

Unlike with SVG, no tags are created within the <canvas> tag on the page; instead, graphics are generated entirely by using the native JavaScript API. As such, the graphical components within the tag cannot be styled with CSS, nor are they accessible for manipulation or assigning to events through the DOM. If you wish to connect DOM events to your graphics to provide user interactivity, use SVG instead.

Only two primitive shapes are permitted within the tag: rectangles and lines, which can be curved and manipulated to create all other required shapes. The graphics themselves are not vector-based, so if you need to perform any resizing of the graphical components within the tag, you must write the code to perform this action yourself, based on the graphics you added to the tag.

An advantage of the <canvas> tag is its good support for embedding and manipulating pictures in image files, which is not easy to achieve using SVG. Performance of the <canvas> tag is superior to SVG, especially with large, complex graphics. This is likely because SVG must maintain references to each graphic component as a DOM element; <canvas> does not have this requirement.

Listing 11-6 shows how to use the <canvas> tag with JavaScript to draw a rectangle shape with a gradient-filled background within an HTML page.

Listing 11-6. *A Simple Canvas Tag Image*

```
<!DOCTYPE html PUBLIC "-//W3C//DTD XHTML 1.0 Strict//EN"  ➥
    "http://www.w3.org/TR/xhtml1/DTD/xhtml1-strict.dtd">
 <html xmlns="http://www.w3.org/1999/xhtml" xml:lang="en" lang="en" >
    <head>
        <title>Canvas demo</title>
    </head>
    <body>
        <h1>Canvas demo</h1>

        <!-- The <canvas> tag takes optional width and height attributes. If these are
             left out, the canvas is usually 300 pixels wide by 150 pixels high -->
        <canvas id="canvas" width="300" height="300"></canvas>

        <!-- The following script is included here for simplicity. You should
             reference the code from a separate file, ideally -->
        <script type="text/javascript">

            // Get a DOM reference to the <canvas> tag
            var canvas = document.getElementById("canvas");

            // The actual drawing surface within the <canvas> tag is known as a
            // rendering context. The drawing methods are associated with the
            // context so we must first get a reference to this context. At present,
            // the <canvas> tag supports only a 2D shape-rendering context. In the
            // future, it is envisioned that 3D shape rendering will be possible
            var context = canvas.getContext("2d");

            // Define a gradient, fading from #000000 to #cccccc horizontally across
            // the space of 200 pixels
            var gradient = context.createLinearGradient(0, 0, 200, 0);
            gradient.addColorStop(0, "#000000");
            gradient.addColorStop(1, "#cccccc");
```

```
            // To use the gradient within a rectangle, we define the gradient as the
            // current fill style and then execute the fillRect method
            context.fillStyle = gradient;

            // Draw the gradient-filled rectangle from position (20, 20) stretching
            // 200 pixels wide and tall from that point
            context.fillRect(20, 20, 200, 200);
        </script>
    </body>
</html>
```

Mozilla provides a useful tutorial on the `<canvas>` tag and its associated API at `https://developer.mozilla.org/en/Canvas_tutorial/`. You can also see demonstrations of what other developers are doing with the `<canvas>` tag at the Canvas Demos web site (`http://www.canvasdemos.com/`).

To tackle the lack of IE support for the `<canvas>` tag, developer Grant Jones attempted to build a reusable Flash component that could provide an implementation of this tag. His code works by duplicating the `<canvas>` tag API within JavaScript in IE and sending the code to a Flash component in this browser instead. His mission was to determine whether this type of approach could enable a more responsive graphics drawing engine to be built in IE without the need for VML-based rendering found in other libraries, such as Raphaël. He describes his experiences in some detail in a blog post at `http://www.azarask.in/blog/post/flash-canvas/`. His conclusion reveals that this approach does not provide a suitably faster graphics rendering capability over any native implementation. The JavaScript-to-Flash communication is fairly slow, and the more cross-communication that occurs, the slower the overall result. In one particular test, he noted that using the Flash technique was 40 times slower than native `<canvas>` rendering in other browsers. For now, it is recommended that you use Raphaël instead of relying on a third-party plug-in that gives no performance benefit.

Summary

In this chapter, you learned about the different technologies that make vector graphics drawing possible in modern browsers. You were introduced to a third-party JavaScript library that allows you to easily create custom dynamic vector graphics within your own web applications. You also were introduced to a new tag in HTML 5 for rendering graphics dynamically on your page.

In the final chapter of this book, I will return to the topic of accessibility, revealing how to make your RIAs as accessible as possible using current techniques and emerging browser standards.

■■■

Accessibility in Rich Internet Applications

As I have emphasized from the very start of this book, accessibility is one of the fundamentals of web development. As web developers, we need to ensure that our web applications can reach and be used by the widest audience possible. Our end users should be able to access the information and interface we provide using whatever browsing technology they have available, to suit their own needs and preferences. This final chapter of the book focuses on designing your RIAs for the greatest accessibility possible.

Whose Needs Are We Meeting?

Web sites and applications are usually simple to navigate and interact with if you are an able-bodied person using a mouse on a computer with an adequate screen size and resolution. Most web sites are designed with this type of user in mind. However, other groups of users do not fit this description, yet are relying on us to provide them with a usable, interactive experience.

Users Using Assistive Technology

Assistive technology is a general term given to software or hardware used to assist those with physical impairments, learning difficulties, or disabilities to perform tasks that they would otherwise be incapable of or have difficulty performing. A number of software developers have built tools to allow such users to access information and interact with sites on the Web. Examples are JAWS (http://www.freedomscientific.com/), which is a screen reader that vocalizes the page contents, and ZoomText (http://www.aisquared.com/), which is a screen magnifier that helps the user read the page contents more easily.

We need to ensure our web applications are usable by individuals using assistive technology.

Users on Mobile Devices

Web browsing on mobile devices has increased in leaps and bounds in just the past few years. What started as plain HTML tags rendered in a default style quickly adapted to basic CSS and JavaScript. We have now reached the point where browsers running on the same rendering and JavaScript engines as desktop versions of Opera, Firefox, Safari, and IE are operating on mobile devices.

Mobile devices typically have very restrictive screen sizes. At the time of writing, some of the largest mobile devices sport a maximum screen resolution of 480 pixels wide by 320 pixels tall. In contrast, the lowest screen resolution seen on desktop computers in recent years is 1024 pixels wide by 768 pixels tall. We need to ensure our web applications are usable by individuals using browsing devices with small screens. Figure 12-1 compares the search results pages of Google and Yahoo! on an Apple iPhone. Notice how Yahoo!'s results are readable at the default screen size, whereas Google's results page requires the user to zoom the page to read its text.

Figure 12-1. *Google's and Yahoo!'s search results on a small screen*

Users Without a Mouse

Pointing and clicking with the mouse has become such an ingrained part of the computer experience that many users can move the pointer on the screen with incredible accuracy and speed. However, some people still do not use a mouse, out of necessity or choice.

The second most common input method for web browsing is the keyboard. Most browsers allow the user to navigate around the page using the Tab key to jump between hyperlinks and form elements—the types of elements that are interactive. Navigating with the keyboard in this way removes the need for the accuracy required when using a mouse.

Note   Many developers use a combination of the mouse and keyboard to interact with elements on the page when browsing. They find it is sometimes faster to use the keyboard to locate elements.

An increasingly popular method for browser and computer interaction in recent times is the touchscreen—users select and interact with elements on the page by actually touching the screen with their fingers. In many ways, this is the ultimate pointing device. In the future, touchscreens may provide more advanced ways of interacting with computers, potentially removing the need for a mouse altogether.

We need to ensure our web applications are usable by individuals interacting with pages using input devices other than a mouse.

Accessibility for All

Clearly, with web browsers providing JavaScript support in scenarios previously unseen, our role as web developers is made all the more difficult. We must ensure that users of all browsers, assistive technologies, devices, and input methods are able to use our web applications intuitively and without difficulty.

Of course, you build your web applications using semantic HTML, ensuring those users without JavaScript are able to use your RIA without difficulty. But now that JavaScript is supported in most browsers and on most devices, it's time to take accessibility to the next level.

Proper Navigation with the Back and Forward Buttons

As web application developers, we must meet the needs and expectations of our users. One of the most fundamental and noticeable issues with web applications is that the browser's Back and Forward toolbar buttons, which typically move the user back and forth through the browser's page history, completely break down when page content is updated via Ajax rather than via a full page refresh. Users can spend hours within a web application, such as a web mail client—navigating to different pages and application states, reading, composing, and deleting messages—but when they click the Back button on the browser's toolbar, they are taken back to the page they viewed before loading that web mail application. Users expect their browser to behave in a certain way and become frustrated when it does not. We must fix this issue within our web applications to avoid frustrating end users.

Pages are added to the browser history when a new URL is loaded, which typically occurs when the user selects a hyperlink or submits a form. The developer may also dynamically alter the location object, which represents the URL, through JavaScript. Most changes made to the URL cause a page refresh, with the exception of changes made to the *hash*—any part of the URL following the # character.

The URL hash is used to navigate to content elsewhere within the same page, which means a page refresh is not required, yet the new URL is still added to the browser's history. You can take advantage of this phenomenon through your web applications, updating the URL hash value at relevant points, such as when new content is loaded via Ajax. When changes are made to the hash value, which will occur when the user navigates the browser history using the Back and Forward toolbar buttons, you can perform the necessary action in your code to return the application to the state it was in at the time that hash value was added. With this technique, you are able to give your users the behavior they expect from their browser history navigation.

Listing 12-1 shows how to write a routine to add browser history items through updates made to the hash part of the URL and a routine for reading back previously stored values from the hash when the user navigates back and forth through their browser history. Add this code to your $ JavaScript library, before the final line in the file, where it is instantiated.

Listing 12-1. *Adding and Retrieving Browser History Items Through JavaScript*

```
// Create a History namespace for managing browser history items
// within our RIAs
$.prototype.History = {

    // The currentValue property holds the current hash value from the URL,
    // which is found via the global location.hash property. This property
    // value contains the # character, so we remove this as it is not needed
    currentValue: location.hash.replace(/#/g, ""),

    // To overcome an issue in Internet Explorer's history handling, we need to
    // add and read back our history items from an <iframe> tag on the page in
    // that browser. Here, we maintain a reference to that element, which we
    // define later
    iframe: null,

    // We will want to perform some action when the user clicks the Back
    // and Forward buttons in their browser and the current history item
    // changes. The onChange method will be called when this change occurs
    onChange: function() {},

    // The enable method starts listening for changes occurring to the current
    // hash portion of the URL and hence the browser's history item list itself
    enable: function() {

        // Internet Explorer behaves differently from the other browsers, so we
        // need to create an <iframe> to contain the changes to the hash
        if (window.ActiveXObject) {
```

```
        // Create a hidden <iframe> and add it to the page
        this.iframe = $.Elements.create("iframe");
        this.iframe.style.display = "none";
        this.iframe.src = "javascript:false;";
        document.body.appendChild(this.iframe);

        // Initialize the <iframe> with a history item to start with. The add
        // method is defined later
        this.add(this.currentValue);
    }

    var self = this;

    // The detectHistoryChange function detects when the current hash value
    // differs from the last and executes the onChange method when it does
    var detectHistoryChange = function() {

        // Get the last saved and latest hash values
        var lastValue = self.currentValue;
        var latestValue = location.hash.replace(/#/g, "");

        // Get the hash slightly different in Internet Explorer
        if (self.iframe) {
            var latestValue = ➡
                self.iframe.contentWindow.document.location.hash.replace( ➡
                    /#/g, "");
        }

        // If the latest and last hash values differ, save the new value and
        // call the onChange property, passing it the latest and previous
        // hash values
        if (latestValue != lastValue) {
            self.currentValue = latestValue;
            self.onChange(latestValue, lastValue);
        }
    }

    // Execute the detectHistoryChange function once every 300 milliseconds -
    // see Chapter 5 for the importance of this number - and begin listening for
    // changes occurring to the hash value
    window.setInterval(detectHistoryChange, 300);
},

// The add method takes a specified text string value and adds it to the URL
// hash, creating a new browser history item with that value
add: function(newValue) {
    if (this.iframe) {
```

```
                // Add the hash to Internet Explorer's <iframe> tag
                var iframeDocument = this.iframe.contentWindow.document;
                iframeDocument.open();
                iframeDocument.close();
                iframeDocument.location.hash = newValue;
            } else {
                // All other browsers can access the hash property of the current page
                location.hash = newValue;
            }
        }
    }
}
```

To see how the code in Listing 12-1 can be used within a web application, take a look at the simple example in Listing 12-2, which uses Ajax to load the contents of other linked pages into a page element on the same page, as shown in Figure 12-2. The browser history list is added to with each Ajax request, allowing the user to navigate back and forth between the content loaded in the Ajax requests using the Back and Forward buttons on the browser toolbar.

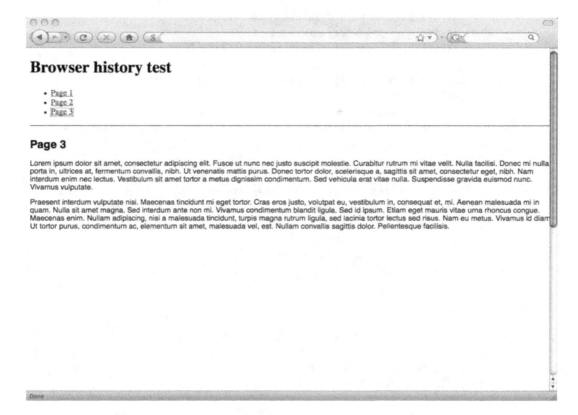

Figure 12-2. *Loading content via Ajax, adding to the browser's page visit history*

Listing 12-2. *Adding and Navigating Page Visit History Items Using Ajax*

```
<!DOCTYPE html PUBLIC "-//W3C//DTD XHTML 1.0 Strict//EN" ➥
    "http://www.w3.org/TR/xhtml1/DTD/xhtml1-strict.dtd">
<html xmlns="http://www.w3.org/1999/xhtml" lang="en" xml:lang="en">
    <head>
        <meta http-equiv="Content-Type" content="text/html; charset=utf-8">
        <title>Browser history test</title>
    </head>
    <body>
        <h1>Browser history test</h1>

        <!-- Create a navigation list of links to other pages -->
        <ul>
            <li><a href="page1.html">Page 1</a></li>
            <li><a href="page2.html">Page 2</a></li>
            <li><a href="page3.html">Page 3</a></li>
        </ul>

        <!-- Create an empty page element to store our Ajax responses -->
        <div id="content"></div>

        <!-- Reference the $ JavaScript library -->
        <script type="text/javascript" src="$.js"></script>

        <!-- In a real web application, you should reference the following code from
             an external file. It is included inline here for simplicity -->
        <script type="text/javascript">
            $.onDomReady(function() {
                // Enable the browser history listener so we can manually add
                // items to the browser's history
                $.History.enable();

                // Assign a function to our new browser history onChange event
                $.History.onChange = function(currentItem, previousItem) {

                    // We will be adding URLs of pages to load via Ajax to the
                    // browser history, so if a URL exists in the current history
                    // item's hash value, load that URL via Ajax, populating the
                    // <div id="content">page element with the result. If there is
                    // no URL in the current history item's hash value, empty the
                    // page element
```

```
                if (currentItem != "") {
                    $.Remote.load({
                        url: currentItem,
                        callback: function(response){
                            document.getElementById("content").innerHTML = ➥
                                response.text;
                        }
                    });
                } else {
                    document.getElementById("content").innerHTML = "";
                }
            }

            // Listen for mouse click events throughout the current page
            $.Events.add(document.body, "click", function(e) {

                // If the user clicks on an anchor <a> tag, stop the default
                // action from occurring and add the URL to the browser history
                // via the URL hash
                if (e.target.tagName.toLowerCase() == "a") {
                    e.preventDefault();

                    // We add the URL of the current link to the history list,
                    // which will, in turn, fire the onChange method we defined
                    // previously, loading the URL via Ajax and displaying its
                    // contents on the page. Navigating through the browser
                    // history using the Back and Forward buttons on the browser
                    // toolbar will cause the different pages to load via Ajax
                    // according to the order they were loaded in the first
                    // place. Click a few links and see for yourself
                    $.History.add(e.target.href);
                }
            });
        });
    </script>
    </body>
</html>
```

Along with adding URLs to the browser history through updates to the URL hash value, you also can add any text values you like. You may even want to consider using a separator character, such as |, to break up multiple text values you wish to store. Consider a web mail application, for example. You may wish to include the value folder|inbox to the history list to inform your application to load the inbox folder, and perhaps use message|display|123 to instruct your application to display message number 123. By building the page-change events using the onChange event, you enable your end users to utilize their Back and Forward toolbar buttons to navigate around your web applications in a way that meets their expectations.

Device-Independent JavaScript

To support the needs of all the users who may potentially use your web application, you will need to update your JavaScript code to remove the reliance on mouse-based interaction. You also will need to improve the flow of your RIA for users who are browsing in a linear fashion—those using a keyboard or software that vocalizes the page contents. You can provide this support by using device-independent events in your JavaScript code.

Device-Independent Events

Throughout this book, you have seen examples of how to assign JavaScript functions to events triggered on DOM elements within the current page. In most cases, you have used the `$.Events.add()` method of the $ JavaScript library you began in Chapter 2. Some of the event types you can listen for using this method are mouse-specific; some are device-independent. Table 12-1 shows the most common event types fired on DOM elements within a page and clarifies whether they are mouse-dependent, keyboard-dependent, or device-independent.

Table 12-1. *Device Dependency of Common JavaScript Events*

Event Type	Input Device	Event Fired
mouseover	Mouse	When the mouse pointer is moved over an element.
mouseout	Mouse	When the mouse pointer is moved away from an element.
mousedown	Mouse	When the mouse button is pressed down.
mouseup	Mouse	When the mouse button is released.
click	Device-independent for hyperlink and form elements Mouse-dependent for all others	When an element is selected by a press and release of the mouse button, the Enter key, a tap of the finger or any other device-specific selection mechanism.
focus	Device-independent	When an element is brought to focus. Occurs when the mouse clicks on a hyperlink or form element, or when the keyboard is used to cycle between all hyperlinks and form elements on a page (usually using the Tab key) or other device-specific focus mechanism.
blur	Device-independent	When focus is moved away from an element. The opposite of focus.
change	Device-independent	When a value in a form field is changed by the user.
select	Device-independent	When text is selected within a form field.
submit	Device-independent	When a form is submitted.
keydown	Keyboard	When a keyboard key is pressed or held down.
keypress	Keyboard	When a key is pressed on the keyboard that causes text to be written to the page, such as in a text field.

From Table 12-1, you can see that the click (only for hyperlink and form elements), focus, blur, change, select, and submit events are input device–independent. Therefore, where possible, you should assign your JavaScript event handlers to these event types to build the most accessible user experience.

Where you still need to use device-dependent event handlers in your code, ensure you provide an alternative means to perform that function using an equivalent event type. Table 12-2 shows which of your code assigned to mouse-specific events should also be assigned to other events to provide a more accessible experience for your end users.

Table 12-2. *Mouse-Dependent and Related Events*

Mouse-Specific Event	Related Event
mouseover	focus
mouseout	blur
mousedown	keydown and/or keypress
mouseup	keyup

For example, suppose your RIA provides an expanded navigation menu when the user hovers the mouse over a single menu item using the mouseover event. You could reveal the same expanded navigation menu when a keyboard-reliant user focuses on that same single menu item by assigning the same code routine to the focus event, which is fired when a keyboard user uses the Tab key in the browser to highlight this element.

Back in Chapter 5, I recommended capturing the mousedown event to execute a code routine, as this event fired before the click event. From what you've learned in this section, you can see that this approach does not meet the criteria for a highly accessible RIA. To improve the accessibility of this technique, apply the same code routine to the keydown event, as shown in Table 12-2. You may also wish to apply the same code routine to the device-independent click event, and execute the code in that routine only if the mousedown or keydown events have not fired first. This gives the perceived performance boost while providing maximum accessibility improvement for all your users.

Device-Independent Event Delegation

In JavaScript, events are raised by the users when they interact with a particular element and *bubble* up the DOM node tree, firing on each element in turn until the top node of the tree, the HTML document itself, is reached. As I explained in Chapter 4, you can use this behavior to your advantage by listening for events occurring throughout the page from a single element near the top of the DOM tree, such as the <body> tag. Since the events bubble up, you can catch them directly on this element rather than attach code to every element you want to react to events on, improving performance within your web applications. For example, to listen for all click events fired within a web application, add the following code to the page:

```
$.Events.add(document.body, "click", function(e) {
    // Code to execute when a click event occurs within the page goes here
});
```

Unfortunately, certain events do not bubble up from the element on which they occurred. This list includes the device-independent focus, blur, change, and submit events. It is suspected that these particular event types do not bubble up because they do not make sense on all elements, though no one really knows for sure why they lack this behavior. A work-around exists to enable you to delegate the focus and blur events, as discussed next; however, no such delegation is possible for the change and submit events.

You could simulate the change event by comparing the value of a field during a focus event handler to the value of the same field during a blur event handler. If the value changed, you know a change event should occur, and you could execute your code accordingly. Unfortunately, a submit event could be fired any number of ways, so in this case, it is best to associate this event handler with a <form> element directly, rather than using event delegation. Thankfully, usually there are not many HTML forms on a page at any one time within a web application, so this should have little performance impact on your code.

To permit event delegation on the focus and blur event types, in IE, you can use the proprietary focusin and focusout events that fire at the same time as focus and blur, respectively. These proprietary event types bubble up just like ordinary events, so you simply associate your code with these event handlers instead, and the problem is resolved.

For other browsers, which use the W3C standard addEventListener() method, you need to turn to the opposite of event bubbling, known as *event capturing*, to delegate events to focus and blur. With event capturing, events fire starting at the top of the DOM node tree, working down toward the element, rather than in the opposite direction you are used to with event bubbling. Unlike event bubbling, event capturing fires events on all elements in the DOM tree, regardless of whether or not it makes sense to fire on a particular element. To listen to events through the event-capturing phase, rather than the bubbling phase, simply set the last parameter of the addEventListener() method to true (in the examples so far, it has been set to false):

```
document.body.addEventListener("focus", function(e) {
    // Code to execute when focus events fire on the page goes here
}, true);
```

To put this all together into a reusable routine to simplify your code, let's alter the event addition code we've been using up to now from the $ JavaScript library to deal with this event anomaly. Listing 12-3 shows the code you should use in place of the current $.Events.add() routine in the $ JavaScript library.

Listing 12-3. *Improving Event Handling Within the $ JavaScript Library*

```
$.prototype.Events.add =  function(element, eventType, callback) {
    var self = this;
    eventType = eventType.toLowerCase();

    if (element.addEventListener) {

        // If the W3C-standard addEventListener method is supported, then associate
        // the event as normal. The final parameter of the method is set to true if
        // the event type is either focus or blur
        element.addEventListener(eventType, function(e){
            callback(self.standardize(e));
        }, (eventType == "focus" || eventType == "blur"));
```

```
    } else if (element.attachEvent) {

        // Detect the event type and switch behavior for focus and blur event types
        // to use the IE-proprietary focusin and focusout event types in their place
        switch (eventType) {
            case "focus":
                element.onfocusin = function(){
                    callback(self.standardize(window.event));
                }
                break;
            case "blur":
                element.onfocusout = function(){
                    callback(self.standardize(window.event));
                }
                break;
            default:
                element.attachEvent("on" + eventType, function(){
                    callback(self.standardize(window.event));
                });
                break;
        }
    }
}
```

Updated Content Alerts and Focus

Most users have no trouble noticing visually when parts of a web application update dynamically via Ajax or DOM manipulation. Such updates usually occur as a result of user interaction with a hyperlink or form element, or on a fixed time interval. However, users with visual impairments and users with assistive technology that vocalizes the page may not be aware of dynamic updates made to other portions of the page away from the section of the page with which they are currently interacting. We need a way to help these users locate updated content when it is appropriate to do so. Additionally, users browsing with a keyboard will not want to frantically use their Tab key to navigate the page to reach the updated page content, so we also need to bring the keyboard focus to the updated content where appropriate. Thankfully, we can meet both needs using the same technique: the DOM element focus() method.

As you saw in Table 12-1, the focus event handler works in a device-independent manner on hyperlinks and form elements. The same is true of the focus() method, which allows you to force the currently focused element to change to one you specify. Focus can also be brought to elements that have a tabindex attribute value set, and this behavior is supported in all modern browsers and assistive technology.

Back in Chapter 1, I advised against using the tabindex attribute within your markup, because this disrupts the natural flow of the page. The better option is to lay out your source code in the order you wish the page to be accessed. This rule is still relevant, but if you set the attribute through JavaScript immediately before bringing the element to focus, you can then remove the attribute immediately, leaving focus on the required element without disruption to the tab order of the page.

In most cases, you should ensure that the updated content appears immediately after the content that causes the update to occur, in order to keep a more natural flow to the page for screen readers and keyboard users, to reduce any confusion.

Caution Use extreme caution and tact when forcing the user's focus to another part of the page. This has the potential to confuse users who are expecting the page to flow in a certain way, which you will be interrupting. Use this technique only when the user would expect a change to occur, such as when following a link or submitting a form. Do not use this technique for content updated on a fixed time interval, which will constantly force users' focus away from the content they are reading, leading to much frustration.

Listing 12-4 shows a way to apply this technique to an HTML form within a web application, which is submitted via Ajax. The server response is placed on the page in place of the form, and focus is brought to the returned content to allow the users to locate and read the response from their form submission and continue browsing from this point. This behavior is depicted in Figure 12-3. The top of the figure shows the page before the form is submitted, and the bottom shows the page after the form is submitted. Often, when an element is brought to focus, an outline appears around it to indicate that this is the current element. In Figure 12-3, this outline is clearly visible around the returned content, showing that this element indeed has the user's current focus.

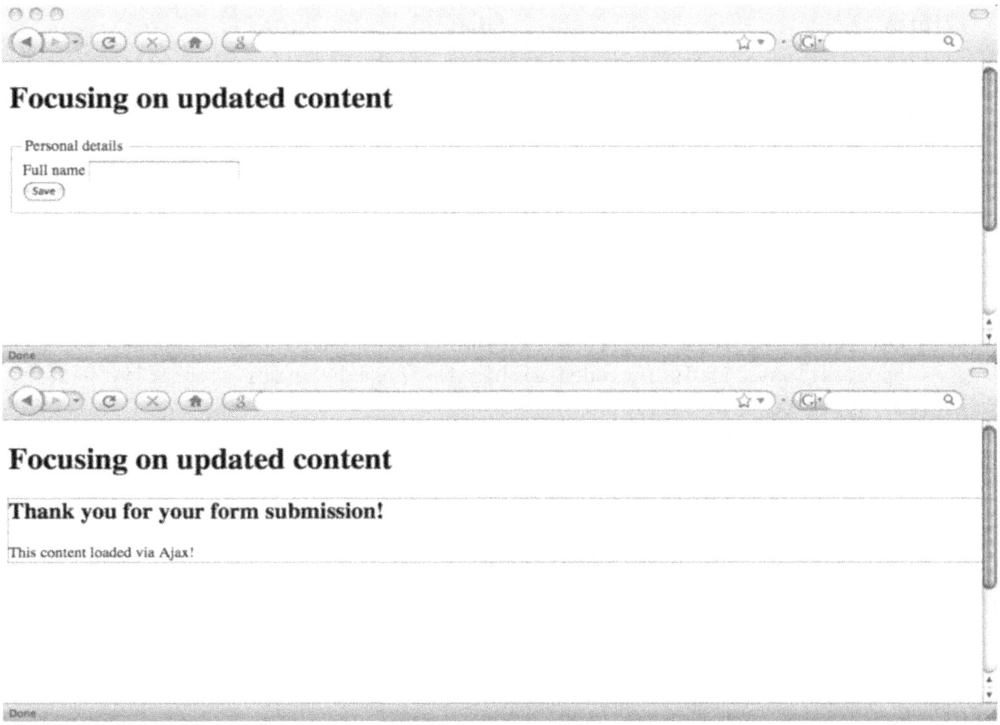

Figure 12-3. *Ajax form submission with focus brought to the returned content*

Listing 12-4. *Alerting Users to Updated Page Content*

```
<!DOCTYPE html PUBLIC "-//W3C//DTD XHTML 1.0 Strict//EN" ➥
    "http://www.w3.org/TR/xhtml1/DTD/xhtml1-strict.dtd">
<html xmlns="http://www.w3.org/1999/xhtml" lang="en" xml:lang="en">
    <head>
        <meta http-equiv="Content-Type" content="text/html; charset=utf-8" />
        <title>Focusing on updated content </title>
    </head>
    <body>
        <h1>Focusing on updated content</h1>

        <!-- Create a form to submit to the server via Ajax -->
        <form id="form" method="post" action="/form-result.html">
            <fieldset>
                <legend>Personal details</legend>

                <div class="field">
                    <label for="full-name">Full name</label>
                    <input type="text" name="full-name" id="full-name" />
                </div>

                <input type="submit" value="Save" />
            </fieldset>
        </form>

        <!-- Create an empty element to be populated with the response of the form
            submission from the server -->
        <div id="result">
        </div>

        <!-- Include the $ JavaScript library -->
        <script type="text/javascript" src="$.js"></script>

        <!-- Reference the following code externally from within your own web
            applications. It is included within the page here for simplicity -->
        <script type="text/javascript">
            $.onDomReady(function() {

                // Store references to the form and result element for use later
                var result = document.getElementById("result");
                var form = document.getElementById("form");
```

```
// When the form is submitted, send the details via Ajax, place the
// response into the <div id="result"> element and bring focus
// to this element
$.Events.add(form, "submit", function(e) {
    e.preventDefault();

    // Send the form details to the server via Ajax
    $.Remote.save({
        url: document.getElementById("form").action,
        data: "full-name=" + document.getElementById( ➥
            "full-name").value,
        callback: function(response) {

            // Place the HTML response from the server into the
            // <div id="result"> page element
            result.innerHTML = response.text;

            // Set the tabIndex property to make the element
            // focusable
            result.setAttribute("tabIndex", 0);

            // Focus on the <div id="result"> page element, which
            // now contains the response from the server
            result.focus();

            // Remove the tabIndex property to prevent any further
            // disruption to the natural focus order of the page
            result.removeAttribute("tabIndex");

            // Remove the <form> element from the page now that the
            // results have been returned
            form.parentNode.removeChild(form);
        }
    });
});
        });
    });
</script>
</body>
</html>
```

Web Accessibility Initiative: Accessible Rich Internet Applications (WAI-ARIA)

The W3C's Web Accessibility Initiative (WAI) group, whose focus is to make the Web more accessible, is addressing the problem of accessibility within RIAs with new recommendations for browser and assistive technology manufacturers, as well as web developers. These recommendations, collectively known as Accessible Rich Internet Applications (shortened to WAI-ARIA or ARIA), deal with alerting the user to updated content; allowing universal access to widgets. form controls, and draggable/droppable elements regardless of browser, device, or input method; and many other topics. You can read the recommendations at http://www.w3.org/TR/wai-aria/.

At the time of writing, support for some or all of the ARIA recommendation has been built into Firefox 3 and up, Opera 9.5 and up, IE 8 and up, Safari 4 and up, and Google Chrome 2 and up. In addition, accessibility software such as JAWS version 10, Window-Eyes, and ZoomText support the ARIA recommendations.

In this section, I will present the essentials of the ARIA recommendations and show you how to add ARIA support to your own web applications to provide the most accessible RIA possible to your end users. You should adopt the ARIA recommendations within your own web applications as soon as you can.

Roles

ARIA roles are a means by which to assign extra semantic meaning to page elements, which allows the browser or assistive technology to better understand what kind of functionality you are intending for the page element and its contents. This can alter how the contents of that element are portrayed to the users of the browser in a way that they, in turn, might understand better.

Roles do not add behavior to an element; they only let the browser and end user know what behavior to expect. You must still add the behavior yourself through JavaScript.

A role is assigned to an element by means of the role attribute on a page element, as in the following example, which denotes an unordered list used for site navigation:

```
<ul id="navigation" role="navigation">
    <li> ... </li>
</ul>
```

The concept of the role attribute was actually introduced by the W3C as part of an extension to XHTML, known as the Role Attribute Module (which you can read about at http://www.w3.org/TR/xhtml-role/). The ARIA recommendation adds the specific attribute values and their meaning. Five role categories are defined within the ARIA recommendation:

User input widget: Elements marked with these types of roles behave like form widgets for collecting user input, such as sliders and custom text boxes.

User interface element: These elements behave like parts of the graphical user interface, such as buttons, menus, tabs, and tool tips.

Document structure: Elements marked with these roles describe structures that organize content within the page. This category includes roles for marking grids, headings, and images.

Application structure: These elements mark self-contained areas representing application user interfaces, such as dialog boxes, progress bars, and timers.

Landmark: These mark regions of the page intended as navigational points of reference within the page, such as the header, navigation, and main content. Browsers are expected to provide a means for users to easily jump between these landmark points using the keyboard or other appropriate mechanism.

This full list of roles is available within the ARIA recommendation. A small subset of this list is shown in Table 12-3.

Table 12-3. *A Selection of ARIA Role Attribute Values*

Role	Category	Meaning
button	User interface	An input that allows for user-triggered actions when pressed
combobox	User input widget	A drop-down list of selectable values that also contains a text box allowing the user to enter a new value not found in the list
dialog	Application structure	An in-page modal window designed to interrupt the application to prompt the user to enter some information or require confirmation
grid	Document structure	Denotes data arranged in rows and columns like a table
heading	Document structure	Indicates a heading for a section of the page
main	Landmark	Denotes the main content of a document
navigation	Landmark	A collection of links for navigating around the page or to other pages
progressbar	Application structure	An element that displays progress for tasks that take a long period of time to complete (like the progress bar presented in Chapter 5)
slider	User input widget	A form control allowing the user to select a value from a range (like the slider control presented in Chapter 8)
toolbar	User interface	Denotes a group of small functional buttons

You can apply the `role` attribute to elements directly in your markup or set it dynamically through JavaScript using the `setAttribute()` DOM method:

```
var list = $.Elements.create("ul");
list.setAttribute("role", "navigation");
```

States and Properties

Whereas roles provide the browser with general information about the type of content contained within a particular element on the page, *states* and *properties* give specific detailed information to the browser. A *state* refers to an element whose value is likely to change throughout the time the web application is being used, whereas a *property* is not likely to change. As with roles, these attribute values do not add behavior. They only present information to the user. You must add the behavior yourself using JavaScript.

States and properties fall into four distinct categories:

Widget attributes: These values are specific to user interface elements that receive user input and process actions. They support the user input and user interface role categories.

Live region attributes: A *live region* is an element on the page that is updated dynamically using JavaScript at some time within use of the web application, such as a live news article feed loaded from the server via Ajax on a fixed time interval. Values of live region attributes indicate to the browser that content updates may occur within the page element while the user does not have that element focused.

Drag-and-drop attributes: These values indicate specific information about draggable elements and their associated drop targets. The extra information allows the browser or screen reader to develop a suitable method to present the information about the draggable and droppable elements.

Relationship attributes: These values describe relationships between different page elements that cannot be determined through the normal page structure.

All state and property attribute names begin with the aria- prefix. Table 12-4 shows a selection of state and property attributes and their meanings. The full list of states, properties, and their permitted values is available within the ARIA documentation.

Table 12-4. *A Selection of ARIA States and Properties*

State or Property	Category	Meaning
aria-activedescendant	Relationship	Denotes the currently active item within a widget as the user interacts with that widget
aria-atomic	Live region	Indicates whether the browser should present the entire contents of the element when an update occurs or whether to simply present the changes that occurred
aria-autocomplete	Widget	Indicates whether the field this property relates to contains autocomplete suggestions when the user types into the field
aria-busy	Live region	Indicates whether the specified live region is currently being updated
aria-checked	Widget	Indicates the current state of a check box, radio button, or other element replicating a similar on/off state
aria-controls	Relationship	Identifies the elements whose contents are controlled by the current element, such as a tab control that changes the currently displayed tab on the page
aria-dropeffect	Drag-and-drop	Indicates the functionality performed when a dragged element is dropped on a target element, such as copy or move operation

State or Property	Category	Meaning
aria-grabbed	Drag-and-drop	Indicates whether an element is currently being "grabbed," ready for dragging to a drop target element
aria-labelledby	Relationship	Identifies the element that provides a label to the current element, such as to a form field
aria-live	Live region	Indicates that an element will be updated dynamically

The value of the aria-live attribute determines how the browser should handle the update:

- A value of off will not alert the user to an update.

- A value of polite, which should be the normal behavior, will alert the users of an update at the next available opportunity, when they have completed their current action.

- A value of assertive will interrupt the users immediately, alerting them to the content update.

Focus Management

You have seen already how important element focus is for accessibility in RIAs. Screen reader users, keyboard users, and others need to focus on elements in order to interact with them. Earlier in this chapter, you saw how assigning a tabindex attribute value allows an element to be selectable using the DOM element's focus() method.

The WAI-ARIA recommendation defines how the behavior of the tabindex attribute should be extended to be more usable, to allow different types of navigation around page elements, as shown in Table 12-5.

Table 12-5. *Behavior of tabindex Based on Its Value*

tabindex Attribute	Behavior
No tabindex attribute	Only hyperlinks and form elements are focusable. Keyboard focus follows source code order.
tabindex="0" (zero)	Allows the element to be focusable, regardless of type. Keyboard focus follows source code order.
tabindex="1" (positive)	Allows the element to be focusable, regardless of type. Keyboard focus follows tabindex value order from 1 upward.
tabindex="-1" (negative)	Allows the element to be focusable through JavaScript but not using the default keyboard key for changing focus. The developer should assign the element focus through JavaScript based on key presses of the arrow keys.

As recommended earlier, where possible, you should attempt to avoid the use of positive values of the `tabindex` attribute and instead rely on document source code to provide the correct focus behavior.

Keyboard Interaction with ARIA Widgets

So far, web developers have been left to their own devices when developing widgets and form components that respond to keyboard interaction—no guidelines had been set regarding which keys to use for what behavior. The ARIA recommendation includes clear suggestions as to which keys to use for navigating within page widgets and components, thus providing clarity for web developers, browser manufacturers, and end users.

Navigating between widgets on the page should be achieved by use of the Tab key, as is the case at present. When the user has focused on a particular widget, the arrow keys, spacebar, and Enter keys should be used to navigate and allow the user to interact with that widget. The recommendation suggests setting the `tabindex` attribute value to 0 on the currently accessed widget when it has the focus. As the user navigates using the arrow keys within the widget, the `aria-activedescendant` property should be set on the currently selected or focused element. This property makes it crystal clear to the browser which element the user has currently selected.

WAI-ARIA Examples

The W3C document WAI-ARIA Best Practices (http://www.w3.org/TR/wai-aria-practices/) is incredibly useful, practical, and highly recommended reading for all web developers. This document describes in great detail how to add ARIA support to your web applications. Here, I'll present a few simple examples to demonstrate how to add ARIA support to your own web applications. I strongly encourage you to read the W3C document thoroughly to get a better understanding of the material and how to apply it to your own web applications.

Marking Up Page Structure Using Roles, States, and Properties

As explained earlier, landmark roles allow you to add extra semantic meaning to page elements that perform a specific duty on the page or as part of the web application as a whole. Listing 12-5 shows an HTML page marked up with ARIA landmark roles to provide this extra meaning to browsers, screen readers, and other assistive technology to allow them to pass that extra meaning onto the users of their software. Figure 12-4 shows how this is structured within an HTML page, as marked with dotted lines around each landmark role area.

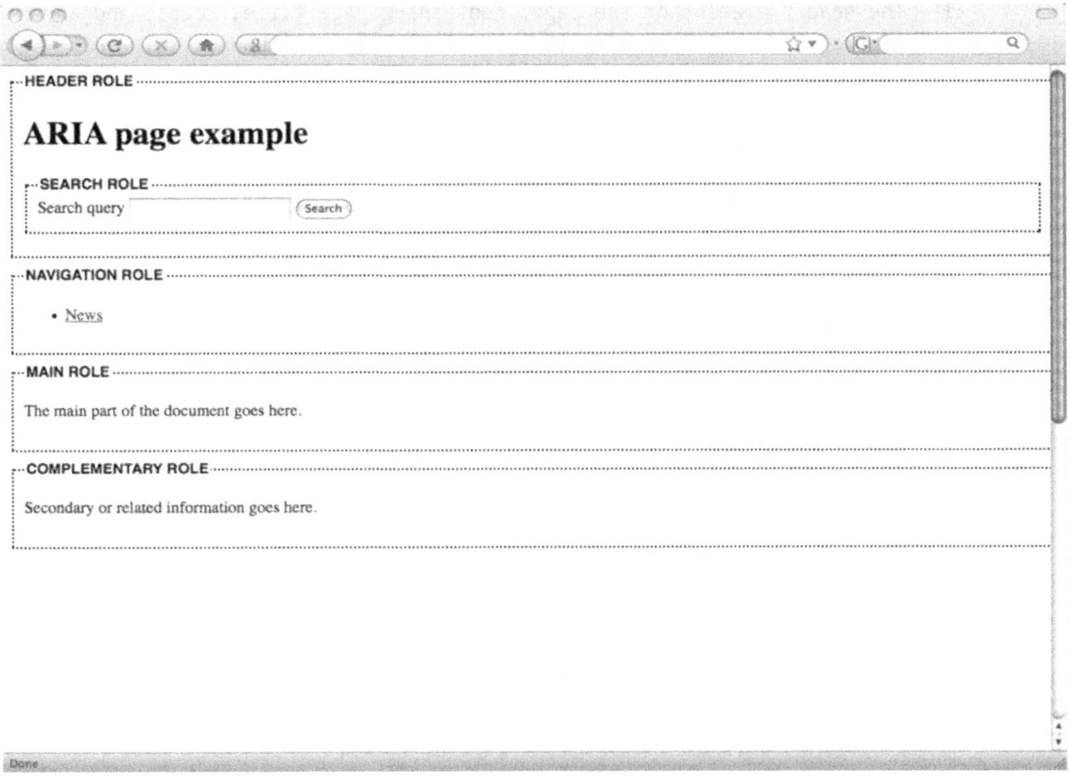

Figure 12-4. *Depiction of ARIA landmark roles within an HTML page*

Listing 12-5. *Marking Up an HTML Page Using ARIA Landmark Roles*

```
<!DOCTYPE html PUBLIC "-//W3C//DTD XHTML 1.0 Strict//EN" ➥
    "http://www.w3.org/TR/xhtml1/DTD/xhtml1-strict.dtd">
<html xmlns="http://www.w3.org/1999/xhtml" lang="en" xml:lang="en">
    <head>
        <meta http-equiv="Content-Type" content="text/html; charset=utf-8" />
        <title>ARIA page example</title>
    </head>

    <!-- The application role denotes a part of the page which acts as a standalone
        RIA - in this case, the entire page is going to represent an RIA so we
        place the role on the <body> tag -->
    <body role="application">
```

```
<!-- The header element of the page, containing page title, logos, and any
     other general site information, is marked with the banner role to
     denote this function -->
<div id="header" role="banner">
    <h1>ARIA page example</h1>

    <!-- A site-wide search functionality should be marked up with the
         search landmark role -->
    <form method="post" action="/search/" role="search">
        <label for="query">Search query</label>
        <input type="text" name="query" id="query" />
        <input type="submit" value="Search" />
    </form>
</div>

<!-- Navigational lists are marked with the navigation role -->
<ul id="navigation" role="navigation">
    <li><a href="/news/">News</a></li>
    <!-- Other navigation links go here -->
</ul>

<!-- The main part of the page is denoted with the main role -->
<div id="main" role="main">
    <p>The main part of the document goes here.</p>
</div>

<!-- Secondary sideline or complementary content, which would make sense
     when read out of the context of the rest of the page, is marked with
     the complementary role -->
<div id="aside" role="complementary">
    <p>Secondary or related information goes here.</p>
</div>
</body>
</html>
```

Dynamically Loading Content via Ajax

Virtually all web applications load or save data via the Ajax technique. Earlier in the chapter, you saw how you would need to write some extra code to draw focus to the updated content once the Ajax communication had completed. This can be greatly simplified with ARIA and its concept of live regions, which are parts of the page that the browser knows might be updated at some point during use of the application. Listing 12-6 shows a simple web application consisting of a live region that updates its contents based on a series of selected links on the page, as shown earlier in Figure 12-2.

Listing 12-6. *Dynamically Loading Content Accessibly via Ajax and ARIA*

```
<!DOCTYPE html PUBLIC "-//W3C//DTD XHTML 1.0 Strict//EN" ➥
    "http://www.w3.org/TR/xhtml1/DTD/xhtml1-strict.dtd">
<html xmlns="http://www.w3.org/1999/xhtml" lang="en" xml:lang="en">
    <head>
        <meta http-equiv="Content-Type" content="text/html; charset=utf-8" />
        <title>ARIA Ajax example</title>
    </head>

    <body role="application">
        <div id="header" role="banner">
            <h1>ARIA Ajax example</h1>
        </div>

        <ul id="navigation" role="navigation">
            <li><a href="/page1.html">Page 1</a></li>
            <li><a href="/page2.html">Page 2</a></li>
            <li><a href="/page3.html">Page 3</a></li>
        </ul>

        <!-- Mark the following element as being a live region using the aria-live
             attribute. The polite value means that users won't be hounded by a
             notification that the content has updated until they have completed
             their current activity. The aria-atomic attribute value of true means
             that users will be notified of the updated contents of the entire live
             region, not just a specific part of the region that changed. The
             aria-busy attribute will be set to true when the live region is being
             updated, resetting to false when no updates are being made at
             that time -->
        <div id="live-region" aria-live="polite" aria-atomic="true" ➥
                aria-busy="false">
            <h2>Default page content</h2>
            <p>Clicking on the navigation links will cause this content to change
            dynamically if JavaScript is enabled. The ARIA attributes ensure
            that screen readers and other assistive technology will be informed
            of the changes.</p>
        </div>

        <!-- Include the $ JavaScript library -->
        <script type="text/javascript" src="$.js"></script>

        <!-- You should move the following script to an external file within a real
             web application. It is included on the page here for simplicity -->
        <script type="text/javascript">
            $.onDomReady(function() {
```

```
            // Locate the live region page element and store a reference to it
            var liveRegion = document.getElementById("live-region");

            // Listen for click events firing within the navigation list
            $.Events.add(document.getElementById("navigation"), "click", ➡
                function(e) {
              if (e.target.tagName.toLowerCase() == "a") {

                    // If the user selected a navigation link, cancel its
                    // default action
                    e.preventDefault();

                    // Inform the browser or any assistive technology being used
                    // that the live region is now being updated
                    liveRegion.setAttribute("aria-busy", "true");

                    // Begin loading the contents of the page specified by the
                    // link URL
                    $.Remote.load({
                        url: e.target.href,
                        callback: function(response) {

                            // When the content has loaded, replace the HTML
                            // within the live region with the new HTML content
                            // loaded from the server
                            liveRegion.innerHTML = response.text;

                            // Inform the browser that the live region has
                            // finished being updated
                            liveRegion.setAttribute("aria-busy", "false");

                            // Users of assistive technology will be informed of
                            // the content update at the next opportunity
                            // after they have completed their current action
                        }
                    });
                }
            });
        });
      </script>
  </body>
</html>
```

Making a Progress Bar More Accessible

Back in Chapter 5, you saw how to construct a progress bar out of two page elements, some CSS, and a little JavaScript. You can update this fairly simply, adopting the ARIA recommendation to provide this information in a usable and accessible way for all users, as follows:

```
<!-- The polite aria-live attribute value will inform the user of a dynamic update
     occurring within the element only when the user is not occupied somewhere
     else on the page  -->
<div class="progress-bar" aria-live="polite">
    <!-- The aria-valuemin attribute denotes the minimum value of a range, the
         aria-valuemax attribute denotes the maximum value of that range, the
         aria-valuenow attribute denotes the current value within that range, and
         the aria-valuetext attribute denotes the current text value related to the
         numeric value -->
    <div class="progress" id="code-progress" role="progressbar" ➥
        aria-valuemin="0" aria-valuemax="100" aria-valuenow="25" ➥
        aria-valuetext="25%">25%</div>
</div>
```

You must then update the value of the `aria-valuenow` attribute at the same time as the width of the progress bar element through JavaScript, as shown in the following line, which denotes the current progress position to be 25%:

```
document.getElementById("code-progress").setAttribute("aria-valuenow", "25");
document.getElementById("code-progress").setAttribute("aria-valuetext", "25%");
```

Validation

Adding the ARIA attributes to HTML elements causes no ill effects in any browser, whether or not that browser supports ARIA. You may, however, notice that attempts to validate your page using the W3C validator online at `http://validator.w3.org/` reveal a series of errors if the ARIA attributes are added directly to your markup. This is because the validator does not recognize the ARIA attributes as valid XHTML, which is correct, since ARIA attributes are an extension of XHTML, and not yet part of the XHTML specification itself. Until the ARIA recommendations are finalized and its support is added to the W3C validator, I suggest you ensure that the rest of your page validates, and simply ignore the ARIA-related errors. These attributes will not cause any rendering issues in any browser.

The way to make sure your markup will still validate is to use JavaScript to set the ARIA-specific attributes and their values programmatically using the `setAttribute()` DOM method:

```
document.getElementById("live-region").setAttribute("aria-live", "polite");
```

Since ARIA is relevant only when JavaScript is enabled, there is no accessibility issue when enabling the attributes within your web application in this way.

Testing

Performing testing of a web application as it affects screen reader users is very difficult if you are not a screen reader user yourself. Simply downloading screen reader software and listening to the output does not give you an accurate representation of how a day-to-day user of this software interacts with the web application. The best testing you can perform in this case is user testing. Take the results of such testing very seriously, and consider every suggestion to improve your web application for assistive technology users.

For more simplistic testing and to ensure you have set your ARIA attributes correctly, try downloading and using the Juicy Studio Accessibility Toolbar for Firefox from `https://addons.mozilla.org/en-US/firefox/addon/9108/`. This add-on enables developers to examine live regions, roles, states, and properties. It also provides other useful accessibility checks, such as color-contrast levels. Figure 12-5 shows the add-on revealing hidden ARIA roles and properties on an HTML page.

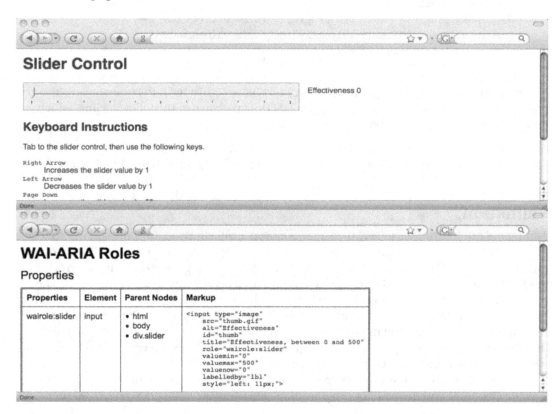

Figure 12-5. *Juicy Studio Accessibility Toolbar revealing ARIA roles and properties on a page*

Try disconnecting your mouse and navigating your web application using solely your keyboard. This is an incredibly effective way of revealing how you can make improvements to your RIA to support your users who prefer or require this input method.

Summary

In this chapter, you have discovered how to improve the accessibility of your RIAs for your end users, regardless of browser, device, or input method. This brings to a close the final part of this book, in which you have discovered how to improve the presentational aspect of your web applications: the user interface.

Throughout this book, I have presented numerous tips, techniques, and technologies that, when used together, allow you to build stable, accessible, high-performing, and well-designed RIAs using JavaScript. I encourage you to stay up-to-date with the constantly evolving web standards, browser updates, and advances in web development techniques. I will maintain an updated list of news, links, and useful advice via my web site at `http://www.denodell.com/` to reflect as many of these advances as possible to keep you well informed.

Continue to experiment, reuse, invent, reinvent, and push the browser to the limit. Learn from others' mistakes. Give back to the wider web development community the fruits of your own labor when you can. Finally, constantly strive to be the best, most thoughtful web developer you can be, and never forget the two most important aspects of any web application: maintainability and accessibility.

Good luck in your endeavors!

Index

Symbols and Numbers

- (hyphen), separating words with, 24
$ JavaScript library. *See also* $ library
   adding client-side database storage code to, 318–321
   adding code for setting and reading cookie values to, 308–310
   adding code to use Flash cookies to, 322–323
   extending with utility methods for dates, 261–264
   implementing cross-browser local storage API in, 324–326
   improving event handling within, 385–386
   using to create, locate, and delete cookies, 310
$ library. *See also* $ JavaScript library
   adding CSS style–related methods to, 92–95
   adding JavaScript methods to, 85–89
   adding methods for locating elements within the page, 95–96
   adding utility functions to, 89–92
   completing, 96–97
   instantiating, 96–97
   loading content dynamically using Ajax, 85–89
% (percent), for font sizing, 40
() (parentheses) in JavaScript, 52–53
/ character. *See also* trailing slash character (/)
   effect of omission of on performance, 148
@font-face directive, 201
@import method, admonition against using, 150
200+ status codes, 125
300+ status codes, 125
400+ status codes, 126

A

abbr tag, 15
Accept header, 122
Accept-Charset request header, 122
Accept-Encoding header, 122
Accept-Language header, 122
Accept-Ranges HTTP response header, 332

access keys, 28
Access-Control-Allow-Origin header, 201, 202
accessibility
   creating web applications for, 375–401
   guidelines for styles, 39–41
   handling of by web developers, 225–226
   principle, 9
   support (JW FLV player), 245
acronym tag, 15
active class
   JavaScript code for applying to wrapper element, 257–258
   writing CSS to hang from, 256–257
addEventListener() method, 385
address tag, 15
Adobe Dreamweaver web site, 46
Adobe web site, 210
Ajax
   adding and navigating page visit history items using, 380–382
   dynamically loading content via, 396–399
   HTML page code for displaying image data via, 352–353
   improving performance of, 170–172
   loading a complete or partial binary file using, 334–336
   loading content on demand with, 85–89
   reading binary files with, 331–339
   using JSON format for responses, 170
Akamai
   web site address, 138
   web site address for page loading study results, 146
alert statement, 63
Alexa information company web site, 159
AlphaImageLoader filter, 151
alt attribute
   using for heading text, 198
   using with img tag, 25
Apache web server
   adding compression configuration to apache.confd file, 142
   enabling compression in, 142
applications, third-party scripts in, 110–111
application/xhtml+xml
   MIME type, 360
   XHTML indicated by, 122

You Need the Companion eBook

Your purchase of this book entitles you to buy the companion PDF-version eBook for only $10. Take the weightless companion with you anywhere.

We believe this Apress title will prove so indispensable that you'll want to carry it with you everywhere, which is why we are offering the companion eBook (in PDF format) for $10 to customers who purchase this book now. Convenient and fully searchable, the PDF version of any content-rich, page-heavy Apress book makes a valuable addition to your programming library. You can easily find and copy code—or perform examples by quickly toggling between instructions and the application. Even simultaneously tackling a donut, diet soda, and complex code becomes simplified with hands-free eBooks!

Once you purchase your book, getting the $10 companion eBook is simple:

❶ Visit **www.apress.com/promo/tendollars/**.

❷ Complete a basic registration form to receive a randomly generated question about this title.

❸ Answer the question correctly in 60 seconds, and you will receive a promotional code to redeem for the $10.00 eBook.

2855 TELEGRAPH AVENUE │ SUITE 600 │ BERKELEY, CA 94705

Offer valid through 11/09.